Network Flow Algorithms

Network flow theory has been used across a number of disciplines, including theoretical computer science, operations research, and discrete math, to model not only problems in the transportation of goods and information but also a wide range of applications from image segmentation problems in computer vision to deciding when a baseball team has been eliminated from contention.

This graduate text and reference presents a succinct, unified view of a wide variety of efficient combinatorial algorithms for network flow problems, including many results not found in other books. It covers maximum flows, minimum-cost flows, generalized flows, multicommodity flows, and global minimum cuts and also presents recent work on computing electrical flows along with recent applications of these flows to classical problems in network flow theory.

DAVID P. WILLIAMSON is a professor at Cornell University in the School of Operations Research and Information Engineering. He has won several awards for his work in discrete optimization, including the 2000 Fulkerson Prize, sponsored by the American Mathematical Society and the Mathematical Programming Society. His previous book, *The Design of Approximation Algorithms*, coauthored with David B. Shmoys, won the 2013 INFORMS Lanchester Prize. He has served on several editorial boards, and was editor-in-chief of the *SIAM Journal on Discrete Mathematics*. He is a Fellow of the ACM and of SIAM.

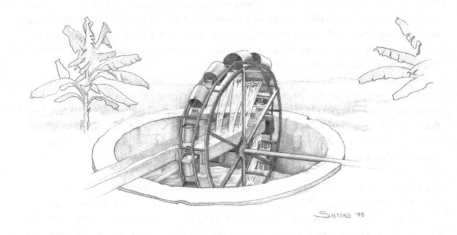

SALTERS '08

Network Flow Algorithms

DAVID P. WILLIAMSON
Cornell University

CAMBRIDGE
UNIVERSITY PRESS

CAMBRIDGE
UNIVERSITY PRESS

University Printing House, Cambridge CB2 8BS, United Kingdom

One Liberty Plaza, 20th Floor, New York, NY 10006, USA

477 Williamstown Road, Port Melbourne, VIC 3207, Australia

314-321, 3rd Floor, Plot 3, Splendor Forum, Jasola District Centre, New Delhi - 110025, India

79 Anson Road, #06-04/06, Singapore 079906

Cambridge University Press is part of the University of Cambridge.

It furthers the University's mission by disseminating knowledge in the pursuit of education, learning and research at the highest international levels of excellence.

www.cambridge.org
Information on this title: www.cambridge.org/9781107185890
DOI: 10.1017/9781316888568

First published 2019

A catalogue record for this publication is available from the British Library

Library of Congress Cataloging in Publication data
Names: Williamson, David P., author.
Title: Network flow algorithms / David P. Williamson, Cornell University, New York.
Description: Cambridge, United Kingdom ; New York, NY, USA : Cambridge
University Press, [2019] | Includes bibliographical references and index.
Identifiers: LCCN 2019011352 | ISBN 9781107185890 (hardback : alk. paper) |
ISBN 9781316636831 (paperback : alk. paper)
Subjects: LCSH: Network analysis (Planning)–Computer programs. |
System theory. | Computer algorithms.
Classification: LCC T57.85 .W56 2019 | DDC 003–dc23
LC record available at https://lccn.loc.gov/2019011352

ISBN 978-1-107-18589-0 Hardback
ISBN 978-1-316-63683-1 Paperback

Contents

Preface   *page* ix
Acknowledgments   xi

1   Preliminaries: Shortest Path Algorithms   1
1.1   Nonnegative Costs: Dijkstra's Algorithm   2
1.2   Negative Costs: The Bellman–Ford Algorithm   6
1.3   Negative-Cost Cycle Detection   11
        Exercises   19
        Chapter Notes   20

2   Maximum Flow Algorithms   23
2.1   Optimality Conditions   26
2.2   Application: Carpool Sharing   33
2.3   Application: The Baseball Elimination Problem   36
2.4   Application: Finding a Maximum Density Subgraph   41
2.5   Most Improving Augmenting Paths   46
2.6   A Capacity Scaling Algorithm   51
2.7   Shortest Augmenting Paths   53
2.8   The Push-Relabel Algorithm   56
        Exercises   69
        Chapter Notes   76

3   Global Minimum Cut Algorithms   80
3.1   The Hao–Orlin Algorithm   82
3.2   The MA Ordering Algorithm   89
3.3   The Random Contraction Algorithm   93
3.4   The Gomory–Hu Tree   100
        Exercises   110
        Chapter Notes   113

4   More Maximum Flow Algorithms   116
4.1   Blocking Flows   116
4.2   Blocking Flows in Unit Capacity Graphs   120
4.3   The Goldberg–Rao Algorithm   122
       Exercises   128
       Chapter Notes   130
       Permissions   130

5   Minimum-Cost Circulation Algorithms   132
5.1   Optimality Conditions   135
5.2   Wallacher's Algorithm   140
5.3   Minimum-Mean Cycle Canceling   146
5.4   A Capacity Scaling Algorithm   154
5.5   Successive Approximation   160
5.6   Network Simplex   167
5.7   Application: Maximum Flow Over Time   170
       Exercises   176
       Chapter Notes   184

6   Generalized Flow Algorithms   188
6.1   Optimality Conditions   190
6.2   A Wallacher-Style GAP-Canceling Algorithm   198
6.3   Negative-Cost GAP Detection   205
6.4   Lossy Graphs, Truemper's Algorithm, and Gain Scaling   209
6.5   Error Scaling   218
       Exercises   221
       Chapter Notes   223

7   Multicommodity Flow Algorithms   224
7.1   Optimality Conditions   225
7.2   The Two-Commodity Case   227
7.3   Intermezzo: The Multiplicative Weights Algorithm   230
7.4   The Garg–Könemann Algorithm   236
7.5   The Awerbuch–Leighton Algorithm   240
       Exercises   249
       Chapter Notes   251

8   Electrical Flow Algorithms   253
8.1   Optimality Conditions   254
8.2   Maximum Flow in Undirected Graphs   266

8.3	Graph Sparsification	271
8.4	A Simple Laplacian Solver	277
	Exercises	285
	Chapter Notes	288
	Permissions	290
9	**Open Questions**	291
	References	294
	Author Index	307
	Index	310

Preface

> I have gathered a posy of other men's flowers, and nothing but the thread that
> binds them is mine own.
>
> — Montaigne

Any new book on network flow would seem to need to justify its existence, since the definitive book on the topic has perhaps already been written. I am referring to the magisterial *Network Flows: Theory, Algorithms, and Applications*, by Ahuja, Magnanti, and Orlin [4], written by some of the premier researchers in the theory and practice of efficient network flow algorithms, and published in 1993; I will refer to the book as AMO, using the initials of its authors. The late 1980s and early 1990s were a golden era for research in combinatorial, polynomial-time algorithms for network flow problems, and not only does AMO discuss most of the work done during this period, it also gives an extensive overview of the entire area of network flows and is full of applications of network flow theory to practical problems. So why another book on the topic? I offer three reasons.

The first is a matter of focus. It is hard to be both definitive and succinct, as I know from having tried to write a definitive book on another topic [206]. AMO is certainly the former; it is my aim here to be the latter. In this volume, I am concerned primarily with combinatorial, polynomial-time algorithms for network flow problems and their analyses. The material for this book comes from having taught several iterations of a graduate-level course in network flow algorithms at Cornell University's School of Operations Research and Information Engineering. The students were primarily in operations research and computer science, but there were also some in electrical and civil engineering. Thus I know from experience that with a bit of selection, the bulk of the material in this book can be taught in a semester-long course. Additionally, because the book is a result of a course, the results covered are ones that I was able to teach successfully in a single lecture. As a consequence, results that are either too long or too complex to cover in a single lecture are not included here. I do not say much concerning other parts of network flow theory, such as applications or algorithms without polynomially bounded running times. Here the existence of AMO is a boon; the interested reader is welcome to refer to that volume for the parts of network flow theory that are not covered in this book.

The second reason is to provide some coverage that AMO does not. Although several of the algorithms covered here for the maximum flow problems and minimum-cost circulation problems are also covered by AMO, there are some important exceptions. As mentioned above, although the late 1980s and early 1990s were a golden era for research in network flow algorithms, there has continued to be work in the area in the last 25 years, which AMO does not cover. One notable example is the 1998 paper of Goldberg and Rao [90], giving what until recently was the theoretically fastest known algorithm for the maximum flow problem. Another is the 1991 algorithm of Wallacher [201] for the minimum-cost circulation problem; the algorithm has a relatively simple analysis. Furthermore, interesting polynomial-time combinatorial algorithms for several types of flow problems were emerging just as AMO went to press, and are not covered there; I am thinking primarily of algorithms for global minimum cut, generalized maximum flow, and multicommodity flow problems. In recent years, specializations of interior-point methods to network flow problems have resulted in still faster algorithms; while these algorithms are not combinatorial and thus do not fall in the scope of this book, I include a few of these results connected to the classical topic of electrical flows.

The third reason is that in the end, I could not really help myself. My main area of research interest is combinatorial, polynomial-time algorithms, but with one exception [173], none of my work has been on network flow problems. So I can say as an unbiased outside observer that the area is one with truly beautiful and useful algorithmic ideas that build on each other in a very aesthetically pleasing way. Following the Montaigne quotation above, my goal in writing this book has been one of selection and arrangement to try to bring out as best I can the beauty that is already inherent in the algorithms and analysis of others; I hope the reader enjoys the resulting bouquet as much as I do.

David P. Williamson
Ithaca, New York
January 2019

Acknowledgments

Beggar that I am, I am even poor in thanks, but I thank you; and sure, dear
friends, my thanks are too dear a halfpenny.
                                    – William Shakespeare, *Hamlet*, Act II, Scene II

This book had its genesis in an advanced algorithms class I taught at Stanford
University in Spring 2003 (CS 361B). The section on network flow algorithms
from that class was expanded into a full-semester course in Spring 2004 when
I moved to Cornell University (ORIE 633). Since then I've taught several
iterations of the class (Spring 2004, Fall 2007, Fall 2012, and Fall 2015),
and tried to make the material into a more cohesive whole. I became familiar
with the material on electrical flows when I taught a spectral graph theory and
algorithms course in Fall 2016. I owe many thanks to my students from these
courses for asking questions and forcing me to clarify my presentation of the
material and the exercises that were part of their problem sets.

My first exposure to this subject came when I was a student at MIT via
courses from Ron Rivest, David Shmoys, and Michel Goemans. Some of the
material they presented, such as the Goldberg-Tarjan minimum-mean cycle
canceling algorithm, was brand new at the time. I am grateful for their clear
and exciting presentations that started my interest in this area.

Over the years I have learned a good deal from the researchers who devel-
oped the material presented in this book, including András Benczúr, Joseph
Cheriyan, Lisa Fleischer, Hal Gabow, Andrew Goldberg, Don Goldfarb,
Nick Harvey, Alan Hoffman, David Karger, Matt Levine, Tom McCormick,
Aleksandr Mądry, Kurt Mehlhorn, Jim Orlin, Satish Rao, David Shmoys,
Martin Skutella, Dan Spielman, Cliff Stein, Éva Tardos, Bob Tarjan, Laci
Vegh, and Kevin Wayne. I am grateful to them all for their development of this
beautiful area of work, and their willingness to share it with me. I apologize to
those I will have inevitably left off the list via oversight.

I am indebted to those who wrote excellent books in this area before me that served as references for me, especially those of Ahuja, Magnanti, and Orlin [4], Ford and Fulkerson [66], and Tarjan [192], as well as more general references in algorithms and combinatorial optimization, such as those by Cook, Cunningham, Pulleyblank, and Schrijver [44], Cormen, Leiserson, Rivest, and Stein [45], Kleinberg and Tardos [134], Korte and Vygen [135], and Schrijver [177].

Several people took the time to look at my manuscript and pointed out various errors and made useful suggestions. I wish to thank Joseph Cheriyan, Jakob Degen, Daniel Fleischman, Daniel Freund, Agustin Garcia, Sam Gutekunst, Harsh Parekh, Glenn Sun, and Jessica Xu. Rajiv Gandhi helped me by finding several students willing to read through a draft of the manuscript.

Jon Kleinberg, Prabhakar Raghavan, and Gary Villa made very timely comments that inspired me to take up the project of writing this book.

This book was written at Cornell University and while I was on sabbatical at the Simons Institute on the Theory of Computing at the University of California, Berkeley. I am grateful to both institutions for their support.

Though I acknowledge the help of so very many people, all mistakes and misunderstandings that remain in this volume are mine alone.

Additional materials related to the book (such as contact information and errata) can be found at the website www.networkflowalgs.com.

Finally, I wish to thank my children, Abigail, Daniel, and Ruth, and my wife Ann especially: without her encouragement to finish this book, it would not have been completed.

David P. Williamson
Ithaca, New York
January 2019

1

Preliminaries: Shortest Path Algorithms

The White Rabbit put on his spectacles. "Where shall I begin, please your
Majesty?" he asked.
"Begin at the beginning," the King said, very gravely, "and go on till you
come to the end: then stop."

— Lewis Carroll, *Alice in Wonderland*

Although we will assume that the reader has previously studied combinatorial
algorithms, it is useful to start by presenting algorithms for computing a
shortest path. Anyone who has studied combinatorial algorithms before will
certainly have encountered these algorithms, but the ideas in them are so
central to the topic of network flow algorithms that a short overview of the
two most fundamental algorithms is in order.

In the shortest path problem we are given a directed graph $G = (V, A)$, and
a distinguished vertex s, which we will call the *source*. For each arc $(i, j) \in A$
we are given a cost $c(i, j)$ of traveling from i to j. A non-empty *path* from s
to i is a sequence of arcs $(s, j_1), (j_1, j_2), (j_2, j_3), \ldots, (j_k, i)$ that starts at s, ends
at i, and such that the head of each arc is the tail of the next. If no vertex is
repeated in the path, it is a *simple* path. A path that starts and ends at the same
vertex is called a *cycle*. A *simple cycle* is a cycle in which only the start and
end vertices are repeated.

For each $i \in V$ we want to compute a path from s to i of minimum total
cost, if such a path exists; we will call it a *minimum-cost* path from s to i.
We will let $d(i)$ denote the cost of such a path. If there is no path from s to i
in G, then we will set $d(i)$ to ∞. As we will see in a moment, it is possible
that the minimum-cost path is not well defined – this can occur if there exists
a cycle such that the total cost of the arcs in the cycle is negative – and we will
eventually discuss this issue. Since we are assigning costs, rather than lengths,

1

to arcs, we could refer to the cheapest path problem, rather than the shortest path problem, but the latter name is standard, and so we will use it.

Throughout the book, we will use n to denote the number of vertices in the graph (that is, $n = |V|$) and m to denote the number of arcs or edges (that is, $m = |A|$).

The shortest path problem is, in some sense, the simplest possible type of flow problem involving costs. Usually flow problems specify a capacity for each arc, capping the rate at which flow can enter the arc. Here we have an *uncapacitated* problem; there are no capacities, and we can send as much flow on an arc as we want. Then if we want to send $a(i)$ units of flow from s to i, we compute the cheapest path from s to i, and the cost of shipping on this path is $a(i)d(i)$.

In what follows, we first discuss an algorithm we can use when all the arc costs are nonnegative. Then we give an algorithm that works when arc costs are negative (subject to the issue of negative-cost cycles).

1.1 Nonnegative Costs: Dijkstra's Algorithm

When arc costs $c(i, j)$ are nonnegative for all arcs $(i, j) \in A$, we can use *Dijkstra's algorithm*, due to Dijkstra [51]. The algorithm maintains a *distance labeling d* on the vertices of the graph; the label $d(i)$ is the algorithm's current guess of the cost of the cheapest path from s to i. As discussed above, we will refer to this as the distance from s to i; henceforward, we will fearlessly interchange the notions of cost and distance. We will maintain the property that the algorithm's guess $d(i)$ is always an upper bound on the true shortest-path distance from s to i. This notion of a distance labeling is one that will recur throughout our discussion of network flow algorithms.

We will also mark vertices as we become certain that their current distance label is correct. Initially, all vertices are unmarked.

Since the algorithm maintains a distance labeling that is an upper bound on the true distance, the easiest place to start is with $d(i) = \infty$ for all $i \in V$. Actually, this is overly pessimistic, because we can set the label of s to zero. Since all arc costs are nonnegative, there cannot be a path from s to s with cost less than zero, and the path with no arcs from s to s trivially has cost zero. Thus we can set $d(s) = 0$, and mark s, since we are certain this label is correct.

What now? Well, we can update the labels for all vertices i such that there is an arc $(s, i) \in A$. Since we know the length of the shortest path from s to s is zero, we know that there exists a path of length at most $d(s) + c(s, i) = c(s, i)$ from s to i (namely, the path consisting of the single arc (s, i)). So $d(s) + c(s, i)$

is a legitimate upper bound on the length of the shortest path from s to i, and we can set $d(i) = \min(d(i), d(s) + c(s,i))$ for i such that $(s,i) \in A$. This update will maintain the property that $d(i)$ is an upper bound on the shortest s-i path.

The key insight for Dijkstra's algorithm is that of all unmarked vertices, we can now correctly mark the one with the minimum distance label; if there is more than one vertex of minimum distance label, then we can choose one arbitrarily. We will prove that this is correct in a moment. Suppose vertex i has minimum distance label $d(i)$ and we mark vertex i. Then as above, for all arcs (i,j), we know that there is a path of length at most $d(i) + c(i,j)$ to vertex j (consisting of the shortest s-i path followed by the arc (i,j)). Thus we can update $d(j) = \min(d(j), d(i) + c(i,j))$ for all j such that $(i,j) \in A$. We then mark the unmarked vertex of minimum distance label, and iterate. Observe that each distance label can only decrease throughout the course of the algorithm.

In addition, by the preceding discussion, we know that the path to vertex j consists of a path from s to some vertex i, followed by the arc (i,j). Hence we can keep track of the current path to j by maintaining a pointer $p(j)$ to the vertex i preceding it on the path; we will call $p(j)$ the *parent* of j. When we update $d(j)$, if we set $d(j) = d(i) + c(i,j)$, we also set $p(j) = i$, so that we know that the current path from s to j is the arc (i,j) added to current path from s to i. To find the path from s to j, we start at j and trace the parent pointers from j back to s. For simplicity, we set the parent of s to be null.

We summarize Dijkstra's algorithm in Algorithm 1.1, and we prove its correctness below.

$d(i) \leftarrow \infty$ for all $i \in V$
$p(i) \leftarrow$ **null** for all $i \in V$
Unmark all $i \in V$
$d(s) \leftarrow 0$
while not all vertices are marked **do**
    Find unmarked $i \in V$ that minimizes $d(i)$ and mark i
    for j such that $(i,j) \in A$ **do**
        if $d(j) > d(i) + c(i,j)$ **then**
            $d(j) \leftarrow d(i) + c(i,j)$
            $p(j) \leftarrow i$

Algorithm 1.1 Dijkstra's algorithm for the shortest path problem.

Theorem 1.1: *If all arc costs are nonnegative, then Dijkstra's algorithm (Algorithm 1.1) correctly determines the shortest distance from the source s to each vertex $i \in V$.*

Proof We argue by induction on the algorithm that when the algorithm marks a vertex j, the value $d(j)$ must be the length of the shortest path from s to j. We have argued previously that $d(s) = 0$, and clearly s is the first vertex marked by the algorithm. Now suppose some iteration of the algorithm is about to mark vertex $j \neq s$, and the algorithm has correctly computed $d(i)$ for all vertices i previously marked by the algorithm. We recall that $d(j)$ is an upper bound on the length of the shortest s-j path, so $d(j)$ is incorrect only if there is a shortest s-j path P that has length strictly less than $d(j)$. Assume that such a path P exists; we will show that we reach a contradiction. We follow path P from s to j until we reach the last vertex $i \neq j$ on the path that was marked; there will be some such vertex because s has already been marked and j is not marked. Let (i, k) be the arc out of i on path P, with k not marked; note that possibly $k = j$. (See Figure 1.1.) By our induction hypothesis, since i has been marked, $d(i)$ is the length of the shortest path from s to i. After we marked i, it must have been the case that $d(k) \leq d(i) + c(i, k)$: either this was already true or we set $d(k) = d(i) + c(i, k)$ after marking i. The length of the remainder of the path P from k to j must be nonnegative, because all the arc costs are nonnegative. Thus $d(k)$ is a lower bound on the length of the path P, which is strictly less than $d(j)$ by assumption. However, we have now reached a contradiction because k is unmarked and has a distance label strictly less than $d(j)$: if $k = j$, then we have $d(j) < d(j)$, or if $k \neq j$, another unmarked vertex has minimum distance label rather than j.   □

It is easy to see that we can implement the algorithm in $O(m+n^2) = O(n^2)$ time by looking for the unmarked vertex of minimum label in each step (recall that $m = |A|$ is the number of arcs in the graph and $n = |V|$ is the number of vertices). Observe that we consider each arc (i, j) in the graph exactly once, when the tail i of the arc is first marked.

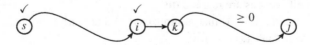

Figure 1.1 Illustration of the proof of Theorem 1.1; this is the shortest s-j path P of length strictly less than $d(j)$. The node i is the last marked node on the path, and k is the next node on the path, and must be unmarked. The proof argues that then $d(k)$ is a lower bound on the length of the path, and thus some node other than j should have been the next to be selected and marked.

$h \leftarrow new\ heap()$;
$d(i) \leftarrow \infty$ for all $i \in V$
$p(i) \leftarrow$ **null** for all $i \in V$
$d(s) \leftarrow 0$
for all $i \in V$ **do**
    $h.insert(i, d(i))$
while not $h.empty?$ **do**
    $i \leftarrow h.extract\text{-}min()$
    for j such that $(i, j) \in A$ **do**
        if $d(j) > d(i) + c(i, j)$ **then**
            $d(j) \leftarrow d(i) + c(i, j)$
            $p(j) \leftarrow i$
            $h.decrease\text{-}key(j, d(j))$

Algorithm 1.2 Dijkstra's algorithm for the shortest path problem using a heap data structure.

We can get a better asymptotic running time by using a data structure known as a *heap*. A heap contains a set of items, and each item has an associated value called its *key*. A heap data structure supports the following operations: *new heap()*, which returns an empty heap; *h.insert(i,k)*, which inserts item i into heap h with key value k; *h.decrease-key(i,k')*, which decreases the key of i to k' (it is assumed that k' is no greater than the current key of item i); *h.extract-min()*, which returns an item i of minimum key value in heap h and removes i from the heap; and *h.empty?*, which returns true if the heap h has no items in it, and returns false otherwise. We can then rewrite Algorithm 1.1 in terms of these operations, which we do in Algorithm 1.2. The items in the heap are the vertices and their keys are the distance labels. Notice that we replace the marking of nodes with non-membership in the heap; if the node is in the heap, then it is unmarked.

Heaps are easy to implement using arrays; we do not give the details here, but point the interested reader to standard books on algorithms (see Chapter Notes for references). The most straightforward implementation of a heap data structure takes $O(1)$ time for a *new heap*, $O(\log n)$ time for an *insert* (given that we are inserting at most n items), $O(\log n)$ time for a *decrease-key*, $O(\log n)$ time for an *extract-min*, and $O(1)$ time for *empty?*. These running times for the data structure yield an overall running time of $O(m \log n)$ time for Dijkstra's algorithm, since we perform n *extract-mins*, n *inserts*, and at most m *decrease-keys*. Faster theoretical running times are known: Using a data structure called a *Fibonacci heap*, it is possible to implement Dijkstra's algorithm in $O(m + n \log n)$ time. See Chapter Notes for more details.

1.2 Negative Costs: The Bellman–Ford Algorithm

We now turn to the case in which the cost of an arc may be negative. While it is difficult to think of instances of problems involving physical travel on networks in which there are arcs of negative length, it is often useful when modeling problems to allow for negative costs; we will encounter this situation many times in the flow algorithms to come.

Once we allow for negative-cost arcs, however, we have to contend with the possibility that there might not be an s-i path of shortest overall length: for any bound B, there might be a path of length less than B. See Figure 1.2 for an example: the s-t path (s,a), (a,t) has cost 2, the path (s,a), (a,b), (b,c), (c,a), (a,t) has cost 1, the path (s,a), (a,b), (b,c), (c,a), (a,b), (b,c), (c,a), (a,t) has cost 0, and so on. Each time we traverse the cycle a-b-c the cost drops by 1. In order to prevent this possibility, we request that our algorithm for the shortest path problem either finds a shortest path or states that it cannot do so because there is a *negative-cost cycle* reachable from s. A cycle has negative cost if the sum of the costs of the arcs in the cycle is negative, while a vertex i is *reachable* from s if there is a path from s to i, and a cycle is reachable from s if any vertex on the cycle is reachable from s. We leave it as an exercise to the reader (Exercise 1.2) to show that there are simple shortest paths from s to each $i \in V$ reachable from s if and only if there are no negative-cost cycles reachable from s (recall that in a simple path, no vertex in the path is repeated). In order to simplify our discussion somewhat, we start by assuming that there are no negative-cost cycles in the input graph, and we then show how to detect them in the next section.

As in Dijkstra's algorithm, this algorithm will maintain a set of distance labels $d(i)$ for all $i \in V$, where initially $d(s) = 0$ and $d(i) = \infty$ for all $i \in V$,

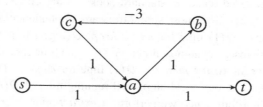

Figure 1.2 A negative-cost cycle on the path from s from t.

$$d(i) \leftarrow \infty \text{ for all } i \in V$$
$$p(i) \leftarrow \textbf{null} \text{ for all } i \in V$$
$$d(s) \leftarrow 0$$
for $k \leftarrow 1$ to $n - 1$ **do**
    for all $(i, j) \in A$ **do**
        if $d(j) > d(i) + c(i, j)$ **then**
            $d(j) \leftarrow d(i) + c(i, j)$
            $p(j) \leftarrow i$

Algorithm 1.3 The Bellman–Ford algorithm for the shortest path problem.

$i \neq s$. The algorithm will have the property that whenever $d(i)$ is finite, it is always the length of *some* path from s to i. Here the central insight is that given an arc (i, j), whenever $d(j) > d(i) + c(i, j)$, we can set $d(j) = d(i) + c(i, j)$; by our invariant, there is some path to i of length $d(i)$, and so we can find a shorter path to j that first visits i and then uses arc (i, j) to get to j. As was the case for Dijkstra's algorithm, we also maintain a set of parent pointers $p(j)$ that point to the previous vertex on the current path to j. Thus when we set $d(j) = d(i) + c(i, j)$, we know that the path to j came from vertex i, and we set $p(j) = i$. Again we observe that distance labels only decrease during the course of the algorithm.

The main idea of the analysis is to show that, after checking all arcs k times, we have correctly found all shortest paths that use at most k arcs. Thus, assuming there are no negative-cost cycles, the algorithm can terminate after $n - 1$ iterations through all the arcs, since any shortest s-i path is simple and will use at most $n - 1$ arcs. This algorithm is traditionally attributed jointly to Bellman and Ford [18, 62], although it was also discovered by others at around the same time; see Chapter Notes for a discussion. We summarize the Bellman–Ford algorithm in Algorithm 1.3. The algorithm will not work correctly if the graph contains negative-cost cycles, but we will first analyze it, and then see how to modify it in order to detect negative-cost cycles.

Lemma 1.2: *Any finite distance label $d(i)$ is the length of some s-i path in the network.*

Proof The lemma follows easily by induction on the algorithm. At the start of the algorithm, the only finite distance label is $d(s) = 0$, which is the length of the s-s path of zero arcs. Then whenever we update a distance label $d(j)$, we set $d(j) = d(i) + c(i, j)$, so that $d(j)$ is the length of the s-i path of length $d(i)$ (which exists by induction) plus the arc (i, j). $\qquad\square$

Lemma 1.3: *After k iterations of the Bellman–Ford algorithm (Algorithm 1.3), each distance label $d(i)$ is at most the length of the shortest s-i path that uses at most k arcs.*

Proof The base case is simple: at the start of the algorithm (at the end of the 0th iteration), there is a path from s to s of length 0; this is the shortest path from s to s with at most 0 arcs. Now for the inductive case. Consider a shortest s-j path P that uses at most k arcs (if one exists), in which the last arc is (i, j). Then the subpath of P from s to i of at most $k - 1$ arcs must be a shortest s-i path that uses at most $k - 1$ arcs, since if there is a shorter s-i path using at most $k - 1$ arcs, then it could be prepended to the arc (i, j) to obtain a shorter s-j path than P using at most k arcs. By the induction hypothesis, after $k - 1$ iterations, $d(i)$ is at most the length of this shortest s-i path of at most $k - 1$ arcs. After the kth iteration, we have updated $d(j)$ to be at most $d(i) + c(i, j)$, so that $d(j)$ is at most the length of path P, as desired.   □

Theorem 1.4: *If there is no negative-cost cycle reachable from s, then the Bellman–Ford algorithm (Algorithm 1.3) correctly determines the length $d(i)$ of the shortest path from the source s to each $i \in V$ if one exists.*

Proof If there are no negative-cost cycles reachable from s, then by Exercise 1.2 for each i the shortest s-i path must be simple and have at most $n - 1$ arcs. Thus by Lemmas 1.2 and 1.3, at the termination of the algorithm, $d(i)$ is the length of a shortest s-i path.   □

Note that we have not yet proven that the parent pointers p give the shortest path in the network. Although they do give the shortest paths, it will be easier to prove this statement once we have considered the issue of negative-cost cycles in the following section; see Corollary 1.13.

Algorithm 1.3 clearly runs in $O(mn)$ time; in fact, we examine each arc exactly $n - 1$ times, and thus the algorithm takes $\Theta(mn)$ time. We can ensure that it is possible for the algorithm to take fewer than $m(n - 1)$ operations by observing that we often don't need to check whether $d(j) > d(i) + c(i, j)$; if $d(i)$ was not decreased in the previous iteration of the algorithm, then none of the arcs (i, j) out of i will lead to a decrease of $d(j)$ in the current iteration. As a step toward making this clearer, it will help to introduce an additional abstraction to the Bellman–Ford algorithm; the abstraction is that of a *scan*. A scan of a vertex i checks all the outgoing arcs (i, j) of i to see whether $d(j) > d(i) + c(i, j)$, and if so, performs the appropriate update; see the Procedure Scan. We rewrite Algorithm 1.3 in terms of scans in Algorithm 1.4. As an exercise, the reader can check that Dijkstra's algorithm can also be rewritten in terms of scans so that we scan a vertex precisely when we mark it.

$d(i) \leftarrow \infty$ for all $i \in V$
$p(i) \leftarrow$ **null** for all $i \in V$
$d(s) \leftarrow 0$
for $k \leftarrow 1$ to $n - 1$ **do**
   for all $i \in V$ **do**
      Scan(i)

Algorithm 1.4 The Bellman–Ford algorithm using scans.

for j such that $(i, j) \in A$ **do**
   if $d(j) > d(i) + c(i, j)$ **then**
      $d(j) \leftarrow d(i) + c(i, j)$
      $p(j) \leftarrow i$

Procedure Scan(i)

Now we note that we only need to scan a vertex i in an iteration if its distance label $d(i)$ was decreased in the previous iteration; if $d(i)$ was unchanged in the previous iteration, then for all arcs (i, j) coming out of i, $d(j)$ will remain at most $d(i) + c(i, j)$. To implement this idea, we use a *queue* data structure. A queue is an ordered list of items and implements the following operations: *new queue()*, which returns an empty queue; *q.add(i)*, which adds an item i to the end of the queue q; *q.remove()*, which removes the item from the front of the queue q and returns it (if there is such an item); *q.empty?*, which checks if the queue q contains any items; and *q.contains?(i)*, which checks if the queue q already contains item i. We assume that *q.contains?* is implemented in $O(1)$ time rather than the $O(n)$ time it would take to scan the queue to check for membership; we can implement the operation this way with an array, for example, when we know in advance, as we do in this case, what elements the queue might contain.

We can then rewrite the scan procedure and the Bellman–Ford algorithm as shown in Procedure QScan and Algorithm 1.5. We place a vertex j in the queue when its distance label has changed during a scan; if vertex j is not in the queue, its label has not changed, and we do not need to perform a scan on it.

We can prove that the algorithm works correctly by an inductive argument similar to that in the proof of Theorem 1.4 in which we replace induction on iterations with induction on passes over the queue.

$d(i) \leftarrow \infty$ for all $i \in V$
$p(i) \leftarrow$ **null** for all $i \in V$
$d(s) \leftarrow 0$
$q \leftarrow new\ queue()$
$q.add(s)$
while not $q.empty?$ **do**
    QScan $(q.remove(), q)$;

Algorithm 1.5 The Bellman–Ford algorithm using queues.

for j such that $(i, j) \in A$ **do**
    if $d(j) > d(i) + c(i, j)$ **then**
        $d(j) \leftarrow d(i) + c(i, j)$
        $p(j) \leftarrow i$
        if not $q.contains?(j)$ **then**
            $q.add(j)$

Procedure QScan(i, q)

Theorem 1.5: *If there are no negative-cost cycles reachable from* s, *then Algorithm 1.5 correctly determines the length* $d(i)$ *of the shortest path from the source* s *to each* $i \in V$ *if one exists.*

Proof As suggested above, we apply induction on passes over the queue. Pass 0 ends after s is initially added to the queue, pass 1 ends after the initial scan of s, and in general pass k ends after the scans of all vertices added to the queue in pass $k - 1$. The induction hypothesis is that at the end of the kth pass, $d(i)$ is at most the length of a shortest s-i path of at most k arcs, and the proof proceeds as in the proof of Theorem 1.4.

If there are no negative-cost cycles reachable from s, then the shortest s-i path can have at most $n - 1$ arcs in it, and thus by the end of the $(n - 1)$st pass, the value of $d(i)$ will be the length of this path. Also, since the $d(i)$ are the lengths of the shortest paths from s to i, $d(j) \leq d(i) + c(i, j)$ for all $(i, j) \in A$ with i reachable from s, since otherwise there would be a shorter path from s to j. Thus no further vertices will be added to the queue, and the algorithm will terminate. Since there are at most $n - 1$ passes, and each pass considers each vertex at most once, at most all m arcs are considered in each pass. Thus the running time of the algorithm is $O(mn)$. $\qquad\square$

1.3 Negative-Cost Cycle Detection

We now wish to modify the Bellman–Ford algorithm so that it terminates with the shortest paths if there are no negative-cost cycles reachable from s, or stops if it detects a negative-cost cycle reachable from s in the input graph. Finding negative-cost cycles is in itself a useful subroutine that we will need later when we discuss minimum-cost circulation algorithms.

To begin our discussion, we return to our initial version of Bellman–Ford in Algorithm 1.3. We show a condition that we can check at the end of the algorithm that lets us convince ourselves that there is no negative-cost cycle.

Lemma 1.6: *There are no negative-cost cycles reachable from s if and only if* $d(j) \leq d(i) + c(i,j)$ *for all* $(i,j) \in A$ *with i reachable from s at the end of Algorithm 1.3.*

Proof If at the end of Algorithm 1.3, $d(j) > d(i) + c(i,j)$ for some $(i,j) \in A$, this implies that we could find a shorter path to j by taking the s-i path of length $d(i)$ (which exists by Lemma 1.2) then arc (i,j); thus the algorithm has not correctly computed the shortest s-j path. Since Theorem 1.4 argues that the algorithm computes the shortest path lengths if there is no negative-cost cycle reachable from s, the hypothesis must be false, and there must exist a negative-cost cycle reachable from s.

If, for all $(i,j) \in A$ with i reachable from s, $d(j) \leq d(i) + c(i,j)$, then given any cycle C reachable from s, we see that

$$\sum_{(i,j) \in C} c(i,j) \geq \sum_{(i,j) \in C} (d(j) - d(i)) = 0,$$

since all the terms cancel. Therefore, C cannot have negative cost. $\square$

Lemma 1.6 gives an immediate method for detecting if there is a negative-cost cycle, though it does not say how to find the cycle: we simply check at the end of algorithm if $d(j) \leq d(i) + c(i,j)$ for all $(i,j) \in A$; if the condition holds, there is no negative-cost cycle, otherwise there is. We summarize this algorithm in Algorithm 1.6.

A disadvantage of this algorithm, in addition to not finding the cycle, is that it takes n iterations and $\Theta(mn)$ time. We would like the algorithm to terminate earlier if possible when a negative-cost cycle is detected. To give such an algorithm, we return to the parent pointers used by the algorithm, and introduce the concept of the *parent graph*, which we denote G_p. The parent graph consists of the set of arcs $(p(j), j)$ for all $j \in V$ for which $p(j)$ is defined. Note that while we follow the parent pointers backward from a node

$d(i) \leftarrow \infty$ for all $i \in V$
$p(i) \leftarrow$ **null** for all $i \in V$
$d(s) \leftarrow 0$
for $k \leftarrow 1$ to $n - 1$ **do**
    for all $(i, j) \in A$ **do**
        if $d(j) > d(i) + c(i, j)$ **then**
            $d(j) \leftarrow d(i) + c(i, j)$
            $p(j) \leftarrow i$
for all $(i, j) \in A$ **do**
    if $d(j) > d(i) + c(i, j)$ **then**
        return "negative-cost cycle exists"

Algorithm 1.6 A negative-cost cycle detection algorithm.

j to s to obtain an s-j path, the parent graph G_p gives the path directed from s to j and contains a subset of arcs from G. We will show below that a negative-cost cycle will appear in the parent graph G_p if and only if there is a negative-cost cycle reachable from s. This will suggest a simple algorithm for finding a negative-cost cycle: at every step check the parent graph G_p for cycles.

Lemma 1.7: *At any point in Algorithm 1.3, if arc (i, j) is in the parent graph G_p, $d(j) \geq d(i) + c(i, j)$.*

Proof At the point at which the arc (i, j) is added to G_p, we have $d(j) = d(i) + c(i, j)$. Recall that distance labels only decrease through the course of the algorithm. Thus if the arc remains in the graph (that is, $p(j)$ and thus $d(j)$ are not updated), $d(i)$ can decrease while $d(j)$ remains the same; therefore, $d(j) \geq d(i) + c(i, j)$. □

Lemma 1.8: *For any h-ℓ path P in the parent graph G_p, the cost of the path, $\sum_{(i,j) \in P} c(i, j)$, is at most $d(\ell) - d(h)$.*

Proof By Lemma 1.7, $\sum_{(i,j) \in P} c(i, j) \leq \sum_{(i,j) \in P} (d(j) - d(i)) = d(\ell) - d(h)$. □

Lemma 1.9: *Suppose a cycle appears in G_p. The first cycle to appear in G_p has negative cost and is reachable from s.*

Proof The first cycle C to appear in the parent graph G_p must have appeared because we added the arc (i, j) to G_p, but j was part of an s-i path in G_p before the update (see Figure 1.3). If P is the path in G_p from j to i, and $d(i)$ and $d(j)$ are the labels before the update, then by the above, and Lemma 1.8, we

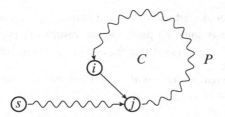

Figure 1.3 Illustration of the proof of Lemma 1.9. The path P with the wavy line is before the update that adds arc (i, j) to the parent graph.

$d(i) \leftarrow \infty$ for all $i \in V$
$p(i) \leftarrow$ **null** for all $i \in V$
$d(s) \leftarrow 0$
for $k \leftarrow 1$ to n **do**
    for all $(i, j) \in A$ **do**
        if $d(j) > d(i) + c(i, j)$ **then**
            $d(j) \leftarrow d(i) + c(i, j)$
            $p(j) \leftarrow i$
            if G_p has a cycle C **then**
                return C

Algorithm 1.7 Another negative-cost cycle detection algorithm.

have that $\sum_{(k,l) \in C} c(k, l) = c(i, j) + \sum_{(k,l) \in P} c(k, l) \leq c(i, j) + d(i) - d(j)$. But since we performed the update, it must have been because $d(j) > d(i) + c(i, j)$, and therefore $c(i, j) + d(i) - d(j) < 0$ and the total cost of the arcs in the cycle C is negative. $\quad\square$

Thus if we find a cycle in the parent graph G_p, the lemma above shows that it must be a negative-cost cycle. As a first attempt at an algorithm using this insight, we modify the Bellman–Ford algorithm to take n iterations, but on each update we check G_p for cycles; we give this algorithm in Algorithm 1.7. This algorithm is not fast because it can take $O(n)$ time to check G_p for a cycle, giving an overall running time of $O(mn^2)$. However, once we prove that this algorithm is correct, we show how we can modify it so that the time to check G_p for a cycle can be amortized over the operations used to update the parent graph.

Lemma 1.10: *If Algorithm 1.7 does not return a cycle, $d(s) = 0$.*

Proof If $d(s)$ is ever altered, then its parent pointer $p(s)$ is changed to a vertex i such that there exists some s-i path, and this results in a cycle in G_p. Thus if no cycle is returned, then $d(s) = 0$ at the end of the algorithm. □

Lemma 1.11: *Throughout the execution of Algorithm 1.7, the parent graph G_p is a tree directed out of s.*

Proof We show by induction on the algorithm that the arcs $(p(j), j)$ for all j such that $p(j) \neq$ **null** form a tree directed out of s. There are initially no arcs in G_p. If we add an arc (i, j) to G_p it is because $d(i)$ is finite, and by induction i is reachable from s in the parent graph G_p. If adding (i, j) to G_p causes a cycle, the algorithm terminates; otherwise we update $p(j)$ to i, and have a path from s to j. □

Theorem 1.12: *Algorithm 1.7 either correctly computes the shortest path from s to all vertices $i \in V$, or it correctly detects and returns a negative-cost cycle reachable from s.*

Proof By Lemma 1.9, if the algorithm returns a cycle C, then C is a negative-cost cycle. We now show that if there is a negative-cost cycle C reachable from s, the algorithm will return a negative-cost cycle C. By Lemma 1.6, if there is a negative-cost cycle reachable from s, then at the end of the algorithm, in the nth iteration, there must be some $(i, j) \in A$ such that $d(j) > d(i) + c(i, j)$ for i reachable from s. Then by Lemma 1.3, after updating $d(j)$ in the nth iteration, $d(j)$ is less than the cost of any simple s-j path, since after $n - 1$ iterations it was no more than the cost of any simple path, and it has since decreased. However, if there is no cycle in G_p, then by Lemmas 1.8 and 1.11, there must be a simple s-j path P in G_p of cost at most $d(j) - d(s)$. By Lemma 1.10, $d(s) = 0$. Thus the cost of the simple path P is at most $d(j)$, but this is a contradiction, since $d(j)$ has cost less than any simple s-j path. Thus if $d(j) > d(i) + c(i, j)$ for some (i, j) in the nth iteration, a cycle must appear in G_p. □

Corollary 1.13: *If there is no negative-cost cycle reachable from s in the graph, then Algorithms 1.3, 1.4, and 1.5 correctly find the shortest path from s to all vertices $i \in V$ in G_p.*

Proof If there is no negative-cost cycle reachable from s in the graph, then $d(i)$ is the length of the shortest s-i path in the graph (by Theorems 1.4 and 1.5), there is a simple s-i path that is shortest (by Exercise 1.2), and there is a simple s-i path in G_p of length at most $d(i)$ (by Lemmas 1.8 and 1.10). Thus the s-i path in G_p must be the shortest s-i path. □

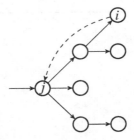

Figure 1.4 Illustration of detecting cycles via subtrees.

Finally, we discuss how we can have the advantage of an algorithm that terminates early if it detects a cycle in G_p together with an $O(mn)$ running time. To do this, we modify the version of the Bellman–Ford algorithm from Algorithm 1.5, which uses queues and the scan operation. We observe that setting $p(j)$ to i causes a cycle in the parent graph G_p exactly when i is in the subtree rooted at j. So we can check whether setting $p(j)$ to i causes a cycle by starting at j and exploring the subtree rooted at j by following arcs in the parent graph. If we find i, then setting $p(j)$ to i will cause a cycle (see Figure 1.4). This operation takes $O(n)$ time, and so it seems that we have not made much progress. However, if we were to traverse each arc at most once, then the time taken to traverse each arc in the subtree rooted at j can be charged to the time at which the arc was created. In order to make sure that we do not traverse an arc multiple times, if there is no cycle – that is, we do not find i in the subtree of j – then we delete every arc in the subtree of j: in particular, for each i' in the subtree rooted at j, we set $p(i')$ to null. We justify deleting the arc as follows: because i' was in the subtree of j in G_p, the shortest s-i' path found so far by the algorithm goes through j, and we have just decreased $d(j)$. So after some number of iterations of the algorithm, the distance label $d(i')$ is also going to decrease, at which point we will add an arc into i' to the parent graph G_p once again. Furthermore, to save ourselves a bit of effort, since we know that $d(i')$ will eventually decrease, we do not scan i' until after this decrease occurs; we can check for the decrease by looking to see if $p(i')$ is not null. We summarize this algorithm in Algorithm 1.8.

We now prove that the algorithm is correct and runs in $O(mn)$ time. Because we now remove edges from the parent graph and do not scan each updated vertex in each pass over the queue, we will need to modify some of our basic helper lemmas and our overall proof approach. As in the proof of Theorem 1.5, we will apply induction on the passes of the algorithm over the queue.

$d(i) \leftarrow \infty$ for all $i \in V$
$p(i) \leftarrow$ **null** for all $i \in V$
$d(s) \leftarrow 0$
$q \leftarrow new\ queue()$
NCCScan(s,q)
while not $q.empty?$ **do**
   $i \leftarrow q.remove()$
   if $p(i) \neq$ **null then**
      NCCScan(i,q)

Algorithm 1.8 A final negative-cost cycle detection algorithm.

---

for j such that $(i, j) \in A$ **do**
   if $d(j) > d(i) + c(i, j)$ **then**
      Traverse subtree of G_p rooted at j
      if i in subtree of G_p rooted at j **then**
         Let C be the cycle closed by (i, j) and j-i path in G_p
         return C
      else
         for all i' in subtree of G_p rooted at j **do**
            $p(i') \leftarrow$ **null**
      $d(j) \leftarrow d(i) + c(i, j)$
      $p(j) \leftarrow i$
      if not $q.contains?(j)$ **then**
         $q.add(j)$

Procedure NCCScan(i, q)

Lemma 1.14: *Throughout the execution of Algorithm 1.8, the parent graph G_p is a tree directed out of s.*

Proof We show by induction on the algorithm that the arcs $(p(j), j)$ for all j such that $p(j) \neq$ **null** form a tree directed out of s. There are initially no arcs in G_p. If we add an arc (i, j) to G_p it is because we scanned i, which we can only do if $p(i)$ is not null; thus by induction i is reachable from s in the parent graph G_p. If adding (i, j) causes a cycle, the algorithm terminates; otherwise we update $p(j)$ to i and remove the entire subtree rooted at j, so that what remains is still a tree rooted at s. $\qquad\square$

Lemma 1.15: *If Algorithm 1.8 does not return a cycle, $d(s) = 0$.*

Proof If $d(s)$ is ever altered, then it is by considering arc (i, s) during a scan of i. We can only scan i if $p(i)$ is defined, so by Lemma 1.14, i is reachable from s in G_p. Thus i is in the subtree rooted at s, and the algorithm will return a negative-cost cycle and terminate. □

Lemma 1.16: *At any point in Algorithm 1.8, for any arc (i, j) in the parent graph G_p, $d(j) = d(i) + c(i, j)$.*

Proof At the point at which the arc (i, j) is added to G_p, we have $d(j) = d(i) + c(i, j)$. If $d(i)$ is updated via a scan to a node h with arc (h, i), and a negative-cost cycle is not returned, then since j is in the subtree of i in G_p, the arc (i, j) is deleted from G_p. □

Lemma 1.17: *Throughout the execution of Algorithm 1.8, any ℓ in the parent graph G_p has $d(\ell)$ equal to the cost of the s-ℓ path in G_p.*

Proof Following the proof of Lemma 1.8 and using Lemmas 1.15 and 1.16, for an s-ℓ path P in G_p,

$$\sum_{(i,j)\in P} c(i, j) = \sum_{(i,j)\in P} (d(j) - d(i)) = d(\ell) - d(s) = d(\ell).$$

□

In the proof of Theorem 1.5, we performed induction on the number of passes to show that after k passes, $d(i)$ is always at most the length of the shortest s-i path of at most k arcs. Now, however, because we may skip the scan of a node i when $p(i)$ is null, we cannot use the same induction. However, we can prove the following.

Lemma 1.18: *Any finite distance label $d(i)$ updated in the kth pass is the length of a simple s-i path with at least k arcs.*

Proof Whenever the distance label $d(i)$ is updated, i becomes part of the tree in G_p, and thus by Lemma 1.17, $d(i)$ is the length of the simple s-i path in the tree. At the end of pass 0, the s-s path is in the tree and $d(s)$ is the length of this path that has zero arcs. If distance label $d(j)$ is updated in the kth pass by considering arc (i, j), then $d(i)$ was updated in pass $k - 1$, and by induction, the s-i path of length $d(i)$ has at least $k - 1$ arcs in it. Therefore, the s-j path formed by the s-i path plus arc (i, j) has at least k arcs in it. □

Because we can now have vertices i with finite distance label $d(i)$ that nevertheless do not have a path from s to i in G_p throughout the algorithm, we need to ensure that there is a path from s to i in the final parent graph G_p. The following lemma shows that this indeed is the case.

Lemma 1.19: *Suppose that there are no negative-cost cycles reachable from s. If $d(j)$ is updated to the length of the shortest s-j path, then $d(j)$ is not updated in future passes and j is part of the tree in G_p throughout the rest of the algorithm.*

Proof Since there are no negative-cost cycles reachable from s, the s-s path of length 0 is the shortest s-s path; initially, $d(s)$ is set to 0 and s is part of the tree in G_p throughout the algorithm. Now consider the shortest s-j path for $j \neq s$; let (i, j) be the final arc of the path. By hypothesis, at some point $d(j)$ is updated to the length of the shortest s-j path. Note that when $d(j)$ is updated to the length of the shortest s-j path, every vertex ℓ on the path already has $d(\ell)$ equal to the length of the shortest s-ℓ path. Note that $d(\ell)$ will not be updated in future iterations: by Lemma 1.18, $d(\ell)$ is always the length of some simple s-ℓ path, and there is no shorter simple s-ℓ path. When $d(j)$ is updated to the length of the shortest s-j path, (i, j) is added to the tree in G_p. The arc (i, j) is never removed because none of the predecessors of j on the path is ever updated.   □

Finally, we can show that the algorithm is correct.

Theorem 1.20: *Algorithm 1.8 runs in $O(mn)$ time and either correctly computes the shortest path from s to each $i \in V$ or correctly detects and returns a negative-cost cycle reachable from s.*

Proof If the algorithm updates a distance label $d(i)$ in the nth pass of the algorithm, then by Lemma 1.18, it is the length of a simple s-i path of at least n arcs, which is a contradiction, and indicates the presence of a negative-cost cycle. Therefore, the algorithm terminates by the end of the nth pass, either by returning a negative-cost cycle or not. If the algorithm returns a cycle C, then by Lemma 1.9 it has negative cost and is reachable from s. Since the algorithm must terminate after the nth pass, and at worst each arc is processed in each pass, the running time is $O(mn)$ except for the operation of traversing subtrees used in detecting cycles. However, we charge the cost of traversing each arc in the subtree to the operation that added the arc to the parent graph in the first place. As the arc is removed after the subtree is traversed, it is clear that we do not charge the event of adding the arc more than once. Thus the algorithm runs in $O(mn)$ time.

If the algorithm terminates without returning a cycle, then there must have been no further updates needed to the distance labels, so that $d(j) \leq d(i) + c(i, j)$ for all $(i, j) \in A$ with i reachable from s; it then follows from Lemma 1.6 that the algorithm correctly states that there are no negative-cost cycles reachable from s. Let P be a shortest s-ℓ path. Then all nodes on P are reachable from s so that $\sum_{(i,j)\in P} c(i,j) \geq \sum_{(i,j)\in P}(d(j) - d(i)) = d(\ell) - d(s)$. By Lemma 1.15, $d(s) = 0$, so that $d(\ell) \leq \sum_{(i,j)\in P} c(i,j)$. Since, by Lemma 1.18, $d(\ell)$ is always the length of a simple s-ℓ path, it cannot be the case that $d(\ell)$ is less than the cost of the path P, so it must equal the cost of the path P. Then by Lemma 1.19, vertex ℓ must be part of the tree in G_p, and by Lemma 1.17, $d(\ell)$ is equal to the length of the path in G_p. $\square$

While this final algorithm seems more complicated that the prior ones, computational studies have shown it to be particularly effective for both shortest-path computation and negative-cost cycle detection; see Chapter Notes for further discussion.

Many of these ideas for negative-cost cycle detection based on the Bellman–Ford algorithm turn out to be very useful for other applications in network flow algorithms. In Exercise 1.4, we ask the reader to extend these ideas to finding a minimum mean-cost cycle, which is the basis for a minimum-cost circulation algorithm given in Section 5.3. Exercise 1.5 generalizes finding the minimum mean-cost cycle to the minimum cost-to-time ratio cycle problem, which gets used in another minimum-cost circulation algorithm in Section 5.2. We'll also see a generalization of the idea of a negative-cost cycle to something called a negative-cost generalized augmenting path in Section 6.3 when we discuss algorithms for the generalized flow problem in Chapter 6.

Exercises

1.1 Suppose that for each arc $(i,j) \in A$, its cost $c(i,j) = 1$. Show that Dijkstra's algorithm can be implemented in $O(m)$ time; we assume that all vertices are reachable from s and thus $m \geq n - 1$.

1.2 Show that there are simple shortest paths from s to each $i \in V$ reachable from s if and only if there are no negative-cost cycles reachable from s.

1.3 A *directed acyclic graph*, or a DAG, is a directed graph with no cycles.

   (a) Prove that any DAG must have a vertex that has no arcs directed into it.

   (b) Given a DAG, let s be a vertex with no arcs directed into it. Give an $O(m)$ time algorithm for finding the shortest path from s to i for each vertex $i \in V$.

   (c) Given a DAG, let s be a vertex with no arcs directed into it. Give an $O(m)$ time algorithm for finding the longest path from s to i for each vertex $i \in V$.

1.4   In this exercise, we want to compute the minimum mean-cost cycle C in
       a directed graph. We are given a directed graph $G = (V, A)$ with costs
       $c(i, j)$ for all $(i, j) \in A$, and we wish to compute

$$\mu = \min_{\text{cycles } \Gamma \in G} \frac{c(\Gamma)}{|\Gamma|},$$

where $c(\Gamma) = \sum_{(i, j) \in \Gamma} c(i, j)$. You may assume that all vertices of G
are reachable from some vertex $s \in V$. Let $d_k(j)$ be the value of the
distance label for j in the kth iteration of the Bellman–Ford algorithm
given in Algorithm 1.3. Show that

$$\mu = \min_{j \in V} \max_{0 \leq k \leq n-1} \left[\frac{d_n(j) - d_k(j)}{n - k} \right],$$

and thus can be computed in $O(mn)$ time. Also show that we can find
the cycle Γ for which $\mu = c(\Gamma)/|\Gamma|$ in the same running time. (Hint:
observe that if we subtract μ from the cost of each arc, then the graph
will have no negative-cost cycles, while if we subtract anything larger,
there will be a negative-cost cycle.)

1.5   In this exercise, we consider the minimum cost-to-time ratio cycle prob-
       lem. This problem generalizes the minimum mean-cost cycle problem
       given in Exercise 1.4. Let $G = (V, A)$ be a directed graph, with
       integer costs $c(i, j)$ and integer times $t(i, j) \geq 0$ for each $(i, j) \in A$.
       Assume that for every cycle Γ, $t(\Gamma) = \sum_{(i, j) \in \Gamma} t(i, j) > 0$. Let
       $T = \max_{(i, j) \in A} t(i, j)$ and $C = \max_{(i, j) \in A} c(i, j)$.

       (a) Give a $O(mn \log(nCT))$ time algorithm for finding a cycle that
           minimizes

$$\min_{\text{cycles } \Gamma \in G} \frac{c(\Gamma)}{t(\Gamma)}.$$

       Note that in the case $t(i, j) = 1$ for all $(i, j) \in A$, this is just the
       problem of finding a minimum mean-cost cycle.

       (b) Now suppose that the times $t(i, j)$ are not integers but rather rational
           numbers such that $\max_{(i, j) \in A} t(i, j) \leq T$ and $\min_{(i, j) \in A} t(i, j) \geq$
           $1/T$. Explain why a $O(mn \log(nCT))$ algorithm is still possible.

Chapter Notes

There are three kinds of lies: lies, damned lies, and statistics.
                                                        – attributed to Mark Twain

There are at least four kinds of lies: lies, damned lies, statistics, and big-oh notation.

– Michael Langston [137, p. 10]

In theory, there is no difference between theory and practice. In practice, there is.

– Often misattributed to Yogi Berra[1]

The literature on algorithms for shortest path problems is vast, and we restrict our overview here to the topics covered in the chapter. See Schrijver [177, chapters 6–8] for more in-depth coverage of the shortest path problem, along with an extensive historical survey on the origins of the algorithms presented here. As the quotes above suggest, we will try in these notes to pay some attention to the experimental studies that have been performed on algorithms discussed, so that we can note when there are differences between what is known in theory and practice.

Dijkstra's algorithm in Section 1.1 is due to Dijkstra [51]. For explanations of the implementation of heaps, see, for instance, chapters 6 and 19 of Cormen, Leiserson, Rivest, and Stein [45] or section 2.5 of Kleinberg and Tardos [134]. As we mentioned, a theoretically faster running time for Dijkstra's algorithm is obtained using a particular implementation of heaps known as *Fibonacci heaps*, introduced by Fredman and Tarjan [71]. The running times of the operations for a Fibonacci heap are *amortized* running times, so that, for instance, an $O(1)$ operation may not truly take $O(1)$ time but can charge some of its running time to operations previously executed. The Fibonacci heap takes amortized $O(1)$ time for each *insert* and *decrease-key*, so that the overall running time of Dijkstra's algorithm is then $O(m + n \log n)$ time. However, Fibonacci heaps are not considered practical compared to array-based heaps or another data structure called a pairing heap [70], though array-based heaps and pairing heaps do not have the same theoretical performance as do Fibonacci heaps. See Larkin, Sen, and Tarjan [138] for an experimental survey of heap data structures.

Ford [62] originally proposed an algorithm in which one looked for arcs (i, j) such that $d(j) > d(i) + c(i, j)$ and updated $d(i) \leq d(j) + c(i, j)$. If these updates are applied in an arbitrary order, then it can take an exponential number of operations to find the shortest paths; see Johnson [117, section 3]. The algorithm in Section 1.3 that applies the updates to all arcs in order $n - 1$ times can be found in Bellman [18] and Moore [149], and hence the algorithm

---

[1] "I really didn't say everything I said." – Yogi Berra.

is sometimes called the Bellman–Ford–Moore algorithm (by Cherkassky and Goldberg [38], for example). However, Schrijver [177, pp. 121–125] points out that in Bellman's paper, Dantzig and Woodbury are mentioned as also having obtained the algorithm independently. In order to avoid a proliferation of people in the name for the algorithm, we follow Schrijver [177] and Cormen et al. [45] in sticking with the historic but inaccurate name of Bellman–Ford.

Cherkassky and Goldberg [38] give an overview of negative-cost cycle detection algorithms, along with an experimental study. They attribute Algorithm 1.6 to Bellman [18], Ford [62], and Moore [149]. Use of the parent graph G_p is unattributed, but they reference a book of Tarjan for a discussion of the method [192]. They attribute the variation of Algorithm 1.8 to Tarjan [191]. Kleinberg and Tardos [134, pp. 304–307] also include a discussion of Algorithm 1.8. Cherkassky and Goldberg found that this algorithm was typically the fastest in their experiments.

Exercise 1.4 is due to Karp [126]. Exercise 1.5 is due to Lawler [139].

2

Maximum Flow Algorithms

This book presents one approach to that part of linear programming theory
that has come to be encompassed by the phrase "transportation problems"
or "network flow problems." We use the latter name, not only because it is
more nearly suggestive of the mathematical content of the subject, but also
because it is less committed to one domain of application. Since many of the
applications that are examined have little to do with transportation [...], it
seems appropriate not to stress one particular applied area over others.
      – L. R. Ford, Jr., and D. R. Fulkerson, *Flows in Networks*

We now turn to the founding problem of network flow theory, the maximum
flow problem, and its dual problem, the minimum s-t cut problem. These two
problems have proven to be enormously useful in modeling various problems
involving networks of all kinds: road networks, railway networks, computer
networks, social networks, and others. Usually we are modeling the flow of
material from one part of the network to the other, and the flow can be cars,
trains, recommendations, bits, trust, and many other items and concepts. Quite
interestingly, these two problems have also proven useful in modeling problems that do not obviously involve networks or the flow of material. We will
give a few examples, one in determining when baseball teams cannot win their
division, another in deciding fair ways to allocate driving duties in carpools,
and yet another in finding the densest subgraph of a given undirected graph.

We formally define the maximum flow problem as follows. We are given as
input a directed graph $G = (V, A)$ and capacities on the arcs $u(i, j)$ that are
nonnegative integers. We also have two distinct vertices $s, t \in V$; we call s the
source and t the *sink*. The source s is the origin of the material of the flow,
and the sink t is its destination. The goal is to find a flow f that maximizes the
net flow coming out of the source, subject to the capacities on the arcs and the
conservation of flow at the vertices. We define a flow as follows.

Definition 2.1: *An s-t flow $f : A \rightarrow \Re^{\geq 0}$ is an assignment of nonnegative reals to the arcs such that the following two properties are obeyed:*

- *for all arcs $(i, j) \in A$,*

$$0 \leq f(i, j) \leq u(i, j); \tag{2.1}$$

- *for all $i \in V$ such that $i \neq s, t$, the total flow entering i is equal to the flow leaving i; that is,*

$$\sum_{k:(k,i)\in A} f(k,i) = \sum_{k:(i,k)\in A} f(i,k). \tag{2.2}$$

The constraints in (2.1) are usually called *capacity constraints* and those in (2.2) are called *flow conservation constraints*. With every flow f we associate a value, which we denote $|f|$. It is the net amount of flow leaving the source; that is, the total amount of flow leaving the source minus the amount of flow entering the source.

Definition 2.2: *The value of an s-t flow f is*

$$|f| \equiv \sum_{k:(s,k)\in A} f(s,k) - \sum_{k:(k,s)\in A} f(k,s).$$

The reader might ask why the value of the flow is the net amount of flow leaving the source rather than the net amount of flow entering the sink, but due to flow conservation, these two amounts are always the same, and we leave it as an exercise to the reader to show this fact (Exercise 2.1).

Thus the goal of the maximum flow problem is to find an *s-t* flow f that maximizes $|f|$. We say that a flow is *maximum* (or *optimal*) if it is a flow of maximum value. Note that because the capacities are nonnegative integers, the flow $f = 0$ (that is $f(i, j) = 0$ for all $(i, j) \in A$) is always an *s-t* flow, so that the value of the maximum flow is always nonnegative. We give a sample instance of the maximum flow problem, and a sample flow in Figure 2.1. The reader should check that the capacity constraints and the flow conservation constraints are obeyed.

It will simplify our proofs to introduce a somewhat unconventional redefinition of a flow, in which we consider only upper bounds on flow values rather than both upper and lower bounds. For each arc $(i, j) \in A$, we will introduce an additional reverse arc (j, i) to A, and we impose the condition that if $f(i, j)$ units of flow are on arc (i, j), then $-f(i, j)$ units of flow are on the reverse arc (j, i). This additional condition is known as *skew symmetry*. Now the lower bound $f(i, j) \geq 0$ on flows can be replaced by the condition that $u(j, i) = 0$, so that $f(j, i) \leq u(j, i)$ implies that $f(i, j) = -f(j, i) \geq -u(j, i) = 0$.

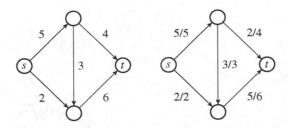

Figure 2.1 An instance of the maximum flow problem (on the left) and a flow (on the right). The flow has value 7. The number next to each arc in figure on the left represents the capacity of the arc. The notation "x/y" next to each arc in the figure on the right represents x units of flow used of the capacity of y.

Furthermore, under the new definition, the sum of the flows on the outgoing arcs from a node i is equal to the net flow out of i under the previous definition. That is, if A' is the new set of arcs (including the reverse arcs), then

$$\sum_{k:(i,k)\in A'} f(i,k) = \sum_{k:(i,k)\in A} f(i,k) - \sum_{k:(k,i)\in A} f(k,i).$$

Thus the flow conservation constraint becomes

$$\sum_{k:(i,k)\in A'} f(i,k) = 0$$

for $i \neq s,t$; see Figure 2.2 for an illustration of the difference between the old and new flow conservation constraints. Similarly, the value of the flow is $|f| = \sum_{k:(s,k)\in A'} f(s,k)$. From now on we will simply refer to the new set of arcs as A. We summarize the new definition of a flow below.

Definition 2.3: *An s-t flow $f : A \to \Re$ is an assignment of reals to the arcs such that the following three properties are obeyed:*

- *for all arcs $(i, j) \in A$,*

$$f(i,j) \leq u(i,j); \tag{2.3}$$

- *for all $i \in V$ such that $i \neq s,t$, the net flow leaving i is zero; that is,*

$$\sum_{k:(i,k)\in A} f(i,k) = 0; \tag{2.4}$$

- *for all $(i, j) \in A$,*

$$f(i,j) = -f(j,i). \tag{2.5}$$

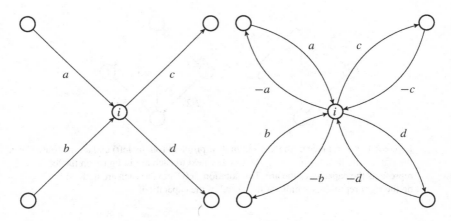

Figure 2.2 Flow conservation in the two different definitions of a flow. On the left, we have a flow according to Definition 2.1. On the right, we have a flow according to Definition 2.3; given skew symmetry, it is sufficient to sum the outgoing arcs to check whether the net flow at a node is zero. In particular, on the left, we have flow out minus flow in is $c + d - (a + b)$, whereas on the right the flow on the outgoing arcs sums to $(-a) + (-b) + c + d$.

2.1 Optimality Conditions

We now start our discussion of the maximum flow problem by asking how one can tell whether a given flow is maximum or not. For instance, consider the flow given in Figure 2.3. Is the flow maximum? The reader should verify that for any s-t path of arcs with positive capacity, we cannot increase the flow along the path without violating capacity constraints.

In fact, the flow of Figure 2.3 is not maximum; we can obtain a larger flow of value $|f| = 5$, as shown in Figure 2.4. We also see from the figure that any unit of flow from s to t must go through one of the arcs from inside the region in the diagram to outside the region; thus we claim that the value of the flow cannot be larger than the total capacity of these arcs, which is $u(a,d) + u(b,d) + u(e,t) = 1 + 2 + 2 = 5$. If the claim is correct, then the flow of value 5 is maximum; it cannot be larger.

We now wish to formalize the intuition we used above. We say that an s-t *cut* is a subset of vertices $S \subseteq V$ such that $s \in S$ and $t \notin S$; this corresponds to the region in the figure. We denote the set of all arcs leaving a set S by $\delta^+(S)$; that is, $\delta^+(S) = \{(i, j) \in A : i \in S, j \notin S\}$. Sometimes we say that the arcs of $\delta^+(S)$ are the arcs *in the cut* defined by S. The set of all arcs entering a set S is denoted $\delta^-(S) = \{(i, j) \in A : i \notin S, j \in S\}$. The *capacity of an s-t cut* S is the sum of the capacities of all the arcs leaving S (or in the cut defined by S), and we write it as $u(\delta^+(S)) \equiv \sum_{(i,j) \in \delta^+(S)} u(i, j)$. We can now prove

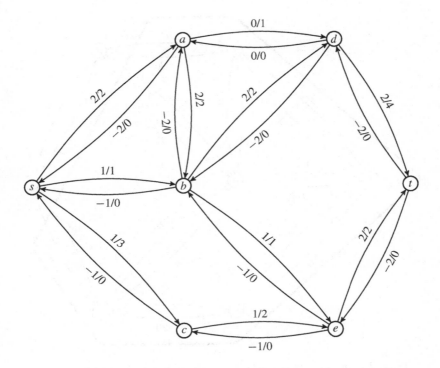

Figure 2.3 Sample maximum flow instance of value $|f| = 4$. Is it maximum?

the claim that we made above; namely, for any flow f and s-t cut S, the value of the flow is at most the capacity of the cut.

Lemma 2.4: *For any s-t flow f and any s-t cut S, $|f| \leq u(\delta^+(S))$.*

Proof Using the definition of the value of the flow f and the flow conservation constraint (2.4) for $i \in S$, $i \neq s$ (and recalling that $t \notin S$), then combining, we can show that the value of the flow is equal to the sum of flow on arcs in $\delta^+(S)$. We see that

$$|f| = \sum_{k:(s,k)\in A} f(s,k) + 0$$

$$= \sum_{k:(s,k)\in A} f(s,k) + \sum_{i\in S:i\neq s} \left(\sum_{j:(i,j)\in A} f(i,j) \right)$$

$$= \sum_{i\in S} \left(\sum_{j:(i,j)\in A} f(i,j) \right).$$

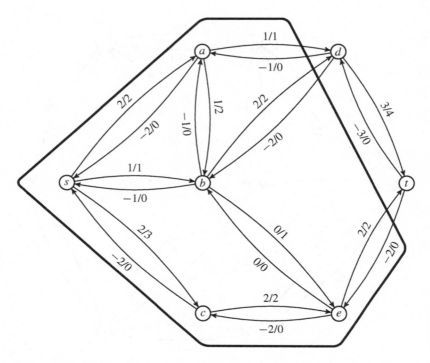

Figure 2.4 Another flow, of value $|f| = 5$. The enclosing thick lines shows that the flow cannot be larger, since only $1 + 2 + 2 = 5$ units of capacity are available on arcs leaving the enclosed set of nodes.

Now we can split this sum into two parts, depending on whether the head of the arc (i, j) is in S or not. Note that if both $i, j \in S$, then the sum includes both $f(i, j)$ and $f(j, i) = -f(i, j)$, and hence these terms all cancel out, so that

$$
\begin{aligned}
|f| &= \sum_{i \in S} \left(\sum_{j:(i,j) \in A} f(i,j) \right) \\
&= \sum_{i \in S} \left(\sum_{j \in S:(i,j) \in A} f(i,j) + \sum_{j \notin S:(i,j) \in A} f(i,j) \right) \\
&= \sum_{i \in S, j \notin S, (i,j) \in A} f(i,j) \\
&= \sum_{(i,j) \in \delta^+(S)} f(i,j)
\end{aligned}
$$

$$\leq \sum_{(i,j)\in\delta^+(S)} u(i,j)$$

$$= u(\delta^+(S)),$$

where the inequality follows from the capacity constraints (2.3).   □

Corollary 2.5: *Let f be an s-t flow and S be an s-t cut. Then $f(i,j) = u(i,j)$ for all $(i,j) \in \delta^+(S)$ if and only if $|f| = u(\delta^+(S))$.*

Proof If $f(i,j) = u(i,j)$ for all $(i,j) \in \delta^+(S)$, then the final inequality of the proof above is an equality. Also, if $|f| = u(\delta^+(S))$, then because the final inequality is an equality, it must be an equality for every term in the sum, $f(i,j) = u(i,j)$ for all $(i,j) \in \delta^+(S)$.   □

Notice that for the flow in Figure 2.4 $f(a,d) = u(a,d)$, $f(b,d) = u(b,d)$ and $f(e,t) = u(e,t)$ for the three arcs in $\delta^+(S)$ given by the s-t cut S in the figure.

We say that a *minimum s-t cut* is an s-t cut S^* of minimum capacity; that is,

$$u(\delta^+(S^*)) = \min_{S\subset V, s\in S, t\notin S} u(\delta^+(S)).$$

By Lemma 2.4, the value of a maximum flow is at most the capacity of a minimum s-t cut. In our example in Figure 2.4, we saw that the two quantities can be equal. Corollary 2.5 gives a condition under which the two quantities are equal. The central result of network flow theory, due to Ford and Fulkerson [63], is that these two quantities are always equal. This result, proved in the 1950s, has led to more than fifty years of research on the topic of network flows.

Theorem 2.6 (Ford and Fulkerson [63]): *The value of a maximum flow is equal to the capacity of a minimum s-t cut.*

This theorem is sometimes known as the maximum flow/minimum cut theorem.

We will shortly provide a proof of this theorem. Before we can do so, we need to define the concept of a *residual graph*. Given flow f on graph $G = (V, A)$, the residual graph with respect to flow f is a graph $G_f = (V, A)$. An arc $(i,j) \in A$ has a *residual capacity* $u_f(i,j) = u(i,j) - f(i,j)$; that is, the difference between the capacity and the flow; note that the residual capacity is always nonnegative because of the capacity constraint. Arcs (i,j) with 0 residual capacity are said to be *saturated*; that is, the flow value $f(i,j)$ equals the capacity $u(i,j)$. It is more traditional to omit these arcs from the residual graph altogether, but it will be useful in our proofs to include them. We denote

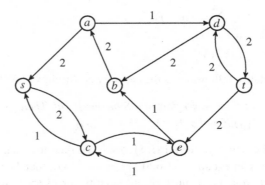

Figure 2.5 Residual graph for the flow of Figure 2.3; arcs of zero residual capacity are omitted. There is an augmenting path s-c-e-b-a-d-t.

by A_f the set of all arcs with positive residual capacity; that is, $A_f = \{(i, j) \in A : u_f(i, j) > 0\}$. Observe that with our definition of flow that uses reverse arcs, the residual capacity of the arc $u_f(j,i) = u(j,i) - f(j,i) = 0 + f(i,j) = f(i, j)$. Thus the residual capacity of such reverse arcs (j, i) corresponds to the amount by which we may decrease the positive amount of flow on the arc (i, j). As an example, in Figure 2.5, we give the residual graph associated with the flow of Figure 2.3; we omit arcs with zero residual capacity.

If there is an s-t path P in the residual graph G_f on arcs in A_f (that is, the arcs with positive residual capacity), then we call P an *augmenting path*; see Figure 2.5 for an example of an augmenting path. The existence of an augmenting path implies that f is not maximum, because we can create a new flow f' of greater value by increasing flow along the arcs in P. Formally, let δ be the capacity of the residual arc of minimum residual capacity in P; that is, $\delta = \min_{(i, j) \in P} u_f(i, j)$. Note that because all arcs in the augmenting path have positive residual capacity, $\delta > 0$. Then we create a new flow f' by setting

$$f'(i, j) = \begin{cases} f(i, j) + \delta & \forall (i, j) \in P \\ f(i, j) - \delta & \forall (j, i) \in P \\ f(i, j) & \forall (i, j) : (i, j), (j, i) \notin P. \end{cases}$$

Sometimes we say that we *push* δ units of flow along P, resulting in flow f'. We also sometimes call δ the residual capacity of the path P.

We need to check that f' is still a flow according to Definition 2.3. We can assume that P is a simple path. Clearly the capacity constraints are obeyed, since by the definition of δ, for all $(i, j) \in P$,

$$f'(i, j) = f(i, j) + \delta \le f(i, j) + u_f(i, j) = f(i, j) + (u(i, j) - f(i, j)) = u(i, j).$$

The skew symmetry constraints continue to be obeyed for all arcs not in P, while if $(i, j) \in P$,

$$f'(i, j) = f(i, j) + \delta = -(f(j, i) - \delta) = -f'(j, i).$$

The flow conservation constraints continue to be obeyed for all nodes i not on the path. If $i \neq s, t$ is on the path, then there are arcs (h, i) and (i, j) on the path, so that $f'(i, j) = f(i, j) + \delta$ and $f'(i, h) = f(i, h) - \delta$ and thus

$$\sum_{k:(i,k)\in A} f'(i, k) = \sum_{k:(i,k)\in A} f(i, k) + \delta - \delta = 0.$$

Similarly, if arc (s, j) is the first arc on the path, then $f'(s, j) = f(s, j) + \delta$ so that

$$|f'| = \sum_{k:(s,k)\in A} f'(s, k) = \sum_{k:(s,k)\in A} f(s, k) + \delta = |f| + \delta.$$

Thus f' is a flow of greater value than f.

We can finally prove a theorem stating when f is a maximum flow; it implies Theorem 2.6.

Theorem 2.7: *The following statements are equivalent for an s-t flow f:*

1. *f is a maximum flow;*
2. *there is no augmenting path in A_f;*
3. *$|f| = u(\delta^+(S))$ for some s-t cut S.*

Proof We have already shown (1) implies (2), since we showed above that if there is an augmenting path in A_f, then f is not maximum. To show that (2) implies (3), let S be the set of vertices that are reachable from s in G_f via arcs of positive residual capacity. Since there are no augmenting paths, then $t \notin S$. Also, for any arc $(i, j) \in A$ such that $i \in S$ and $j \notin S$, it must be the case that $u_f(i, j) = 0$ and thus $f(i, j) = u(i, j)$. Then by Corollary 2.5, $|f| = u(\delta^+(S))$. Finally, to show that (3) implies (1), we recall that Lemma 2.4 states that $|f| \leq u(\delta^+(S))$ for every s-t cut S and every flow f, so that $|f| = u(\delta^+(S))$ implies that f must be a maximum flow and S a minimum s-t cut.   □

Theorem 2.7 leads immediately to an algorithmic idea (summarized in Algorithm 2.1): start with the flow $f = 0$, look for an augmenting path, then update the flow as described previously. The problem with this algorithm is that if the augmenting paths are not chosen carefully, the algorithm is not polynomial-time; see Exercise 2.2 for an example. However, this algorithm does lead to one useful conclusion: if all the capacities $u(i, j)$ are integer, then

---

$f(i, j) \leftarrow 0$ for all $(i, j) \in A$
while there is an augmenting path P in A_f **do**
    Push flow along P
    Update f
return f

Algorithm 2.1 Generic augmenting path algorithm for the maximum flow problem.

there is a maximum flow such that all $f(i, j)$ are integer and Algorithm 2.1 finds such a flow f. If all $f(i, j)$ are integer, we say that f is *integral*. This statement follows, since initially all $f(i, j)$ are integer, and thus if all $u(i, j)$ are integer, all residual capacities $u_f(i, j)$ are integer, and thus δ is integer, so that the new flow f' also has all $f'(i, j)$ integer. This statement is enormously useful, as we will see, and it is often called the *integrality property* of the maximum flow problem.

Property 2.8 (Integrality property): *If all capacities $u(i, j)$ are integer, then there is an integral maximum flow f.*

If the capacities are integer, then we can bound the number of iterations of the algorithm (that is, the number of times we find an augmenting path) by $O(mU)$, where U is the maximum capacity; that is, $U = \max_{(i, j) \in A} u(i, j)$ (recall that m is the number of arcs and n the number of vertices). Since the maximum flow is the net flow out of the source, at worst in the maximum flow we have all m arcs out of the source with flow equal to the maximum capacity, so that the value of a maximum flow is at most mU. If all capacities are integer, then in each iteration we increase the value of the flow by at least 1; the value of the flow starts at zero and can be at most mU, and hence the bound on the number of iterations follows. We can find an augmenting path in the graph in $O(m)$ time, so this leads to an overall running time of $O(m^2U)$ (we assume G is connected so that $m \geq n - 1$).

Although the number U is part of the input, this running time is not a polynomial in the input size of the problem, because we assume that the input of numeric data is given in binary. The number of bits used to encode a number U is then at most $\lceil \log_2 U \rceil + 1$. Thus U is exponential in the input size of the encoding of U. The algorithm is polynomial time if we assume that the numeric data is given in *unary*: that is, a number U is encoded by U 1s (so that 5 is encoded as 11111). If we have an algorithm whose number of operations can be bounded by a polynomial in the size of the input if the numeric data is encoded in unary, then we say we have a *pseudopolynomial-time* algorithm.

Definition 2.9: *An algorithm is said to be* pseudopolynomial-time *if the number of operations of the algorithm can be bounded above by a polynomial in the size of the input if the numeric data in the input is encoded in unary.*

Thus if all capacities are integers, the augmenting path algorithm is a pseudopolynomial-time algorithm for the maximum flow problem. We would like to give a polynomial-time algorithm, however: one in which the running time can be bounded above by a polynomial in the size of the input if the numeric data is encoded in binary. We will see such algorithms in subsequent sections.

Another important distinction in running times is that of a *strongly polynomial-time* algorithm. We say we have such an algorithm if the running time of the algorithm can be bounded above by a polynomial in the number of input items; that is, the polynomial doesn't depend on the size of the encoding of the numeric inputs at all. For the maximum flow problem, this means that the running time is given as a polynomial in m and n, with no dependence on the size of the encoding of the capacities; that is, the running time bound does not depend on $\log_2 U$.

Definition 2.10: *An algorithm is said to be* strongly polynomial-time *if the number of operations of the algorithm can be bounded above by a polynomial in number of items in the input, and the number of operations does not depend on the size of the encoding of the numeric inputs.*

We will see examples of strongly polynomial-time algorithms for the maximum flow problem in Sections 2.7 and 2.8.

2.2 Application: Carpool Sharing

Before we turn to devising polynomial-time algorithms for the maximum flow problem, we first give a few sample applications of maximum flow that do not obviously involve flows or even networks.

The first application involves the fair allocation of driving responsibilities for a set of people who carpool together. Each week the people in the carpool announce which days they will be using the carpool. They would like to come up with a way to allocate the driving responsibilities fairly, and they hit upon the following idea. On a day in which k people use the carpool, each person will receive a $1/k$ share of the responsibility to drive. Let r_i be the total share of the ith person for the week. Then each person should drive at most $\lceil r_i \rceil$ times that week. For instance, here is a sample week with four people.

	M	T	W	Th	F
1	X	X	X		
2	X		X		
3	X	X	X	X	X
4		X	X	X	X

Persons 1, 2, and 3 receive a 1/3 share for the trip on Monday, persons 1, 3, and 4 receive a 1/3 share for the trip on Tuesday, persons 1, 2, 3, and 4 receive a 1/4 share for the trip on Wednesday, and persons 3 and 4 each receive a 1/2 share for both Thursday and Friday. So the total shares are $r_1 = \frac{1}{3} + \frac{1}{3} + \frac{1}{4} = \frac{11}{12}$, $r_2 = \frac{1}{3} + \frac{1}{4} = \frac{7}{12}$, $r_3 = \frac{1}{3} + \frac{1}{3} + \frac{1}{4} + \frac{1}{2} + \frac{1}{2} = \frac{23}{12}$, and $r_4 = \frac{1}{3} + \frac{1}{4} + \frac{1}{2} + \frac{1}{2} = \frac{19}{12}$. Note that $\sum_i r_i = 5$, since $\sum_i r_i$ gives the sum of the fractional responsibilities for each of the 5 days.

We now set up a maximum flow problem to decide who should drive each day. To do this, we set up a graph in which there is one node per person, and one node per day of the week; to these we add a source node s and a sink node t. We add an arc of capacity $\lceil r_i \rceil$ from the source s to each person i, and an arc of capacity 1 from each day of the week to the sink t. Then for each person we add an arc of capacity 1 from the person to the days of the week in which the person takes the carpool. For the example given above, the corresponding maximum flow instance appears in Figure 2.6.

We claim that if the network has a flow f of value 5 such that f is integral, then there is a feasible way to assign driving responsibilities. Note that the cut $S = V - \{t\}$ has capacity 5 (for the five arcs of capacity 1 from the day nodes to t), so if such a flow exists, it is a maximum flow. Thus each arc from a day node to t must be saturated (recall this means the flow equals the capacity), and the flow on the arc is 1. For each day node, we know that the flow entering the node is equal to the flow leaving the node, and f is integral, so there must be a positive flow of 1 entering each day node coming from some person node who is using the carpool that day. We can assign the driving responsibility for the day to the corresponding person whose arc to the day node has positive flow. Since the flow leaving each person node is equal to the flow entering each person node, and the flow entering person node i is at most $\lceil r_i \rceil$ (by the capacity constraint on the single arc entering person node i), person i can be assigned to at most $\lceil r_i \rceil$ days, which is what we wanted.

It now remains to show that the network has a flow f of value 5 such that f is integral. What we will do instead is give a fractional flow of value 5 instead, and then appeal to the integrality property (Property 2.8) to conclude that since there exists a maximum flow of value 5 and all capacities are integer,

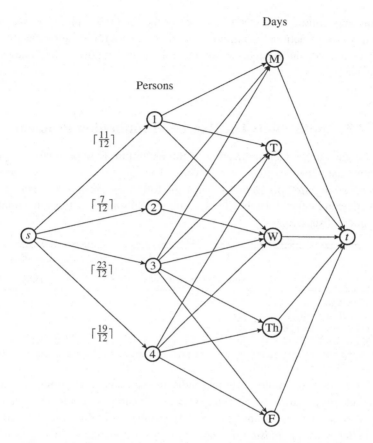

Figure 2.6 Instance of the flow network for the carpool problem. All unlabeled arcs have capacity 1.

then there must exist an integral maximum flow of value 5. Our fractional flow corresponds to the fractional assignment of responsibility that we made initially. In particular, for a given day, if k persons were using the carpool, we assigned each a share of $1/k$, so in the network for that day, we put a flow of value $1/k$ on each arc from a person node using the carpool that day to the corresponding day node. Since the sum of the flow entering the day node is 1, we set the flow to 1 for the arc from the day node to the sink t. Note then that the flow leaving each person node i is exactly r_i, so we set the flow on the arc from s to person node i to be r_i. We now have a feasible flow of value $\sum_i r_i = 5$.

This application illustrates the power of the integrality property: we only need to show a fractional maximum flow in a graph with integer capacities in order to conclude the existence of an integral maximum flow of the same value or greater.

2.3 Application: The Baseball Elimination Problem

We now turn to another application of the maximum flow problem that does not obviously involve flow or networks. The application is known as the *baseball elimination problem*. Consider the following example of teams from the American League East division (omitting the Tampa Bay Rays, to simplify subsequent discussion):

			Remaining schedule			
Team	Wins	Games to play	NYY	BOS	TOR	BAL
New York Yankees (NYY)	93	8	–	1	6	1
Boston Red Sox (BOS)	89	4	1	–	0	3
Toronto Blue Jays (TOR)	88	7	6	0	–	1
Baltimore Orioles (BAL)	86	5	1	3	1	–

The "remaining schedule" columns indicate the number of games the given team must play against the other teams in the division; we assume that none of the teams has any remaining games to play outside the division. We will say that a team *wins the division* if it wins more games than any other team in the division. A team is *eliminated* if it cannot win the division given *any* outcome of the remaining games. For instance, in the example above, Baltimore is eliminated, since it can win at most 91 games – the 86 it has already won plus its 5 remaining games – but New York has already won 93. One can also show that Boston is eliminated. Boston can win at most 93 games: the 89 games it has already won plus the 4 remaining games. However, either New York wins at least 94 games by winning at least one of its remaining games, or it will lose all of its remaining games, including all 6 games played against Toronto. In the latter case, Toronto will win at least $88 + 6 \geq 94$ games. In either case, a team other than Boston wins the division; hence, Boston is eliminated.

We will show that we can decide if a given team is eliminated by computing a maximum flow. We first need to introduce some notation for the general problem. Let T be the set of teams in a division. Let $w(i)$ be the number of wins that team $i \in T$ currently has; let $g(i)$ be the number of games that team i has left to play, and let $g(i, j)$ be the number of games that team i and team j have left to play against each other. Let $w(R)$ be the total number of wins of teams in $R \subseteq T$, so that $w(R) = \sum_{i \in R} w(i)$. Let $g(R)$ be the number of games remaining to play for teams in R against each other, so that $g(R) = \frac{1}{2} \sum_{i \in R, j \in R} g(i, j)$ (we divide by 2, since the sum double-counts each game). Finally, for $R \subseteq T$, let $a(R) = \frac{1}{|R|}(w(R) + g(R))$. We can then prove the following.

Lemma 2.11: *For any $R \subseteq T$, some team $i \in R$ will win at least $a(R)$ games by the end of the season.*

Proof The total number of wins for teams in R at the end of the season is at least $w(R) + g(R)$: some team in R wins each of the $g(R)$ games played between two teams in R. Thus the average number of wins at the end of the season for the teams in R is at least $a(R)$, and some team in R must have at least this many wins. □

Corollary 2.12: *If for some $k \in T$ and $R \subseteq T - \{k\}$, $a(R) > w(k) + g(k)$, then team k is eliminated.*

Proof Since some team in R must win more than $w(k) + g(k)$ games, and team k can win at most $w(k) + g(k)$ games by the end of the season, team k cannot win the division, and must therefore be eliminated. □

In the example above, with $R = \{\text{NYY}, \text{TOR}\}$, and $k = \text{BOS}$, $w(R) = 93 + 88$, $g(R) = 6$, $w(k) + g(k) = 89 + 4 = 93$, while $a(R) = \frac{1}{2}((93 + 88) + 6) = 93.5 > 93$. Thus Boston is eliminated.

We will now set up a maximum flow problem to decide if a given team $k \in T$ is not eliminated. We know that team k is not eliminated if there is some outcome to the remaining games in which it has at least as many wins as every other team. Let Z be all teams other than k, so that $Z = T - \{k\}$. Let $x(i, j)$ represent the number of remaining games in which team i defeats team j. Clearly in each of the $g(i, j)$ remaining games between teams i and j either team i defeats j or team j defeats i, so that

$$x(i, j) + x(j, i) = g(i, j). \tag{2.6}$$

We may as well assume that if team k is not eliminated, then it wins all of its remaining games, and has $w(k) + g(k)$ wins. Any other team i will have $w(i) + \sum_{j \in Z} x(i, j)$ wins (the number of wins it currently has plus the number of the remaining games it wins against teams in Z; recall it loses all games to team k). Thus in order for team k not to be eliminated, we need that

$$w(k) + g(k) \geq w(i) + \sum_{j \in Z} x(i, j) \qquad \forall i \in Z. \qquad (2.7)$$

Finally, we need that the $x(i, j)$ are nonnegative integers. Thus, if we can find nonnegative integers $x(i, j)$ such that (2.6) and (2.7) are obeyed, then team k is not eliminated. We will set up a maximum flow problem such that either we find such nonnegative integers $x(i, j)$ or we find a set $R \subseteq Z$ with $a(R) > w(k) + g(k)$; in the first case, there is an outcome of games such that team k is not eliminated, while in the second case, team k is eliminated by Corollary 2.12.

We set up the maximum flow problem as follows. We will have a source node s, a sink node t, one node for every pair of distinct teams in Z (the *pair nodes*), and one node for every team in Z (the *team nodes*). From each team node $i \in Z$, we include an arc to the sink of capacity $w(k) + g(k) - w(i)$. Note that if $w(i) > w(k) + g(k)$, team k is already eliminated; thus we assume $w(i) \leq w(k) + g(k)$ so that this capacity is nonnegative. From the source node s to each pair node for pair i, j, we include an arc of capacity $g(i, j)$, the number of games remaining between teams i and j. From the pair node for the pair i, j, we include one arc to the team node for i of infinite capacity, and another arc to the team node for j of infinite capacity. The graph is shown in Figure 2.7. In Figure 2.8, we show the flow instance corresponding to our

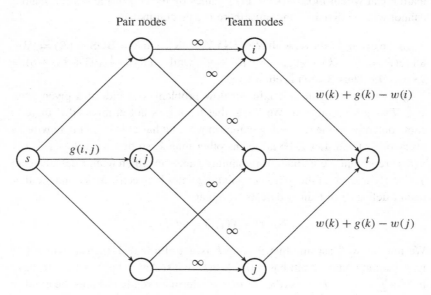

Figure 2.7 Illustration of the maximum flow instance for the baseball elimination problem.

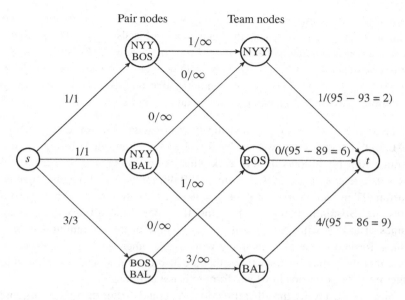

Figure 2.8 Illustration of the maximum flow instance and a maximum flow for our example of the baseball elimination problem, checking if Toronto is eliminated.

example above, checking whether or not Toronto is eliminated; we also give a maximum flow.

Note that $g(Z)$ is the number of games played between all teams in Z, the teams other than team k. We can now show that team k is not eliminated if and only if there is a flow of value $g(Z)$ in the flow instance.

Lemma 2.13: *If there is a flow of value $g(Z)$ in the maximum flow instance, then team k is not eliminated.*

Proof We note that the s-t cut $S = \{s\}$ has capacity $g(Z)$, so if there is a flow of value $g(Z)$, then by Corollary 2.5 and Theorem 2.7 it is a maximum flow and all arcs from the source to the pair nodes must be saturated. By the integrality property, we know that if there is a maximum flow of value $g(Z)$, then there is an integral maximum flow of value $g(Z)$. We set $x(i, j)$ to be the flow from the pair node for i, j to the team node for i, and $x(j, i)$ to be the flow from the pair node for i, j to the team node for j. Because the flow is integral, $x(i, j)$ must be a nonnegative integer. Because the flow into the pair node for i, j is equal to the flow out, and the flow in must be $g(i, j)$ because the incoming arc is saturated, we have that $x(i, j) + x(j, i) = g(i, j)$. The total flow into the team node for a team $i \in Z$ is then $\sum_{j \in Z} x(i,j)$; by flow conservation at the team node for i, the flow leaving the team node for i is also $\sum_{j \in Z} x(i,j)$. Since there is a single arc leaving the team node for i of capacity $w(k) + g(k) - w(i)$, it must be the case that $\sum_{j \in Z} x(i,j) \leq w(k) + g(k) - w(i)$, or $w(k) + g(k) \geq w(i) + \sum_{j \in Z} x(i,j)$. Thus we have nonnegative integers $x(i,j)$ that satisfy conditions (2.6) and (2.7), and therefore team k is not eliminated. $\square$

Returning to our example, and the flow in Figure 2.8, for $Z = \{$NYY, BAL, BOS$\}$, there is a flow of value $1 + 1 + 3 = 5$, and thus Toronto is not eliminated. This follows if New York wins its one game against Boston and loses its one game against Baltimore, and Baltimore wins all 3 games against Boston. Then New York has $93 + 1 = 94$ wins, Baltimore has $86 + 4 = 90$ wins, and Boston has $89 + 0 = 89$ wins. If Toronto wins all of its remaining games, it has 95 wins. So there is some outcome of the remaining games in which Toronto has at least as many wins as the other teams in the division. Note that there may be other flows that are also maximum that correspond to other possible scenarios in which Toronto is not eliminated.

Now we must prove the other direction. We could do this directly by arguing that any outcome of games in which team k is not eliminated leads to a flow of value $g(Z)$; instead we give a proof based on the value of minimum s-t cut and Corollary 2.12.

Lemma 2.14: *If the value of the maximum flow is less than $g(Z)$, then team k is eliminated.*

Proof Since the value of the maximum flow is equal to the capacity of a minimum s-t cut, if the value of the maximum flow is less than $g(Z)$, then there is a minimum s-t cut S of capacity less than $g(Z)$. We observe that if the pair node for i, j is in S, then both team nodes i and j are in S; if one or both of the team nodes is not in S, then the arc from the pair node i, j to the team node (or both team nodes) is in the cut defined by S, and the capacity of the cut is then infinite, which is a contradiction. Let R be the set of all teams whose team node is in S. Then the arcs in $\delta^+(S)$ will include those that go from the team nodes in R to the sink t, and those from the source s to any pair node of teams not both in R, since if a pair node i, j is in S, then we have observed that both i and j must be in R. The latter set of arcs has total capacity $g(Z) - g(R)$. Thus the capacity of the cut S is at least

$$g(Z) - g(R) + \sum_{i \in R} (w(k) + g(k) - w(i))$$
$$= g(Z) - g(R) + |R|(w(k) + g(k)) - w(R);$$

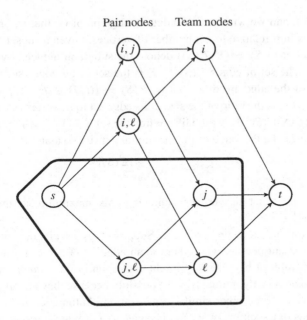

Figure 2.9 Illustration of an s-t cut in the max flow instance for the baseball elimination problem. For this cut, $R = \{j, \ell\}$.

see Figure 2.9 for an illustration. By hypothesis, the capacity of the cut is less than $g(Z)$ so that

$$g(Z) - g(R) + |R|(w(k) + g(k)) - w(R) < g(Z),$$

or

$$w(k) + g(k) < \frac{g(R) + w(R)}{|R|} = a(R).$$

Thus by Corollary 2.12, team k is eliminated. $\qquad\square$

Exercise 2.3 asks the reader to show that it is possible to determine all the teams that have been eliminated in the division by using $O(\log |T|)$ maximum flow computations.

2.4 Application: Finding a Maximum Density Subgraph

In this section, we turn to a third application of the maximum flow problem that does not obviously involve flow. Here we are given an undirected graph

$G = (V, E)$, and we wish to find a dense subgraph of G; that is, one that has many edges in it relative to the number of vertices. Given a subset of vertices $S \subseteq V$, we let $G(S) = (V, E(S))$ denote the subgraph induced by the set of vertices S. The set of edges $E(S) \subseteq E$ is the set of all edges such that both endpoints of the edge are in S; that is, $E(S) = \{(i, j) \in E : i, j \in S\}$. The *density* of $G(S)$ is the ratio of the size of its edge set to its vertex set; that is, the density is $|E(S)|/|S|$. We would like to find the set $S \subseteq V, S \neq \emptyset$ of maximum density. Let D^* be the value of the maximum density so that

$$D^* = \max_{S \subseteq V, S \neq \emptyset} \frac{|E(S)|}{|S|}.$$

We let S^* be a set of vertices achieving this maximum so that $D^* = |E(S^*)|/|S^*|$.

Why is this an interesting problem? Suppose G is a social network, and the vertices represent people, while there is an edge (i, j) if i and j are friends. Then a subgraph of high density might correspond to a *community*: a set of people who are mostly mutual friends, possibly because they are all part of the same school or some other similar organization. Automatically finding such communities in a social network has been an area of intense research.

We will show below that we can find the densest subgraph by performing $O(\log n)$ maximum flow computations. The basic idea is that we will start with a guess γ of the value of D^*. We will then use a maximum flow computation to determine if $\gamma \geq D^*$ or not. Then by using a technique called bisection search (or binary search), we can update the value of γ until the value of γ is sufficiently close to D^* that we can find the exact value of D^* and the corresponding densest subgraph.

Given a guess γ, we construct an instance of the maximum flow problem in a new graph G' as follows. We create a vertex i for each $i \in V$, and add a source vertex s and a sink vertex t, so that $V' = V \cup \{s, t\}$. For each edge $(i, j) \in E$, we add two arcs (i, j) and (j, i), each of capacity 1. For each $i \in V$, we add an arc (s, i) of capacity m, and an arc (i, t) of capacity $m + 2\gamma - d_i$, where d_i is the degree of node i in the original graph (that is, the number of edges incident on i). Since $d_i \leq m$, the capacity is nonnegative. See Figure 2.10 for an illustration of the construction.

We then compute a maximum flow in the graph G'. To help bound the value of the maximum flow, consider the s-t cut $\{s\} \cup S$, for $S \subseteq V$. The capacity of this cut includes all arcs from s to $i \in V - S$, from $i \in S$ to t, and from $i \in S$ to $j \in V - S$; see Figure 2.11. Let $\delta(S)$ represent the set of edges in G such that exactly one endpoint of each edge is in S. We observe that $\sum_{i \in S} d_i = 2|E(S)| + |\delta(S)|$, since $\sum_{i \in S} d_i$ double-counts all edges with both

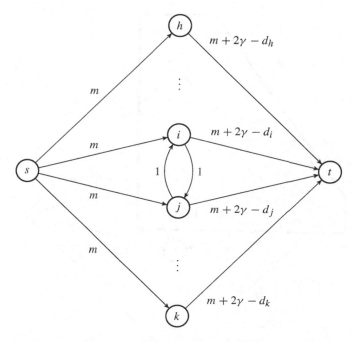

Figure 2.10 Illustration of the max flow instance for the maximum densest subgraph problem for guess γ.

endpoints in S and counts each edge in $\delta(S)$ exactly once. Then the capacity of the s-t cut $\{s\} \cup S$ is

$$m|V - S| + |\delta(S)| + \sum_{i \in S}(m + 2\gamma - d_i)$$
$$= mn - m|S| + |\delta(S)| + m|S| + 2\gamma|S| - \sum_{i \in S} d_i$$
$$= mn + |\delta(S)| + 2\gamma|S| - (2|E(S)| + |\delta(S)|)$$
$$= mn + 2|S|\left(\gamma - \frac{|E(S)|}{|S|}\right). \tag{2.8}$$

We can then prove the following lemma.

Lemma 2.15: *The value of the maximum flow is mn if and only if $\gamma \geq D^*$.*

Proof First of all, we observe that the s-t cut $\{s\}$ has capacity mn, so the value of the maximum flow can be at most mn. If $\gamma < D^*$, then for set S^* the capacity of the corresponding s-t cut $\{s\} \cup S^*$ is $mn + 2|S^*|(\gamma - |E(S^*)|/|S^*|) = mn + 2|S^*|(\gamma - D^*) < mn$ by Equation (2.8), since $S^* \neq \emptyset$.

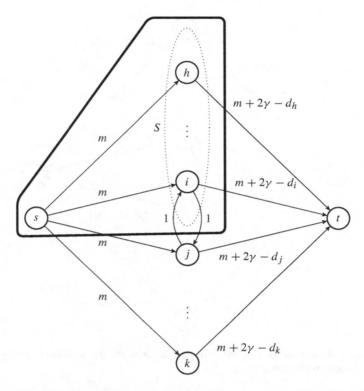

Figure 2.11 Illustration of the s-t cut for $\{s\} \cup S$ for the max flow instance for the maximum density subgraph problem. The dashed circle gives the nodes in S from the original graph.

Thus the maximum flow in this case must be strictly less than mn, since we have shown an s-t cut whose capacity is strictly less than mn. Similarly, suppose the value of the maximum flow is less than mn. Let $\{s\} \cup S$ be the minimum s-t cut; by Theorem 2.7, it has capacity equal to the value of the maximum flow, and so is less than mn, and thus we must have $S \neq \emptyset$. By Equation (2.8) the capacity of the cut is $mn + 2|S|(\gamma - |E(S)|/|S|) < mn$, so it must be the case that $\gamma < |E(S)|/|S| \leq D^*$, and the lemma is proven.   □

In what follows, let D' be the second largest density, so that $D' < D^*$ and for any $S \neq \emptyset$ either $|E(S)|/|S| = D^*$ or $|E(S)|/|S| \leq D'$.

Corollary 2.16: *If $D' \leq \gamma < D^*$, then for the minimum s-t cut $\{s\} \cup X$ corresponding to the maximum flow in the instance, it must be that X is the maximum density subgraph.*

Proof By Equation (2.8), the capacity of any s-t cut $\{s\} \cup S$ that has density $D' \leq \gamma$ is $mn + 2|S|(\gamma - |E(S)|/|S|) = mn + 2|S|(\gamma - D') \geq mn$, and so is not the minimum s-t cut. But since $\gamma < D^*$, by Lemma 2.15 the value of the maximum flow is strictly less than mn, and so the minimum s-t cut $\{s\} \cup X$ must have capacity $mn + 2|S|(\gamma - |E(X)|/|X|) < mn$, and thus $\gamma < |E(X)|/|X|$. Since γ is at least the second largest density, it must be that X is a maximum density subgraph. $\square$

We now explain how to use the maximum flow computation as a subroutine to find a guess γ between D' and D^* so that we can be certain we have found a subgraph of maximum density D^*. To do this, we use bisection search (sometimes also called binary search). Throughout the search, we maintain an interval $(\ell, u]$ such that we are certain that $D^* \in (\ell, u]$. Assuming $E \neq \emptyset$ (since if $E = \emptyset$, then $D^* = 0$ trivially), we can initialize the interval to $(0, m]$, since it is clear that $0 < D^* \leq m$. We then compute a maximum flow in the instance as given above with a guess γ set to the midpoint of the interval, so that $\gamma = (u + \ell)/2$. By Lemma 2.15, if the value of the maximum flow is mn, then $D^* \leq \gamma = (u + \ell)/2$, so we then know that $D^* \in (\ell, (u + \ell)/2]$, and we reset the value of u to $(u + \ell)/2$. Otherwise, if the value of the maximum flow is less than mn, then $D^* > \gamma = (u + \ell)/2$, so that $D^* \in ((u + \ell)/2, u]$, and we can reset the value of ℓ to be $(u + \ell)/2$. In either case, the size of the interval $(\ell, u]$ has dropped by a factor of 2, and still correctly contains D^*.

We will show below that if the interval $(\ell, u]$ is sufficiently small, then we can apply Corollary 2.16 and ensure that we have found a subgraph of maximum density.

Lemma 2.17: *When $u - \ell < \frac{1}{n^2}$, then for $\gamma = \ell$, $D' \leq \gamma < D^*$.*

Proof We let $\mathcal{S}$ be the set of all possible subgraph densities for a graph with $m \geq 1$ edges and n vertices; that is,

$$\mathcal{S} = \left\{ \frac{m'}{n'} : 1 \leq m' \leq m, 1 \leq n' \leq n \right\}.$$

We let Δ be the smallest possible difference between two distinct values of $\mathcal{S}$, so that $\Delta = \min_{a,b \in \mathcal{S}: a \neq b} |a - b|$. How small can Δ be? We know that $a = m_1/n_1$ and $b = m_2/n_2$ for $1 \leq m_1 \leq m$, $1 \leq n_1 \leq n$, $1 \leq m_2 \leq m$, and $1 \leq n_2 \leq n$. Thus

$$\Delta = \left| \frac{m_1}{n_1} - \frac{m_2}{n_2} \right| = \left| \frac{m_1 n_2 - m_2 n_1}{n_1 n_2} \right| \geq \frac{1}{n^2};$$

because $\Delta > 0$, $|m_1 n_2 - m_2 n_1| \geq 1$, and $n_1 n_2 \leq n^2$.

Thus when we know $D^* \in (\ell, u]$ and $u - \ell < 1/n^2$, then $D' \leq \ell$. Thus for $\gamma = \ell$, $D' \leq \gamma < D^*$. $\square$

---

if $E = \emptyset$ **then return** $\{i\}$ `// Return an arbitrary` $i \in V$
$\ell \leftarrow 0$
$u \leftarrow m$
$X \leftarrow \emptyset$
while $u - \ell \geq 1/n^2$ **do**
    Compute maximum flow f, minimum s-t cut $\{s\} \cup S$ in maximum
    flow instance with guess $\gamma = (u + \ell)/2$
    if $|f| = mn$ **then**
        $u \leftarrow (u + \ell)/2$
    else
        $\ell \leftarrow (u + \ell)/2$
        $X \leftarrow S$
return X

Algorithm 2.2 Algorithm for computing a maximum density subgraph.

We can then summarize the algorithm in Algorithm 2.2, and we finish showing the result in the following theorem.

Theorem 2.18: *Algorithm 2.2 finds a maximum density subgraph in $O(\log n)$ maximum flow computations.*

Proof If $E = \emptyset$, then any single vertex is a densest subgraph, and the algorithm returns a single vertex. Otherwise, the algorithm maintains that $D^* \in (\ell, u]$ and maintains that X corresponds to the minimum s-t cut $\{s\} \cup X$ obtained with guess $\gamma = \ell$. By Lemma 2.17 and Corollary 2.16, once $u - \ell < 1/n^2$, it must be the case that X is a maximum density subgraph, and the algorithm terminates and returns X.

To complete the proof, we must determine the number of iterations of the while loop. Initially the size of the interval $(\ell, u]$ is m, and the algorithm terminates once $u - \ell < 1/n^2$, and in each iteration, the size of the interval shrinks by a factor of 2. Thus it takes at most $\lceil \log_2 \frac{m}{1/n^2} \rceil = O(\log mn^2) = O(\log n^4) = O(\log n)$ iterations until the algorithm terminates, since there are at most $\binom{n}{2} = O(n^2)$ edges in any undirected graph. $\qquad\square$

2.5 Most Improving Augmenting Paths

We now return to the question we posed at the end of Section 2.1 about how we might obtain a polynomial-time version of the augmenting path algorithm. We start with a very natural idea: we look for the augmenting path that increases

---

$f(i, j) \leftarrow 0$ for all $(i, j) \in A$
while there is an augmenting path in A_f **do**
    Let P be augmenting path that maximizes $\min_{(i,j) \in P} u_f(i, j)$
    Push flow along P
    Update f
return f

Algorithm 2.3 Most improving augmenting path algorithm for the maximum flow problem.

the flow value as much as possible. In other words, we want the augmenting path whose minimum residual capacity arc is as large as possible; we will call this the *most improving* augmenting path. We give this version of the augmenting path algorithm in Algorithm 2.3.

The basic idea of the analysis of the algorithm is fairly simple. We will show that the difference between the maximum flow f^* and the current flow f can be decomposed into at most m augmenting paths. Since we always augment along the most improving such path, the path increases $|f|$ by at least a $1/m$ factor of $|f^*| - |f|$, the difference in values between the maximum and current flows. We can show that after m such augmentations, the difference has decreased by a constant factor, and this allows us to show that after a polynomially bounded number of augmentations, the current flow must be maximum. This basic idea of showing a decomposition into m objects, and showing that the algorithm performs an update as least as good as any one of these objects, leading to a constant factor improvement after m updates, is an algorithmic idea we will see several times in the course of the book.

We now flesh out the details of this idea. We first prove a *flow decomposition* lemma, showing that any flow can be decomposed into flows on at most m s-t paths and cycles. In what follows, for flows f, f', and f'', we write $f = f' + f''$ (or $f = f' - f''$) if $f(i, j) = f'(i, j) + f''(i, j)$ (respectively, $f(i, j) = f'(i, j) - f''(i, j)$) for all arcs $(i, j) \in A$. The following lemma is easy but useful.

Lemma 2.19: *If f' and f'' obey flow conservation and skew symmetry, then so do $f = f' + f''$ and $f = f' - f''$. Also, $|f| = |f' + f''| = |f'| + |f''|$ and $|f| = |f' - f''| = |f'| - |f''|$.*

Proof Suppose $f = f' + f''$. For all $i \neq s, t$,

$$\sum_{k:(i,k) \in A} f(i,k) = \sum_{k:(i,k) \in A} f'(i,k) + \sum_{k:(i,k) \in A} f''(i,k) = 0,$$

since both f' and f'' obey flow conservation. Furthermore,

$$|f| = \sum_{k:(s,k)\in A} f(s,k) = \sum_{k:(s,k)\in A} f'(s,k) + \sum_{k:(s,k)\in A} f''(s,k) = |f'| + |f''|.$$

Also, $f(i,j) = f'(i,j) + f''(i,j) = -f'(j,i) - f''(j,i) = -f(j,i)$, since f' and f'' obey skew symmetry. The case of $f = f' - f''$ is similar. □

Now we give the flow decomposition lemma.

Lemma 2.20: *Given an s-t flow f, there exists flows $f_1, \ldots, f_\ell$, for some $\ell \leq m$, such that $f = \sum_{i=1}^{\ell} f_i$, $|f| = \sum_{i=1}^{\ell} |f_i|$, and for each i, the arcs of f_i with positive flow form either a simple s-t path or a cycle.*

Proof We prove the statement by induction on the number of arcs with positive flow; in fact, we prove a stronger statement for ℓ, the number of arcs with positive flow. Obviously, $\ell \leq m$. Clearly if $\ell = 0$ the statement is trivially true. Suppose the statement holds for $\ell < p$, and that f has $\ell = p$ arcs with positive flow. Pick any arc $(i,j) \in A$ such that $f(i,j) > 0$. If $i \neq s$, then by flow conservation there must be some node h such that $f(h,i) > 0$, and if $j \neq t$, then there must be some node k such that $f(j,k) > 0$. We can continue this argument until either we have a simple s-t path P of arcs that all have positive flow on them, or a cycle C of arcs that all have positive flow on them. Suppose we have a simple s-t path P; the case for a cycle C is similar. We set $\delta = \min_{(i,j)\in P} f(i,j)$; we also set $f_p(i,j) = \delta$, $f_p(j,i) = -\delta$ for $(i,j) \in P$, and $f_p(i,j) = 0$ otherwise. We claim that it is easy to check that f_p is a flow. Let $f' = f - f_p$. Then f' has at least one fewer arc with positive flow on it than f (in particular, the arc $(i,j) \in P$ such that $f(i,j) = \delta$). By Lemma 2.19 f' obeys flow conservation and skew symmetry because f and f_p do; f' also obeys the capacity constraints because for $f(i,j) > 0$, $f'(i,j) = f(i,j) - f_p(i,j) \leq f(i,j) \leq u(i,j)$, and thus by skew symmetry for $f(i,j) < 0$, $f'(i,j) = f(i,j) - f_p(i,j) \leq 0 \leq u(i,j)$. Thus f' is a flow with at most $p-1$ arcs of positive flow, and can be written as $f' = \sum_{i=1}^{p-1} f_i$ by induction. Hence $f = f' + f_p = \sum_{i=1}^{p} f_i$, and the lemma statement follows. □

Next, we need to show that we can apply this decomposition theorem not to flows in the original graph G, but to flows in the residual graph G_f with residual capacities u_f, and that flows in the residual graph have a natural relationship to flows in G.

Lemma 2.21: *Let f be an s-t flow in G, and let f^* be a maximum s-t flow in G. Then the maximum flow in the residual graph G_f has value $|f^*| - |f|$.*

Proof Consider $f' = f^* - f$; we need to argue that f' is a flow in G_f. Flow conservation and skew symmetry hold by Lemma 2.19; for capacity constraints, we note that $f'(i, j) = f^*(i, j) - f(i, j) \leq u(i, j) - f(i, j) = u_f(i, j)$. The value of f' in G_f is $|f^*| - |f|$. We now argue that there cannot be a flow of larger value. Consider a minimum s-t cut S in G, so that $|f^*| = u(\delta^+(S))$. Then for each arc $(i, j) \in \delta^+(S)$, we know by Corollary 2.5 that $f^*(i, j) = u(i, j)$, so that $f'(i, j) = f^*(i, j) - f(i, j) = u(i, j) - f(i, j) = u_f(i, j)$. Then also by Corollary 2.5, we have that $|f'| = u_f(\delta^+(S))$ and hence f' is a maximum flow in G_f. □

We now show that the residual capacity of a most improving path is relatively large by combining the two lemmas above.

Lemma 2.22: *Let f^* be a maximum flow in G, and let f be any s-t flow. Then the residual capacity of a most improving path is at least $\frac{1}{m}(|f^*| - |f|)$.*

Proof By Lemma 2.21, the value of a maximum flow in G_f is $|f^*| - |f|$, and by Lemma 2.20, the maximum flow in G_f can be decomposed into at most m flows on paths such that the value of the flow is at most the minimum residual capacity arc on the path. Thus the value of one of the flows is at least $\frac{1}{m}(|f^*| - |f|)$, and the residual capacity of each arc on the path is also at least this much. Hence a most improving augmenting path will also have residual capacity at least $\frac{1}{m}(|f^*| - |f|)$. □

We can now use the lemma to bound the number of iterations of the most improving augmenting path algorithm. To give a bound on the number of iterations, we let U be the largest capacity over all the arcs; that is, $U = \max_{(i,j) \in A} u(i, j)$. As mentioned previously, the style of the proof of the following theorem is something we will encounter many times in the analysis of network flow algorithms.

Theorem 2.23: *If capacities are integers, Algorithm 2.3 computes a maximum flow in $O(m \ln(mU))$ iterations.*

Proof An easy upper bound on the value of a maximum flow is mU: potentially every arc leads out of the source and is saturated at the maximum capacity U. If f is the flow in some iteration of the algorithm, let $f^{(k)}$ be the resulting flow after k iterations. Then by Lemma 2.22

$$|f^{(1)}| \geq |f| + \frac{1}{m}(|f^*| - |f|),$$

or

$$|f^*| - |f^{(1)}| \leq \left(1 - \frac{1}{m}\right)(|f^*| - |f|).$$

Similarly,

$$|f^{(2)}| \geq |f^{(1)}| + \frac{1}{m}(|f^*| - |f^{(1)}|),$$

or

$$|f^*| - |f^{(2)}| \leq \left(1 - \frac{1}{m}\right)(|f^*| - |f^{(1)}|) \leq \left(1 - \frac{1}{m}\right)^2 (|f^*| - |f|).$$

In general,

$$|f^*| - |f^{(k)}| \leq \left(1 - \frac{1}{m}\right)^k (|f^*| - |f|).$$

Thus after $k = m \ln(mU)$ iterations after starting with flow $f = 0$, we have that

$$|f^*| - |f^{(k)}| \leq \left(1 - \frac{1}{m}\right)^{m \ln(mU)} (|f^*| - |f|) < e^{-\ln(mU)}|f^*|,$$

using $1 - x < e^{-x}$ for $x \neq 0$. Then

$$|f^*| - |f^{(k)}| < e^{-\ln(mU)}|f^*| = \frac{1}{mU}|f^*| \leq 1.$$

By the integrality property, since all capacities are integer, the value $|f^*|$ is an integer. Furthermore, by the properties of the augmenting path algorithm $|f^{(k)}|$ is an integer. Thus if $|f^*| - |f^{(k)}| < 1$, then we must have that $|f^{(k)}| = |f^*|$, and $f^{(k)}$ is a maximum flow. $\qquad\square$

To complete our analysis, we need to bound the overall running time of the algorithm; to do that, we need to bound the time taken to compute a most improving path. Here we give a very simple-minded algorithm. First, we sort all arcs in order of nonincreasing residual capacity in $O(m \log m)$ time. We then introduce arcs one at time (in order of nonincreasing residual capacity) until there exists an s-t path in the graph. Then the path must be a most improving path; there cannot be any other path with greater residual capacity. The overall running time of this algorithm to find a path is $O(m^2)$. We give another algorithm in Exercise 2.8 that has running time $O(m + n \log n)$. Thus we have the following theorem.

Theorem 2.24: *Algorithm 2.3 can be implemented to run in $O(m \log(mU)$ $(m + n \log n))$ time.*

2.6 A Capacity Scaling Algorithm

To achieve a better running time, we will see that it is sufficient for the analysis if we find an augmenting path that is almost most improving, and finding a good path gives a better running time than always finding a most improving path. The savings in running time will not be too large, but the idea of finding a good improvement rather than the best possible improvement is one we will see in other contexts, and the running time improvements there will be more significant.

We return to our algorithm for finding the most improving path given at the end of the last section, and introduce a *scaling parameter* Δ. Rather than sorting arcs by nonincreasing residual capacity, and then introducing arcs one at a time until there is an s-t path, we start by setting Δ to a large value, and introduce all arcs that have residual capacity at least Δ, and check if there is an s-t path. If there is one, we push flow on it; otherwise, we divide Δ by 2, and check again. Intuitively, if there is no s-t path on arcs of residual capacity at least Δ, but there is one on arcs of capacity at least $\Delta/2$, then the path has residual capacity within a factor of 2 of that of a most improving path; we will see that this is good enough for our purposes. Also, if there is no s-t path in the residual graph on arcs of residual capacity at least Δ, then the value of the maximum flow in the residual graph cannot be too large, which means the current flow must be close to a maximum flow.

To formalize this idea, we let $G_f(\Delta) = (V, A_f(\Delta))$ be the subgraph of G_f of all arcs (i, j) whose residual capacity is at least Δ; that is, $A_f(\Delta) = \{(i, j) \in A : u_f(i, j) \geq \Delta\}$. Then we give a capacity scaling version of the augmenting path algorithm in Algorithm 2.4. In the algorithm, the innermost loop is performed for a fixed value of Δ; we call these iterations of the algorithm for a fixed Δ a Δ-*scaling phase* of the algorithm.

$f(i, j) \leftarrow 0$ for all $(i, j) \in A$
$\Delta \leftarrow 2^{\lfloor \log_2 U \rfloor}$
while $\Delta \geq 1$ **do**
    while there is an s-t path P in $G_f(\Delta)$ **do**
        Push flow along P
        Update f
    $\Delta \leftarrow \Delta/2$
return f

Algorithm 2.4 A capacity scaling augmenting path algorithm for the maximum flow problem.

We first bound the value of a maximum flow in the residual graph at the start of a Δ-scaling phase.

Lemma 2.25: *At the start of a Δ-scaling phase, the value of a maximum flow in the residual graph G_f is at most $2m\Delta$.*

Proof At the start of the algorithm, $\Delta \geq U/2$ and $f = 0$. An upper bound on the value of the maximum flow is mU, and this is an upper bound on the value of the maximum flow in the residual graph, and thus the lemma statement holds initially.

At the end of any Δ-scaling phase, there are no s-t paths in $G_f(\Delta)$; thus there must be an s-t cut S such that each arc in $\delta^+(S)$ has residual capacity less than Δ. This implies the residual capacity of the cut is at most $m\Delta$ at the end of the Δ-scaling phase. Since we divide Δ by 2 before we start the next phase, the residual capacity of the cut is at most $2m\Delta$ at the start of the next phase. Thus the value of the maximum flow in the residual graph G_f is at most $2m\Delta$. $\square$

We can now bound the number of iterations in any Δ-scaling phase.

Lemma 2.26: *There are at most $2m$ iterations per Δ-scaling phase.*

Proof First, we observe that each iteration in a Δ-scaling phase increases the value of the flow by at least Δ: since all arcs in the s-t path have residual capacity at least Δ, pushing flow along the path will increase the flow value by at least Δ. Let f be the flow at the beginning of the Δ-scaling phase, and let f^* be a maximum flow. Then by Lemmas 2.21 and 2.25, $|f^*| - |f| \leq 2m\Delta$. Thus if $2m$ iterations occur, the value of the resulting flow must be at least $|f| + 2m\Delta \geq |f| + (|f^*| - |f|) = |f^*|$, so the flow must be maximum and no further augmenting paths are found. $\square$

Theorem 2.27: *If the capacities are integers, Algorithm 2.4 computes a maximum flow in $O(m \log U)$ iterations.*

Proof Since Δ is initially $2^{\lfloor \log_2 U \rfloor}$ and is divided by 2 each Δ-scaling phase until it is less than 1, there are $O(\log U)$ scaling phases; by Lemma 2.26 there are at most $2m$ iterations per Δ-scaling phase. Thus there are at most $O(m \log U)$ iterations overall. When $\Delta = 1$, the Δ-scaling phase finds any s-t path in the residual graph such that each arc has residual capacity at least 1. Since the capacities are all integer, if there are no augmenting paths with residual capacity at least 1 in each arc, then there are no augmenting paths in G_f. Thus when the algorithm terminates, there are no augmenting paths in G_f, and by Theorem 2.7, the flow must be maximum. $\square$

Note that it takes only $O(m)$ time to detect whether there is an s-t path in $G_f(\Delta)$, so we obtain the following overall bound on the running time.

Theorem 2.28: *Algorithm 2.4 can be implemented to run in $O(m^2 \log U)$ time.*

2.7 Shortest Augmenting Paths

> We will show that these theoretical difficulties, which could conceivably be a practically serious matter, can be avoided. In particular, by making a refinement of the labeling method which is so simple that it is likely to be incorporated innocently into a computer implementation...
>
> – Jack Edmonds and Richard M. Karp [57]

In this section, we look at yet another natural variant of the augmenting path algorithm. As the quote above (from the paper that proposed it) attests, it is so simple that one might simply write an algorithm to find such a path without thinking about it. In this variant, we always augment along the *shortest* augmenting path; that is, the path with the fewest number of arcs. The algorithm is summarized in Algorithm 2.5.

For the sake of the analysis, we introduce distance labels on the nodes; in the algorithm of the next section, these labels will appear in the algorithm itself. We let $d(i)$ be the number of arcs in the shortest path from node $i \in V$ to the sink t in the current residual graph G_f using only arcs in A_f. Note that this notion of distance is flipped from the notion we used in Chapter 1; in that chapter, $d(i)$ represented the distance *from* the source s, whereas here it represents the distance *to* the sink t. Thus our notion of correct distance labels is flipped as well: here we know that for any arc (i, j) with positive residual capacity it must be the case that $d(i) \leq d(j)+1$. Otherwise, if $d(i) > d(j)+1$, then there is a shorter path from i to t by taking the arc (i, j) and the path from

---

$f(i, j) \leftarrow 0$ for all $(i, j) \in A$
while there is an augmenting path in A_f **do**
    Let P be a shortest augmenting path in A_f
    Push flow along P
    Update f
return f

Algorithm 2.5 Shortest augmenting path algorithm for the maximum flow problem.

j to the sink. In particular, we have that $d(i) = \min_{(i,j) \in A_f}(d(j) + 1)$, and thus for an arc (i, j) that is on a shortest path, $d(i) = d(j) + 1$.

A crucial observation that we will use repeatedly from this point forward in our analysis is that if an arc (i, j) has residual capacity of zero in one iteration of the augmenting path algorithm, and positive residual capacity in the next, it must have been the case that we pushed flow on the arc (j, i).

Observation 2.29: *If $u_f(i, j) = 0$ in the current iteration, f' is the flow in the next iteration, and $u_{f'}(i, j) > 0$, it must be that $f'(i, j) < f(i, j)$, and thus by skew symmetry, $f'(j, i) > f(j, i)$.*

Proof If $u_f(i, j) = 0$ in the current iteration, and in the next iteration (with flow f'), $u_{f'}(i, j) > 0$, then the algorithm must have increased the flow on the arc (j, i) from the current iteration to the next. Thus it is the case that $f'(j, i) > f(j, i)$, and, by skew symmetry, that $f(i, j) > f'(i, j)$. $\square$

The first lemma we need to show is that for any node i, the distance label for i does not decrease at any point in the algorithm.

Lemma 2.30: *For any $i \in V$, let $d(i)$ be its distance to the sink in the residual graph in the current iteration, and let $d'(i)$ be its distance to the sink in the residual graph in the next iteration. Then $d'(i) \geq d(i)$.*

Proof We give a proof by contradiction. Pick some iteration of the algorithm for which the lemma statement is false, and let i be a vertex of minimum $d'(i)$ such that $d'(i) < d(i)$; note $i \neq t$, since $d(t) = d'(t) = 0$. Let P' be the path from i to t of distance $d'(i)$; P' is not an empty path because $i \neq t$. Note that by the choice of i, for any j with $d'(j) < d'(i)$, $d'(j) \geq d(j)$. Thus the first arc (i, j) in the path P' must have had residual capacity zero in the previous iteration, since otherwise $d(i) > d'(i) = 1 + d'(j) \geq 1 + d(j)$, which contradicts the inequality $d(i) \leq d(j) + 1$ for all $(i, j) \in A_f$. If (i, j) had residual capacity zero in the previous iteration, and has positive residual capacity in this iteration, by Observation 2.29 flow was increased on the arc (j, i). Therefore, (j, i) must have been on some shortest path to the sink, so that $d(j) = d(i) + 1$. But then $d'(i) = 1 + d'(j) \geq d(j) + 1 \geq d(i) + 2$, which contradicts $d'(i) < d(i)$. $\square$

Corollary 2.31: *For any i, the distance label $d(i)$ is nondecreasing during the execution of Algorithm 2.5.*

We next show that Corollary 2.31 implies a limit on the number of times during the algorithm a given arc (i, j) can become saturated; recall that an arc

(i, j) is saturated if $f(i, j) = u(i, j)$, and thus arc (i, j) becomes saturated if in the previous iteration $f(i, j) < u(i, j)$ and after pushing flow $f(i, j) = u(i, j)$. Since the augmenting path algorithm saturates at least one arc in each iteration, the limit on the number of times a given arc can be saturated will translate into an overall bound on the number of iterations of the algorithm.

Lemma 2.32: *A given arc $(i, j) \in A$ becomes saturated $O(n)$ times during the execution of Algorithm 2.5.*

Proof Suppose arc (i, j) becomes saturated; it then has zero residual capacity. If it was saturated, then it must have been on a shortest path to the sink, so that $d(i) = d(j) + 1$ using the current distance labels d. In order for it to become saturated again in a later iteration, it must first have nonzero residual capacity. By Observation 2.29, it can have nonzero residual capacity if the flow is increased on arc (j, i); this happens only if (j, i) is on a shortest path to the sink. Let d' be the distance labels in this later iteration; it must be the case that $d'(j) = d'(i) + 1$. By Corollary 2.31, the distance label for i is nondecreasing, so that $d'(j) = d'(i) + 1 \geq d(i) + 1 = (d(j) + 1) + 1$, or $d'(j) \geq d(j) + 2$. Thus, between the iteration in which (i, j) is saturated and the iteration in which it again has positive residual capacity and can become saturated again, the distance label of j must have increased by at least 2. The maximum distance of any vertex to the sink is at most $n - 1$, since there are at most $n - 1$ arcs on a simple path from any vertex to the sink. Thus the arc (i, j) can be saturated $O(n)$ times. □

An overall bound on the number of iterations of the algorithm is an almost immediate consequence of the previous lemma.

Theorem 2.33: *Algorithm 2.5 computes a maximum flow in $O(mn)$ iterations.*

Proof By Lemma 2.32, a given arc can become saturated $O(n)$ times during the algorithm. Each iteration of the augmenting flow algorithm saturates at least one arc. Since there are m arcs, there can be at most $O(mn)$ iterations. □

We can compute a shortest path in a connected unweighted graph in $O(m)$ time (Exercise 1.1), so we get the following running time.

Theorem 2.34: *Algorithm 2.5 can be implemented in $O(m^2 n)$ time.*

We observe that this running time shows that Algorithm 2.5 is a strongly polynomial-time algorithm, according to Definition 2.10.

2.8 The Push-Relabel Algorithm

In the previous three sections, we have given algorithms for the maximum flow problem that are different implementations of the generic augmenting path algorithm given in Algorithm 2.1. In this section, we turn to a quite different algorithm for solving the maximum flow problem, one that has proven to be among the fastest in practice.

One issue with the running time of augmenting path algorithms is illustrated in Figure 2.12. In the figure, there are M nodes to the right of s and another M to the left of t and a very long path in the center. Each time we augment the flow, we can only send a single unit, and we must push the single unit of flow down the very long path. It would be better if we could somehow push all M units of flow down the very long path just once. The algorithm we are about to discuss, called *push-relabel*, will be able to do this. While augmenting path algorithms always maintain a feasible flow f and in the end find an s-t cut of value equal to the flow, the push-relabel algorithm does the opposite: it maintains an infeasible flow and a feasible s-t cut, and gradually modifies the infeasible flow so that it becomes feasible, and equals the value of the s-t cut.

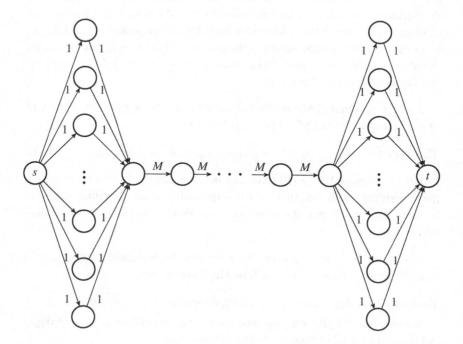

Figure 2.12 A bad instance for augmenting path algorithms.

The algorithm maintains a particular type of infeasible flow called a *preflow*. It has all the properties of a flow as given in Definition 2.3 except that of flow conservation; instead of enforcing that the net flow out of i is zero for $i \neq s, t$, we ensure that the net flow into i is nonnegative for $i \neq s$. We call the net flow into i the *excess* at i, and for a given preflow f, we denote it by $e_f(i)$. We define preflow and excess formally below.

Definition 2.35: *An s-t preflow* $f : A \rightarrow \Re$ *is an assignment of reals to the arcs such that the following three properties are obeyed:*

- *for all arcs* $(i, j) \in A$, $f(i, j) \leq u(i, j)$;
- *for all* $i \in V$ *such that* $i \neq s$, *the net flow entering* i *is nonnegative; that is,* $\sum_{k:(k,i)\in A} f(k, i) \geq 0$;
- *for all* $(i, j) \in A$, $f(i, j) = -f(j, i)$.

The excess *at* i *for a preflow* f *is defined as* $e_f(i) = \sum_{k:(k,i)\in A} f(k, i)$.

The push-relabel algorithm has some similarities with the shortest augmenting path algorithm of the previous section. Whereas the shortest augmenting path algorithm used distance labels in the analysis, the push-relabel algorithm maintains distance labels $d(i)$ for each $i \in V$; in the case of the push-relabel algorithm, if $d(i) \leq n$, the label $d(i)$ is a lower bound on the distance from i to the sink on the arcs of positive residual capacity In this algorithm, we say that we have a *valid* distance labeling if the $d(i)$ obey the following properties with respect to a preflow f.

Definition 2.36: *In the push-relabel algorithm, we have a* valid *distance labeling* $d(i)$ *for* $i \in V$ *for preflow* f *if:*

- $d(s) = n$;
- $d(t) = 0$;
- $d(i) \leq d(j) + 1$ *for all arcs* $(i, j) \in A_f$.

One immediate consequence of a valid distance labeling is that for a preflow f, there is an s-t cut in the residual graph; that is, there are no augmenting paths in the residual graph.

Lemma 2.37: *Given a preflow* f *and a valid distance labeling* d, *there is no augmenting path in* G_f.

Proof Suppose there is a simple s-t path P such that each arc $(i, j) \in P$ has $(i, j) \in A_f$. Then since P is simple, the number of arcs in P is at most $n - 1$, and since d is a valid distance labeling, $d(i) \leq d(j) + 1$ for each arc $(i, j) \in P$. We know that $d(t) = 0$, since d is a valid distance labeling, but then this implies that $d(s) \leq d(t) + |P| \leq n - 1$, which contradicts the properties of a valid distance labeling. $\square$

Thus our goal in the push-relabel algorithm is to gradually convert the preflow to a flow while maintaining a valid distance labeling; once we have a flow f and a valid distance labeling for f, we know by Lemma 2.37 that there is no augmenting path in G_f, and thus the flow is maximum.

The main idea for converting a preflow to a flow is to gradually push as much positive excess as possible toward the sink; following the shortest augmenting path algorithm, we will only do so along arcs that appear to be part of a shortest path toward the sink. If a node i has positive excess $e_f(i) > 0$ and there is some arc (i, j) with positive residual capacity, we can obtain another preflow by increasing the amount of flow on the arc (i, j): increasing $f(i, j)$ reduces the excess at i but increases it at j. To ensure that we are pushing on arcs that are on a short path to the sink, we only push on arcs (i, j) such that $d(i) = d(j) + 1$; that is, j is closer to the sink than i. To introduce some terminology that we will begin to use frequently, we say that an arc (i, j) is *admissible* if $(i, j) \in A_f$ and $d(i) = d(j) + 1$; we will only increase flows on admissible arcs. We try to push as much flow as possible along the arc (i, j) while maintaining that f is a preflow, so we will push as much excess as we can given the residual capacity $u_f(i, j)$ of the arc; thus we will push the minimum of $e_f(i)$ and $u_f(i, j)$.

What if we have a node i with positive excess but no admissible arcs (i, j) leading out of i, since $d(i) < d(j)+1$ for all arcs $(i, j) \in A_f$? In this case, our intuition is that the current distance label for i must be too low: all neighbors of i via admissible arcs have distance to the sink at least as large as i, and so it must be the case that i is even further from the sink than its current distance label indicates. Thus, in the case there are no admissible arcs out of a node i with positive excess, we will *relabel* the distance label $d(i)$; we will increase it to be the minimum of $d(j) + 1$ over all arcs $(i, j) \in A_f$, and introduce at least one admissible arc out of i on which we can push an excess from i, while maintaining that d is a valid distance labeling. Note that if i has positive excess, then $f(k, i) > 0$ for some arc (k, i) entering i, which implies that there is positive residual capacity on at least one arc leading out of i, the reverse arc (i, k), so that there will be some arc leaving i in A_f. We formally define the push and relabel operations in Procedure Push and Procedure Relabel.

Another useful perspective on the notion of a distance label is to view it as giving the height of the node. The condition $d(i) \leq d(j) + 1$ for arcs (i, j) with positive residual capacity ensures that a node isn't much higher than a neighboring node to which flow can be pushed. We only push excess when

$d(i) = d(j) + 1$, since we want flows to go "downhill," from a higher node to a lower one. The relabel operation raises the height of a node so that there is some neighboring node that is downhill from it.

In our discussion above, we have not said what happens if the excess cannot be pushed to the sink. In instances for which this happens, we will push the excess back to the source: if a distance label $d(i)$ becomes n or greater, then $d(i) - n$ is a lower bound on its distance to the source, and the excess at the node will be pushed back to the source. We will have more to say about this later.

We can now give the entire push-relabel algorithm, shown in Algorithm 2.6. We say that a node $i \neq s, t$ is *active* if it has positive excess ($e_f(i) > 0$). If we have an active node, then we don't yet have a flow f, so we look for some admissible arc (i, j). If there is some admissible arc (i, j), we push as much flow as possible along it: we push the minimum of the excess at i and the residual capacity of (i, j). If there is no admissible arc (i, j), we relabel i.

$\delta \leftarrow \min(e_f(i), u_f(i, j))$
$f(i, j) \leftarrow f(i, j) + \delta$
$f(j, i) \leftarrow f(j, i) - \delta$

Procedure Push(i, j)

$d(i) \leftarrow \min_{(i, j) \in A_f}(d(j) + 1)$

Procedure Relabel(i)

$f(i, j) \leftarrow 0$ for all $(i, j) \in A$
$f(s, j) \leftarrow u(s, j), f(j, s) \leftarrow -u(s, j)$ for all $(s, j) \in A$
$d(s) \leftarrow n$
$d(i) \leftarrow 0$ for all $i \in V, i \neq s$
while there is an active i ($e_f(i) > 0$ for $i \neq s, t$) **do**
    if there is j such that (i, j) is admissible ($(i, j) \in A_f$ and
    $d(i) = d(j) + 1$) **then**
        Push((i, j))
    else
        Relabel(i)
return f

Algorithm 2.6 The basic push-relabel algorithm.

We first argue that the push-relabel algorithm is correct and returns a maximum flow. We start by proving that it maintains a preflow f and a valid distance labeling d.

Lemma 2.38: *Algorithm 2.6 maintains a preflow f.*

Proof First we must show that f is initialized to a preflow; then we show that every push operation maintains that f is a preflow. For any node k such that (s,k) is an arc, initially $e_f(k) = u(s,k)$; for all other nodes $i \neq s,t$, $e_f(i) = 0$. Capacity constraints and skew symmetry are clearly obeyed. Now consider a push on arc (i,j); let f' be the result if we start with preflow f. We push $\delta = \min(e_f(i), u_f(i,j))$ units of flow. Thus capacity constraints are obeyed, since $f'(i,j) = f(i,j) + \delta \leq f(i,j) + u_f(i,j) \leq u(i,j)$ and $f'(j,i) = f(j,i) - \delta \leq u(j,i)$. Skew symmetry is maintained, since $f'(i,j) = f(i,j) + \delta = -f(j,i) + \delta = -(f(j,i) - \delta) = -f'(j,i)$. Finally, nodes continue to have nonnegative excess, since we did a push at a node $i \neq s,t$ and $e_{f'}(i) = e_f(i) - \delta \geq 0$ and $e_{f'}(j) = e_f(j) + \delta \geq 0$. Thus f' is also a preflow. □

Lemma 2.39: *Algorithm 2.6 maintains a valid distance labeling d.*

Proof We initially set $d(s) = n$, $d(t) = 0$, and $d(i) = 0$ for all $i \neq s,t$. The only arcs (i,j) for which possibly $d(i) > d(j) + 1$ are the arcs (s,k), since $d(s) = n$ and $d(k) = 0$. However, these arcs are initially saturated, so that $u_f(s,k) = 0$ and we do not need $d(s) \leq d(k) + 1$ for these arcs, since they are not in A_f. We now need to show that d continues to be a valid distance labeling during the course of the algorithm. The distance labeling d remains valid after a relabel operation by construction. Now consider a push operation on the arc (i,j). Increasing the flow $f(i,j)$ may cause the residual capacity of the arc (j,i) to become positive. However, since we only pushed on (i,j) if $d(i) = d(j) + 1$, it is the case that $d(j) = d(i) - 1 \leq d(i) + 1$, so the labeling is valid for the arc (j,i). Finally, we never relabel s or t because s and t are never active, so $d(s) = n$ and $d(t) = 0$ throughout the algorithm. □

To show that the algorithm terminates eventually with a flow f, we first must prove the following lemma.

Lemma 2.40: *For any preflow f, for any node i with $e_f(i) > 0$ there always exists a simple path from i to s such that each arc in the path has positive residual capacity.*

Proof Let i be a node with $e_f(i) > 0$, and let S be the set of all nodes reachable from i using only arcs of positive residual capacity. Suppose that $s \notin S$. Note that for any arc (j,k) with $j \in S$, $k \notin S$, $u_f(j,k) = 0$, so that

$f(j,k) = u(j,k)$. Thus by skew symmetry, $f(k,j) = -f(j,k) = -u(j,k) \leq 0$. Now consider $\sum_{j \in S} e_f(j)$. By definition,

$$\sum_{j \in S} e_f(j) = \sum_{j \in S} \sum_{k:(k,j) \in A} f(k,j)$$

$$= \sum_{j \in S} \left(\sum_{k \in S:(k,j) \in A} f(k,j) + \sum_{k \notin S:(k,j) \in A} f(k,j) \right).$$

By skew symmetry, the terms in the sum $\sum_{j \in S} \sum_{k \in S:(k,j) \in A} f(k,j)$ all cancel, and by the previous argument, the terms in the sum $\sum_{j \in S} \sum_{k \notin S:(k,j) \in A} f(k,j)$ are all nonpositive. Thus we have that $\sum_{j \in S} e_f(j) \leq 0$. But since f is a preflow, $e_f(j) \geq 0$ for all $j \neq s$. This implies that $\sum_{j \in S} e_f(j) = 0$ and $e_f(j) = 0$ for all $j \in S$, which contradicts $e_f(i) > 0$, since $i \in S$. We have reached a contradiction, so it must be the case that $s \in S$. $\square$

While Lemma 2.40 at first seems rather innocuous, it has the consequence of making sure that the distance labels remain bounded, and this will lead directly to bounds on the running time of the algorithm.

Lemma 2.41: *For any $i \in V$, $d(i) \leq 2n - 1$.*

Proof Note that we only relabel nodes i with positive excess, and by Lemma 2.40, there is always a simple path $P \subseteq A_f$ from i to s on arcs with positive residual capacity. Since P is simple, $|P| \leq n - 1$, and since d is a valid distance labeling and all $(i,j) \in P$ have $(i,j) \in A_f$, it must be that $d(i) \leq d(s) + |P| = n + |P| \leq 2n - 1$. $\square$

Using Lemma 2.41, we can immediately bound the number of relabel operations performed by the algorithm, and with a little more work we can also bound the number of push operations. Let's start by bounding the number of relabel operations.

Lemma 2.42: *The number of relabel operations performed in Algorithm 2.6 is $O(n^2)$.*

Proof All distance labels for $i \neq s$ are set at $d(i) = 0$, and each time a relabel is performed, we increase the distance label by at least 1. By Lemma 2.41, each distance label can be at most $2n - 1$, and there are at most $n - 2$ different nodes that can be relabeled, so that the overall number of relabel operations that can be performed is at most $(n - 2)(2n - 1) = O(n^2)$. $\square$

To bound the number of push operations performed by the algorithm, we separate them into two types. Recall that in a push operation, we increase the flow on an arc (i, j) by the minimum of $e_f(i)$ and $u_f(i, j)$. We call a push that increases the flow on $f(i, j)$ by $u_f(i, j)$ a *saturating* push, because afterwards the arc (i, j) is saturated. We call a push that increases flow by $e_f(i) < u_f(i, j)$ a *nonsaturating* push. We can bound the number of saturating pushes performed by the algorithm with a proof essentially identical to one we used for the shortest augmenting path algorithm (Lemma 2.32).

Lemma 2.43: *The number of saturating pushes performed in Algorithm 2.6 is* $O(mn)$.

Proof The proof of this lemma closely follows the proof of Lemma 2.32 for the shortest augmenting path algorithm. Fix an arc (i, j). If we perform a saturating push on arc (i, j), then the arc was admissible and $d(i) = d(j) + 1$; since the arc becomes saturated, it has zero residual capacity. By Observation 2.29, it can have nonzero residual capacity again only if the flow is increased on arc (j, i), which happens if flow is pushed on arc (j, i). Let d' be the distance labels in the iteration in which flow is pushed on (j, i); flow can only be pushed if (j, i) is admissible, or $d'(j) = d'(i) + 1$. Since distance labels are nondecreasing during the course of the algorithm, $d'(j) = d'(i) + 1 \geq d(i) + 1 = d(j) + 2$. Thus the distance label of j must have been increased by at least two units before the arc (i, j) again has any positive residual capacity, and thus before another saturating push can be performed on arc (i, j). Since over the course of the algorithm $d(j) \leq 2n - 1$ by Lemma 2.41, it must be the case that we can perform at most n saturating pushes on the arc (i, j). Taken over all m arcs, we can perform $O(mn)$ saturating pushes. $\square$

If we adopt the perspective that the distance label represents the height of a node, then the proof above notices that a saturating push on (i, j) pushes flow from i downhill one unit to j, and to be able to push from i to j again, we must first push from j to i. To push downhill, we must raise the height of j by two units. Since the height of j is never more than $2n - 1$ units, we can perform at most n saturating pushes on (i, j).

Finally, we bound the number of nonsaturating pushes of the algorithm. In this argument, as well as others in the book, we will use a *potential function argument*. We set up a potential function Φ in terms of some of the parameters of the algorithm such that Φ is nonnegative during the course of the algorithm, and is some nonnegative number P at the start. Typically, each algorithmic step that we are interested in counting (for instance, each nonsaturating push) causes Φ to decrease by at least one unit. Other steps of the algorithm cause Φ to increase. Then to bound the number of the steps we wish to count, we only need to bound the total amount by which Φ increases: the number of these steps can be at most P plus the total increase. We can view Φ as something like a bank account; each algorithmic step we want to count withdraws at least a unit from the account, and because the account never becomes negative, to bound the total number of withdrawals, we only need to give a bound on the total amount initially in the account and that deposited into the account.

Lemma 2.44: *The number of nonsaturating pushes performed in Algorithm 2.6 is $O(n^2m)$.*

Proof As stated above, we use a potential function argument. Let $\Phi = \sum_{i \text{ active}} d(i)$. Then $\Phi = 0$ at both the start and end of the algorithm, since at the start all active nodes have distance label 0, and at the end there are no active nodes. Now we consider what causes Φ to increase and to decrease over the course of the algorithm. The decreases in Φ are due to nonsaturating pushes, since these take a currently active node i and make it inactive, thus removing it from the sum; since a push on arc (i, j) requires $d(i) = d(j) + 1$, even if the nonsaturating push makes j active, the change in Φ is $d(j) - d(i) = d(j) - (d(j) + 1) = -1$. The increases in Φ are due to relabel operations and saturating pushes that create a newly active vertex; a relabel can increase Φ by the change in the distance label, and adding a new active vertex j to the sum can increase Φ by $d(j) \leq 2n - 1$. Thus the total amount by which Φ can increase over the algorithm is $O(n^2)$ due to relabels plus $O(nm) \cdot (2n - 1) = O(n^2m)$ due to saturating pushes. Thus the total amount by which Φ can increase over the course of the algorithm is $O(n^2 + n^2m) = O(n^2m)$. Since at the start and end of the algorithm $\Phi = 0$, the total number of nonsaturating pushes is $O(n^2m)$. ☐

Putting everything together gives the following time bound.

Theorem 2.45: *The push-relabel algorithm (Algorithm 2.6) takes $O(n^2m)$ time overall to compute a maximum flow.*

Proof Each push operation takes $O(1)$ time, so the algorithm takes $O(n^2m)$ time overall for push operations. For each vertex i, we maintain an ordered list of its outgoing arcs (i, j), and we keep a pointer to the last arc (i, j) on which we pushed flow. When searching for an admissible arc out of i, we start with this last previous arc on which we pushed flow; if it is no longer admissible, we move to the next arc in the list. If we reach the end of the list, then there are no longer any admissible arcs out of i, and we can perform a relabel of i, and reset the pointer to the beginning of the list. Examining all of the arcs out of i takes $O(|\delta^+(\{i\})|)$ time. By Lemma 2.41, we relabel i $O(n)$ times, so that

the overall time taken for relabel operations and for scanning the arcs out of all
nodes for an admissible arc is $O(n \sum_{i \in V} |\delta^+(\{i\})|) = O(nm)$.

When the algorithm terminates, the preflow f is a flow, since $e_f(i) = 0$ for
all $i \neq s, t$. By Lemma 2.37, there are no augmenting paths in G_f, and thus by
Theorem 2.7, f must be a maximum flow.   □

We observe from the proof above that the running time is dominated by
the push operations. The push-relabel algorithm is quite flexible; we have
a good deal of choice in selecting arcs to push and nodes to relabel. By
taking some advantage of this flexibility, we can give a better bound on the
overall run time. In particular, we need to do something to obtain a better
bound on the number of nonsaturating pushes, since the $O(n^2 m)$ bound of
Lemma 2.44 is what yields the $O(n^2 m)$ running time. To help us do this,
we introduce a new operation, called *discharge*, and we choose a particular
order of applying discharge to active nodes. The discharge operation takes
an active node i and continues to apply push operations (and relabels when
necessary) until it is no longer active; note that the discharge operation causes
at most one nonsaturating push, since only the last push out of active node i
can be nonsaturating. Additionally, we will apply the discharge operation to the
active node with the highest distance label. In order to support this ordering, we
maintain an integer d^* which is equal to the maximum label of an active node
(that is, $d^* = \max_{\text{active } i} d(i)$). We also maintain *buckets* $b[0], \ldots, b[2n-1]$,
where each bucket $b[k]$ contains a list of active nodes whose distance label

---

while i is active **do**
    for all j such that $(i, j) \in A$ **do**
        if (i, j) is admissible **then**
            Push(i, j)
    if $e_f(i) > 0$ **then**
        Relabel(i)

Procedure Discharge(i)

$\delta \leftarrow \min(e_f(i), u_f(i, j))$
$f(i, j) \leftarrow f(i, j) + \delta$
$f(j, i) \leftarrow f(j, i) - \delta$
if j active and not $b[d(j)].contains?(j)$ **then**
    $b[d(j)].add(j)$

Procedure Push(i, j)

$b[d(i)].remove(i)$
$d(i) \leftarrow \min_{(i,j) \in A_f}(d(j) + 1)$
$b[d(i)].add(i)$
if $d(i) > d^*$ **then**
    $d^* \leftarrow d(i)$

Procedure Relabel(i)

$f(i, j) \leftarrow 0$ for all $(i, j) \in A$
$f(s, j) \leftarrow u(s, j), f(j, s) \leftarrow -u(s, j)$ for all $(s, j) \in A$
$d(s) \leftarrow n$
$d(i) \leftarrow 0$ for all $i \in V, i \neq s$
$d^* \leftarrow 0$
$b[0].add(i)$ for all $i \in V, i \neq s, t$
while $d^* \geq 0$ **do**
    if not $b[d^*].empty?$ **then**
        Discharge $(b[d^*].remove())$
    else
        $d^* \leftarrow d^* - 1$
return f

Algorithm 2.7 The highest label version of the push-relabel algorithm.

is k. Each bucket $b[k]$ supports the operations $b[k].add(i)$, which adds node i to the list for bucket k; $b[k].remove()$, which removes and returns some node from the list for bucket k (if there is one); $b[k].remove(i)$, which removes node i from bucket k if it is present; $b[k].contains?(i)$, which checks if the bucket k contains node i; and $b[k].empty?$, which checks if the list for bucket k is empty or not. We give a formal presentation of this version of the algorithm in Procedure Discharge and Algorithm 2.7. This version is often called the *highest label* version of push-relabel. We will show below that this version reduces the number of nonsaturating pushes (and hence the running time of the algorithm) to $O(n^2\sqrt{m})$.

Lemma 2.46: *The number of nonsaturating pushes in Algorithm 2.7 is* $O(n^2\sqrt{m})$.

Proof We let K be a parameter; ultimately we will set $K = \sqrt{m}$. Let $N(i)$ be the set of nodes with distance label at most that of i, so that $N(i) = \{j \in V : d(j) \leq d(i)\}$. Note that $i \in N(i)$, so $|N(i)| \geq 1$. As in our proof of the bound of $O(n^2m)$ on nonsaturating pushes (in Lemma 2.44), we give a potential function argument, this time with the potential function $\Phi = \frac{1}{K} \sum_i$ active $|N(i)|$. Note that at the start of the algorithm $\Phi \leq n^2/K$, and at termination $\Phi = 0$, since there are no longer any active nodes. Once again, we need to consider which operations make the potential function increase and which make it decrease. As observed previously, Φ is initially at most n^2/K. A relabel of node i can increase Φ by at most n/K, since it could be the case that $|N(i)|$ increases to n; note that all other $|N(j)|$, $j \neq i$, do not increase. A saturating push can increase Φ by at most n/K by creating a newly active node. Thus by Lemmas 2.42 and 2.43, the total amount by which Φ can increase over the course of the algorithm is $O(n^2/K + (n^2 + mn)n/K) = O(mn^2/K)$.

A nonsaturating push on arc (i, j) must decrease Φ, since i is no longer active and is removed from the sum, and $|N(i)| \geq 1$; even if j becomes active due to the push, because (i, j) is admissible, $d(i) = d(j) + 1$, which implies that $N(j) \subset N(i)$ and thus $|N(j)| < |N(i)|$, since $i \notin N(j)$. Thus Φ decreases by at least $(|N(i)| - |N(j)|)/K \geq 1/K$.

To analyze the number of nonsaturating pushes, we divide the algorithm into phases: we end a phase when d^* changes, and start a new phase. We first bound the total number of phases. Note that initially $d^* = 0$ and this is also true at the end of the algorithm. If d^* increases (causing the end of a phase), this must be due to a relabel operation on a node i of label d^*, since we always discharge an active node of highest label. The increase in d^* is equal to the amount of change in the label of node i. By Lemma 2.42, the total amount by which d^* can increase due to increases in the labels of all the nodes is $O(n^2)$. A decrease in d^* also causes the end of a phase, and since the number of decreases of d^* can be at most the total amount of increase of d^*, the number of phases is $O(n^2)$.

We will call a phase *short* if there are at most K nonsaturating pushes during the phase, and a phase is *long* otherwise. Since there are $O(n^2)$ phases, there are $O(n^2 K)$ nonsaturating pushes during the short phases. The key claim is that during a long phase, since there are at least K nonsaturating pushes, then Φ must decrease by at least one for each nonsaturating push. Each nonsaturating push on (i, j) is made from a node i of the highest label, so that $d(i) = d^*$, and the phase ends either when all nodes of label d^* are not active, or when a node of label d^* is relabeled. Thus if there are $Q > K$ nonsaturating pushes in the phase, there must have been at least Q nodes of distance label d^* at the start of the phase. Thus for each nonsaturating push on an admissible arc (i, j) during a long phase, $|N(i)| - |N(j)| \geq Q > K$, and each push reduces Φ by at least $(|N(i)| - |N(j)|)/K \geq 1$. Since Φ increases by $O(mn^2/K)$ during the course of the algorithm, the number of nonsaturating pushes in long phases is $O(mn^2/K)$. Thus the overall number of nonsaturating pushes is $O(n^2 K + mn^2/K)$. Choosing $K = \sqrt{m}$ to balance the two terms gives us that the number of nonsaturating pushes is $O(n^2 \sqrt{m})$. □

Theorem 2.47: *The highest label version of push-relabel (Algorithm 2.7) runs in $O(n^2 \sqrt{m})$ time.*

Goldberg and Tarjan [92] show that by using a data structure known as a dynamic tree (discussed in Exercise 4.3), the push-relabel algorithm can be implemented in $O(mn \log(n^2/m))$ time.

As we mentioned at the beginning of the section, the push-relabel algorithm and its variants are among the fastest maximum flow algorithms in practice; the highest label version of the algorithm given above typically has been the fastest variant of push-relabel. We now describe a number of implementation details that have no effect on the theoretical running time of the algorithm but are useful in improving the overall speed of implementations of the highest label algorithm.

The first is to redefine an active node $i \neq t$ to be one such that $d(i) < n$, in addition to having positive excess $e_f(i) > 0$; we show below that only nodes i with $d(i) < n$ can push their excess to the sink, and that once there are no active nodes of this type, we have found a minimum s-t cut. Often, as in the baseball elimination problem, we are only interested in the value of the flow and not the actual values $f(i, j)$, and so it is sufficient to have such an algorithm. The basic idea of the proof is to consider a set S such that all arcs $(i, j) \in \delta^+(S)$ are saturated. If all nodes with positive excess are in this set S, then we show that if we continue to run the push-relabel algorithm, the arcs in $\delta^+(S)$ continue to be saturated, and so by Corollary 2.5 S is a minimum s-t cut when the algorithm terminates. We will give a set S such that all i with $d(i) \geq n$ are in S and such that all arcs $(i, j) \in \delta^+(S)$ are saturated.

If we are interested in the flow values $f(i, j)$, it is possible to take a preflow f and an s-t cut S, with all nodes of positive excess in S and all arcs in $\delta^+(S)$ saturated, and convert the preflow to a flow in $O(mn)$ time; we give this as an exercise (Exercise 2.13).

Lemma 2.48: *Let f be a preflow, and let S be any s-t cut such that if $(i, j) \in \delta^+(S)$ then $u_f(i, j) = 0$, and if $j \notin S$ and $j \neq t$, then $e_f(j) = 0$. Then S is a minimum s-t cut.*

Proof We would like to apply Corollary 2.5 to show that then S must be a minimum s-t cut, but f is a preflow, not a flow. So instead we argue that if we continue to run the basic push-relabel algorithm (Algorithm 2.6), the arcs in $\delta^+(S)$ continue to be saturated. To see this, note that the flow on an arc $(i, j) \in \delta^+(S)$ changes only if we perform a push either on (i, j) or on (j, i). We will not perform a push on (j, i), since $j \notin S$, and therefore $e_f(j) = 0$. We also cannot perform a push on (i, j), since $u_f(i, j) = 0$. Thus inductively, it continues to be the case that $u_f(i, j) = 0$ for arcs $(i, j) \in \delta^+(S)$ and $e_f(j) = 0$ for $j \notin S$, $j \neq t$, and so when the algorithm terminates with a flow f, by Corollary 2.5, S must be a minimum s-t cut. □

Lemma 2.49: *If $d(i) \geq n$, then i cannot reach the sink t via arcs of positive residual capacity.*

Proof Suppose otherwise, and let P be a simple path from i to t via arcs of positive residual capacity. Then since d is a valid distance labeling, $d(i) \leq d(t) + |P| \leq 0 + n - 1 = n - 1$, which is a contradiction. □

Corollary 2.50: *If we terminate the algorithm when $e_f(i) > 0$ implies $d(i) \geq n$ for $i \neq t$, then the set S of all vertices that cannot reach t via arcs in A_f is a minimum s-t cut.*

Proof Note that for the set S, $(i, j) \in \delta^+(S)$ implies that $u_f(i, j) = 0$. Then the corollary follows immediately from Lemmas 2.49 and 2.48. □

Note that from the corollary above, if we redefine an active node i to be one such that $d(i) < n$ (and $e_f(i) > 0$), then when there are no longer any active nodes, we can find a minimum s-t cut by looking for the set S of all vertices that cannot reach t via arcs in A_f.

As mentioned above, we leave the proof of the following lemma as an exercise (Exercise 2.13).

Lemma 2.51: *Let f be a preflow and S an s-t cut such that if $e_f(i) > 0$ for $i \neq s$, then $i \in S$, and also $u_f(i, j) = 0$ for all $(i, j) \in \delta^+(S)$. Then it is possible to find a flow f in $O(mn)$ time such that $|f| = u(\delta^+(S))$.*

Two additional heuristics are used in practical variants of the push-relabel algorithm. The first is called the *gap relabeling* heuristic. It checks to see whether there is a "gap" in the distance labels; that is, if there is some value $k < n$ such that there are active nodes i with distance label $d(i) > k$, but no nodes j of distance $d(j) = k$. If so, it takes every node i with distance label $k < d(i) < n$ and sets $d(i) = n$. Since now a node i is active only if $d(i) < n$, effectively this makes all of these nodes inactive. The central idea in proving the correctness of this heuristic is to show that the new distance labeling continues to be a valid distance labeling. We ask the reader to prove this in Exercise 2.14. It is easy to implement the heuristic, also: during a relabel operation, we check when we remove node i from its bucket $b[d(i)]$ if the bucket is now empty. If so, then since i is active, and will receive label greater than its current label of $d(i)$, we can set the label of every active node of label greater than $d(i)$ to n. Both Lemma 2.48 and gap relabeling will play a role in the Hao–Orlin algorithm we discuss in Section 3.1.

The second heuristic is called *global relabeling*. We observed that the distance label $d(i)$ is meant to be used as an estimate of the distance of each node to the sink using arcs of positive residual capacity. It turns out to be useful to calculate the actual distance of i to t using arcs of positive residual capacity and update $d(i)$ to be this distance; these give a valid distance labeling, and the update takes $O(m)$ time (as we observed in Exercise 1.1). Since global relabeling is a relatively time-consuming operation, we do not want to perform it too frequently. Experimentally, it seems that performing a global relabeling once every n relabels is very useful. Since there are $O(n^2)$ relabel operations total during the course of the algorithm, this adds an additional $O(mn)$ to the running time.

As we mentioned previously, not only is the push-relabel algorithm quite practical, but it is very flexible, and variants of it can be used in many settings. We will see versions of the push-relabel algorithm applied to several different flow problems in the exercises and upcoming sections. For instance, we apply ideas from the push-relabel algorithm to finding a global minimum cut in Section 3.1, to finding a minimum-cost circulation in Section 5.5, and to finding a generalized maximum flow in Exercise 6.5. We also see variants of the push-relabel algorithm in the exercises known as FIFO push-relabel (Exercise 2.10), excess scaling (Exericse 2.11), and wave scaling (Exercise 2.12).

Exercises

2.1 Let f be an s-t flow according to Definition 2.1. Show that the value of the flow is equal to the net flow entering the sink; that is, show that

$$|f| = \sum_{k:(k,t)\in A} f(k,t) - \sum_{k:(t,k)\in A} f(t,k).$$

2.2 Consider the maximum s-t flow problem shown below, where M is a large integer. Show that an algorithm that chooses arbitrary augmenting paths from the residual graph does not run in polynomial time.

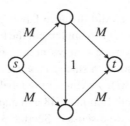

2.3   In this problem, we return to the baseball elimination problem of Section
       2.3; we use the same notation as that section.

       (a) Prove that if team k is eliminated, and $w(k) + g(k) \geq w(i) + g(i)$,
            then team i is also eliminated.
       (b) Prove that we can determine which teams in the division have been
            eliminated and which have not with $O(\log |T|)$ executions of a
            maximum flow algorithm, where T is the set of teams in the division.

2.4   We now consider the *quidditch elimination problem*, to determine
       whether a given professional league quidditch team has been eliminated
       from the championship at some point in the middle of the season. The
       only rules of professional quidditch that we need to know are that there
       are 3 points awarded for each game. If a team has the highest score and
       captures the Golden Snitch, then 3 points go to the winner and 0 go to the
       loser; if the team has the highest score but does not capture the Golden
       Snitch, it gets 2 points and the other team gets 1 point. Another way to
       view this is that the team with the highest score gets 2 points, and the
       team that captures the Golden Snitch gets 1 point. The team with the
       most points at the end of the season wins the championship. Assume
       that each team plays the same number of games, in total, in the course of
       the season. Show how to determine whether a given quidditch team has
       been eliminated via a single maximum flow computation.

2.5   A type of problem in computer vision is called *image segmentation*. In
       this problem, we would like to identify objects that are present in the
       image; we do so by assigning labels to the pixels in the image, such
       that the pixels for a given objects are all labeled with the same label.
       The problem can be formulated as follows. We are given as input an
       undirected graph $G = (V, E)$ in which the vertices represent the pixels
       of the image and the edges connect adjacent pixels. We are also given
       labels L, assignment costs $c(i, \ell) \geq 0$ for all $i \in V$ and $\ell \in L$, and
       separation costs $p(i, j) \geq 0$ for all $(i, j) \in E$. We would like to assign
       each vertex a single label of L. There is a cost $c(i, \ell)$ for assigning label
       ℓ to vertex $i \in V$. Also, all things being equal, we want nearby vertices

assigned the same labels, so there is a penalty $p(i, j)$ for edge $(i, j) \in E$ if i and j are assigned different labels. The goal is to find a labeling that minimizes the overall cost (assignment costs plus penalties). More formally, we want to find a labeling of the vertices $f : V \to L$ that minimizes

$$\sum_{i \in V} c(i, f(i)) + \sum_{(i,j) \in E : f(i) \neq f(j)} p(i, j).$$

Show that if there are only two labels (that is, $|L| = 2$), then we can find the labeling of minimum cost via a minimum s-t cut computation.

2.6 Consider an undirected graph $G = (V, E)$ with nonnegative integer weights $w(i, j) \geq 0$ for all $(i, j) \in E$. Suppose we now wish to find the weighted maximum density subgraph. Let $w(E(S)) = \sum_{(i,j) \in E(S)} w(i, j)$; we want to find $S \subseteq V$, $S \neq \emptyset$, that maximizes $w(E(S))/|S|$. Show how the algorithm of Section 2.4 can be adapted to find the weighted maximum density subgraph in $O(\log W)$ maximum flow computations, where $W = \sum_{(i,j) \in E} w(i, j)$.

2.7 (Hoffman's circulation theorem) Let $G = (V, A)$ be a directed graph, with bounds $0 \leq \ell(i, j) \leq u(i, j)$ for all $(i, j) \in A$. We say that f is a feasible *circulation* if for all $i \in V$,

$$\sum_{j:(j,i) \in A} f(j, i) - \sum_{j:(i,j) \in A} f(i, j) = 0,$$

and for all $(i, j) \in A$, $\ell(i, j) \leq f(i, j) \leq u(i, j)$. For $S \subset V$, recall that $\delta^+(S) = \{(i, j) \in A : i \in S, j \notin S\}$ and $\delta^-(S) = \{(i, j) \in A : i \notin S, j \in S\}$. Also, for a subset $A' \subseteq A$ of arcs, define $u(A') = \sum_{(i,j) \in A'} u(i, j)$ and $\ell(A') = \sum_{(i,j) \in A'} \ell(i, j)$. Prove that there exists a feasible circulation f if and only if for all subsets $S \subset V$, $S \neq \emptyset$, $u(\delta^+(S)) \geq \ell(\delta^-(S))$. As part of the proof, show that a feasible circulation can be found (if it exists) with a single maximum flow computation.

2.8 Show that it is possible to find the most improving augmenting path (that is, the augmenting path whose arc of minimum residual capacity is maximized) in a residual graph in $O(m + n \log n)$ time.

2.9 Consider the following problem. We are given as input a directed graph $G = (V, A)$, source and sink vertices s and t, integer capacities $u(i, j) \geq 0$ for all $(i, j) \in A$, and a positive integer k. The goal of the problem is to find the maximum amount of flow that can be sent from s to t if flow is sent on exactly k paths and each path must send the same amount of flow.

We claim that a max flow/min cut theorem can be shown for this problem for a suitable definition of cut. For a cut S, $s \in S$, consider a bin packing problem in which there is a bin of capacity $u(i,j)$ for each arc $(i,j) \in \delta^+(S)$. Let λ be the maximum item size such that k items of size λ can be packed in these bins. Then we define the capacity of cut S, $\hat{c}(S)$, to be $k\lambda$.

Prove that the maximum s-t flow of the type above is equal to the minimum capacity s-t cut as defined above; i.e. $\min_{S \subseteq V: s \in S, t \notin S} \hat{c}(S)$.

2.10 Another variant of the push-relabel algorithm is called *FIFO* push-relabel. This version maintains a queue of active nodes; initially all active nodes are added to the queue (if needed, see page 9 in Section 1.2 for definitions of operations supported by a queue). The algorithm takes a node i from the front of the queue and performs a discharge operation on it. If pushing flow from i to j causes j to become active, and j is not already in the queue, the algorithm adds j to the end of the queue.

To bound the running time of the algorithm, we need to bound the number of nonsaturating pushes performed by the algorithm. To do this, we use a potential function argument on *passes* over the queue. The first pass over the queue ends when the algorithm has performed a discharge operation on all the nodes initially added to the queue. In general, the kth pass to the queue ends when the algorithm has performed a discharge operation on all the nodes added to the queue in the $(k-1)$st pass. Consider the potential function $\Phi = \max_{\text{active } i} d(i)$.

(a) Use the potential function to prove that the algorithm makes $O(n^2)$ passes.

(b) Argue that the bound on the number of passes implies there are $O(n^3)$ nonsaturating pushes.

(c) Finally, argue that the FIFO version of push-relabel takes $O(n^3)$ time.

2.11 Yet another variant of the push-relabel algorithm is known as *excess scaling*. In this variant of the algorithm we maintain a parameter Δ which is initially $2^{\lceil \log_2 U \rceil}$; we proceed in a sequence of Δ-*scaling phases*. At the start of each Δ-scaling phase, we maintain that the current preflow f is Δ-*optimal*. A preflow f is Δ-optimal if the excess $e_f(i) \le \Delta$ for all $i \ne s, t$. In each Δ-scaling phase, we run a slightly modified push-relabel algorithm in which we ensure that we do not create any new nodes i with $e_f(i) > \Delta$.

(a) Explain how to modify the push operation so that the algorithm does not create any new nodes i with $e_f(i) > \Delta$.

(b) Assuming that for each node $i \in V$, $i \neq s$, there is at most one arc from the source s to i, explain why after the usual initialization of the push-relabel algorithm, the initial preflow is Δ-optimal for $\Delta = 2^{\lceil \log_2 U \rceil}$.

Within a Δ-scaling phase, we say that a node i is $\Delta/2$-*active* if $e_f(i) > \Delta/2$. In the push-relabel algorithm for a Δ-scaling phase, we pick the $\Delta/2$-active node i that has minimum distance label $d(i)$, and we push excess from i on admissible arcs (i, j) (recall that an arc is admissible if it has positive residual capacity and $d(i) = d(j) + 1$); we continue to push on i until either $e_f(i) \leq \Delta/2$ or we need to relabel i. We then pick the next $\Delta/2$-active node of minimum distance label. The Δ-scaling phase ends when there are no more $\Delta/2$-active nodes. We then divide Δ by 2, and continue to the next Δ-scaling phase; observe that since there were no $\Delta/2$-active nodes at the end of the previous phase, once we divide Δ by 2, the preflow is Δ-optimal for the new value of Δ.

(c) Argue that for the $\Delta/2$-active node of minimum distance label, either a push or a relabel operation always applies, and thus if we can bound the number of push-relabel operations, each Δ-scaling phase must terminate in finite time.

(d) Argue that if capacities are integer, then once $\Delta < 1$ the algorithm has computed a maximum flow.

(e) Prove that the number of nonsaturating pushes is $O(n^2)$ per Δ-scaling phase (Hint: use the potential function $\Phi = \sum_{i \in V : i \neq s,t} e_f(i) d(i) / \Delta$).

(f) Prove that the overall running time of the algorithm (including the time needed to find the minimum distance label $\Delta/2$-active node in each iteration) is $O(mn + n^2 \log U)$.

2.12 In Problem 2.11, we looked at a variation of the push-relabel algorithm called excess scaling. In this variant of the algorithm we maintain a parameter Δ which is initially $2^{\lceil \log_2 U \rceil}$; we proceed in a sequence of Δ-*scaling phases*. At the start of each Δ-scaling phase, we maintain that the current preflow f is Δ-*optimal*. A preflow f is Δ-optimal if the excess $e_f(i) \leq \Delta$ for all $i \neq s, t$. In each Δ-scaling phase, we run a slightly modified push-relabel algorithm in which we ensure that we do not create any new nodes i with $e_f(i) > \Delta$; recall from Part (a) of Exercise 2.11 that this variant involves modifying the push operation.

In this problem, we consider a variant called *wave scaling*. In order to implement wave scaling, we need to implement our push operations in a particular way, which we will call *stack push*, given in Procedure

---

Add i to empty stack S
while stack S is nonempty **do**
    Let i be the vertex at the top of S
    Let (i, j) be the current arc out of i
    if (i, j) not admissible **then**
        if (i, j) last arc out of i **then**
            Set current arc out i to be first arc out of i
            Pop i from S
            `Relabel`(i)
        else
            Set current arc out of i to be next arc out of i
    else if $e_f(j) \geq \Delta/2$ and $j \neq t$ **then**
        Push j onto stack S
    else
        `Push`$((i, j))$
        if $e_f(i) = 0$ **then** pop i from stack S

Procedure StackPush(i)

StackPush. For each node i, we will have some ordering of the outgoing arcs, and we will maintain an arc called the *current arc*. We will always try to push on the current arc, and if we can't, then we proceed to the next arc in the ordering. Once we have finished pushing on the last arc, we know that we will need to relabel node i, and we reset the current arc to the first arc in the ordering.

Wave scaling happens in a series of *waves*. For each wave, we sort the nodes other than s and t in nonincreasing order by distance label (which we can do in $O(n)$ time using a type of sorting called a radix sort), and we then consider each node i in the ordering. If i is active, and has not yet been relabeled in this wave, we perform a stack push on i.

Define the total excess E_f as the sum over all excess of nodes that are not s or t; that is, $E_f = \sum_{i \in V : i \neq s, t} e_f(i)$. Let ℓ be a parameter to be named later. The algorithm will keep performing waves until the total excess is at most $n\Delta/\ell$. It will then behave as the excess scaling algorithm and perform a stack push on any node i with excess greater than $e_f(i) > \Delta/2$. It will do this until there are no more nodes with excess greater than $\Delta/2$, at which point the current Δ-scaling phase will end, and we divide Δ by 2. The algorithm is summarized in Algorithm 2.8.

$\Delta \leftarrow 2^{\lfloor \log_2 U \rfloor}$

$f(i,j) \leftarrow 0$ for all $(i,j) \in A$

$f(s,j) \leftarrow u(s,j)$, $f(j,s) \leftarrow -u(s,j)$ for all $(s,j) \in A$

$d(s) \leftarrow n$

$d(i) \leftarrow 0$ for all $i \in V$, $i \neq s$

while $\Delta \geq 1$ **do**

    while $E_f \geq n\Delta/\ell$ **do** // Start new wave

       Let L be ordering of nodes except s,t sorted in nonincreasing

       order by $d(i)$

       for i next node in L **do**

          if $e_f(i) > 0$ and i not yet relabeled in this wave **then**

             StackPush(i)

    while $\exists i \neq t : e_f(i) \geq \Delta/2$ **do**

       StackPush(i)

    $\Delta \leftarrow \Delta/2$

return f

Algorithm 2.8 The wave scaling version of the push-relabel algorithm.

Call any push during a Δ-scaling phase that pushes at least $\Delta/2$ units of flow a *big* push and a push that pushes less than $\Delta/2$ units of flow a *small* push.

(a) Argue that for each time node i is on the stack during a stack push, there are at most two nonsaturating pushes, and only one nonsaturating push can be a small push.

(b) Argue that at the end of a wave, it must be the case that any vertex with positive excess must have been relabeled.

(c) Explain why we must push from nodes with excess at least $\Delta/2$ after we have finished with the waves.

(d) Prove that there can be at most $O(n^2 + (n^2/\ell) \log U)$ nonsaturating big pushes during the course of the entire algorithm (Hint: use the same potential function as in Problem 2.11 Part (e)).

(e) Prove that there can be at most $O(n^2 + (n^2/\ell) \log U)$ nonsaturating small pushes plus $O(n)$ nonsaturating small pushes per wave during the course of the entire algorithm.

(f) Prove that for any wave except the last one in a Δ-scaling phase, there must be at least $O(n/\ell)$ relabels during the wave.

(g) Prove that if there are no relabels during a wave, there are no nodes with positive excess at the end of the wave, and thus the algorithm terminates.

(h) Use the preceding items to argue that there are at most $O(\min(n^2, n\ell + \log U))$ waves during the algorithm.

(i) Prove that if $\ell = \sqrt{\log U}$, the running time of the wave scaling version of push-relabel takes $O(mn + n^2\sqrt{\log U})$.

2.13 Prove Lemma 2.51.

2.14 In this exercise, we prove the correctness of the gap relabeling heuristic. Suppose there is a value $k < n$ such that there are no nodes i with $d(i) = k$, but there are active nodes j of distance $k < d(j) < n$. Prove that setting $d(j) = n$ for all such nodes gives a valid distance labeling.

2.15 In a variation of the normal maximum flow problem, we have a *parametric* network, in which the capacities of arcs leaving the source and entering the sink vary with a parameter λ. Let $u(i, j, \lambda)$ be the capacity of arc (i, j) for parameter λ. In particular, we have

- $u(s, j, \lambda)$ is a nondecreasing function of λ for all $j \neq t$;
- $u(i, t, \lambda)$ is a nonincreasing function of λ for all $i \neq s$;
- $u(i, j, \lambda) = u(i, j)$ for all $i \neq s$ and $j \neq t$.

In the parametric max flow problem, in addition to the usual input for the maximum flow problem, we are also given the values $\lambda_1 < \lambda_2 < \cdots < \lambda_\ell$, and the capacities of the arcs $u(i, j, \lambda_k)$ for all $(i, j) \in A$, $1 \leq k \leq \ell$. The goal is to find flow values $f_1, \ldots, f_\ell$ and minimum s-t cuts $S_1, \ldots, S_\ell$ for the flow problems associated with the capacities given by the input $\lambda_1, \ldots, \lambda_k$.

(a) Show that the push-relabel algorithm for the maximum flow problem can be used to solve the parametric maximum flow problem in $O(n^2(\ell + m))$ time. (Hint: Start by solving the flow problem for λ_1. What should you do after that?)

(b) Show that $S_1 \subseteq S_2 \subseteq \cdots \subseteq S_\ell$.

(c) Show that there are at most $n - 1$ distinct sets among the S_k.

Chapter Notes

Schrijver ([176], [177, section 10.8e]) gives an overview of the history of the maximum flow problem. The problem was posed to Ford and Fulkerson in 1954 by T. E. Harris as one of finding the maximum amount of railway traffic through a railway network. Schrijver notes that a formerly classified report shows that the problem of interest was that of finding a minimum s-t cut in the network sending rail traffic between the Soviet Union and its satellite countries in Eastern Europe. Ironically, this potential split between East and West would soon manifest itself in the maximum flow literature.

Ford and Fulkerson [63] proved the maximum flow/minimum cut theorem (Theorem 2.6) and developed the various ideas in Section 2.1, including that of a residual graph, augmenting paths, and the augmenting path algorithm (Algorithm 2.1). Other proofs of the maximum flow/minimum cut theorem soon followed, including one by Elias, Feinstein, and Shannon [58] and one by Dantzig and Fulkerson [49] that showed that the result follows from linear programming duality theory. Fulkerson and Dantzig [75] showed how to adapt the simplex method for linear programming to the problem. A number of results in graph theory and combinatorics were shown soon thereafter to follow from the maximum flow/minimum cut theorem, including the König-Egerváry theorem, Menger's theorem, Hall's theorem, and Dilworth's theorem; these applications of the theorem are discussed in the classical text of Ford and Fulkerson [66, chapter 2].

The maximum flow/minimum cut theorem predated the notion of polynomial-time algorithms by a decade, and so algorithms with provably polynomial running times did not appear until some time later. Here we encounter the split between the mathematical literature in the Soviet Union and West alluded to earlier; some of the history of this split is discussed (from the Soviet perspective) in a paper of Dinitz [54]. Many developments on each side of the Iron Curtain were unknown to the other side until some years later, and so algorithmic ideas were developed independently. Maximum flow algorithms based on blocking flows were developed by Dinitz in the Soviet Union [52]; we will discuss blocking flow algorithms in Chapter 4. The idea of using a preflow, along with a push operation, was given by Karzanov [128]. He used preflows to obtain a blocking flow in $O(n^2)$ time, which led to a $O(n^3)$ time algorithm. In the West, Edmonds and Karp [57] gave the most improving path algorithm of Section 2.5 and the shortest augmenting path algorithm of Section 2.7. The scaling algorithm of Section 2.6 is due to Ahuja and Orlin [6].

The push-relabel algorithm in Section 2.8 is due to Goldberg and Tarjan [92]. The algorithm is quite flexible, and there are quite a number of variants discussed in the literature. Section 2.8 discusses the highest label push-relabel algorithm, and others are given in the exercises. The bound on nonsaturating pushes for highest label push-relabel as given in Lemma 2.46 was originally shown by Cheriyan and Maheshwari [34]. We give a proof by Cheriyan and Mehlhorn [35].

The list of developments in polynomial-time algorithms for the maximum flow problem is very long, and we will not give an survey here. A recent overview was given by Goldberg and Tarjan [95]. Older references include the textbook-length treatment of Ahuja, Magnanti, and Orlin [4] and surveys of Frank [68] and Goldberg, Tardos, and Tarjan [91]. In Chapter 4, we will give an $O(\min(m^{1/2}, n^{2/3})(m \log n \log(mU))$ time algorithm due to Goldberg and Rao [90]. In 2013, Orlin [159] achieved a long-standing goal of the field by giving an $O(mn)$ time algorithm for the maximum flow problem, which remains the fastest strongly polynomial-time algorithm known. More recent progress using interior-point methods for maximum flows has been made; we discuss these results in the Chapter Notes of Chapter 8 on electrical flows.

Experimental work prior to the advent of the push-relabel algorithm showed Dinitz's algorithm outperforming other known algorithms such as the augmenting path algorithm, the simplex method, and Karzanov's algorithm (see, for instance, Cheung [39], Glover, Klingman, Mote, and Whitman [81, 82], and Imai [115], though Imai found that Dinitz's and Karzanov's algorithms were the best two of several algorithms). Once Goldberg and Tarjan introduced the push-relabel algorithm, studies showed that the push-relabel algorithm, especially the highest label variant, outperformed other algorithms known at the time (see Derigs and Meier [50], Anderson and Setubal [9], Nguyen and Venkateswaran [153], and Cherkassky and Goldberg [37]). These implementation studies showed the usefulness of the global relabeling heuristic (which was proposed by Goldberg and Tarjan [92]) and the gap relabeling heuristic (which was discovered independently by Cherkassky [36] and Derigs and Meier [50]). These implementations also use the idea discussed at the end of Section 2.8 of having only active nodes with distance label less than n, and using an algorithm such as that of Lemma 2.13 to convert the resulting preflow to a flow. Since that period, however, there have been additional studies suggesting that other algorithms are competitive with, or even surpass, the push-relabel algorithm. Goldberg [85] defines a version of push-relabel that pushes flow over two arcs in succession, and shows that it outperforms highest label push-relabel. Hochbaum [107] introduces a maximum flow algorithm based on *pseudoflows* and experimental work by Chandran and Hochbaum [31] shows that this algorithm also outperforms hightest label push-relabel (a pseudoflow obeys capacity constraints, but may allow excesses or deficits; see Section 5.4). Goldberg, Hed, Kaplan, Kohli, Tarjan, and Werneck [86] also introduce an algorithm based on pseudoflows that they show typically outperforms other algorithms, with Hochbaum's pseudoflow algorithm or Goldberg's two-level push-relabel algorithm being usually the best performer on instances in which the Goldberg et al. algorithm is not the fastest algorithm. They also compare their algorithm with a flow algorithm of Boykov and Kolmogorov [28] that is widely used in the computer vision community but has no strongly polynomial-time running bound.

For the applications in this chapter, the carpool sharing application of Section 2.2 was suggested to the author by Jon Kleinberg in a personal communication. The baseball elimination problem of Section 2.3 is a classical application of maximum flow given by Schwartz [178]. We follow the presentation of Wayne [203], who credits Alan Hoffman with popularizing this application of maximum flow. The algorithm we give for finding a maximum density subgraph in Section 2.4 is due to Goldberg [83].

Exercise 2.3 is due to Wayne [203]. Exercise 2.7 is due to Hoffman (see [108]). Exercise 2.9 is from Baier, Köhler, and Skutella [14]. Exercise 2.10 is due to Goldberg and Tarjan [92]. The excess scaling algorithm of Exercise 2.11 is due to Ahuja and Orlin [5]. The wave scaling algorithm of Exercise 2.12 is due to Ahuja, Orlin, and Tarjan [7]. Exercise 2.15 is due to Gallo, Grigoriadis, and Tarjan [78].

3

Global Minimum Cut Algorithms

Think globally, act locally.
– Common Ithaca bumper sticker

While the details of the push-relabel algorithm are still fresh in our minds, we take a detour out of the topic of maximum flow algorithms to discuss global minimum cut algorithms; we'll return to maximum flow algorithms with a discussion of blocking flow style algorithms in the next chapter.

In the preceding chapter, we saw that computing a maximum s-t flow also computes a minimum capacity s-t cut S^*, one that minimizes $u(\delta^+(S))$ over all $S \subseteq V$ with $s \in S$ and $t \notin S$. However, sometimes we are interested in computing the minimum capacity cut S over all nontrivial sets $S \subseteq V$. We say that this is a *global* minimum cut. Formally, for the global minimum cut problem, we are given as input a directed graph $G = (V, A)$ and capacities $u(i, j) \geq 0$ for all arcs $(i, j) \in A$, and we wish to find a subset of vertices $S \subset V$, $S \neq \emptyset$, that minimizes $u(\delta^+(S))$. We will also consider the global minimum cut problem in undirected graphs $G = (V, E)$: for such problems we wish to find a subset of vertices $S \subset V$, $S \neq \emptyset$, that minimizes $u(\delta(S)) = \sum_{(i,j) \in \delta(S)} u(i, j)$, where $\delta(S)$ is the set of undirected edges with exactly one endpoint in S (that is, $\delta(S) = \{(i, j) \in E : i \in S, j \notin S \text{ or } i \notin S, j \in S\}$).

It is not hard to see that we can solve the global minimum cut problem in directed graphs via some number of minimum s-t cut problems. For instance, we could try all $n(n-1)$ possible pairs of vertices $s, t \in V$, $s \neq t$, and compute the minimum s-t cut problem for each one, and take the minimum over all the cuts. Certainly for a global minimum cut S, there is some $s \in S$ and $t \notin S$, and so this algorithm will find a global minimum cut.

However, we can be somewhat smarter. Define the minimum s-cut problem as follows: we are given a directed graph $G = (V, A)$, capacities $u(i, j) \geq 0$

for all $(i, j) \in A$, and a vertex $s \in S$. The goal is to find a nontrivial subset $S \subset V$ with $s \in S$ of minimum capacity $u(\delta^+(S))$. To find a minimum s-cut, we can compute a minimum s-t cut for all $t \neq s$ with $n - 1$ minimum s-t cut computations, and take the minimum cut found; since for a minimum s-cut S, there will be some $t \notin S$, this algorithm will find a minimum s-cut. Now how do we use this to find a global minimum cut? We first pick an arbitrary $s \in V$, and compute a minimum s-cut S as above. We now want to compute a minimum cut S' over all $S' \subset V$, $S' \neq \emptyset$, such that $s \notin S'$. The minimum capacity cut of S and S' will give the global minimum cut. We find such a cut S' by considering the reverse graph $G_R = (V, A_R)$ in which we reverse the direction of each arc but keep the capacity the same; that is, $A_R = \{(j, i) : (i, j) \in A\}$ where $u_R(j, i) = u(i, j)$. Now we compute the minimum s-cut S' in G_R. We observe that $u_R(\delta^+(S')) = u(\delta^+(V - S'))$, so that $V - S'$ is a cut of minimum capacity in the original graph G over sets that do not contain s. Thus we can find the global minimum cut in a directed graph by two minimum s-cut calculations, or $2(n - 1)$ minimum s-t cut calculations, rather than $n(n - 1)$ minimum s-t cut calculations.

In the next section, however, we will see that we can do better still. We will show that we can compute a minimum s-cut in the time it takes to run a single execution of the push-relabel algorithm. Thus we can infer a global minimum cut simply by the very local operations of the push-relabel algorithms, in agreement with the bumper sticker quoted at the start of the chapter.

For undirected graphs, it is possible to reduce the global minimum cut problem to the case in directed graphs by replacing each undirected edge (i, j) of capacity $u(i, j)$ with two directed arcs (i, j) and (j, i), each of the same capacity. However, here we will see that we can find a global minimum cut by using ideas that do not involve flows at all. In Section 3.2, we will see how to find a global minimum cut via an algorithm that computes an ordering of the vertices then *contracts* the last two vertices in the ordering; we say that we contract two vertices if we merge two vertices (and associated edges) into a single vertex. Then in Section 3.3, we will get our first taste of how randomization can be useful in network flow algorithms by looking at an algorithm that picks random pairs of vertices to contract. Finally, in Section 3.4, we will see an algorithm that computes a global minimum cut with $n - 1$ minimum s-t cut computations but also gives the value of the minimum s-t cut for every possible pair of vertices $s, t \in V$.

For an example of why finding a global minimum cut might be interesting, we consider the *network reliability problem*. Suppose that we are given an undirected graph $G = (V, E)$ with probabilities $p(i, j)$ for all $(i, j) \in E$, where $0 < p(i, j) \leq 1$ for each edge (i, j). The probability $p(i, j)$ is the probability that edge (i, j) will fail during a given time period. We assume that edge failures are independent of each other. We want to find the set $S \subset V$, $S \neq \emptyset$, that maximizes the probability that all edges in $\delta(S)$ fail during the time period, where $\delta(S)$ is the set of all edges such that exactly one endpoint of the edge is in S. If all edges in $\delta(S)$ fail, then the graph will become disconnected. Thus we want to find a nontrivial S that maximizes $\prod_{(i,j) \in \delta(S)} p(i, j)$. Suppose we let $u(i, j) = -\log p(i, j)$. Then maximizing $\prod_{(i,j) \in \delta(S)} p(i, j)$ is equivalent to minimizing

$$-\log \prod_{(i,j) \in \delta(S)} p(i, j) = - \sum_{(i,j) \in \delta(S)} \log p(i, j) = \sum_{(i,j) \in \delta(S)} u(i, j) = u(\delta(S)).$$

Thus finding the cut with the maximum probability of edge failures of all edges in the cut is equivalent to finding a global minimum cut in an undirected graph.

3.1 The Hao–Orlin Algorithm

In the introduction to this chapter, we showed how to use an algorithm for the minimum s-cut problem to solve the problem of finding the minimum global cut. Now we show how to use an algorithm for yet another problem, which we call the minimum X-t cut problem, to solve the minimum s-cut problem. We then give an algorithm for the minimum X-t cut problem due to Hao and Orlin [104] that is based on the push-relabel algorithm of Section 2.8.

In the minimum X-t cut problem, we are given an directed graph $G = (V, A)$ with capacities $u(i, j) \geq 0$ on the arcs $(i, j) \in A$. We are also given a set $X \subset V$ and a vertex $t \in V - X$. The goal is to find a set S such that $X \subseteq S$ and $t \notin S$ that minimizes the capacity $u(\delta^+(S))$. Given an algorithm for the minimum X-t cut problem, we can now solve the minimum s-cut problem as follows; the algorithm is summarized in Algorithm 3.1. We first set $X = \{s\}$, pick some arbitrary $t \in V - X$, and find a minimum X-t cut S_t. We then add t to X and repeat until all vertices are in X. We then return the cut S_t that minimizes $u(\delta^+(S_t))$. Note that $s \in S_t$, so the cut is an s-cut. We now argue that it must be a minimum s-cut. Let S^* be a minimum s-cut. Consider the first iteration of the algorithm in which we pick some $t \notin S^*$. Since in all prior iterations, we picked a $t \in S^*$, it must be the case in this iteration that $X \subseteq S^*$ and $t \notin S^*$, so that the X-t cut S_t found in this iteration has capacity $u(\delta^+(S_t)) \leq u(\delta^+(S^*))$. Since S_t is also an s-cut, it must also be that $u(\delta^+(S_t)) \geq u(\delta^+(S^*))$, and thus

---

$X = \{s\}$
while $X \neq V$ **do**
　　Pick some $t \in V - X$
　　Compute minimum X-t cut S_t
　　$X \leftarrow X \cup \{t\}$
$t' \leftarrow \operatorname{argmin}_{t \in V - \{s\}} u(\delta^+(S_t))$
return $S_{t'}$

Algorithm 3.1 Using a minimum X-t cut algorithm to find a minimum s-cut.

the cut S_t found in this iteration will have the same capacity as a minimum s-cut S^*.

At first blush, it seems that we have only made things more complicated: to find a minimum s-cut, we are now running $n - 1$ iterations of an algorithm to find a minimum X-t cut! But we will now show that we can perform all of these iterations in a single run of the push-relabel algorithm. To get this to work, we need to tinker slightly with the definitions of a preflow and a valid distance labeling to treat the nodes in X analogously to the way the source vertex s is treated in the push-relabel algorithm. We do this by introducing the notion of an X-preflow and an X-valid distance labeling. An X-preflow is a preflow in which we only enforce that nodes $i \in V - X$ have nonnegative excess; an X-valid distance labeling is one in which all nodes $i \in X$ have $d(i) = n$, and we weaken the condition $d(t) = 0$ to $d(t) \leq |X| - 1$; note that for $X = \{s\}$ this gives $d(t) \leq 0$.

Definition 3.1: *An X-preflow f for $X \subseteq V$ is a preflow as in Definition 2.35 except that we allow $e_f(i) < 0$ for $i \in X$.*

Definition 3.2: *An X-valid distance labeling $d(i)$ for $i \in V$ for X-preflow f obeys the following:*
- $d(j) = n$ *for all* $j \in X$;
- $d(i) \leq d(j) + 1$ *for all arcs* $(i, j) \in A_f$;
- $d(t) \leq |X| - 1$;
- $d(t) \leq d(i)$ *for all* $i \in V$.

We can show that as in the case of the push-relabel algorithm, if we maintain an X-preflow and an X-valid distance labeling, then there is no path in G_f from X to t of arcs in A_f (that is, arcs with positive residual capacity).

Lemma 3.3: *Given an X-preflow f and an X-valid distance labeling d, there is no path in G_f from any node in X to t of arcs in A_f.*

Proof Suppose otherwise, and let $P \subseteq A_f$ be such a path; let $j \in X$ be the first node of P. We can assume j is the only node of P in X, since otherwise we could take the path starting from the last node of X in P. There are at most $n - |X|$ arcs in the path, so that by the properties of an X-valid distance labeling, $d(j) \le d(t) + |P| \le (|X| - 1) + (n - |X|) = n - 1$, but this contradicts the requirement that $d(j) = n$ for $j \in X$. Hence there is no path in G_f from X to t of arcs in A_f, and this implies that there is always an X-t cut S_t such that all arcs in $\delta^+(S_t)$ have no residual capacity. $\qquad\square$

We would like to use a lemma similar to Lemma 2.48 that says that as long as all nodes with positive excess are inside S_t, then S_t is a minimum X-t cut; we will leave the proof of the following lemma as an exercise (Exercise 3.1).

Lemma 3.4: *Let f be a X-preflow, and let S be any X-t cut such that if $(i, j) \in \delta^+(S)$ then $u_f(i, j) = 0$ and if $j \notin S$ and $j \ne t$, then $e_f(j) = 0$. Then S is a minimum X-t cut.*

We will shortly define the concept of a cut level, which is defined in terms of the value $d < n$ of a distance label. One of the main ideas of the algorithm is that the cut level naturally defines an X-t cut S of all vertices i with distance label $d(i) \ge d$, such that if we can guarantee that $e_f(j) = 0$ for all $j \ne t$ with $d(j) < d$, then we can apply Lemma 3.4 and show that we have found the minimum X-t cut.

To define a cut level, we first define the concept of a distance level; these are sets containing all nodes i with the same distance label, and hence are analogous to the buckets $b[k]$ we used in the implementation of the highest label variant of push-relabel (Algorithm 2.7). We denote them $B(k)$.

Definition 3.5: *The distance level k, denoted $B(k)$, is the set of all nodes i with $d(i) = k$; that is $B(k) = \{i \in V : d(i) = k\}$. The distance level k is empty if $B(k) = \emptyset$.*

We now define the *cut level* as a particular kind of distance level.

Definition 3.6: *The distance level k is a cut level if for all $i \in B(k)$ and all arcs $(i, j) \in A_f$, $d(i) \le d(j)$.*

Observation 3.7: *If distance level k is empty, then it is trivially a cut level.*

As discussed above, if all nodes i with positive excess have distance label $d(i) \ge d$ for some cut level d, then we can show that an application of Lemma 3.4 proves that the set $S(k) = \{i \in V : d(i) \ge d\}$ is a minimum X-t cut; we show this in the following lemma and corollary.

Lemma 3.8: *Suppose distance level k is a cut level, and let $S(k) = \{i \in V :$ $d(i) \geq k\}$. Then if $(i, j) \in \delta^+(S(k))$, $u_f(i, j) = 0$ (and $(i, j) \notin A_f$).*

Proof We need to show that for any $(i, j) \in \delta^+(S(k))$, $u_f(i, j) = 0$. By the definition of $S(k)$, $d(i) \geq k$ and $d(j) < k$. If $d(i) = k$, then by the definition of a cut level, $u_f(i, j) = 0$, since $d(i) > d(j)$. If $d(i) > k$, then $d(i) - d(j) \geq 2$, so we cannot have $d(i) \leq d(j) + 1$, so that $u_f(i, j) = 0$ by the definition of a valid distance labeling. □

Corollary 3.9: *If distance level k is a cut level for $d(t) < k \leq n$, and for all nodes $i \neq t$ such that $d(i) < k$, $e_f(i) = 0$, then $S(k)$ is a minimum X-t cut.*

Proof The set $S(k)$ is an X-t cut because all nodes $i \in X$ have $d(i) = n$, and thus $i \in S(k)$, since $S(k)$ contains all nodes of distance label at least $k \leq n$. Additionally, $t \notin S(k)$, since $k > d(t)$. Then the statement follows from the combination of Lemmas 3.8 and 3.4. □

We can now give the Hao–Orlin algorithm, which is summarized in Algorithm 3.2 (the given algorithm is slightly simplified from the one given in [104] for pedagogical purposes). The algorithm has the same overall structure as Algorithm 3.1; it starts with $X = \{s\}$, picks some $t \in V - X$, computes a minimum X-t cut S_t, adds t to X, and repeats until $X = V$. Then the algorithm returns the cut S_t of minimum capacity. To compute the minimum X-t cut, the algorithm runs a modification of the push-relabel algorithm (Algorithm 2.7) in which we consider a node i to be active if $e_f(i) > 0$ and its distance label $d(i) \leq \ell$, where ℓ is a cut level maintained by the algorithm. The cut level ℓ is initially set to $n - 1$, which we later show is always a cut level. The central idea is that we would like to get to the point in which we have the cut level ℓ and no nodes $i \neq t$ of positive excess with $d(i) < \ell$. In that case, we know by Corollary 3.9 that $S(\ell)$ is a minimum X-t cut. We then add the current sink t to X. In order to ensure that d remains an X-valid distance labeling and f a valid X-preflow, for the current sink t, when we add it to X, we set $d(t) = n$ and saturate all the arcs out of t. For the sink t in the next iteration, we choose a node t with smallest current distance label in order to maintain the property of an X-valid distance labeling.

We also need some modifications of the basic algorithm. First, if relabeling node i would make the distance level $d(i)$ empty, then we don't perform the relabel, but instead update the current cut level ℓ to $d(i)$; if we wanted to relabel i, and i is the only node on the distance level $d(i)$, then $d(i)$ must be a cut level, since we relabel i precisely when $d(i) \leq d(j)$ for all $(i, j) \in A_f$. This modification has some similarities to the gap heuristic mentioned at the end of

---

$X = \{s\}$

Pick $t \in V - X$

$f(i, j) \leftarrow 0$ for all $(i, j) \in A$

$f(s, j) \leftarrow u(s, j), f(j, s) \leftarrow -u(s, j)$ for all $(s, j) \in A$

$d(s) \leftarrow n$

$d(i) \leftarrow 0$ for all $i \in V, i \neq s$

$\ell \leftarrow n - 1$

while $X \neq V$ **do**

    Run push-relabel as normal except:

        – Only select nodes i for pushes if $d(i) < \ell$

        – For a call to relabel i with $|B(d(i))| = 1$, don't change $d(i)$ but
          set ℓ to $d(i)$

        – If relabel of i makes $d(i) \geq \ell$, set ℓ to $n - 1$

    $S_t \leftarrow S(\ell)$

    $X \leftarrow X \cup \{t\}$

    $d(t) \leftarrow n$

    $f(t, j) \leftarrow u(t, j), f(j, t) \leftarrow -u(t, j)$ for all $(t, j) \in A$

    $t \leftarrow \text{argmin}_{i \in V - X} d(i)$

    if $d(t) \geq \ell$ **then**

        $\ell \leftarrow n - 1$

$t' \leftarrow \text{argmin}_{t \in V - \{s\}} u(\delta^+(S_t))$

return $S_{t'}$

Algorithm 3.2 The Hao–Orlin algorithm for computing a minimum s-cut.

Section 2.8, and has a nice consequence that we will observe below. Second, if we relabel a node to a distance level at least ℓ, we reset ℓ to $n - 1$. Finally, if we reach the point of choosing the next sink t and $d(t) = \ell$, we reset ℓ to be $n - 1$.

Our first lemma shows that the algorithm maintains that the non-empty distance levels k are consecutive for $k < n - 1$; that is, there is no distance level $k < n - 1$ such that $B(k)$ is empty while $B(k + 1)$ and $B(k - 1)$ are not; the proof explains why we do not want to relabel i when $|B(d(i))| = 1$.

Lemma 3.10: *The non-empty distance levels k for $k < n - 1$ are consecutive.*

Proof The statement is true initially, since all nodes except s are in $B(0)$ and $d(s) = n$. If some distance level $B(k)$ for $k < n - 1$, becomes empty, let i be the last node removed from $B(k)$. The node i was removed from $B(k)$ either because i was relabeled or because i was the sink vertex. In the first case, by our modification of the relabel operation, we do not remove i from $B(k)$ if it is the last node in $B(k)$. In the second case, if i is the sink t, then at the end of the previous iteration it was chosen because it had the minimum distance label; that is, $B(d(i) - 1)$ is empty. During this iteration, $d(i)$ is not changed, since we do not relabel the sink vertex. Thus i is still a vertex of minimum distance label, and since $B(d(i) - 1)$ continues to be empty, removing i from $B(d(i))$ does not contradict the lemma statement. Finally, if a relabel of node i adds i to set $B(k)$, then it must be the case that there is some j with $d(j) = k - 1$, so that $B(k - 1)$ is also non-empty. □

Note that the following lemma, which we need in order to have an X-valid distance labeling, is now immediate.

Lemma 3.11: $d(t) \leq |X| - 1$.

Proof We prove the statement by induction on the algorithm. The statement is true initially, since $X = \{s\}$ and $d(t) = 0$. During the execution of push-relabel within the main loop, we do not alter the distance label of t. At the end of each iteration of the main loop, we add t to X, to get $X' = X \cup \{t\}$, and choose the new sink t' to be the one of minimum distance level. Since the distance labels are consecutive, the distance label of the new sink t' can be at most one more than the distance label of the previous sink t, so that $d(t') \leq d(t) + 1 \leq (|X| - 1) + 1 = |X'| - 1$, and the inequality continues to hold. □

Lemma 3.12: *The algorithm maintains an X-preflow and an X-valid distance labeling.*

Proof The proof that the algorithm maintains an X-preflow follows from the proof of Lemma 2.38; at the end of each iteration of the main loop, we saturate all arcs coming out of the current sink t, so that then $e_f(t)$ is possibly negative; however, we then add t to X, maintaining the properties of an X-preflow.

The proof that the algorithm maintains an X-valid distance labeling follows mostly from Lemmas 3.11 and 2.39, since the algorithm changes distance labels as in the standard push-relabel algorithm. However, the one case in which it does not do so is at the end of a loop, when we relabel the current sink t to have distance label $d(t) = n$. However, we then saturate all arcs out of t, so that for any arc (t, j), $u_f(t, j) = 0$, and thus the condition $d(t) \leq d(j) + 1$ does not apply. □

We now begin to show that ℓ is always a cut level during the course of the algorithm.

Lemma 3.13: *If $i \notin X$, then $d(i) \leq n - 2$.*

Proof We prove this by induction on X. Let $i \notin X$ be the node with maximum distance label. By Lemma 3.10, we know that the distance levels $d(t), d(t) + 1, \ldots, d(i)$ are all non-empty. There are $n - |X| - 1$ nodes other than t and those in X, so that $d(i) \leq d(t) + (n - |X| - 1) \leq (|X| - 1) + (n - |X| - 1) = n - 2$, because $d(t) \leq |X| - 1$ by Lemma 3.11. □

Lemma 3.14: *Throughout the algorithm, ℓ is a cut level with $d(t) < \ell \leq n - 1$.*

Proof We note that $n - 1$, by Observation 3.7, is trivially a cut level because by Lemma 3.13 it is empty, so whenever $\ell = n - 1$, it is a cut level. As argued previously, when the relabel operation sets ℓ to $d(i)$ when $|B(d(i))| = 1$, it is a cut level. The distance level ℓ is maintained as a cut level, since we only push on a node i with distance level less than ℓ (resetting ℓ to $n - 1$ if an active i is relabeled to have a distance label at least ℓ). By induction on the algorithm, $\ell \leq n - 1$: it starts at $n - 1$, and we only push on nodes with level less than ℓ, so we only attempt to relabel nodes of label less than ℓ, which means that the cut level can only be set to values at most $n - 1$. Furthermore, we will never set ℓ to $d(t)$: we would only change ℓ to $d(t)$ if $|B(d(t))| = 1$, so that only $t \in B(d(t))$, but we never relabel t. □

Lemma 3.15: *At the end of each iteration, $S_t = S(\ell)$ is a minimum X-t cut.*

Proof The push-relabel procedure in each iteration terminates when there are no more active nodes; that is, when there are no nodes $i \neq t$ with positive excess and distance label $d(i) < \ell$. Since we also have that $d(t) < \ell \leq n - 1$, Corollary 3.9 applies. □

We can now analyze the running time. However, for the most part the proofs of the running time are identical to the ones for the push-relabel algorithm, and hence we omit them.

Lemma 3.16: *The number of relabel operations is $O(n^2)$.*

Proof Each relabel operation either increases the distance label of a node by at least 1 (and potentially resets the cut level ℓ), or decreases the value of the cut level ℓ. Each time the latter happens we charge it to the next relabel that resets the cut level or to the end of the iteration. Thus since overall the relabels will increase at most n nodes from distance label 0 to at most distance label $n - 2$, the number of relabel operations is $O(n^2)$ overall. □

Lemma 3.17: *The number of saturating pushes is $O(nm)$.*

Proof The proof follows as in the proof of Lemma 2.43. $\square$

Lemma 3.18: *The number of nonsaturating pushes is $O(n^2m)$.*

Proof The proof follows as in the proof of Lemma 2.44. $\square$

Theorem 3.19: *The running time of the Hao–Orlin algorithm given in Algorithm 3.2 is $O(n^2m)$.*

Hao and Orlin have shown that a more sophisticated version of the algorithm can be implemented in $O(mn \log(n^2/m))$ time.

3.2 The MA Ordering Algorithm

In this section, we turn to finding global minimum cuts in undirected graphs; we will give algorithms for this problem in this section and the next section. Let $G = (V, E)$ be an undirected graph, and let $u(i, j)$ be the capacity of the undirected edge (i, j). For $S \subseteq V$, let $\delta(S)$ be the set of all edges with exactly one endpoint in S. The goal is to find a nontrivial cut $S \subset V$ that minimizes $u(\delta(S)) = \sum_{(i,j) \in \delta(S)} u(i, j)$. Note that $u(\delta(S)) = u(\delta(V - S))$ for undirected graphs, which is not true for directed graphs. For $A, B \subseteq V$, A and B disjoint, let $\delta(A, B) = \{(i, j) \in E : i \in A, j \in B\}$; to simplify notation, if $B = \{v\}$, we simply write $\delta(A, v)$ rather than $\delta(A, \{v\})$, and similarly we write $\delta(v)$ instead of $\delta(\{v\})$. Then $u(\delta(A, B)) = \sum_{(i,j) \in \delta(A,B)} u(i, j)$. We extend the notion of a minimum s-t cut in undirected graphs to be a set S with $s \in S$, $t \notin S$ that minimizes $u(\delta(S))$.

We can find a global minimum cut in an undirected graph by computing $n - 1$ minimum s-t cuts in a directed graph. We create a directed graph $G' = (V, A)$ by introducing directed arcs (i, j) and (j, i), each of capacity $u(i, j)$. We can find the global minimum cut in G by picking a vertex s arbitrarily, then solving $n - 1$ minimum s-t cut problems in G' for all possible $t \neq s$, and choosing the cut of minimum overall capacity. Consider the global minimum cut S^* for G. Because $u(\delta(S^*)) = u(\delta(V - S^*))$, we can assume without loss of generality that $s \in S^*$. Thus since there must be some vertex $t \notin S^*$, one of the minimum s-t cut problems will choose this vertex t and will compute a cut of capacity S^*.

We can, however, compute a global minimum cut in undirected graphs without using flows at all. We give two such algorithms, one in this section and a randomized algorithm in the next. Our first algorithm is based on computing a particular ordering of the vertices called a *maximum adjacency ordering*, or an *MA ordering*. In an MA ordering, we start with an arbitrary vertex v_1, and we

---

Pick v_1 arbitrarily from V
$W_1 \leftarrow \{v_1\}$
$k \leftarrow 2$
while $k \leq |V|$ **do**
    Choose $v_k \in V - W_{k-1}$ to maximize $u(\delta(W_{k-1}, v_k))$
    $W_k \leftarrow W_{k-1} \cup \{v_k\}$
    $k \leftarrow k + 1$

Algorithm 3.3 The MA ordering algorithm.

choose the vertex v_2 to be the vertex $v \in V - \{v_1\}$ that maximizes $u(\delta(v_1, v))$. In general, let $W_{k-1} = \{v_1, \ldots, v_{k-1}\}$; the vertex v_k is chosen as the vertex $v \in V - W_{k-1}$ that maximizes $u(\delta(W_{k-1}, v))$. In words, in each iteration we choose the next vertex in the ordering to be the one that maximizes the total capacity of its edges to the vertices already chosen thus far; hence the name of maximum adjacency ordering. We summarize the algorithm in Algorithm 3.3. We can compute an MA ordering in $O(m + n \log n)$ time by using Fibonacci heaps mentioned at the end of Section 1.1; we give this as an exercise (Exercise 3.2).

MA orderings have several interesting and useful properties. The main property of interest for this section is the following lemma.

Lemma 3.20: *For an MA ordering $v_1, \ldots, v_\ell$ of an undirected graph with ℓ vertices, $\{v_\ell\}$ is a minimum v_ℓ-$v_{\ell-1}$ cut.*

For now, let us discuss why this lemma is useful for finding a global minimum cut, and we will later come back to the proof of the lemma. Suppose the graph has n vertices, so that the lemma states that $\{v_n\}$ is a minimum v_n-v_{n-1} cut. The lemma is useful because either some global minimum cut S^* is a minimum v_n-v_{n-1} cut (that is, $v_n \in S^*$, $v_{n-1} \notin S^*$ or vice versa), or no global minimum cut is a v_n-v_{n-1} cut. If some global minimum cut S^* is a minimum v_n-v_{n-1} cut, then by the lemma we know that $\{v_n\}$ is a minimum v_n-v_{n-1} cut, and so $u(\delta(S^*)) = u(\delta(\{v_n\}))$, and we have found a global minimum cut. If no global minimum cut is also a v_n-v_{n-1} cut, then in any global minimum cut S^*, either both $v_n, v_{n-1} \in S^*$ or both $v_n, v_{n-1} \notin S^*$. In this case, we can effectively treat both nodes as a single node. We say that we *contract* the nodes v_n and v_{n-1}: we remove both nodes from V, replace them with a new node v', and replace any edge (v_n, v_j) of capacity $u(v_n, v_j)$ with a new edge (v', v_j) of capacity $u(v_n, v_j)$, and similarly for an edge (v_{n-1}, v_j). If both edges (v_n, v_j) and (v_{n-1}, v_j) exist, then we replace them both with

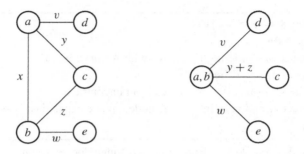

Figure 3.1 Example of contracting two nodes a and b. The edge between a and b is removed, while edges (a,c) of capacity y and (b,c) of capacity z are combined into a single edge of capacity $y+z$.

a single edge (v', v_j) of capacity $u(v', v_j) = u(v_n, v_j) + u(v_{n-1}, v_j)$. See Figure 3.1 for an example of contracting two nodes into a single node. We can implement a contraction in $O(n)$ time, which is the time needed to update the capacity of edges between the contracted node and all other nodes. Note that if no global minimum cut is a minimum v_n-v_{n-1} cut, then the capacity of any global minimum cut is not changed by contracting the two nodes.

Thus either $\{v_n\}$ is a global minimum cut or we can contract v_n and v_{n-1} into a single node, since this will not change the capacity of any global minimum cut. We do not know which statement is true, but we can keep track of the capacity of the cut $\{v_n\}$, contract v_n and v_{n-1} into a single node, and compute a new MA ordering in the resulting graph. We repeat until there are only two nodes left. If we have not found a global minimum cut in any of the previous iterations, then the capacity of the edge between the two remaining nodes will be the capacity of a global minimum cut. We give the overall algorithm in Algorithm 3.4; we keep track of the value of the smallest cut $\{v_\ell\}$ found thus far, as well as the associated cut (that is, all the nodes that were contracted in to the current node v_ℓ). We return the best cut found overall. An example of the algorithm is given in Figure 3.2. The running time of the algorithm is dominated by finding $n-1$ MA orderings. The preceding argument proves the following theorem.

Theorem 3.21: *Algorithm 3.4 finds a global minimum cut in an undirected graph in $O(n(m + n \log n))$ time.*

We now prove Lemma 3.20.

Lemma 3.20: *For an MA ordering $v_1, \ldots, v_\ell$ of an undirected graph with ℓ vertices, $\{v_\ell\}$ is a minimum v_ℓ-$v_{\ell-1}$ cut.*

$val \leftarrow \infty; S \leftarrow \emptyset; \ell \leftarrow |V|$
while $\ell > 1$ **do**
    Compute MA ordering $v_1, \ldots, v_\ell$ with Algorithm 3.3
    if $u(\delta(v_\ell)) < val$ **then**
        $val \leftarrow u(\delta(v_\ell)); S \leftarrow$ nodes from uncontracted v_ℓ
    Contract v_ℓ and $v_{\ell-1}$ into single node; update capacities; $\ell \leftarrow \ell - 1$
return S

Algorithm 3.4 The MA ordering-based algorithm for computing a global minimum cut in an undirected graph.

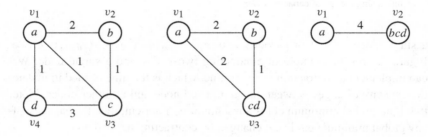

Figure 3.2 Sample execution of Algorithm 3.4. The first ordering is a,b,c,d; the cut $\{d\}$ is of capacity 4, and c and d are contracted. The second ordering is a, b, cd; the cut $\{cd\}$ has capacity 3. The third ordering has the two vertices a and bcd; the cut $\{bcd\}$ has capacity 4. So a global minimum cut is $\{c,d\}$, and it has capacity 3.

Proof Let C be a minimum v_ℓ-$v_{\ell-1}$ cut in the graph with ℓ vertices. Given the MA ordering, let $W_k = \{v_1, \ldots, v_k\}$ be the first k vertices in the ordering, and let $E_k = E(W_k) \subseteq E$ be all edges both of whose endpoints are in W_k. We say that a vertex u is *separated* from v if either $u \in C$ and $v \notin C$ or vice versa. Notice that v_ℓ is separated from $v_{\ell-1}$, since C is a v_ℓ-$v_{\ell-1}$ cut.

We will show by induction on vertices v_k separated from v_{k-1} that $u(\delta(W_{k-1}, v_k)) \leq u(\delta(C) \cap E_k)$ for all such vertices v_k. This will imply the lemma because for $k = \ell$, we will have that $u(\delta(W_{\ell-1}, v_\ell)) \leq u(\delta(C) \cap E_\ell)$, since v_ℓ and $v_{\ell-1}$ are separated. But $u(\delta(v_\ell)) = u(\delta(W_{\ell-1}, v_\ell))$ and E_ℓ is all the edges in the graph, so that $u(\delta(C) \cap E_\ell) = u(\delta(C))$. Thus we will have shown that $u(\delta(v_\ell)) \leq u(\delta(C))$. Since $\{v_\ell\}$ is a v_ℓ-$v_{\ell-1}$ cut, this will prove that it is a minimum v_ℓ-$v_{\ell-1}$ cut.

Suppose v_k is the vertex of minimum index in the ordering such that v_k is separated from v_{k-1}; without loss of generality, suppose that $v_k \notin C$, so

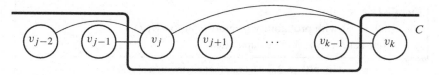

Figure 3.3 Illustration of the inductive proof in Lemma 3.20. The cut C separates v_{j-1} and v_j, and v_{k-1} and v_k.

that then $v_1, \ldots, v_{k-1} \in C$ (otherwise some earlier vertex v_j is separated from v_{j-1}). Then clearly $u(\delta(W_{k-1}, v_k)) = u(\delta(C) \cap E_k)$, as desired. Now suppose that we have shown the inequality for all vertices v_j separated from v_{j-1} for $j < k$, and v_k is separated from v_{k-1}. Let j be the largest index less than k such that v_j is separated from v_{j-1}, so that we know $u(\delta(W_{j-1}, v_j)) \leq u(\delta(C) \cap E_j)$ by induction. Since the edges from v_k to W_{k-1} either are incident on vertices in W_{j-1} or on the remaining vertices in $W_{k-1} - W_{j-1}$, we have that

$$u(\delta(W_{k-1}, v_k)) = u(\delta(W_{j-1}, v_k)) + u(\delta(W_{k-1} - W_{j-1}, v_k));$$

see Figure 3.3. Because the algorithm chose v_j before v_k in the MA ordering, we know that $u(\delta(W_{j-1}, v_j)) \geq u(\delta(W_{j-1}, v_k))$. Furthermore, v_k must be separated from all vertices in $W_{k-1} - W_{j-1}$: by the choice of index j, all vertices $v_j, v_{j+1}, \ldots, v_{k-1}$ are separated from v_k. Thus all edges in $\delta(W_{k-1} - W_{j-1}, v_k)$ are in $\delta(C) \cap E_k$, and furthermore, since none of these edges can be in E_j, none of these edges are in $\delta(C) \cap E_j$. Thus we have that

$$
\begin{aligned}
u(\delta(W_{k-1}, v_k)) &= u(\delta(W_{j-1}, v_k)) + u(\delta(W_{k-1} - W_{j-1}, v_k)) \\
&\leq u(\delta(W_{j-1}, v_j)) + u(\delta(C) \cap (E_k - E_j)) \\
&\leq u(\delta(C) \cap E_j) + u(\delta(C) \cap (E_k - E_j)) = u(\delta(C) \cap E_k),
\end{aligned}
$$

as desired. $\qquad\square$

MA orderings have other uses as well. In Exercise 3.3, we have the reader show that they can be used to give a maximum s-t flow algorithm, and in Exercise 3.5, we show that MA orderings can be used to find the minimum of a kind of function called a *symmetric submodular function*; such functions generalize the capacity of cuts of an undirected graph.

3.3 The Random Contraction Algorithm

In this section, we introduce an algorithm that uses randomization to find a global minimum cut in an undirected graph. The algorithm is not guaranteed

---

while $|V| > 2$ **do**

    Pick (i, j) with probability proportional to $u(i, j)$

    Contract i and j; update capacities

Algorithm 3.5 The random contraction algorithm.

to find the global minimum cut, but will do so *with high probability*; that is, the probability that it fails to find such a cut can be bounded by $1/n^c$ for a constant $c \geq 1$ that can be made as large as we would like, if we are willing to increase the overall running time. In the algorithm of the previous section, in each iteration we either found the global minimum cut or we identified a pair of vertices that could be contracted. Here we make the simplest conceivable use of randomization and contraction: we select a pair of vertices at random and contract them. More precisely, we pick an edge (i, j) in the graph with probability proportional to its capacity $u(i, j)$, and then contract i and j into a single vertex. We do this until there are only two vertices left in the graph; the set of vertices which have been contracted into one of these vertices identifies a cut which is returned by the algorithm. The intuition for this algorithm is that because any particular global minimum cut S has small capacity, we are unlikely to choose an edge from $\delta(S)$. For the sake of completeness, we state this very simple algorithm in Algorithm 3.5.

We can now start analyzing the algorithm. Let S^* be a global minimum cut, and let $\lambda^* = u(\delta(S^*))$; our calculations will be made with reference to this single global minimum cut. We let $W = \sum_{(i, j) \in E} u(i, j)$ denote the total capacity of all edges in the graph. Thus in the first iteration of the algorithm, we pick edge (i, j) to contract with probability $u(i, j)/W$. Let us say that cut S^* *survives* a contraction if the selected edge $(i, j) \notin \delta(S^*)$. Then the probability that S^* does not survive the first contraction is λ^*/W, so that the probability that it does survive is $1 - \frac{\lambda^*}{W}$. The following lemma allows us to bound the probability in terms of more useful quantities.

Lemma 3.22: $W \geq n\lambda^*/2$.

Proof For each $i \in V$, $u(\delta(i)) \geq \lambda^*$. Since the capacity of each edge (i, j) is counted once in $u(\delta(i))$ and once in $u(\delta(j))$, we get that $W = \frac{1}{2} \sum_{i \in V} u(\delta(i)) \geq n\lambda^*/2$. $\qquad\qquad\square$

Corollary 3.23: *The probability that cut S^* survives the first contraction is at least* $1 - \frac{2}{n}$.

Let W_k be a random variable denoting the total capacity of the graph after k contractions. Then since for any contracted node i, $u(\delta(i)) \geq \lambda^*$ (since λ^* is the capacity of a minimum global cut), and since there are $n - k$ nodes remaining in the graph after k contractions, we also get the following corollary.

Corollary 3.24: $W_k \geq (n - k)\lambda^*/2$.

Now we can prove the following lemma, which is central to the analysis of the random contraction algorithm. Note that the algorithm performs $n - 2$ contractions.

Lemma 3.25: *The probability that a given global minimum cut S^* is returned by the algorithm is at least $1/\binom{n}{2}$.*

Proof From the discussion above, the probability that S^* survives the kth contraction given that it survived the $(k - 1)$st contraction is the probability that no edge in the cut of capacity λ^* is chosen from the edges of W_{k-1} total capacity. Let Z_k be the event that S^* survives the first k contractions; thus this probability is

$$\Pr[Z_k | Z_{k-1}] = 1 - \frac{\lambda^*}{W_{k-1}} \geq 1 - \frac{2}{n - k + 1},$$

using Corollary 3.24. Then we want to know $\Pr[Z_{n-2}]$, and we can bound it as follows:

$$\Pr[Z_{n-2}] = \Pr[Z_1] \cdot \Pr[Z_2 | Z_1] \cdot \Pr[Z_3 | Z_2] \cdots \Pr[Z_{n-2} | Z_{n-3}]$$

$$\geq \prod_{k=1}^{n-2} \left(1 - \frac{2}{n - k + 1} \right)$$

$$= \prod_{k=1}^{n-2} \frac{n - k - 1}{n - k + 1}$$

$$= \prod_{\ell=3}^{n} \frac{\ell - 2}{\ell} = \frac{(n - 2)!}{n!/2} = \frac{1}{\binom{n}{2}}.$$

$\square$

As discussed in the previous section, we can implement a contraction in $O(n)$ time, which is the time needed to update the capacities of the edges. We can now show the following.

Theorem 3.26: *The random contraction algorithm (Algorithm 3.5) takes $O(n^2)$ time.*

Proof There are $n - 2$ contractions, each of which takes $O(n)$ time. We now argue that we can select an edge at random to contract in $O(n + \log(mU))$ time, where $U = \max_{(i,j) \in E} u(i,j)$; it is possible to reduce this running time to $O(n)$, but we omit the proof. To obtain the running time of $O(n + \log(mU))$, we maintain a quantity $D(i) = \sum_{j:(i,j) \in E} u(i,j)$ for all nodes i currently in the graph; it is easy to update the $D(i)$ each time we do a contraction. Note that after k contractions, $\sum_{i \in V} D(i) = 2W_k$, since the sum counts every edge twice. Assume that $V = \{1, 2, \ldots, n\}$, and consider the array $[D(1), D(1) + D(2), D(1) + D(2) + D(3), \ldots, \sum_{i=1}^{n} D(i)]$. To select a random edge after k contractions, we pick a random number $r \in [0, 2W_k)$, and we use bisection search on the array to identify the entry i such that $r \in [\sum_{\ell=1}^{i} D(\ell), \sum_{\ell=1}^{i+1} D(\ell))$. Then we consider all the edges incident on i, and select an edge with probability proportional to its capacity $u(i,j)$. The probability that we select entry i is $D(i)/2W_k$, and the probability that we select (i,j) given that we select i is $u(i,j)/D(i)$, so that the overall probability that we choose edge (i,j) is

$$\Pr[\text{select } (i,j)|\text{select } i]\Pr[\text{select } i] + \Pr[\text{select } (i,j)|\text{select } j]\Pr[\text{select } j]$$

$$= \frac{u(i,j)}{D(i)} \frac{D(i)}{2W_k} + \frac{u(i,j)}{D(j)} \frac{D(j)}{2W_k} = \frac{u(i,j)}{W_k}.$$

We need $O(\log W_k)$ time to perform the bisection search to select an entry i from the array, then $O(n)$ time to select the edge (i,j). Since $W_k \leq mU$, we get a running time of $O(n + \log(mU))$ per edge selection. □

Since the probability that the algorithm returns the cut S^* is quite low, in order to obtain an algorithm that returns the cut with high probability, we simply run the algorithm many times. This gives the following theorem.

Theorem 3.27: *Any fixed global minimum cut S^* can be found in $O(n^4 \ln n)$ time with high probability.*

Proof We run the random contraction algorithm $c\binom{n}{2} \ln n$ times for some constant $c \geq 1$. Since the event that the algorithm fails to return S^* in a given run is independent of whether it is returned in any other run, the probability that S^* is not returned in any of the $c\binom{n}{2} \ln n$ runs is at most

$$\left(1 - \frac{1}{\binom{n}{2}}\right)^{c\binom{n}{2} \ln n} \leq e^{-c \ln n} = \frac{1}{n^c},$$

using $1 - x \leq e^{-x}$. Each run of the random contraction algorithm takes $O(n^2)$, and we run it $O(n^2 \log n)$ times, for an overall running time of $O(n^4 \ln n)$. □

We would like a faster algorithm than this one. We observe that the probability of the cut S^* surviving a contraction is very high initially but becomes steadily lower as more vertices are contracted. Perhaps we should execute part of the random contraction algorithm to make the graph somewhat smaller, and then use some other global minimum cut algorithm on the reduced graph; the cut S^* would survive with a reasonable probability. Below we analyze the probability that cut S^* survives if we stop the random contraction algorithm when there are t vertices left.

Lemma 3.28: *The probability that a given global minimum cut S^* survives after $n - t$ contractions is at least $\binom{t}{2}/\binom{n}{2}$.*

Proof The desired probability is

$$\Pr[Z_{n-t}] = \Pr[Z_1] \cdot \Pr[Z_2|Z_1] \cdot \Pr[Z_3|Z_2] \cdots \Pr[Z_{n-t}|Z_{n-t-1}]$$

$$\geq \prod_{k=1}^{n-t} \left(1 - \frac{2}{n-k+1}\right)$$

$$= \prod_{k=1}^{n-t} \frac{n-k-1}{n-k+1}$$

$$= \prod_{\ell=t+1}^{n} \frac{\ell-2}{\ell} = \frac{(n-2)!/(t-2)!}{n!/t!} = \frac{\binom{t}{2}}{\binom{n}{2}}.$$

$\square$

In particular, we note that if we run the random contraction algorithm on an n-node graph until $t = \lceil n/\sqrt{2} + 1 \rceil$ nodes are left, then by Lemma 3.28, the probability that a given global minimum cut survives is

$$\frac{\binom{t}{2}}{\binom{n}{2}} = \frac{t(t-1)}{n(n-1)} \geq \frac{(1+n/\sqrt{2})(n/\sqrt{2})}{n(n-1)} \geq \frac{n^2/2}{n^2} = \frac{1}{2}. \tag{3.1}$$

Thus if we run the random contraction algorithm to contract the graph to $t = \lceil n/\sqrt{2} + 1 \rceil$ twice, we expect that at least one of the two times the given global minimum cut survives. The final idea of the section is that we should then run the algorithm recursively on each of these two smaller graphs to find a global minimum cut, and return the smaller of the two cuts found. We state the algorithm formally in Algorithm 3.6.

We can now analyze the algorithm.

Lemma 3.29: *The recursive random contraction algorithm (Algorithm 3.6) runs in $O(n^2 \log n)$ time.*

> **Algorithm:** RecursiveRandomContraction(G,n)
>
> **if** $n \leq 6$ **then**
>   Find global minimum cut in G by exhaustive search
> **else**
>   **for** $i \leftarrow 1$ to 2 **do**
> $H_i \leftarrow$ random contraction of G down to $\lceil n/\sqrt{2} + 1 \rceil$ vertices
> $S_i \leftarrow$ RecursiveRandomContraction(H_i, $\lceil n/\sqrt{2} + 1 \rceil$)
>   **if** $u(\delta(S_1)) \leq u(\delta(S_2))$ **then**
>   **return** S_1
>   **else**
>   **return** S_2

Algorithm 3.6 The recursive random contraction algorithm.

Proof We let $T(n)$ denote the running time of the algorithm on n vertices. As we argued before, running the contraction algorithm on a graph with n vertices takes $O(n^2)$ time. Thus we have the following recurrence relation for the running time:

$$T(n) = 2T(\lceil n/\sqrt{2} + 1 \rceil) + O(n^2).$$

The recurrence is solved by $T(n) = O(n^2 \log n)$. □

Lemma 3.30: *The probability that a given global minimum cut S^* is returned by the algorithm is $\Omega(1/\log n)$.*

Proof We let $P(n)$ be the probability that S^* survives starting from an n node graph. Then $P(n) = 1$ if $n \leq 6$, while if $n > 6$, we note that $1 - P(n)$ is the probability that S^* does not survive, which is the probability that S^* does not survive either recursive call. The probability that S^* survives a recursive call is $\Pr[Z_{n-t}] \cdot P(t) \geq \frac{1}{2} P(t)$, for $t = \lceil 1 + n/\sqrt{2} \rceil$ by (3.1), so that for $n \geq 7$,

$$P(n) \geq 1 - \left(1 - \frac{1}{2}P(t)\right)^2 = P(t) - \frac{1}{4}P(t)^2.$$

To analyze this probability, we set p_k to be the probability of success for the kth recursive call of the algorithm, where $p_0 = 1$. Then by the above we have that

$$p_{k+1} \geq p_k - \frac{1}{4}p_k^2 = p_k\left(1 - \frac{p_k}{4}\right).$$

Substitute $z_k = -1 + 4/p_k$ so that $p_k = 4/(z_k + 1)$. Then we have that $z_0 = 3$ and we set

$$\frac{4}{z_{k+1} + 1} = \frac{4}{z_k + 1}\left(1 - \frac{1}{z_k + 1}\right),$$

or

$$z_{k+1} + 1 = (z_k + 1)\left(1 + \frac{1}{z_k}\right)$$
$$= z_k + 2 + \frac{1}{z_k},$$

so that

$$z_{k+1} = z_k + 1 + \frac{1}{z_k}.$$

From this recurrence, we see that z_k grows by at least one and at most two for each increase in k, so that $k < z_k < 3 + 2k$. Thus $p_k = \Theta\left(\frac{1}{k}\right)$. Since $P(n) \geq p_k$ for $k = \Theta(\log n)$ (we need $\Theta(\log n)$ recursive calls for an n node graph), we have that $P(n) = \Omega(1/\log n)$. $\qquad\square$

Theorem 3.31: *Any fixed global minimum cut S^* can be found in $O(n^2 \log^3 n)$ time with high probability.*

Proof We run the recursive random contraction algorithm $c \ln n \cdot O(\log n)$ times for some constant $c \geq 1$. Since the event that the algorithm fails to return S^* in any given run is independent of whether it is returned in any other run, the probability that S^* is not returned in any of these runs is at most

$$\left(1 - \Omega\left(\frac{1}{\log n}\right)\right)^{c \ln n \cdot O(\log n)} \leq e^{-c \ln n} = \frac{1}{n^c},$$

using $1 - x \leq e^{-x}$. $\qquad\square$

Not only is the random contraction algorithm a simple algorithm with an easy analysis, it is also one that has made it remarkably easy to prove properties of global minimum cuts and near-minimum cuts. In Exercise 3.6, we have the reader use Lemma 3.25 to infer that the number of distinct global minimum cuts is at most $\binom{n}{2}$. In Exercise 3.7, the reader is asked to give an algorithm for finding near-minimum cuts, and to bound the number of distinct near-minimum cuts.

3.4 The Gomory–Hu Tree

Suppose we call two n-node networks *flow-equivalent*, or briefly, *equivalent*, if they have the same flow function v. Thus every network is equivalent to a tree. Is there some way of constructing an equivalent tree that is better than first determining v explicitly by solving a large number of flow problems, and the constructing a v-maximal spanning tree?

Gomory and Hu have answered this question decidely in the affirmative. Their procedure involves successive solution of precisely $n - 1$ maximal flow problems. Moreover, many of these problems involve smaller networks than the original one. Thus one could hardly ask for anything better.

– L. R. Ford, Jr., and D. R. Fulkerson, Flows in Networks

Recall from the introduction of this chapter that we compute maximum s-t flows and minimum s-t cuts in undirected graphs by replacing each undirected edge (i, j) of capacity $u(i, j)$ with two directed arcs (i, j) and (j, i), each of the same capacity $u(i, j)$. Recall also that in Section 3.2 we described how to find a global minimum cut in an undirected graph via $n - 1$ minimum s-t cut computations. The final algorithm in this chapter will also compute a global minimum cut in an undirected graph by using $n - 1$ minimum s-t cut computations, but in the process will compute a tree known as a *Gomory–Hu tree* that contains information about all of the minimum s-t cuts in the graph. The existence of the Gomory–Hu tree, along with an algorithm to compute it in $n - 1$ maximum flow computations, was initially shown by Gomory and Hu [101]. We will give another algorithm (which also uses $n - 1$ minimum s-t cut computations) that is due to Gusfield [103] and is simpler to implement.

For a given undirected graph $G = (V, E)$ with capacities $u(i, j)$ for all $(i, j) \in E$, a Gomory–Hu tree is a spanning tree T on the nodes of V in which each edge $e \in T$ is labeled with a value $\ell(e)$. Note that T may contain edges that are not in E, so T is not necessarily a spanning tree from the graph G. If we remove edge $e = (i, j) \in T$, the tree is split into two connected components; let $S(e)$ be the nodes in one of these two connected components. Then a Gomory–Hu tree has the following property. For any pair of vertices $s, t \in V$, $s \neq t$, there is a unique path in the tree T between s and t. Let e be the edge in this path that has minimum label value $\ell(e)$. Then $\ell(e) = u(\delta(S(e)))$ is the capacity of a minimum s-t cut in G. It follows that $S(e)$ is a minimum s-t cut, since either $s \in S(e)$ and $t \notin S(e)$ or vice versa (in this section, since graphs are undirected, we assume an s-t cut S can have $s \in S$ and $t \notin S$ or vice versa). A Gomory–Hu tree is sometimes called a *cut-equivalent tree*. Suppose we treat the labels $\ell(e)$ as the capacities of the edges

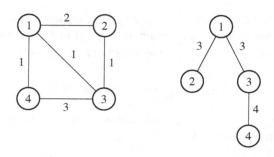

Figure 3.4 An example of a Gomory–Hu tree. The tree on the right represents the minimum s-t cuts of the graph on the left.

in tree T. Then the minimum s-t cut in the tree is $S(e)$ for the edge e that has minimum label on the s-t path in T, and by the properties of the Gomory–Hu tree, this cut is also a minimum s-t cut in the graph. Thus for any $s \neq t$, the minimum s-t cut in the tree is the same as the minimum s-t cut in the graph. In Exercise 3.8, we consider a tree with weaker properties called a *flow-equivalent tree*. We give an example of a graph and its associated Gomory–Hu tree in Figure 3.4.

Thus for all $s, t \in V$, $s \neq t$, a Gomory–Hu tree encodes both a minimum s-t cut and its capacity. Although there are $\binom{n}{2}$ possible s-t pairs, we can determine this information with only $n - 1$ minimum s-t cut computations.

Before we give the algorithm, we show that in order to have a Gomory–Hu tree, it is sufficient to show that for each edge $e = (i, j)$ in the tree T that $S(e)$ is a minimum i-j cut and $\ell(e)$ is the capacity of this cut.

Lemma 3.32: *Suppose we are given an undirected graph $G = (V, E)$ with capacities $u(i, j)$ for all $(i, j) \in E$, and a tree T spanning V with labels $\ell(e)$ on all $e = (i, j) \in T$ such that the label $\ell(e)$ is equal to the capacity of the cut $S(e)$, and $S(e)$ is a minimum i-j cut: that is, $\ell(e) = u(\delta(S(e)))$ and $u(\delta(S(e))) = \min_{S: i \in S, j \notin S} u(\delta(S))$. Then the tree T is a Gomory–Hu tree.*

Proof We assume that for any edge e the tree T, $\ell(e) = u(\delta(S(e)))$. We must show that for any pair of vertices $s, t \in V$ with $s \neq t$, that for the edge e of minimum label on the s-t path in T, $\ell(e)$ is the capacity of the minimum s-t cut. We notice that since e is on the s-t path in T, it must be that $S(e)$ is an s-t cut: either $s \in S(e)$, $t \notin S(e)$, or vice versa. Then if $\ell(e) = u(\delta(S(e)))$ is the capacity of a minimum s-t cut, it must be that $S(e)$ is a minimum s-t cut.

Pick an arbitrary $s, t \in V$, $s \neq t$. Let $s \equiv v_1, v_2, \ldots, v_k \equiv t$ be the sequence of vertices in the unique path P in the tree T between s and t, and let e_i

denote the edge (v_i, v_{i+1}) in T. For any pair of distinct vertices $p, q \in V$, let $c(p, q)$ be the capacity of a minimum p-q cut in G. We will show that $c(s, t) \geq \min_{i=1,\ldots,k-1} c(v_i, v_{i+1})$ and that $c(s, t) \leq \min_{i=1,\ldots,k-1} c(v_i, v_{i+1})$, so that

$$c(s, t) = \min_{i=1,\ldots,k-1} c(v_i, v_{i+1}).$$

Since for each i, $e_i = (v_i, v_{i+1})$ is an edge in T, by hypothesis $c(v_i, v_{i+1}) = \ell(e_i)$. Then it will follow that

$$c(s, t) = \min_{i=1,\ldots,k-1} c(v_i, v_{i+1}) = \min_{e \in P} \ell(e),$$

as desired.

It is easy to show that $c(s, t) \leq c(v_i, v_{i+1})$ for each $e_i = (v_i, v_{i+1}) \in T$. Because e_i is on the unique s-t path in T, each set $S(e_i)$ is an s-t cut, since s will be in one of the two connected components when e_i is removed from T, and t will be in the other. Thus the capacity of the minimum s-t cut will be at most the capacity $u(\delta(S(e_i))) = c(v_i, v_{i+1})$ for $i = 1, \ldots, k-1$.

It is also easy to see that it cannot be the case that $c(s, t) < c(v_i, v_{i+1})$ for all $i = 1, \ldots, k-1$. Let S^* be a minimum s-t cut with $s \in S^*$ and $t \notin S^*$. Because $s = v_1$ and $t = v_k$, it must be the case that for some i, $1 \leq i < k$, $v_i \in S^*$ and $v_{i+1} \notin S^*$. Then S^* is also a v_i-v_{i+1} cut, so it must be the case that $c(v_i, v_{i+1}) \leq c(s, t)$, and $c(s, t) \geq \min_{i=1,\ldots,k-1} c(v_i, v_{i+1})$. ☐

The algorithm for constructing a Gomory–Hu tree depends on the fact that the capacity of a cut in an undirected graph is a symmetric submodular function on the sets of vertices. A function $f(S)$ on sets of vertices $S \subseteq V$ is *submodular* if

$$f(A) + f(B) \geq f(A \cap B) + f(A \cup B) \tag{3.2}$$

for any $A, B \subseteq V$. If $f(S) = u(\delta(S))$, then f is a submodular function; we ask the reader to prove this statement in Exercise 3.4. Furthermore, in an undirected graph, the function f is also *symmetric*: that is, $u(\delta(S)) = u(\delta(V - S))$ so that $f(S) = f(V - S)$ for any $S \subseteq V$. A function f is symmetric submodular if it is both symmetric and submodular. For symmetric submodular functions, it is also the case that

$$f(A) + f(B) \geq f(A - B) + f(B - A), \tag{3.3}$$

which we ask the reader to prove in Exercise 3.4. While we concentrate in this section on showing that a Gomory–Hu tree exists for functions $f(S) = u(\delta(S))$, such a tree exists for any symmetric submodular function; we will say more about such trees at the end of the section.

To give the algorithm for constructing a Gomory–Hu tree, we first need to show that minimum s-t cuts have some nice properties.

Lemma 3.33: *Let $c(s,t)$ be the capacity of a minimum s-t cut. Given three vertices, $r,s,t \in V$, then $c(s,t) \geq \min(c(r,s), c(r,t))$.*

Proof Let S be a minimum s-t cut, with $s \in S$. Then either $r \in S$ or $r \notin S$. In the first case, S is also an r-t cut, and so $c(r,t) \leq c(s,t)$. In the second case, S is also an s-r cut, and so $c(r,s) \leq c(s,t)$. $\qquad\qquad\square$

Corollary 3.34: *Given three vertices, $r,s,t \in V$, the minimum of $c(r,s)$, $c(r,t)$, and $c(s,t)$ is not unique.*

Proof Suppose without loss of generality that $c(s,t)$ is the unique minimum; then the lemma statement above is contradicted. $\qquad\qquad\square$

Lemma 3.35: *Let R be a minimum r-s cut, with $r \in R$, and S a minimum s-t cut, with $s \in S$. Assume $t \notin R$.*

1. *If $r \in S$, then $R \cap S$ is a minimum r-s cut and $R \cup S$ is a minimum s-t cut.*
2. *If $r \notin S$, then $R - S$ is a minimum r-s cut, $S - R$ is a minimum s-t cut, and $c(r,t) = c(r,s)$.*

Proof See Figure 3.5.

The statements are shown by noting that since $u(\delta(S))$ is symmetric submodular, then by (3.2),

$$c(r,s) + c(s,t) = u(\delta(R)) + u(\delta(S)) \geq u(\delta(R \cap S)) + u(\delta(R \cup S)), \quad (3.4)$$

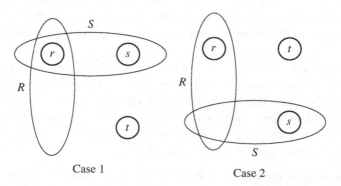

Case 1   Case 2

Figure 3.5 Illustration of the two different cases of Lemma 3.35. R is a minimum r-s cut, with $t \notin R$, and S is a minimum s-t cut.

and, by (3.3),

$$c(r,s) + c(s,t) = u(\delta(R)) + u(\delta(S)) \geq u(\delta(R - S)) + u(\delta(S - R)). \quad (3.5)$$

We then note that in Case 1, $R \cap S$ is an r-s cut and $R \cup S$ is an s-t cut, so that $u(\delta(R \cap S)) \geq c(r,s)$ and $u(\delta(R \cup S)) \geq c(s,t)$. These inequalities together with Inequality (3.4) imply that $u(\delta(R \cap S)) = c(r,s)$ and $u(\delta(R \cup S))) = c(s,t)$ so that $R \cap S$ is a minimum r-s cut, and $R \cup S$ is a minimum s-t cut.

In Case 2, $R - S$ is an r-s cut and $S - R$ is an s-t cut so that $u(\delta(R - S)) \geq c(r,s)$ and $u(\delta(S - R)) \geq c(s,t)$. These inequalities together with Inequality (3.5) imply that $R - S$ is a minimum r-s cut and $S - R$ is a minimum s-t cut. Furthermore in Case 2, since R is also an r-t cut in this case, we have that $c(r,t) \leq c(r,s)$, and since S is also an s-r cut in this case, we have that $c(r,s) \leq c(s,t)$. Then by Corollary 3.34, it must be the case that $c(r,t) = c(r,s)$. □

We can now begin to describe the algorithm. The algorithm maintains a partition of the vertices, $\mathcal{V} = \{V_1, V_2, \ldots, V_k\}$; initially there is a single part with all the vertices so that $\mathcal{V} = \{V\}$. The algorithm also maintains a *representative* $r_i \in V_i$ for each part V_i and a labeled set of edges T that form a spanning tree on the representatives. In each iteration of the algorithm, we pick some part $V_i \in \mathcal{V}$ with $|V_i| \geq 2$. We pick some vertex $t \in V_i$ with $t \neq r_i$, and compute a minimum r_i-t cut X, with $r_i \in X$. We then split V_i into two parts, $V_i \cap X$ and $V_i - X$. The vertex r_i is the representative of $V_i \cap X$, while t becomes the representative of $V_i - X$. We add the edge $e = (r_i, t)$ with label $\ell(e) = u(\delta(X))$. Finally, for any edge $(r_i, r_j) \in T$ with $r_j \notin X$, we replace the edge (r_i, r_j) in the tree with (r_j, t), and keep the same label for the edge. The algorithm terminates when $|V_i| = 1$ for all i, and thus we have a labeled spanning tree T on the vertices V. We will show that the spanning tree meets the condition of Lemma 3.32, and thus is a Gomory–Hu tree. We summarize the algorithm in Algorithm 3.7, and illustrate one iteration of the algorithm in Figure 3.6.

For an edge $e = (r_i, r_j) \in T$, we observe that removing edge e splits the vertices of V into two parts; let $S(e)$ be the vertices in one of the two parts with $r_i \in S(e)$. We claim that the algorithm will maintain that $S(e)$ is a minimum r_i-r_j cut, and we label edge e with the capacity of the minimum r_i-r_j cut so that $\ell(e) = u(\delta(S(e)))$. The correctness of the algorithm is implied by the following lemma, together with Lemma 3.32.

Lemma 3.36: *At the end of each iteration of Algorithm 3.7, for each edge $e = (r_i, r_j) \in T$, $S(e)$ is a minimum r_i-r_j cut, and $\ell(e)$ is the capacity of a minimum r_i-r_j cut.*

$\mathcal{V} \leftarrow \{V\}$
Assign arbitrary $r \in V$ as representative for V
$T \leftarrow \emptyset$
while there is $V_i \in \mathcal{V}$ with $|V_i| > 1$ **do**
    Let r_i be representative of V_i
    Pick $t \in V_i$, $t \neq r_i$
    Compute minimum r_i-t cut X with $r_i \in X$
    forall $(r_i, r_j) \in T$ **do**
        if $r_j \notin X$ **then**
            Replace (r_i, r_j) in T with (r_j, t)
    Remove V_i from $\mathcal{V}$, and add $V_i \cap X$ and $V_i - X$
    Assign r_i as representative of $V_i \cap X$ and t as representative of $V_i - X$
    Add (r_i, t) to T with label $u(\delta(X))$
return T

Algorithm 3.7 An algorithm for computing a Gomory–Hu tree.

Proof We prove the statement by induction on the algorithm. In the first iteration, there are initially no edges in the tree T. We have one representative $r_1 \in V_1 = V$, and pick another vertex $t \in V$, and compute a minimum r_1-t cut X. We partition V into $V_1 = X \cap V$ and $V_2 = V - X$, and insert edge $e = (r_1, t)$ into the tree T with label $\ell(e) = u(\delta(X))$. Assume $r_1 \in S(e) = X$; then $S(e) = X$, and $S(e)$ is indeed an r_1-t minimum cut.

Now suppose the lemma statement is true at the end of the previous iteration. Note that for all edges e unaffected by the algorithm, the cut $S(e)$ remans unchanged, and so the lemma statement continues to hold for these edges. The algorithm picks a part V_i of the partition with $|V_i| \geq 2$, and picks a $t \in V_i$, where $t \neq r_i$, for $r_i \in V_i$ the representative of V_i. The algorithm then computes a minimum r_i-t cut X, splits V_i into $V_i \cap X$ and $V_i - X$, and adds edge (r_i, t) to the tree.

We suppose that for any edge $e \in T$, $r_i \notin S(e)$; this is without loss of generality, since the capacity of the cut function is symmetric. Pick any edge $e = (r_i, r_j)$. We want to apply Lemma 3.35 with $s = r_i$, $t = t$, $r = r_j$, $R = S(e)$, and $S = X$. Observe that $r_i \notin S(e)$ by assumption, and hence $S(e) \cap V_i = \emptyset$, so that $t \notin S(e)$; thus the lemma applies. If $r_j \in X$, then Case 1 of the lemma applies, so $S(e) \cup X$ is also a minimum r_i-t cut. If $r_j \notin X$, then by Case 2 of the lemma applies, so $X - S(e)$ is also a minimum r_i-t cut, and $c(r_j, t) = c(r_j, r_i)$. Thus if we replace edge $e = (r_i, r_j)$ with $e' = (r_j, t)$,

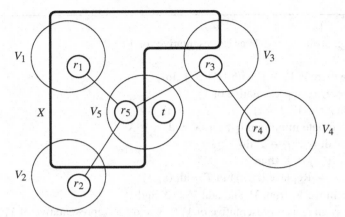

At start of iteration. The r_5-t cut X is shown in bold.

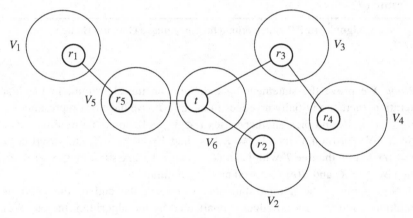

After iteration

Figure 3.6 Illustration of an iteration of Algorithm 3.7. The algorithm picks part V_5 and $t \in V_5$ with $t \neq r_5$. It computes a minimum r_5-t cut X, and splits V_5 into $X \cap V_5$ and $V_5 - X$. The latter set becomes a new part V_6 with representative $t \equiv r_6$. In the example above, $r_1 \in X$, while $r_2, r_3 \notin X$, and so we keep edge $(r_1, r_5) \in T$ but remove (r_2, r_5) and (r_3, r_5) and replace them with (r_2, t) and (r_3, t), respectively. We also add the edge (r_5, t).

we still have that $S(e') = S(e)$ and $S(e')$ is a minimum r_j-t cut. Applying these results repeatedly for all edges $e = (r_i, r_j)$ incident on r_i, we have that there is a minimum r_i-t cut that is the union of X and all $S(e)$ for $e = (r_i, r_j)$ with $r_j \in X$, minus all the $S(e)$ for $e = (r_i, r_j)$ with $r_j \notin X$. Note that this cut is exactly the one induced by taking the union of $V_i \cap X$ with all $S(e)$ for

$e = (r_i, r_j)$ with $r_j \in X$. Thus if we split V_i into $V_i \cap X$ and $V_i - X$ and add edge (r_i, t) to the tree with label $u(\delta(X))$, the statement of the lemma is true for the edge (r_i, t). □

The proof of the following theorem is then almost immediate.

Theorem 3.37: *Algorithm 3.7 computes a Gomory–Hu tree with $n - 1$ minimum s-t cut computations.*

Proof The algorithm starts with one part in the partition and computes a minimum s-t cut in each iteration, creating one new part, until there are n parts in the partition; thus there are $n - 1$ iterations in total. By Lemma 3.32, it is sufficient for a Gomory–Hu tree to prove that for each edge $e = (r_i, r_j)$ in the tree, $S(e)$ is a minimum r_i-r_j cut, and $\ell(e)$ is the capacity of this cut. By Lemma 3.36, we know that this is true of the final tree. □

We can now state Gusfield's algorithm as a method of implementing Algorithm 3.7. Let us index the vertices so that $V = \{1, \ldots, n\}$. The algorithm will maintain a directed tree D in which each vertex i has a directed path to the vertex 1. Each vertex $i \neq 1$ has an edge directed out of it, from i to $p(i)$; we call $p(i)$ be the *parent* of i. We maintain the partition, the representatives, and the tree of Algorithm 3.7 as follows: every vertex that is a parent of some vertex (and therefore is not a leaf of D) is a representative of some set in the partition. All leaves that point at a particular parent are the vertices in that part of the partition. Each arc between one representative (non-leaf) and another corresponds to an edge of the tree T from Algorithm 3.7. We label such an edge from i to $p(i)$ with a label $\ell(i)$.

Gusfield's algorithm works as follows. Initially we set $p(i) = 1$ for all i (notice that for $i = 1$ this creates a self-loop), so that 1 is the representative of the entire set of vertices. We iterate from vertex 2 through n; let t denote the current vertex, and let $s = p(t)$ be its parent. We compute a minimum s-t cut X: the vertex t will always be a leaf, so effectively we choose the part V_i of the partition that contains t, and compute a minimum cut X between the representative of the part, $s = p(t)$, and the chosen vertex t in the part. We label (t, s) with $\ell(t) = u(\delta(X))$. We then move all the vertices pointing at s that are not in X to point at t instead, so that t becomes the representative of these vertices. We have to be somewhat careful if the parent of s is not in X; in order to mimic the behavior of Algorithm 3.7, we need to have t connected to this vertex, so we point t at this vertex and point s at t, while keeping the labels of the corresponding edges the same. We summarize Gusfield's algorithm in Algorithm 3.8. The correctness of the algorithm follows by Theorem 3.37. A sample execution of the algorithm is shown in Figure 3.7.

---

forall $i \in V$ **do** $p(i) \leftarrow 1$
for $t \leftarrow 2$ to n **do**
   $s \leftarrow p(t)$
   Compute minimum s-t cut X
   $\ell(t) \leftarrow u(\delta(X))$
   for $i \leftarrow 1$ to n **do**
      if $i \notin X$ and $i \neq t$ and $p(i) = s$ **then**
         $p(i) \leftarrow t$
   if $p(s) \notin X$ **then**
      $p(t) \leftarrow p(s)$
      $p(s) \leftarrow t$
      $\ell(t) \leftarrow \ell(s)$
      $\ell(s) \leftarrow u(\delta(X))$

Algorithm 3.8 Gusfield's algorithm for computing a Gomory–Hu tree.

The original Gomory–Hu algorithm works as in Algorithm 3.7, but when computing a minimum r_i-t cut X for $r_i, t \in V_i$, we contract each part V_j for $j \neq i$ into a single node v_j. Then if $v_j \in X$, we place all the vertices of V_j on the same side of the cut as r_i, whereas if $v_j \notin X$, we place all the vertices of V_j on the same side of the cut as t. The result is the same as that of Algorithm 3.7, but there is a computational trade-off in the work performed by contracting and uncontracting parts of the partition versus the work saved by running the minimum r_i-t cut algorithm on a smaller graph. See the Chapter Notes for further discussion.

The Gomory–Hu tree is one of several different structures for representing cuts in a graph. Some discussion of other cut structures are in the Chapter Notes.

Recall that we earlier defined symmetric submodular functions f on a set of vertices V. We now argue that Algorithm 3.7 can be used to find an analogous tree for any symmetric submodular f, but first we need to define what we mean by a Gomory–Hu tree for a symmetric submodular function f. For a spanning tree T on V, let $S(e) \subseteq V$ be the cut defined by removing an edge $e = (i, j)$ from T (note that because f is symmetric, it does not matter which of the two connected components defines the cut). Suppose we label the edges of the tree T with labels $\ell(e)$. We say that S^* is a minimum s-t cut for f if $S^* \subseteq V$ is a set that minimizes the function value over all sets S such that $s \in S$ and $t \notin S$; that is, $f(S^*) = \min_{s \in S, t \notin S} f(S)$. Then we say we have a Gomory–Hu tree T for f if the following is satisfied for any pair of vertices $s, t \in V$, $s \neq t$:

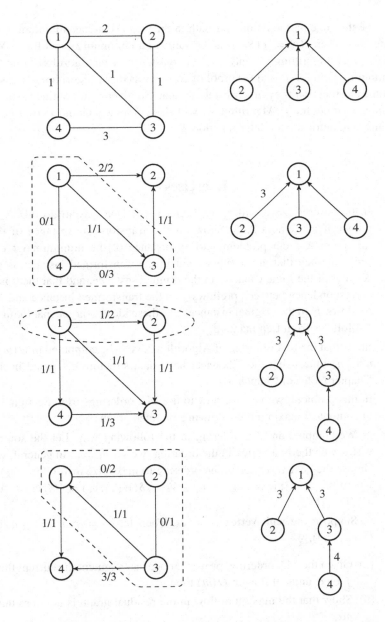

Figure 3.7 Sample execution of Algorithm 3.8. The undirected graph on the top left is the original input. The algorithm finds a minimum 1-2 cut, a minimum 1-3 cut, and a minimum 3-4 cut: the corresponding flows and graphs are shown on the left-hand side, where the flows are shown with our usual f/c notation, and the cuts are shown in dashed lines. The corresponding tree from the algorithm is shown on the right-hand side, and the final Gomory–Hu tree is in the lower right-hand corner.

Let e be the edge on the unique s-t path in the tree T that has minimum label value $\ell(e)$. Then $\ell(e) = f(S(e))$ is the value of a minimum s-t cut for f. We observe that Algorithm 3.7 only uses the existence of an algorithm to find a minimum s-t cut for f, and the proof of correctness of the algorithm only uses that the cut function is symmetric submodular. So given a subroutine to find a minimum s-t cut for f, Algorithm 3.7 will also compute a Gomory–Hu tree T for any symmetric submodular function f.

Exercises

3.1   In this exercise, we will prove Lemma 3.4. One way to do this is to reduce it to Lemma 2.48. Show how to transform an instance of the minimum X-t cut problem into an instance of the minimum s-t cut problem such that any finite s-t cut in the transformed instance is an X-t cut of the same capacity in the original instance, and that there is a correspondence between preflows f in the transformed instance and X-preflows f' in the original instance. Use these ideas to argue that Lemma 3.4 follows from Lemma 2.48.

3.2   Show that the MA ordering of Algorithm 3.3 can be computed in $O(m + n \log n)$ time using the Fibonacci heap data structure discussed in the Chapter Notes of Chapter 1.

3.3   In this problem, we will see how to use MA orderings from Section 3.2 to compute a maximum s-t flow in a directed graph.

We compute an MA ordering in the following way. Let the source vertex s be the first vertex in the ordering; we set $v_1 = s$. In general, we choose the next vertex v_k in the ordering to maximize $u_f(\delta(W_{k-1}, v_k))$, where $W_{k-1} = \{v_1, \ldots, v_{k-1}\}$, $v_k \notin V_{k-1}$, $\delta(W_{k-1}, v_k) = \{(j, v_k) \in A : j \in W_{k-1}\}$.

Suppose the sink vertex $t = v_\ell$. Then let $\alpha = \min_{k=2,\ldots,\ell} u_f(\delta (W_{k-1}, v_k))$.

(a) Given the MA ordering, prove that one can augment the current flow f by α units of flow in $O(m)$ time.

(b) Show that the maximum flow in the residual graph is no more than $n\alpha$.

(c) Given an $O(m + n \log n)$ time algorithm for finding an MA ordering, use the items above to give an $O((m + n \log n)n \log(mU))$ time algorithm for finding a maximum s-t flow.

3.4   A function f on subsets $S \subseteq V$ is called *submodular* if for any $S, T \subseteq V$,

$$f(S) + f(T) \geq f(S \cap T) + f(S \cup T).$$

The function f is *symmetric* if for all $S \subseteq V$, $f(S) = f(V - S)$. We say f is symmetric submodular if it is both symmetric and submodular.

(a) Let $G = (V, A)$ be a directed graph, with capacities $u(i, j) \geq 0$ for all $(i, j) \in A$. Prove that $f(S) = u(\delta^+(S))$ is a submodular function.

(b) Let $G = (V, E)$ be an undirected graph, with capacities $u(i, j) \geq 0$ for all $(i, j) \in E$. Prove that $f(S) = u(\delta(S))$ is a symmetric submodular function.

(c) Prove that a function f is submodular if and only if for any $S \subseteq T \subseteq V$, and any $\ell \notin T$,

$$f(S \cup \{\ell\}) - f(S) \geq f(T \cup \{\ell\}) - f(T).$$

(d) Prove that if f is symmetric submodular, then for any $S, T \subseteq V$,

$$f(S) + f(T) \geq f(S - T) + f(T - S).$$

3.5   Recall the definition of a symmetric submodular function $f : 2^V \to \Re$ from Exercise 3.4. Algorithm 3.9 is a generalization of the MA ordering given in Algorithm 3.3. Again, we start with an arbitrary vertex v_1, and to compute the next vertex v_k in the ordering, we look for the vertex v_k that minimizes $f(\{v_1, \ldots, v_k\}) - f(\{v_1, \ldots, v_{k-1}\})$.

(a) Suppose that $|V| = \ell$. Prove that if we compute the ordering of vertices as in Algorithm 3.9, then $\{v_\ell\}$ minimizes f over all sets S that contain v_ℓ but not $v_{\ell-1}$. (Hint: prove by induction on $i \leq \ell - 1$ that for all $X \subseteq W_{i-1}$ and all $v \in V - W_i$ that $f(W_i) + f(\{v\}) \leq f(W_i - X) + f(X \cup \{v\})$. Explain why this implies the desired conclusion.)

Pick v_1 arbitrarily from V
$W_1 \leftarrow \{v_1\}$
$k \leftarrow 2$
while $k \leq |V|$ **do**
    Choose $v_k \in V - W_{k-1}$ to minimize $f(W_{k-1} \cup \{v_k\}) - f(W_{k-1})$
    $W_k \leftarrow W_{k-1} \cup \{v_k\}$
    $k \leftarrow k + 1$

Algorithm 3.9 MA ordering for symmetric submodular functions.

(b) Give an algorithm to find a set $S \subseteq V$ that minimizes f, and prove
    that it finds the set that minimizes f.

3.6 Use Lemma 3.25 to prove that there can be at most $\binom{n}{2}$ distinct global
     minimum cuts.

3.7 Given an undirected graph G, let λ be the value of the global minimum
     cut. An *α-approximate global min-cut* is a set of vertices $S \subset V$,
     $S \neq \emptyset$, such that $u(\delta(S)) \leq \alpha\lambda$. This problem considers applying the
     random contraction algorithm (Algorithm 3.5) to the problem of finding
     α-approximate global min-cuts.

     Suppose that α is a half-integer greater than 1 (e.g. $\frac{3}{2}, 2, \frac{5}{2}, \ldots$), and
     is a fixed constant.

     (a) Prove that the probability that a given α-approximate global min-cut
         survives contraction of the graph from n vertices down to 2α vertices
         is at least $1/\binom{n}{2\alpha}$.
     (b) Use the previous result as the basis for an algorithm that outputs an
         α-approximate global min-cut with probability at least $1/\left(2^{2\alpha}\binom{n}{2\alpha}\right)$.
     (c) Argue that there can be at most $O((2n)^{2\alpha})$ α-approximate global
         min-cuts.
     (d) (A harder problem) Give an algorithm that finds all α-approximate
         global min-cuts. Get the best running time that you can.

3.8 In this exercise, we consider a *flow-equivalent* tree T, a tree with weaker
     properties than a cut-equivalent (or Gomory–Hu) tree. Suppose we are
     given an undirected graph $G = (V, E)$ with capacities $u(i, j)$ for all
     $(i, j) \in E$. Consider a spanning tree T on the nodes of V in which each
     edge $e \in T$ is labeled with a value $\ell(e)$. For any pair of vertices $s, t \in V$,
     $s \neq t$, there is a unique path in the tree T between s and t. Let e be
     the edge in this path that has minimum label value $\ell(e)$. Then in a *flow-
     equivalent tree T*, $\ell(e)$ is the capacity of the minimum s-t cut in G. This
     property is weaker than that of a cut-equivalent tree because it is not
     necessarily the case that $\ell(e)$ is the capacity of the cut $S(e)$. The tree
     is flow-equivalent because if we treat the labels as capacities, then the
     maximum s-t flow we can send in the tree is equal to the maximum s-t
     flow we can send in the graph.

     Consider Algorithm 3.10. As with Algorithm 3.7, let us index the
     vertices so that $V = \{1, \ldots, n\}$. The algorithm will maintain a tree T
     in which each vertex i has a directed path to the vertex 1. Each vertex
     $i \neq 1$ has an edge directed out of it, from i to $p(i)$; we call $p(i)$ be the
     parent of i. Initially we set $p(i) = 1$ for all i (notice that for $i = 1$ this
     creates a self-loop). We will gradually compute labels for the edges of

---

forall $i \in V$ **do** $p(i) \leftarrow 1$
for $t \leftarrow 2$ to n **do**
  $s \leftarrow p(t)$
  Compute minimum s-t cut X
  $\ell(t) \leftarrow u(\delta(X))$
  for $i \leftarrow t$ to n **do**
    if $i \notin X$ and $i \neq t$ and $p(i) = s$ **then**
      $p(i) \leftarrow t$

Algorithm 3.10 An algorithm for computing a flow-equivalent tree.

the tree, and we will label the edge $(i, p(i))$ with $\ell(i)$. The main loop of the algorithm iterates over all the vertices $t \geq 2$, and computes a minimum s-t cut X between $s = p(t)$ and t, with $s \in X$, so that the algorithm computes $n - 1$ minimum s-t cuts overall. The algorithm then labels the edge $(t, p(t))$ with $\ell(t) = u(\delta(X))$.

Show that Algorithm 3.10 produces a flow-equivalent tree.

Chapter Notes

Until early 1990s, there were no algorithms known for finding a global minimum cut in a directed graph (or an undirected graph) other than computing $2(n - 1)$ maximum s-t flow computations (or $n - 1$ such computations in the case of undirected graphs). Several algorithms were known for the *unit capacity* case in undirected graphs, in which $u(i, j) = 1$ for all $(i, j) \in E$. Podderyugin [165] gives an $O(mn)$ time algorithm, while Karzanov and Timofeev [129] give an $O(\lambda^* n^2)$ algorithm, where λ^* is the number of edges in the global minimum cut. For directed unit capacity graphs, Gabow [76] gives a method based on packing spanning arborescences running in $\tilde{O}(\lambda m)$ time, when the capacity of the minimum cut is λ (Recall that $\tilde{O}(f(n)) = O(f(n) \log^c n)$ for some constant c; that is, the $\tilde{O}$ notation hides polylogarithmic factors). Then in the early 1990s, a slew of methods were developed, including several described in this chapter. The MA ordering algorithm was developed by Nagamochi and Ibaraki [151] to find a global minimum cut in undirected graphs; a simpler version of the algorithm as described in Section 3.2 was given in two independent papers, one by Stoer and Wagner [187] and the other by Frank [69]. Fujishige [72] also gave a simple proof. The analysis we give here is due to Stoer and Wagner. The Hao–Orlin algorithm of Section 3.1 was given by Hao and Orlin [104] for directed graphs. The version of the algorithm that we give is somewhat simplified from the version given in [104]: the full Hao–Orlin algorithm keeps sophisticated track of nodes that are *awake* and those that are *dormant* (corresponding here to the nodes below the current cut level, and the remainder not in X, respectively). Even in our version of the algorithm, we could maintain a stack of cut levels, and whenever we need to reset the cut level, we simply pop the stack to the appropriate cut level (rather than resetting the cut level to $n - 1$). The full version of the Hao–Orlin algorithm can be implemented in $O(mn \log(n^2/m))$ time. Karger and Stein [125] developed the recursive contraction algorithm of Section 3.3. Karger [123] gives a near-linear time randomized algorithm for finding a global minimum cut in undirected graphs; the algorithm runs in $O(m \log^3 n)$ time. Kawarabayashi and Thorup [130] give a deterministic near-linear time algorithm for the unit capacity undirected case, with the algorithm running in $O(m \log^{12} n)$ time. Henzinger, Rao, and Wang [106] improve this running time to $O(m \log^2 n \log \log n)$.

Gomory and Hu [101] gave their algorithm for finding a Gomory–Hu tree in 1961. The algorithm due to Gusfield [103], which we give in Section 3.4, was developed later in 1990. The original Gomory–Hu algorithm required contracting parts of the graph and computing minimum s-t cuts in the contracted graph. Gusfield's algorithm was developed to avoid graph contractions. It remains an intriguing open question of whether a Gomory–Hu tree can be computed in time faster than $n - 1$ maximum s-t flows. Some initial work along these lines has been given by Bhalgat, Hariharan, Kavitha, and Panigrahi [23], who give an $\tilde{O}(mn)$ time algorithm for unit capacity undirected graphs.

Several experimental papers have studied the question of which algorithm is the most efficient in finding a global minimum cut in an undirected graph. Chekuri, Goldberg, Karger, Levine, and Stein [32] (see also Levine [144]) compare the Hao–Orlin algorithm, the MA ordering algorithm, the recursive contraction algorithm, and Karger's algorithm experimentally, and find that the Hao–Orlin algorithm is overall the best algorithm, with the MA ordering algorithm second best. Their implementations included heuristics due to Padberg and Rinaldi [160] to speed up running time. Nagamochi, Ono, and Ibaraki [152] implement the Padberg-Rinaldi heuristics and also incorporate them into the MA ordering algorithm to obtain a hybrid algorithm; they find that the hybrid algorithm outperforms both the MA ordering algorithm and the Padberg-Rinaldi heuristics on their own. Jünger, Rinaldi, and Thienel [119] studied implementations of Gusfield's algorithm, the Padberg-Rinaldi heuristics, the MA ordering algorithm, the Nagamochi-Ono-Ibaraki hybrid algorithm, the Hao–Orlin algorithm, and the recursive contraction algorithm. They also found the hybrid algorithm generally outperformed the others.

For Gomory–Hu trees, Goldberg and Tsioutsiouliklis [96] compare the computational performance of the original Gomory–Hu algorithm versus Gusfield's algorithm. They find that when some heuristics are added to the original Gomory–Hu algorithm, it performs better overall than Gusfield's algorithm. While performing contractions in the graph results in some overhead, the smaller resulting instances for the maximum s-t flow problem gives a performance boost to the Gomory–Hu algorithm.

Numerous other cut structures besides the Gomory–Hu tree have been developed; we mention four here. Picard and Queyranne [163] give a data structure for representing all minimum s-t cuts in a graph. Dinitz, Karzanov, and Lomonosov [53] proposed the *cactus tree* structure to represent all the global minimum cuts in an undirected graph. Fleischer [60] and Gabow [77] show how to compute the cactus tree from a single run of the Hao–Orlin algorithm; Karger and Panigrahi [124] give a randomized $\tilde{O}(m)$ algorithm. Benczúr and Goemans [19] give a structure for representing all cuts in the graph of capacity within a factor of 6/5 of that of a global minimum cut. Finally, Cheng and Hu [33] give an algorithm to compute a structure they call an *ancestor tree*, which encodes all $\binom{n}{2}$ values of an arbitrary s-t cut function, for all pairs $s, t \in V$, by using only $n-1$ computations of the same cut function.

The maximum flow algorithm in Exercise 3.3 is due to Fujishige [73]. The algorithm and analysis in Exercise 3.5 are due to Queyranne [167]. Exercises 3.6 and 3.7 are due to Karger and Stein [125]. The algorithm in Exercise 3.8 is due to Gusfield [103].

4

More Maximum Flow Algorithms

I got rhythm, I got music, I got my girl, who could ask for anything more?
– Ira Gershwin, *I Got Rhythm*

Who could ask for anything more,
I hear you query;
Who could ask for anything more, let me tell you dearie...
– Stephen Sondheim, *More*

In this chapter, we pick up where we left off in Chapter 2 with a discussion of additional polynomial-time algorithms for the maximum flow problem. Our main reason for discussing these additional algorithms is so that we can introduce one of the fastest polynomial-time algorithms known: the Goldberg–Rao algorithm, due to Goldberg and Rao [90]. To build up to this algorithm, it is first useful to discuss a type of flow called a *blocking flow*, and see how blocking flows can be used to give polynomial-time algorithms for the maximum flow problem.

4.1 Blocking Flows

In Section 2.7, we discussed a variant of the augmenting path algorithm in which we always select the shortest augmenting path along which to push flow. In this section, we consider an expansion of that idea in which we push as much flow as possible along all shortest paths simultaneously. To define what we mean by this, we introduce the concept of a *blocking flow*.

Definition 4.1: *A flow f is* blocking *if for each s-t path P in G of arcs of positive capacity, there is some saturated arc; that is, there is some $(i, j) \in P$ such that $f(i, j) = u(i, j) > 0$.*

As an example, the flow in Figure 2.3 is a blocking flow. Recall that the flow in Figure 2.3 is not a maximum flow: the residual graph is given in Figure 2.5 and a flow of larger value is given in Figure 2.4. Thus a blocking flow is not in general a maximum flow, although by Corollary 2.5 every maximum flow is a blocking flow. In Exercise 4.2, we give some types of graphs in which a blocking flow is a maximum flow.

We said previously that we want to push as much flow as we can along all the shortest augmenting paths; by this we mean that we want to compute a blocking flow along the current shortest paths of positive capacity arcs to the sink. In the shortest augmenting path algorithm of Section 2.7, we showed that the distances to the sink did not decrease. In this section's algorithm, we will see that each blocking flow computation will make the source vertex at least one distance unit farther away from the sink. We will show that this means we find blocking flows at most n times before there are no more augmenting paths in the residual graph, and the flow is maximum.

We now describe the algorithm more precisely. Given a flow f, we compute the shortest path distance $d(i)$ from each $i \in V$ to the sink node t along arcs of positive residual capacity, which can be done in $O(m)$ time by Exercise 1.1. If an arc (i, j) is on a shortest path to t, then $d(i) = d(j) + 1$. Let $\hat{A}$ be the set of all admissible arcs: that is, all arcs (i, j) such that $d(i) = d(j) + 1$ and such that the residual capacity $u_f(i, j) > 0$. We compute a blocking flow $\hat{f}$ in the graph $G = (V, A)$ in which the capacity $\hat{u}(i, j) = u_f(i, j)$ for all admissible arcs $(i, j) \in \hat{A}$, and $\hat{u}(i, j) = 0$ otherwise. We will show below that $f + \hat{f}$ is a valid flow in the original instance, and that if we compute the new distances, then $d(s)$ must have increased by at least one. We give the summary of the algorithm in Algorithm 4.1.

We first show that the algorithm maintains a flow f.

$f \leftarrow 0$
while there is an augmenting path in G_f **do**
    Compute the distance $d(i)$ from i to t for all $i \in V$ on arcs of positive
    residual capacity
    $\hat{A} \leftarrow \{(i, j) \in A_f : d(i) = d(j) + 1\}$
    $\hat{u}(i, j) \leftarrow \begin{cases} u_f(i, j) & \text{if } (i, j) \in \hat{A} \\ 0 & \text{if } (i, j) \in A - \hat{A} \end{cases}$
    Compute blocking flow $\hat{f}$ in G with capacities $\hat{u}$
    $f \leftarrow f + \hat{f}$
return f

Algorithm 4.1 A blocking flow algorithm for the maximum flow problem.

Lemma 4.2: *Algorithm 4.1 maintains a flow f.*

Proof The flow $f = 0$ is initially a flow. Each blocking flow $\hat{f}$ computed is a flow, so by Lemma 2.19, we know that the new flow $f' = f + \hat{f}$ obeys flow conservation and skew symmetry. Furthermore, for $(i, j) \in \hat{A}$, we know that $f'(i, j) = f(i, j) + \hat{f}(i, j) \leq f(i, j) + u_f(i, j) = u(i, j)$ and for $(i, j) \in A - \hat{A}$, $f'(i, j) = f(i, j) + \hat{f}(i, j) \leq f(i, j) \leq u(i, j)$, so the new flow also obeys the capacity constraints. Thus at the end of each iteration f is a flow. □

The following lemma is the key to the analysis of the running time of the algorithm.

Lemma 4.3: *The distance $d(s)$ from s to t increases by at least one in each iteration of Algorithm 4.1.*

Proof Let f and d be the flow and distances (respectively) at the start of one iteration of the algorithm, and let f' and d' be the flow and distances (respectively) at the start of the next iteration. Consider any shortest augmenting path P in $A_{f'}$, the arcs of positive residual capacity from the next iteration. We want to show that $d'(s) = |P| > d(s)$. To do this, we will show that for all arcs $(i, j) \in P$, it must be the case that $d(i) \leq d(j) + 1$ and for at least one arc $d(i) \leq d(j)$. This will prove that

$$d'(s) = |P| = \sum_{(i,j)\in P} 1 > \sum_{(i,j)\in P} (d(i) - d(j)) = d(s),$$

where the strict inequality follows, since $d(i) - d(j) < 1$ for at least one arc $(i, j) \in P$.

We first show that $d(i) \leq d(j) + 1$ for all arcs $(i, j) \in P$. Since $(i, j) \in P$, it must have positive residual capacity for the flow f'. For the arc to have positive residual capacity, either (i, j) had positive residual capacity in the previous iteration, or we increased the flow on the reverse arc (j, i). If (i, j) had positive residual capacity in the previous iteration, then it must have been the case that $d(i) \leq d(j) + 1$ in order for $d(i)$ to be the length of the shortest path to t on arcs of positive residual capacity in the previous iteration. If we increased flow on (j, i) in the previous iteration, then since we only increased flow on admissible arcs, it must have been that $d(j) = d(i) + 1$ in the previous iteration, so that $d(i) = d(j) - 1 \leq d(j) + 1$.

Next, we want to show that $d(i) \leq d(j)$ for some arc $(i, j) \in P$. To see this, we observe that by the properties of a blocking flow, it cannot be the case that all arcs in P were admissible in the previous iteration; if they were, then by the properties of a blocking flow, at least one arc $(i, j) \in P$ must have become saturated in the previous iteration so that $u_{f'}(i, j) = 0$, contradicting the statement that P is an augmenting path in $A_{f'}$. So it must be the case that for some arc $(i, j) \in P$, either $d(i) < d(j) + 1$ so that $d(i) \leq d(j)$ as desired, or $u_f(i, j) = 0$. In this latter case, as we argued above, if $u_{f'}(i, j) > 0$, then we increased flow on (j, i) so that $d(j) = d(i) + 1$ and $d(i) = d(j) - 1 \leq d(j)$. □

Corollary 4.4: *There are at most n iterations of the main loop of Algorithm 4.1 before the algorithm terminates with a maximum flow.*

Proof Initially $d(s) \geq 0$, and increases by at least one in each iteration. Note that the length of any simple augmenting path can be at most $n - 1$, so that once $d(s) \geq n$, there is no augmenting path in G_f, and f must be a maximum flow. □

Now we show that we can compute a blocking flow in $O(mn)$ time if there are no cycles of positive capacity arcs. In Exercise 4.3, we ask the reader to show that this can be done in the same class of graphs in $O(m \log n)$ time using a data structure called a dynamic tree.

Lemma 4.5: *A blocking flow can be computed in $O(mn)$ time in a graph with no cycles of positive capacity arcs.*

Proof We start at the source s and follow arcs of positive capacity for at most $n-1$ steps; that is, we pick an arc (s, j) of positive capacity, then pick a positive capacity arc (j, k) going out of j, and so on. Within n steps, we will either have reached t, in which case we will have an s-t path P, or we will reach a vertex i that has no outgoing arcs of positive capacity. Notice that we will not repeat a vertex in our search because there are no cycles of positive capacity arcs. If we find an s-t path P, we send as much flow as possible on the path, and reduce the capacity of all arcs on the path by the amount of flow sent; notice that at least one arc will be saturated, and so will have zero capacity. If we find a node i with no outgoing positive capacity arcs, we remove the arc (k, i) that we traversed leading into i. In either case, we remove at least one positive capacity arc from the graph, and thus we can have at most m iterations before we are done. Since no s-t path of positive capacity arcs remain, it is clear that we have computed a blocking flow. □

The following statement of running time is then almost immediate.

Theorem 4.6: *The blocking flow algorithm for computing maximum flows in Algorithm 4.1 runs in $O(mn^2)$ time, or $O(mn \log n)$ time by using dynamic trees.*

Proof In each iteration, we compute shortest paths in the residual graph, which we can do in $O(m)$ time by Exercise 1.1, and compute a blocking flow, which we can do in either $O(mn)$ time or $O(m \log n)$ time, assuming that the blocking flow is computed in a graph with no positive capacity cycles. Thus we only need show that in the set of admissible arcs $\hat{A}$ selected each time, there cannot be any cycle $C \subseteq \hat{A}$. There cannot be such a cycle: since $d(i) = d(j)+1$ for all arcs $(i, j) \in \hat{A}$, this cannot be true for all arcs $(i, j) \in C$, since this would imply that $|C| = \sum_{(i,j) \in C}(d(i) - d(j))$. However, since all terms in the sum cancel, $\sum_{(i,j) \in C}(d(i) - d(j)) = 0$, which is a contradiction, so there cannot be a cycle of admissible arcs.   □

4.2 Blocking Flows in Unit Capacity Graphs

We can state somewhat better running times for the blocking flow algorithm of Algorithm 4.1 if it is the case that $u(i, j) \in \{0, 1\}$ for all $(i, j) \in A$; this special case is sometimes known as the *unit capacity* case. In the unit capacity case, we are able to give tighter bounds on the number of iterations taken by the algorithm. To begin our discussion of this case, we recall that in Section 3.1, we defined the *distance level* k as the set of all nodes i such that $d(i) = k$, and we used the notation $B(k) = \{i \in V : d(i) = k\}$. Also, recall that we defined the cut determined by distance level k as $S(k) = \{i \in V : d(i) \geq k\}$. We now define some notation that we will use frequently in the rest of this chapter.

Definition 4.7: *Let $\Lambda = \min(\sqrt{m}, 2n^{2/3})$.*

Lemma 4.8: *In the unit capacity case, Algorithm 4.1 takes $O(\Lambda)$ iterations.*

Proof We show first that the algorithm takes $O(\sqrt{m})$ iterations, and then that it takes $O(n^{2/3})$ iterations; the combination shows the lemma.

We note that by Lemma 4.3 that after $\sqrt{m}$ iterations, $d(s) \geq \sqrt{m}$, and there are at least $\sqrt{m}$ distinct, non-empty distance levels $0, 1, 2, \ldots, \sqrt{m}$ (each of these distance levels must be non-empty, since otherwise any path from s to t would have an arc (i, j), where $d(i) > d(j) + 1$). Consider the cuts $S(1), \ldots, S(\sqrt{m})$. Note that any arc $(i, j) \in \delta^+(S(k))$ must have $d(i) = k$ and $d(j) = k - 1$, since otherwise $d(i) > d(j) + 1$; thus any arc in a cut $S(k)$

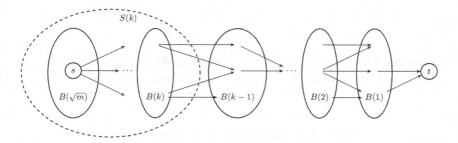

Figure 4.1 Illustration of the proof in Lemma 4.8.

for $k = 0, 1 \ldots, \sqrt{m}$ belongs to exactly one such cut (see Figure 4.1). Since there are at most m arcs, there must be some k such that there are at most $\sqrt{m}$ arcs in $\delta^+(S(k))$. Since each arc $u(i, j) \in \{0, 1\}$, then $u_f(i, j) \in \{0, 1\}$ so that $u_f(\delta^+(S(k))) \leq \sqrt{m}$. Then by Lemma 2.21, we know that for the current flow f and any maximum flow f^*, it must be that $|f^*| - |f| \leq \sqrt{m}$. Since the capacities are integers, and the flow value increases by at least one in each iteration of the algorithm, the algorithm can perform at most $\sqrt{m}$ more iterations before it terminates. Thus the algorithm will have performed $O(\sqrt{m})$ iterations overall.

Similarly, after $2n^{2/3}$ iterations, there are at least $2n^{2/3}$ distinct, non-empty distance levels $0, 1, 2, \ldots, 2n^{2/3}$. Consider the cuts $S(1), \ldots, S(2n^{2/3})$. Since there are n nodes, there must be some k such that both distance levels k and $k - 1$ have at most $n^{1/3}$ nodes, since otherwise at least half of the $2n^{2/3}$ levels will have more than $n^{1/3}$ nodes. Then there can be at most $n^{2/3}$ arcs from distance level k to distance level $k - 1$ (at most one arc (i, j) for each i with $d(i) = k$ and each j with $d(j) = k - 1$). Thus $u_f(\delta^+(S(k))) \leq n^{2/3}$, and by the same argument as above, the algorithm can perform at most $n^{2/3}$ more iterations before it terminates. Thus the algorithm will have performed $O(n^{2/3})$ iterations overall. □

Corollary 4.9: *After Λ iterations of finding blocking flows, there is some s-t cut $S(k)$ with $|\delta^+(S(k))| \leq \Lambda$.*

We will use Corollary 4.9 when we discuss the Goldberg–Rao algorithm in the next section. In this case, since all the arcs have unit capacity, the capacity of the s-t cut in the residual graph has capacity at most Λ, which implies that there are at most Λ iterations remaining. In the case of a unit capacity graph, we can compute a blocking flow in $O(m)$ time; we give this as Exercise 4.1. Thus we have the following.

Theorem 4.10: *The blocking flow algorithm in Algorithm 4.1 computes a maximum flow in unit capacity graphs in $O(\Lambda m)$ time.*

4.3 The Goldberg–Rao Algorithm

The Goldberg–Rao algorithm extends the analysis of the blocking flow algorithm for unit capacity graphs to arbitrary capacities. We will show that this gives an $O(\Lambda m \log n \log(mU))$ time algorithm. This is one of the best theoretical running times for a maximum flow algorithm. Suppose we can ensure in running the algorithm that each arc from distance level k to distance level $k - 1$ has residual capacity at most Δ for some parameter Δ for all distance levels k. Initially we set $\Delta = U$. Then Corollary 4.9 shows that after Λ iterations of the blocking flow algorithm, there must be some s-t cut $S(k)$ in the residual graph such that there are at most Λ arcs in the cut, and thus the total residual capacity of the cut is at most $\Lambda \Delta$. We then decrease Δ by a factor of 2, and repeat. Thus after each Λ blocking flow computations, we will reduce the size of the minimum s-t cut in the residual graph by a factor of 2. If we start with the zero flow, the minimum s-t cut in the residual graph initially has capacity at most mU, so after $O(\Lambda \log(mU))$ iterations, we will have found the maximum flow. Using the $O(m \log n)$ time algorithm to find a blocking flow, this gives the running time previously mentioned. What we have just described is the basic intuition of the algorithm, although implementing these ideas will introduce some additional complications.

How can we make it be the case that an arc going from distance level k to distance level $k - 1$ has residual capacity at most Δ? To do this, we note that so far when we have been computing the shortest path distances $d(i)$ from each vertex i to the sink, we have assumed that the length of each positive residual capacity arc is 1. We now introduce the idea of lengths $\ell(i, j)$ for each arc, and calculate the distance to the sink using these lengths. In particular, we set $\ell(i, j) = 1$ only if the residual capacity $u_f(i, j) \leq \Delta$, and set $\ell(i, j) = 0$ otherwise. Then since $d(i) \leq d(j) + \ell(i, j)$, if the arc (i, j) goes from distance level k to distance level $k - 1$, we must have $d(i) = k$, $d(j) = k - 1$, and $\ell(i, j) = 1$, so that it must be the case that the residual capacity of (i, j) is at most Δ. An admissible arc remains one with positive residual capacity that is on a shortest s-t path, but now an arc (i, j) is on the shortest path if $d(i) = d(j) + \ell(i, j)$, so that $\hat{A} = \{(i, j) \in A_f : d(i) = d(j) + \ell(i, j)\}$.

We now make a small change in which arcs are admissible, which will be mysterious for the time being but will be needed later in the proofs. We call an arc (i, j) a *special arc* if i and j are in the same distance level (that is, $d(i) = d(j)$), $\Delta/2 \leq u_f(i, j) \leq \Delta$, and $u_f(j, i) > \Delta$. If an arc (i, j) is special, then we set $\ell(i, j) = 0$ (it otherwise would have been 1, since $u_f(i, j) \leq \Delta$). Observe that this does not change the distances at all (since already $d(i) = d(j)$), but it does make arc (i, j) admissible, since now $d(i) = d(j) + \ell(i, j)$.

Changing the notion of the length of an arc to be either 0 or 1 (instead of just 1) then allows us to assume that after Λ iterations of the blocking flow algorithm, the capacity of the minimum s-t cut is at most $\Lambda\Delta$ for our choice of parameter Δ, but it raises questions about previous parts of the proof of the blocking flow algorithm. For one, it is not clear that the analog of Lemma 4.3 will hold; that is, it is not clear if we can assert that the distance from s to t will increase with each blocking flow computation. We will set that issue aside for the moment and come back to it later. A second issue is that we used subroutines that assume that there is no cycle of positive capacity arcs in $\hat{A}$; our proof that no such cycles exist in $\hat{A}$ relied crucially on the fact that the length of each arc was one; there could not be any cycles in the admissible arcs, since they were all on shortest paths to the sink. However, now that we allow length zero arcs, it is possible for there to be a cycle in $\hat{A}$ of length zero arcs between nodes all from the same distance level.

The second issue is easier to deal with; before we compute a blocking flow we will take any strongly connected component of length zero admissible arcs and contract them into a single node (see Figure 4.2). Now we will be able to do the blocking flow computation in a graph in which there are no cycles in the positive capacity arcs. How then will we route flow in the

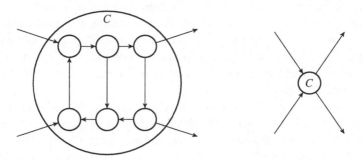

Figure 4.2 An illustration of contracting a strongly connected component C to a single node.

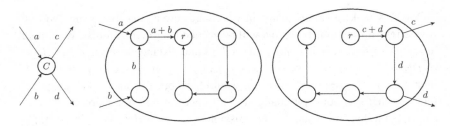

Figure 4.3 An illustration of decomposing the strongly connected component of Figure 4.2 into an intree and an outtree, and routing flow from the contracted graph on the two trees. We take all incoming flow and send it to the root r on the arcs in the intree. Then we take all the flow sent to the root and send it to the outgoing arcs via the arcs on the outtree. By flow conservation, the two amounts must be equal (that is, $a + b = c + d$).

original, uncontracted graph? Suppose we limit the amount of flow entering the contracted node to be at most $\Delta/4$. In the strongly connected component, we will pick a single root node r, and pick two subsets of the arcs of the component, an intree in which there is a directed path from each node of the connected component to r, and an outtree in which there is a directed path from r to each node of the component (we can use an arc in both the intree and the outtree). We route the flow from all the arcs coming in to the component to r, then all the flow from r to the outgoing arcs; see Figure 4.3 for an illustration. Because each arc (i, j) in the strongly connected component has length 0, either $u_f(i, j) > \Delta$ or (i, j) is a special arc and $u_f(i, j) \geq \Delta/2$. In either case, we are able to route $\Delta/4$ units of flow over arc (i, j) if it is in the intree and another $\Delta/4$ units if it is in the outtree.

In order to limit the amount of flow through such nodes to be at most $\Delta/4$, we change the goal of each iteration of the algorithm; either we find a blocking flow or we find a flow of value $\Delta/4$. We can achieve this goal by adding an extra arc (s', s) of capacity $\Delta/4$ in each blocking flow computation and changing the source to be s'. Clearly we will not find a flow of value more than $\Delta/4$, and if we find a flow of value less than $\Delta/4$ it will be a blocking flow in the contracted graph without the arc (s', s).

We can now give the algorithm in Algorithm 4.2. We keep track of a quantity F; we will show below that this quantity always gives an upper bound on the value of the maximum flow in the residual graph G_f. Initially we set the flow f to the zero flow, and F to mU, since this gives an upper bound on the value of the maximum flow. In each iteration, we set Δ to be $F/2\Lambda$. Then do the following 5Λ times. We compute distances and admissible arcs.

$f \leftarrow 0$
$F \leftarrow mU$
while $F \geq 1$ **do**
    $\Delta \leftarrow F/2\Lambda$
    repeat 5Λ times **do**
        $\ell(i,j) \leftarrow \begin{cases} 0 & \text{if } u_f(i,j) > \Delta \\ 1 & \text{otherwise} \end{cases}$
        Compute distances $d(i)$ from i to t using lengths ℓ on arcs of
        positive residual capacity
        $\hat{A} \leftarrow \{(i,j) \in A : d(i) = d(j) + \ell(i,j), u_f(i,j) > 0\}$
        Add special arcs (i,j) to $\hat{A}$
        Shrink strongly connected components in $\hat{A}$
        Find either flow $\tilde{f}$ of value $\Delta/4$ or blocking flow $\tilde{f}$ in resulting
        graph
        Compute $\hat{f}$, by routing flows of $\tilde{f}$ in uncontracted components
        $f \leftarrow f + \hat{f}$
    $F \leftarrow F/2$
return f

Algorithm 4.2 The Goldberg–Rao algorithm.

We contract the graph as necessary and compute either a blocking flow or a flow of value $\Delta/4$ in the contracted graph, then compute the resulting flow $\hat{f}$ in the original uncontracted graph. We add $\hat{f}$ to f and continue. Once we have computed the flow $\hat{f}$ 5Λ times, we divide F by 2, and repeat as long as $F \geq 1$. If F is indeed an upper bound on the flow in the residual graph, and if the capacities are integers, then once $F < 1$, we have a maximum flow and the algorithm terminates.

The technical heart of the proof is the following lemma; we defer its proof for a moment.

Lemma 4.11: *For each iteration in which we compute a blocking flow, the distance $d(s)$ from s to t increases by at least one.*

We can now show that F indeed behaves as claimed using Lemma 4.11.

Lemma 4.12: *F is an upper bound on the value of the maximum flow in G_f.*

Proof We show by induction on the algorithm that F is always an upper bound on the value of the maximum flow in G_f. Initially f is the zero flow, so the value of the maximum flow is at most $F = mU$. In each iteration of the main

while loop, after 5Λ flow computations, either we will have increased the value
of the flow f by $4\Lambda \cdot (\Delta/4)$, or we will have found Λ blocking flows, so that
there is an s-t cut $S(k)$ such that $|\delta^+(S(k))| \leq \Lambda$ by Corollary 4.9.

In the first case, we have increased the value of the flow f by $\Lambda\Delta = F/2$.
Thus the value of the maximum flow in G_f has decreased by $F/2$. Since at the
start of the iteration it was at most F, it is now at most $F - F/2 = F/2$, and
we correctly divide F by 2.

In the second case, since there is an s-t cut $S(k)$ with $|\delta^+(S(k))| \leq \Lambda$,
then since we know that each arc $(i, j) \in \delta^+(S(k))$ has residual capacity
$u_f(i, j) \leq \Delta$, we have that $u_f(\delta^+(S(k))) \leq \Lambda\Delta = F/2$. Since we have an
s-t cut in the residual graph of value at most $F/2$, the value of the maximum
flow in the residual graph is at most $F/2$, and again we can correctly divide
F by 2.   □

Finally, the main technical proof is to show that Lemma 4.11, the analog of
Lemma 4.3, still holds.

Proof of Lemma 4.11.   Let f, d, and ℓ be the flow, distances, and lengths,
respectively, at the start of the blocking flow computation; let f', d', and ℓ'
be the flow, distances, and lengths, respectively, from the next iteration, after
computing a blocking flow. We let ℓ be the lengths after we have determined
the special arcs for the previous iteration, and let ℓ' be the lengths before we
have determined the special arcs for the next iteration; since special arcs do not
change the distances at all, we can make this distinction.

We follow the same structure as the proof of Lemma 4.3. Pick any shortest
augmenting path P in $A_{f'}$, the arcs of positive residual capacity from the next
iteration. We want to show that $d'(s) = \sum_{(i,j)\in P} \ell'(i, j) > d(s)$. To do this,
we will show that for all arcs $(i, j) \in P$, it must be the case that $d(i) \leq
d(j) + \ell'(i, j)$, and for at least one arc $d(i) < d(j) + \ell'(i, j)$. Then

$$d'(s) = \sum_{(i,j)\in P} \ell'(i, j) > \sum_{(i,j)\in P} (d(i) - d(j)) = d(s) - d(t) = d(s).$$

We first want to show that for all arcs $(i, j) \in P$ that $d(i) \leq d(j) + \ell'(i, j)$;
as a first step, we show that $d(i) \leq d(j) + \ell(i, j)$. Since $(i, j) \in P$, it must
have positive residual capacity for the flow f', so that $u_{f'}(i, j) > 0$. For the arc
to have positive residual capacity, either (i, j) had positive residual capacity in
the previous iteration, or we increased flow on the reverse arc (j, i). If (i, j)
had positive residual capacity in the previous iteration, then we know by the
properties of shortest paths that $d(i) \leq d(j) + \ell(i, j)$. If we increased flow on

(j,i) in the previous iteration, then (j,i) was admissible and $d(j) = d(i) + \ell(j,i)$, so that $d(i) = d(j) - \ell(j,i) \le d(j) + \ell(i,j)$.

Now we have established that $d(i) \le d(j) + \ell(i,j)$ for all $(i,j) \in P$; how can it be the case that $d(i) \not\le d(j) + \ell'(i,j)$? It can only happen if $d(i) = d(j) + \ell(i,j)$, $\ell(i,j) = 1$, and $\ell'(i,j) = 0$. Since $d(i) = d(j) + 1$, it must be the case that (j,i) is not admissible. Thus the flow (i,j) can only increase, and the residual capacity can only decrease; that is, $u_f(i,j) \ge u_{f'}(i,j)$. However, since $\ell'(i,j) = 0$, we have that $u_{f'}(i,j) > \Delta$, which then implies that $u_f(i,j) > \Delta$ (recall that ℓ' is set before we have determined the special arcs for the next iteration), which contradicts $\ell(i,j) = 1$. Hence this case cannot occur, and it must be that $d(i) \le d(j) + \ell'(i,j)$.

We now want to prove that there must be some arc $(i,j) \in P$ such that $d(i) < d(j) + \ell'(i,j)$. By the properties of a blocking flow, it cannot be the case that all arcs in P were admissible in the previous iteration, since the blocking flow must have saturated an arc of P. So it must be the case that some arc $(i,j) \in P$ was not admissible in the previous iteration, and thus either $u_f(i,j) = 0$ or $d(i) < d(j) + \ell(i,j)$.

Suppose (i,j) was not admissible because $u_f(i,j) = 0$. Then since $(i,j) \in P$, we must have pushed flow on (j,i), which implies that (j,i) was admissible and $d(j) = d(i) + \ell(j,i)$ or $d(i) = d(j) - \ell(j,i)$. Then the only way we could have $d(i) \not< d(j) + \ell'(i,j)$ would be if $\ell'(i,j) = 0$, which implies $u_{f'}(i,j) > \Delta$. However, we had $u_f(i,j) = 0$ in the previous iteration; this can only happen if we push more than Δ units of flow on (j,i). The algorithm only pushes $\Delta/4$ units of flow per iteration, which results in at most $\Delta/2$ units of flow on any arc (possibly $\Delta/2$ on an arc in a contracted component). Thus we never push more than Δ units of flow on an arc, and if $u_f(i,j) = 0$, then it must be the case that $d(i) < d(j) + \ell'(i,j)$.

Now we suppose that (i,j) was not admissible because $d(i) < d(j) + \ell(i,j)$ and $u_f(i,j) > 0$. Then the only way we can have $d(i) \not< d(j) + \ell'(i,j)$ is if $\ell(i,j) = 1$, $d(i) = d(j)$, and $\ell'(i,j) = 0$. Since $\ell(i,j) = 1$, then $u_f(i,j) \le \Delta$, and since $\ell'(i,j) = 0$, $u_{f'}(i,j) > \Delta$. Because we assume that (i,j) was not admissible, it cannot be a special arc, and thus $u_f(i,j) < \Delta/2$. In order to have $u_{f'}(i,j) > \Delta$ in the next iteration, we must have pushed more than $\Delta/2$ units of flow on (j,i), which is a contradiction, since the algorithm only pushes $\Delta/4$ units of flow per iteration (possibly we route $\Delta/2$ units of flow on an arc in a contracted component). Thus in this case it is also true that $d(i) < d(j) + \ell'(i,j)$. $\square$

Theorem 4.13: *The Goldberg–Rao algorithm of Algorithm 4.2 runs in* $O(\Lambda m \log n \log(mU))$ *time.*

Proof The outermost while loop runs $O(\log(mU))$ times, and the inner repeat loop runs $O(\Lambda)$ times, and in each innermost iteration a blocking flow computation is run, taking $O(m \log n)$ time. The overall running time follows.   □

The Goldberg–Rao algorithm was the theoretically fastest polynomial-time algorithm for the maximum flow problem for almost fifteen years. Faster algorithms based on ideas for interior-point methods from linear programming are now known; see the Chapter Notes for details.

Exercises

4.1   Recall that a unit capacity graph is one such that $u(i, j) \in \{0, 1\}$ for all $(i, j) \in A$. Give an $O(m)$ time algorithm to find a blocking flow in a unit capacity graph if there are no cycles of positive capacity.

4.2   In some graphs, a blocking flow is also a maximum flow. This is true in *series-parallel* graphs. Series-parallel graphs can be constructed inductively. A graph with a single arc from s to t is the simplest series-parallel graph (Figure 4.4).

Two series-parallel graphs G_1 and G_2 can be combined into a new series-parallel graph through either a *series composition* or a *parallel composition*. In a series composition, the t node of G_1 is identified with the s node of G_2, and the s node of G_1 becomes the s node of the new graph, while the t node of G_2 becomes the t node of the new graph. See Figure 4.5.

In a parallel composition, the s nodes of G_1 and G_2 are identified, and the t nodes of G_1 and G_2 are identified. The identified s nodes are the s node of the new graph, and the identified t nodes are the t node of the new graph. See Figure 4.6.

(a) Prove that a blocking flow in a series-parallel graph is also a maximum flow.

(b) Show that series-parallel graphs have no positive capacity cycles, and conclude that there is an $O(mn)$ time algorithm for finding a maximum flow in series-parallel graphs.

Figure 4.4 The simplest series-parallel graph.

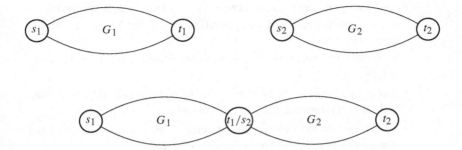

Figure 4.5 Series composition.

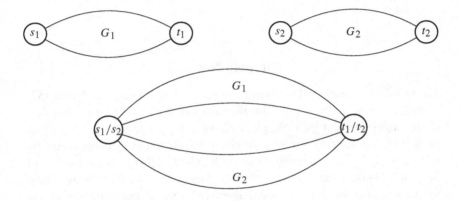

Figure 4.6 Parallel composition.

4.3   Lemma 4.5 gives an $O(mn)$ time algorithm for finding a blocking flow in
      a graph with no positive capacity cycles. We can derive a faster algorithm
      assuming the existence of a special data structure called *dynamic trees*.
      The data structure maintains a vertex-disjoint set of rooted trees. Each
      rooted tree is a directed tree with a specific vertex called the root; every
      other vertex in the tree has a single arc directed out of the vertex, and can
      reach the root vertex via a directed path. Each vertex has a real-valued
      cost. The data structure can perform each of the following operations in
      $O(\log n)$ amortized time:

      • *maketree(i)*: Create a new tree containing the single vertex i of cost
        zero; i is the root of the new tree.

      • *findroot(i)*: Return the root of the tree containing vertex i.

- *findcost(i)*: Return (j, x), where x is the minimum cost of a vertex on the tree path from i to findroot(i) and j is the last vertex on this path of cost x.
- *addcost(i, x)*: Add x to the cost of every vertex on the path from i to findroot(i).
- *link(i, j)*: Combine the two trees containing vertices i and j by adding the arc (i, j) directed from i to j. i must be the root of a tree.
- *cut(i)*: Divide the tree containing vertex i into two trees by deleting the arc out of i. i must not be the root of a tree.

Show that by using the dynamic trees data structure one can obtain an $O(m \log n)$ time algorithm for finding a blocking flow in a graph with no positive capacity cycles.

Chapter Notes

The blocking flow algorithm given in Section 4.1 is attributed to Dinitz [52] (sometimes written Dinic); see also the survey of Dinitz [54] for an overview of this algorithm and its subsequent modifications. The time bounds given in Section 4.2 for unit capacity graphs were discovered independently by Karzanov [127] and Even and Tarjan [59]. The Goldberg–Rao algorithm of Section 4.3 is due, naturally enough, to Goldberg and Rao [90]. Interestingly, the early paper by Edmonds and Karp [57] had already introduced the idea of considering different arc lengths $\ell(i, j)$ for shortest augmenting path algorithms. Lecture notes of Mehlhorn [147] present the perspective of the Goldberg–Rao algorithm in terms of blocking flows used in the section.

Hoffman [109, 110] attributes Exercise 4.2 to folklore: "It is well known that sequential greediness for any sequence of s-t paths solves the max flow problem for series-parallel graphs." He conceives of the blocking flow algorithm as a greedy maximum flow algorithm that does not require reducing flow on an arc. Exercise 4.3 is due to Sleator and Tarjan [182].

Permissions

5

Minimum-Cost Circulation Algorithms

> In this chapter we take up the problem of constructing network flows that minimize cost. The practical importance of this problem area is affirmed by the fact that a sizeable fraction of the linear programming literature has been devoted to it, and an even larger share of the many concrete industrial and military applications of linear programming have been in this domain.
> – L. R. Ford, Jr., and D. R. Fulkerson, *Flows in Networks*

We now turn to flow problems that involve a cost per unit flow, and in which the goal is to minimize the overall cost of the flow meeting certain conditions. We saw that in some cases we could model problems in which we wished to minimize costs as a minimum *s-t* cut problem (as in the image segmentation problem of Exercise 2.5). However, in many problems it makes sense to have a cost per unit flow; this allows us to model problems in minimizing the transport of goods, for instance, in which there are per-unit costs for transportation.

The fundamental problem we will study is the *minimum-cost circulation problem*. In this problem we are given as input a directed graph $G = (V, A)$, integer costs $c(i, j)$ for all $(i, j) \in A$, integer capacities $u(i, j) \geq 0$ for all $(i, j) \in A$, and integer lower bounds $\ell(i, j)$ such that $0 \leq \ell(i, j) \leq u(i, j)$ for all $(i, j) \in A$. The goal is to find a *circulation* f of minimum cost. We define a circulation as follows.

Definition 5.1: *A circulation* $f : A \to \Re^{\geq 0}$ *is an assignment of nonnegative reals to the arcs such that the following two properties are obeyed:*

• *for all arcs* $(i, j) \in A$,

$$\ell(i, j) \leq f(i, j) \leq u(i, j); \tag{5.1}$$

- *for all $i \in V$, the total flow entering i is equal to the flow leaving i; that is,*

$$\sum_{k:(k,i)\in A} f(k,i) = \sum_{k:(i,k)\in A} f(i,k). \tag{5.2}$$

The cost *of the circulation is* $\sum_{(i,j)\in A} c(i,j)f(i,j)$ *and is denoted* $c(f)$.

As with the maximum flow problem, the constraints (5.1) are called capacity constraints, and (5.2) are called flow conservation constraints. Note that unlike the maximum flow problem, it is possible that no feasible circulation exists. However, it is possible to determine whether a feasible circulation exists, and find such a circulation if one exists, using a single maximum flow computation. This result is known as *Hoffman's circulation theorem*, and is given as Exercise 2.7.

Another popular type of flow problem involving costs is known as the *minimum-cost flow problem*. In this problem, we are given as input a directed graph $G = (V, A)$, integer costs $c(i, j)$ for all $(i, j) \in A$, integer capacities $u(i, j) \geq 0$ for all $(i, j) \in A$, and integer demands $b(i)$ for all $i \in V$. A *flow* $f : A \to \Re^{\geq 0}$ in this problem is an assignment of nonnegative reals to the arcs such that $0 \leq f(i, j) \leq u(i, j)$ and such that the demands are met at all nodes; that is, the difference between the flow out of i and the flow into i is exactly $b(i)$ for all $i \in V$, or

$$b(i) = \sum_{k:(i,k)\in A} f(i,k) - \sum_{k:(k,i)\in A} f(k,i).$$

If $b(i) > 0$ we call i a *supply node* (since there must be positive net flow out of i) and $b(i)$ is the *supply* of node i. If $b(i) < 0$ we call i a *demand node* and $-b(i)$ is the *demand* of node i. The goal of the minimum-cost flow problem is to minimize the cost of the flow, which is $\sum_{(i,j)\in A} c(i,j)f(i,j)$. We observe that in order to have a feasible solution f, it must be the case that $\sum_{i\in V} b(i) = 0$, since if we sum the demand constraints over all $i \in V$ we get

$$\sum_{i\in V} b(i) = \sum_{i\in V}\left(\sum_{k:(i,k)\in A} f(i,k) - \sum_{k:(k,i)\in A} f(k,i) \right) = 0;$$

the sum is zero, since each term $f(i, j)$ appears once positively and once negatively in the sum. It makes intuitive sense that $\sum_{i\in V} b(i) = 0$, since then the total demand over all demand nodes equals the total supply over all supply nodes.

We claim that any instance of the minimum-cost flow problem can be reduced to a minimum-cost circulation problem, allowing us to focus our attention on the latter problem (it is also the case that any instance of the

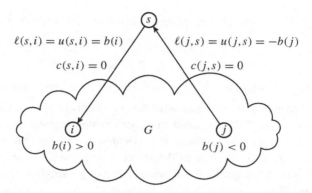

Figure 5.1 Illustration of reduction from the minimum-cost flow problem to the minimum-cost circulation problem.

minimum-cost circulation problem can be reduced to a minimum-cost flow problem; see Exercise 5.2). Given an instance of the minimum-cost flow problem with graph G, capacities u, and demands b, we create an instance of the minimum-cost circulation problem as follows. We create a new node s. For any supply node i (with $b(i) > 0$), we add an arc (s, i) with $\ell(s, i) = u(s, i) = b(i)$ and cost $c(s, i) = 0$, and for any demand node j (with $b(j) < 0$), we add an arc (j, s) with $\ell(j, s) = u(j, s) = -b(j)$ and cost $c(j, s) = 0$; see Figure 5.1. Then it is easy to check that any circulation in this instance gives a flow in the original instance of the same cost, and vice versa. So for the remainder of the chapter, we will only consider the minimum-cost circulation problem.

As in the maximum flow problem, it will be useful to consider a somewhat unconventional redefinition of a circulation. We will add an arc (j, i) for each arc $(i, j) \in A$, and impose a skew symmetry constraint, so that $f(j, i) = -f(i, j)$. We can then replace the lower bound $\ell(i, j)$ in the definition of the circulation with a capacity constraint $u(j, i) = -\ell(i, j)$ on the reverse arc. We observe that if $f(j, i) \leq u(j, i)$, then $-f(i, j) \leq -\ell(i, j)$ or $f(i, j) \geq \ell(i, j)$ as desired. Furthermore, we set $c(j, i) = -c(i, j)$ so that $c(i, j)f(i, j) + c(j, i)f(j, i) = 2c(i, j)f(i, j)$. Now we define the cost of a circulation to be $\frac{1}{2}\sum_{(i,j)\in A} c(i, j)f(i, j)$, so that the cost of a circulation in the new definition is the same as the cost under the previous definition. Finally, as in the case of the maximum flow problem, the flow conservation constraints now become

$$\sum_{k:(i,k)\in A} f(i, k) = 0.$$

We summarize the new definition below.

Definition 5.2: *A circulation* $f : A \to \Re$ *is an assignment of reals to the arcs such that the following three properties are obeyed:*

- *for all arcs* $(i, j) \in A$,

$$f(i, j) \leq u(i, j); \tag{5.3}$$

- *for all* $i \in V$, *the total flow leaving* i *is zero; that is,*

$$\sum_{k:(i,k)\in A} f(i, k) = 0; \tag{5.4}$$

- *for all* $(i, j) \in A$,

$$f(i, j) = -f(j, i). \tag{5.5}$$

The cost *of the circulation is* $\frac{1}{2}\sum_{(i,j)\in A} c(i, j)f(i, j)$ *and is denoted* $c(f)$.

5.1 Optimality Conditions

As in the case of the maximum flow problem, we would like to develop a set of conditions that let us know when we have found a circulation of minimum cost.

To begin with, we need the concept of a residual graph. The residual graph in the case of the minimum-cost circulation problem is identical to that used in the maximum flow problem. Given a circulation f on the graph $G = (V, A)$ with capacities $u(i, j)$ for all $(i, j) \in A$, the residual graph with respect to the circulation f is $G_f = (V, A)$. Each arc $(i, j) \in A$ has residual capacity $u_f(i, j) = u(i, j) - f(i, j)$; notice again that the residual capacity is always nonnegative, even though in the case of the minimum-cost circulation problem the capacities $u(i, j)$ might be negative. As in the case of the maximum flow problem, we define A_f to be the subset of arcs that have positive residual capacity; that is, $A_f = \{(i, j) \in A : u_f(i, j) > 0\}$.

The object analogous to an augmenting path in a residual graph for the maximum flow problem is a *negative-cost cycle* in the residual graph for the minimum-cost circulation problem. A negative-cost cycle Γ is a simple cycle in the residual graph G_f such that all arcs of Γ have positive residual capacity and the sum of the costs of the arcs is negative; that is, $\Gamma \subseteq A_f$ and $\sum_{(i,j)\in\Gamma} c(i, j) < 0$. We denote the cost of the arcs in Γ by $c(\Gamma) = \sum_{(i,j)\in\Gamma} c(i, j)$. Suppose we have a circulation f, and there is a negative-cost cycle $\Gamma \subseteq A_f$. Let $\delta = \min_{(i,j)\in\Gamma} u_f(i, j)$; since all the arcs in Γ have positive residual capacity, $\delta > 0$. Then we create a new circulation f' by setting

$$f'(i,j) = \begin{cases} f(i,j) + \delta & \forall (i,j) \in \Gamma, \\ f(i,j) - \delta & \forall (j,i) \in \Gamma, \\ f(i,j) & \forall (i,j) : (i,j), (j,i) \notin \Gamma. \end{cases}$$

Sometimes we say that we *push* δ units of flow around the cycle Γ. We also say that we *cancel* the cycle Γ because in the new circulation f' some arc in Γ must have zero residual capacity; that is, $\Gamma \not\subseteq A_{f'}$.

We need to check that f' is still a circulation. One way to do this is to consider a circulation $\tilde{f}$ in the residual graph G_f that has

$$\tilde{f}(i,j) = \begin{cases} \delta & \forall (i,j) \in \Gamma, \\ -\delta & \forall (j,i) \in \Gamma, \\ 0 & \forall (i,j) : (i,j), (j,i) \notin \Gamma. \end{cases}$$

Since $\delta \leq u_f(i,j)$ for all $(i,j) \in \Gamma$, the circulation $\tilde{f}$ obeys all the capacity constraints of the residual graph. It clearly obeys skew symmetry and flow conservation for any node i not on the cycle. For a node i on the cycle, we have that $\sum_{k:(k,i)\in A} \tilde{f}(k,i) = f(k,i) + f(j,i) = \delta - \delta = 0$ for arcs (k,i) and (i,j) on the cycle. Thus $\tilde{f}$ is indeed a circulation. Since $f' = f + \tilde{f}$, and both f and $\tilde{f}$ obey flow conservation and skew symmetry, so does f' (by Lemma 2.19). Finally, $f'(i,j) = f(i,j) + \tilde{f}(i,j) \leq f(i,j) + u_f(i,j) = u(i,j)$, so the capacity constraints are obeyed and f' is indeed a circulation.

Now we show that $c(f') < c(f)$. We first observe that $c(\tilde{f}) = \delta c(\Gamma)$, since

$$c(\tilde{f}) = \frac{1}{2} \sum_{(i,j)\in\Gamma} (\delta c(i,j) - \delta c(j,i)) = \frac{1}{2}\delta \sum_{(i,j)\in\Gamma} (c(i,j) + c(i,j)) = \delta c(\Gamma).$$

Then

$$c(f') = c(f + \tilde{f}) = c(f) + c(\tilde{f}) = c(f) + \delta c(\Gamma) < c(f),$$

since $c(\Gamma) < 0$ and $\delta > 0$.

The natural analogy with the maximum flow problem would now lead us to believe that we have a minimum-cost circulation f if and only if there are no negative-cost cycles in G_f (just as a flow f is maximum if and only if there are no augmenting paths in G_f). Indeed, this is the case. However, to prove this statement, it is helpful to introduce one more concept. A node *potential* (or *price*) $p : V \rightarrow \Re$ is an assignment of reals to the nodes. Then we define the *reduced cost* of an arc (i,j) with respect to potentials p as $c_p(i,j) = c(i,j) + p(i) - p(j)$. Observe that $c_p(j,i) = c(j,i) + p(j) - p(i) = -(c(i,j) + p(i) - p(j)) = -c_p(i,j)$. Also notice that the reduced cost of a cycle Γ, $c_p(\Gamma)$, is exactly equal to the cost $c(\Gamma)$ of the cycle:

$$c_p(\Gamma) = \sum_{(i,j)\in\Gamma} (c(i,j) + p(i) - p(j)) = c(\Gamma) + \sum_{(i,j)\in\Gamma} (p(i) - p(j)) = c(\Gamma),$$

since the potentials all cancel out. In Exercise 5.3 we have the reader prove the stronger statement that for a circulation f, $c(f) = c_p(f)$, where $c_p(f) = \frac{1}{2}\sum_{(i,j)\in A} c_p(i,j)f(i,j)$.

Intuitively, we can think of $p(i)$ as the length of a shortest s-i path for some source vertex s. Then, we know from Lemma 1.6 that $p(j) \leq p(i) + c(i,j)$ for all $(i,j) \in A_f$ if and only if there are no negative-cost cycles reachable from s in G_f; rewriting, we have that $c_p(i,j) = c(i,j) + p(i) - p(j) \geq 0$ for all $(i,j) \in A_f$ if and only if there are no negative-cost cycles in G_f, which we have stated above is a condition for having a minimum-cost circulation. Note that if we have potentials p such that $c_p(i,j) \geq 0$ for all $(i,j) \in A_f$, the potentials serve as a witness that there are no negative-cost cycles, since $c(\Gamma) = c_p(\Gamma) \geq 0$ for any cycle $\Gamma \subseteq A_f$. The intuition we have given above leads to the following theorem that gives equivalent optimality conditions for minimum-cost circulations.

Theorem 5.3: *The following statements are equivalent for a circulation f:*

1. *f is a minimum-cost circulation;*
2. *there is no negative-cost cycle in A_f;*
3. *there are potentials p such that $c_p(i,j) \geq 0$ for all $(i,j) \in A_f$.*

Proof We argued above that (1) implies (2), since we showed that if there is a negative-cost cycle in G_f, then there is a new circulation f' such that $c(f') < c(f)$.

To show that (2) implies (3), we consider a new graph obtained by adding a source vertex s to the residual graph G_f, with arcs (s,j) of cost $c(s,j) = 0$ for all nodes $j \in V$; see Figure 5.2. Now we let $p(i)$ be the length of the shortest path from s to i using arcs in A_f, where the length of arc (i,j) is the arc cost $c(i,j)$. As discussed in Section 1.3 and Lemma 1.6, we can compute these shortest paths if there is no negative-cost cycle in the residual graph G_f reachable from s. Also as discussed in that section, we have that $p(j) \leq p(i) + c(i,j)$ for any $(i,j) \in A_f$ (that is, the cost of the shortest s-j path is at most the shortest s-i path plus the cost of (i,j)). Thus $c_p(i,j) = c(i,j) + p(i) - p(j) \geq 0$ for all $(i,j) \in A_f$.

Now we wish to show that (3) implies (1). Let $\tilde{f}$ be any other circulation in G, and consider $f' = \tilde{f} - f$; we claim that f' must be a circulation in the residual graph G_f. By Lemma 2.19, f' obeys skew symmetry and flow conservation, and $f'(i,j) = \tilde{f}(i,j) - f(i,j) \leq u(i,j) - f(i,j) = u_f(i,j)$,

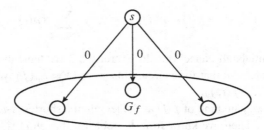

Figure 5.2 Proof of (2) implies (3) in Theorem 5.3.

so f' obeys the capacity constraints in the residual graph; thus if $f'(i, j) > 0$, then $(i, j) \in A_f$. Then

$$c(\tilde{f}) - c(f) = c(\tilde{f} - f) = c(f')$$

$$= c(f') + \frac{1}{2} \sum_{i \in V} p(i) \left(\sum_{k:(i,k) \in A} f'(i,k) - \sum_{k:(k,i) \in A} f'(k,i) \right)$$

using the flow conservation constraints. It follows that

$$c(\tilde{f}) - c(f) = c(f') + \frac{1}{2} \sum_{i \in V} p(i) \left(\sum_{k:(i,k) \in A} f'(i,k) - \sum_{k:(k,i) \in A} f'(k,i) \right)$$

$$= c(f') + \frac{1}{2} \sum_{(i,j) \in A} (p(i) - p(j)) f'(i,j)$$

$$= \frac{1}{2} \sum_{(i,j) \in A} (c(i,j) + p(i) - p(j)) f'(i,j)$$

$$= \frac{1}{2} \sum_{(i,j) \in A} c_p(i,j) f'(i,j)$$

$$= \sum_{(i,j) \in A: f'(i,j) > 0} c_p(i,j) f'(i,j) \geq 0,$$

where the final equality follows, since $c_p(i,j) f'(i,j) + c_p(j,i) f'(j,i) = 2c_p(i,j) f'(i,j)$ for $f'(i,j) > 0$, and the final inequality follows, since when $f'(i,j) > 0$ then $(i,j) \in A_f$, so that $c_p(i,j) \geq 0$. So $c(\tilde{f}) \geq c(f)$, and since $\tilde{f}$ was an arbitrary circulation, it follows that f is a minimum-cost circulation. □

We note the following corollary of the proof, which follows from the calculation of the potentials in showing that condition (2) implies condition (3).

Corollary 5.4: *If costs c are integer and f is optimal, there exist integer potentials p such that $c_p(i, j) \geq 0$ for all $(i, j) \in A_f$.*

Just as the optimality conditions for the maximum flow problem suggests the augmenting path algorithm of Ford and Fulkerson, the optimality conditions above suggest a natural negative-cost cycle canceling algorithm due to Klein [132], which we give in Algorithm 5.1. Given any feasible circulation f, we repeatedly look for a negative-cost cycle Γ in the residual graph G_f, then cancel Γ and update f. Recall that in Section 1.3 we gave $O(mn)$ time algorithms for finding negative-cost cycles if they exist. Once there are no more such cycles, we have a minimum-cost circulation. The algorithm does not specify how we find an initial feasible circulation. Hoffman's Circulation Theorem given in Exercise 2.7 gives a necessary and sufficient condition for the existence of a feasible circulation, and if the condition is met and capacities u are integral, we can find a feasible circulation f that is integral with a single maximum flow computation.

One consequence of Algorithm 5.1 is that an integrality property holds for the minimum-cost circulation property. If the capacities u are integral, then by the discussion above the initial circulation f is integral. Then the residual capacities u_f are integral, and thus the quantity $\delta = \min_{(i, j) \in \Gamma} u_f(i, j)$ is integer, and the resulting circulation f' is also integral.

Property 5.5: *If capacities $u(i, j)$ are integer, then the minimum-cost circulation f is integral.*

If both the capacities u and the costs c are integer, then we can show that Algorithm 5.1 is a pseudopolynomial-time algorithm. Recall that we let $U = \max_{(i, j) \in A} u(i, j)$. Let $C = \max_{(i, j) \in A} |c(i, j)|$. The maximum value of a circulation is mCU; each arc can have flow at most U and thus cost at most CU. It follows similarly that the minimum value of a circulation is $-mCU$. Each negative-cost cycle Γ found must have cost $c(\Gamma) \leq -1$, so that in each iteration the cost of the circulation must go down by at least 1. Thus there are

---

Let f be any feasible circulation
while there is a negative-cost cycle Γ in A_f **do**
    Cancel Γ
    Update f
return f

Algorithm 5.1 Klein's [132] negative-cost cycle canceling algorithm for the minimum-cost circulation problem.

$O(mCU)$ iterations of the algorithm in total. We know from Section 1.3 that we can find a negative-cost cycle in a graph (or determine that none exists) in $O(mn)$ time. Thus Algorithm 5.1 takes $O(m^2nCU)$ time plus the time to find the initial feasible circulation (via a single maximum flow computation), and thus is $O(m^2nCU)$ time overall.

Just as choosing an arbitrary augmenting path does not result in an polynomial-time algorithm for the maximum flow problem (as we saw in Exercise 2.2), choosing an arbitrary negative-cost cycle to cancel does not result in a polynomial-time algorithm for the minimum-cost circulation problem (see Exercise 5.4). However, we will see in subsequent sections that choosing the appropriate cycle to cancel in each iteration results in a polynomial-time algorithm.

5.2 Wallacher's Algorithm

A reasonable first guess at the cycle to choose for a polynomial-time version of the negative-cost cycle canceling algorithm is the cycle that gives the greatest overall improvement in cost; this cycle is analogous to choosing the most improving augmenting path for the maximum flow problem, as we did in Section 2.5. Unfortunately, it is NP-hard to find such a cycle; we leave the proof as an exercise (Exercise 5.5). However, suppose for a moment that we could find such a cycle. Let $f^{(k)}$ be the circulation resulting from k iterations of canceling the most improving cycle starting with circulation f, and let f^* be a minimum-cost circulation. Then, in Exercise 5.5, we ask the reader to show that

$$c(f) - c(f^{(1)}) \geq \frac{1}{m}(c(f) - c(f^*)). \tag{5.6}$$

Rearranging terms, this inequality is equivalent to

$$c(f^{(1)}) - c(f^*) \leq \left(1 - \frac{1}{m}\right)(c(f) - c(f^*)).$$

Thus after k iterations, we have that

$$c(f^{(k)}) - c(f^*) \leq \left(1 - \frac{1}{m}\right)^k (c(f) - c(f^*)).$$

Using $1 - x < e^{-x}$ for $x \neq 0$, and the fact that $c(f) - c(f^*) \leq 2mCU$, after $k = m \ln(2mCU)$ iterations, we have that

$$c(f^{(k)}) - c(f^*) < e^{-\ln(2mCU)}(c(f) - c(f^*)) \leq \frac{1}{2mCU} \cdot 2mCU = 1.$$

Since $f^{(k)}$ and f^* are integral, if the costs and capacities are integer, then after $k = m \ln(2mCU)$ iterations we have that the difference between the cost of $f^{(k)}$ and the cost of a minimum-cost circulation f^* is less than 1, which implies that $c(f^{(k)}) = c(f^*)$, and we have found a minimum-cost circulation. We can summarize this line of reasoning in the following theorem.

Theorem 5.6: *If costs and capacities are integer, and if Inequality (5.6) holds for each iteration of Algorithm 5.1, then the algorithm finds a minimum-cost circulation in $O(m \ln(mCU))$ iterations.*

The reader may wonder why we have analyzed the most improving negative-cost cycle algorithm given that we do not know how to implement it in polynomial time. It turns out that several minimum-cost circulation algorithms look for cycles or collections of cycles to cancel that give the same type of improvement as the most improving negative-cost cycle, namely the improvement given by Inequality (5.6). We will now see such an algorithm, one due to Wallacher [201] and hence known as Wallacher's algorithm (we give another such algorithm in Exercise 5.7). The ideas for Wallacher's algorithm also turn out to extend to other problems such as the generalized flow problem; other algorithmic ideas in this chapter do not extend as easily. We start by presenting an algorithm that requires finding a complicated cycle to cancel, and then show how these ideas can be used in an algorithm that merely requires finding any negative-cost cycle.

In Wallacher's algorithm, we look for a cycle that trades off large residual capacity arcs against negative-cost arcs. As argued in the previous section, canceling the cycle Γ gives an improvement in cost of $c(\Gamma) \min_{(i,j) \in \Gamma} u_f(i,j)$, and thus we would like to find the cycle $\Gamma \subseteq A_f$ that minimizes this quantity (we want to minimize, since $c(\Gamma) < 0$). We rewrite this improvement as

$$\frac{c(\Gamma)}{\max_{(i,j) \in \Gamma} \frac{1}{u_f(i,j)}};$$

recall that we have asserted that it is NP-hard to find the cycle Γ that minimizes this quantity. Thus we look for a cycle Γ that minimizes a related quantity, such that we are able to find the cycle minimizing the quantity in polynomial time. For a given circulation f and a cycle $\Gamma \subseteq A_f$, we define $\beta(\Gamma)$ as follows:

$$\beta(\Gamma) = \frac{c(\Gamma)}{\sum_{(i,j) \in \Gamma} \frac{1}{u_f(i,j)}}.$$

That is, $\beta(\Gamma)$ is the ratio of the cost of the cycle to the sum of the inverse residual capacities of the cycle; observe that in the denominator we have replaced taking the maximum of the inverses of the residual capacities with the sum. We let $\beta(f)$ define the minimum ratio cycle; that is,

$$\beta(f) = \min_{\text{cycle } \Gamma \subseteq A_f} \beta(\Gamma).$$

Note that if f is not a minimum-cost circulation, then $\beta(f)$ must be negative. By using the algorithm to find the minimum cost-to-time ratio algorithm of Exercise 1.5, we can compute a cycle Γ of minimum ratio in $O(mn \ln(nCU))$ time.

We will now show that $\beta(f)$ is at least a $1/m$ fraction of the difference in cost of an optimal circulation and the cost of f. To prove this statement, we first need the analog of the flow decomposition lemma in Lemma 2.20; since the proof is also the analog of the proof there, we leave it as an exercise to the reader (Exercise 5.1).

Lemma 5.7: *Given a circulation f, there exists circulations $f_1, \ldots, f_\ell$, for $\ell \le m$, such that $f = \sum_{i=1}^{\ell} f_i$, $c(f) = \sum_{i=1}^{\ell} c(f_i)$, and for each i, the arcs of f_i with positive flow are a simple cycle.*

We can now prove our earlier statement about $\beta(f)$.

Lemma 5.8: *Given a circulation f that is not minimum-cost and a minimum-cost circulation f^*, $\beta(f) \le \frac{1}{m}(c(f^*) - c(f))$.*

Proof We start by showing that $f^* - f$ is a feasible circulation in the residual graph G_f. Because f^* and f are both circulations, $f^* - f$ obeys skew symmetry and flow conservation (as shown in Lemma 2.19). It also obeys the capacity constraints with respect to the residual capacities, since $f^*(i, j) - f(i, j) \le u(i, j) - f(i, j) = u_f(i, j)$.

Now we apply Lemma 5.7 to decompose the circulation $f^* - f$ in G_f into circulations $f_1, \ldots, f_\ell$ in G_f, where each circulation f_i has positive flow only on a simple cycle; let Γ_i be the cycle corresponding to circulation f_i. Since f_i is a circulation, the positive flow on each arc is identical: let δ_i be this positive amount of flow on each arc of Γ_i. Then $c(f_i) = \delta_i c(\Gamma_i)$. Then we have that

$$c(f^*) - c(f) = \sum_{k=1}^{\ell} c(f_k) = \sum_{k=1}^{\ell} \delta_k c(\Gamma_k)$$

$$= \sum_{k=1}^{\ell} \delta_k \beta(\Gamma_k) \sum_{(i,j) \in \Gamma_k} \frac{1}{u_f(i, j)}$$

$$\ge \beta(f) \sum_{k=1}^{\ell} \delta_k \sum_{(i,j) \in \Gamma_k} \frac{1}{u_f(i, j)},$$

since $\beta(f) \le \beta(\Gamma_k)$ for any cycle Γ_k. Then, rewriting the initial sum over the edges rather than over k, we get

$$c(f^*) - c(f) = \beta(f) \sum_{k=1}^{\ell} \delta_k \sum_{(i,j) \in \Gamma_k} \frac{1}{u_f(i,j)}$$

$$= \beta(f) \sum_{(i,j) \in A_f} \frac{\sum_{k:(i,j) \in \Gamma_k} \delta_k}{u_f(i,j)}$$

$$\ge m\beta(f),$$

where the final inequality holds, since the total flow on arc $(i,j) \in A_f$, $\sum_{k:(i,j) \in \Gamma_k} \delta_k$, is at most the residual capacity $u_f(i,j)$, and since $\beta(f)$ is nonpositive. We obtain the lemma statement by rearranging terms. □

Corollary 5.9: *Suppose costs and capacities are integer. Then if $\beta(f) > -\frac{1}{m}$, then f is a minimum-cost circulation.*

Proof If $\beta(f) > -\frac{1}{m}$, then by the lemma $c(f^*) - c(f) > -1$. Since the capacities are integral, by the integrality property f^* is integral and in each iteration f is integral. Since the costs are integral, $c(f^*) - c(f)$ is an integer, and thus if $c(f^*) - c(f) > -1$, then $c(f^*) - c(f) = 0$, and thus f has minimum cost. □

Thus we can now give Wallacher's algorithm in Algorithm 5.2: we start with any feasible circulation f. While $\beta(f)$ is at most $-1/m$, we cancel the minimum ratio cycle Γ.

The analysis of the algorithm is relatively straightforward. We first show that each cycle Γ we cancel decreases the cost of the circulation by $-\beta(\Gamma)$. Then we use Lemma 5.8 to show that we must be a factor closer to the optimal circulation.

Let f be any feasible circulation
while $\beta(f) \le -\frac{1}{m}$ **do**
    Let $\Gamma \subseteq A_f$ be the cycle such that $\beta(f) = \beta(\Gamma)$
    Cancel Γ
    Update f
return f

Algorithm 5.2 Wallacher's algorithm for the minimum-cost circulation problem.

Lemma 5.10: *Let f be a circulation that is not minimum-cost. Suppose we cancel cycle Γ, and let $f^{(1)}$ be the result of canceling Γ. Then $c(f^{(1)}) - c(f) \leq \beta(\Gamma)$.*

Proof Let $\delta = \min_{(i,j) \in \Gamma} u_f(i,j)$ be the amount of flow we push around Γ to cancel it. Then

$$c(f^{(1)}) - c(f) = \delta c(\Gamma) = \delta \beta(\Gamma) \sum_{(i,j) \in \Gamma} \frac{1}{u_f(i,j)} = \beta(\Gamma) \sum_{(i,j) \in \Gamma} \frac{\delta}{u_f(i,j)} \leq \beta(\Gamma),$$

since $\delta = u_f(i,j)$ for some $(i,j) \in \Gamma$, and $\beta(\Gamma) < 0$. □

If $f^{(1)}$ is the circulation resulting from circulation f after one iteration of the algorithm in which the cycle Γ which attains the minimum for $\beta(f)$ is canceled, and f^* is a minimum-cost circulation, then the combination of Lemmas 5.8 and 5.10 yields that

$$c(f^{(1)}) - c(f) \leq \beta(\Gamma) = \beta(f) \leq \frac{1}{m}(c(f^*) - c(f)),$$

or

$$c(f) - c(f^{(1)}) \geq \frac{1}{m}(c(f) - c(f^*)).$$

Notice that this is exactly Inequality (5.6) from the beginning of this section, giving an improvement in cost similar to what we could get by canceling the most improving cycle. Thus we can apply Theorem 5.6 to bound the iterations of the algorithm and the running time.

Theorem 5.11: *Suppose costs and capacities are integer. Then Wallacher's algorithm (Algorithm 5.2) takes $O(m \ln(mCU))$ iterations, and runs in $O(m^2 n \ln^2(mCU))$ time.*

For the maximum flow problem, we started out with the most improving augmenting path algorithm in Section 2.5, which required finding a particular s-t path in each iteration. We then used capacity scaling in Section 2.6 to allow us to find any s-t path in a selected set of edges, which resulted in an augmenting path that increased the flow value nearly as much as the most improving path. Here we will perform a similar simplification. Rather than finding the cycle Γ such that $\beta(\Gamma) = \beta(f)$, we maintain an estimate $\hat{\beta}$ on the value $\beta(f)$. Given the current circulation f, consider the costs $\bar{c}(i,j) = c(i,j) - \hat{\beta}/u_f(i,j)$. Observe that for a cycle $\Gamma \subseteq A_f$,

$$\bar{c}(\Gamma) < 0 \quad \text{iff} \quad c(\Gamma) < \hat{\beta} \sum_{(i,j) \in \Gamma} \frac{1}{u_f(i,j)} \quad \text{iff} \quad \hat{\beta} > \beta(\Gamma). \tag{5.7}$$

Let f be any feasible circulation
$\hat{\beta} \leftarrow -CU$
while $\hat{\beta} \leq -\frac{1}{2m}$ **do**
    if there exists cycle Γ with $\bar{c}(\Gamma) < 0$ **then**
        Cancel Γ
        Update f
    else
        $\hat{\beta} \leftarrow \hat{\beta}/2$
return f

Algorithm 5.3 Scaling version of Wallacher's algorithm for the minimum-cost circulation problem.

Thus Γ is a negative-cost cycle with respect to the costs $\bar{c}$ if and only if $\hat{\beta}$ is an upper bound on the value of $\beta(\Gamma)$. Thus given a current estimate $\hat{\beta}$, we find and cancel negative-cost cycles with respect to costs $\bar{c}$; once there are no more such cycles, we divide $\hat{\beta}$ by two and repeat. Since the cost of each arc is at least $-C$ and has residual capacity at most U, $\beta(f) \geq -CU$, and we can use $-CU$ as our initial estimate for $\hat{\beta}$. We summarize the algorithm in Algorithm 5.3.

We now turn to the analysis of the algorithm. Let us call the iterations in which $\hat{\beta}$ maintains the same value a $\hat{\beta}$-*scaling phase*. We start by arguing that the algorithm terminates with a minimum-cost circulation. To prove this, we use the following lemma.

Lemma 5.12: *At the start of any $\hat{\beta}$-scaling phase, $\hat{\beta} \leq \beta(f)/2$.*

Proof Initially $\hat{\beta} = -CU$, and we know for any cycle Γ,

$$\bar{c}(\Gamma) = c(\Gamma) + CU \sum_{(i,j)\in\Gamma} \frac{1}{u_f(i,j)} \geq c(\Gamma) + C|\Gamma| \geq 0.$$

Thus $\hat{\beta} \leq \beta(\Gamma)$ for any cycle Γ and so $\hat{\beta} \leq \beta(f) \leq \beta(f)/2$ (recall that $\beta(f) < 0$ if f is not a minimum-cost circulation). At the end of any $\hat{\beta}$-scaling phase, we have that $\bar{c}(\Gamma) \geq 0$ for any $\Gamma \subseteq A_f$, so that $\hat{\beta} \leq \beta(f)$ by (5.7); we then divide $\hat{\beta}$ by two, so that $\hat{\beta} \leq \beta(f)/2$. $\qquad\square$

Corollary 5.13: *Suppose costs and capacities are integer. If $\hat{\beta} > -1/2m$ at the start of a $\hat{\beta}$-scaling phase, then the circulation f is optimal.*

Proof By the lemma, we then have that $-1/2m < \hat{\beta} \leq \beta(f)/2$, so that $\beta(f) > -1/m$. Applying Corollary 5.9, the circulation f is optimal. $\qquad\square$

We now wish to bound the number of iterations of the algorithm in a $\hat{\beta}$-scaling phase. We can prove the following analog of Lemma 2.26 to obtain a bound.

Lemma 5.14: *There are at most $2m$ iterations per $\hat{\beta}$-scaling phase.*

Proof Let f be the circulation at the start of a $\hat{\beta}$-scaling phase, and let f^* be a minimum-cost circulation. Then by Lemmas 5.8 and 5.12, we have that $\hat{\beta} \leq \beta(f)/2 \leq \frac{1}{2m}(c(f^*) - c(f))$. By Lemma 5.10, we know that if we cancel Γ, then the cost of the current circulation changes by $\beta(\Gamma) < \hat{\beta} < \frac{1}{2m}(c(f^*) - c(f))$. After $2m$ iterations, the cost of the current circulation is then at most

$$c(f) + \frac{2m}{2m}(c(f^*) - c(f)) = c(f^*).$$

Thus after $2m$ iterations, the $\hat{\beta}$-scaling phase must end, since otherwise f will be an optimal circulation. □

Thus we have the following theorem.

Theorem 5.15: *The scaling version of Wallacher's algorithm (Algorithm 5.3) takes $O(m \log(mCU))$ iterations, and runs in $O(m^2 n \log(mCU))$ time.*

Proof Initially $\hat{\beta} = -CU$; within $\lceil \log_2(mCU) \rceil + 2$ $\hat{\beta}$-scaling phases, the value of $\hat{\beta} > -1/2m$ and the algorithm terminates. In each phase, there are at most $2m$ iterations, and so there are $O(m \log(mCU))$ iterations overall. Each iteration requires a negative-cost cycle detection, which can be done in $O(mn)$ time by the algorithm of Section 1.3. □

We will see similar ideas in Section 6.2 for the generalized flow problem.

5.3 Minimum-Mean Cycle Canceling

Our next algorithm for the minimum-cost circulation problem also uses the negative-cost cycle canceling algorithm of Algorithm 5.1; in each iteration it finds a *minimum-mean cycle* to cancel. A minimum-mean cycle Γ is one that minimizes the average cost of the arcs in the cycle; that is, it minimizes $c(\Gamma)/|\Gamma|$. We showed in Exercise 1.4 that we can find a minimum-mean cycle in $O(mn)$ time. For Wallacher's algorithm we gave an analysis that showed that each cycle canceled brings the cost of the circulation closer to the cost of a minimum-cost circulation; for the minimum-mean cycle canceling algorithm, we will use the optimality condition from Theorem 5.3 that states that a

---

Let f be any feasible circulation
while $\mu(f) < 0$ **do**
　　Let Γ be a minimum-mean cycle in A_f so that $\mu(f) = c(\Gamma)/|\Gamma|$
　　Cancel Γ
　　Update f
return f

Algorithm 5.4 Minimum-mean cycle canceling algorithm for the minimum-cost circulation problem.

circulation f has minimum cost if and only if there are potentials p such that $c_p(i, j) \geq 0$ for all $(i, j) \in A_f$. To achieve this condition, we allow the reduced cost of all the arcs in A_f to be negative, but gradually make the reduced cost closer and closer to zero. One of the advantages of this algorithm is that we are rather easily able to modify the analysis to give a strongly polynomial running time for the same algorithm. After defining the algorithm, we first give a polynomial-time analysis of the algorithm, then turn to the strongly polynomial-time analysis.

For a cycle Γ, we define $\mu(\Gamma)$ to be the average cost of arcs in the cycle; that is,

$$\mu(\Gamma) = \frac{c(\Gamma)}{|\Gamma|}.$$

For a given circulation f, we let $\mu(f)$ be the ratio $\mu(\Gamma)$ of a cycle Γ achieving the minimum ratio over all cycles in A_f; that is,

$$\mu(f) = \min_{\text{cycle } \Gamma \subseteq A_f} \frac{c(\Gamma)}{|\Gamma|}.$$

Observe that $\mu(f) < 0$ if and only if there is a negative-cost cycle in A_f. We give the resulting algorithm in Algorithm 5.4.

Recall we said above that we use the optimality condition that states that a circulation f has minimum cost if and only if there are potentials p such that $c_p(i, j) \geq 0$ for all $(i, j) \in A_f$. We will gradually make the reduced costs of arcs in A_f closer and closer to zero. To show how we will do this, we need the following definition.

Definition 5.16: *A circulation f is ϵ-optimal if there exist potentials p such that $c_p(i, j) \geq -\epsilon$ for all $(i, j) \in A_f$.*

Notice that any circulation is C-optimal, since for potentials $p(i) = 0$ for all $i \in V$, $c_p(i, j) = c(i, j) \geq -C$ for all $(i, j) \in A$. Furthermore, a minimum-cost circulation f is 0-optimal, since by Theorem 5.3, there exist potentials p such that $c_p(i, j) \geq 0$ for all $(i, j) \in A_f$. In fact, if costs are integer, then we can say something slightly more interesting about when a circulation is optimal.

Lemma 5.17: *Suppose the costs $c(i, j)$ are integer. If circulation f is ϵ-optimal for $\epsilon < 1/n$, then f is a minimum-cost circulation.*

Proof Let f be a circulation that is ϵ-optimal for $\epsilon < 1/n$. Thus there exist potentials p such that $c_p(i, j) \geq -\epsilon > -1/n$ for all arcs $(i, j) \in A_f$. Consider any simple cycle Γ of arcs of positive residual capacity. Then

$$c(\Gamma) = c_p(\Gamma) \geq -|\Gamma|\epsilon > -|\Gamma|/n \geq -1,$$

since $|\Gamma| \leq n$. Since the costs are integer, if $c(\Gamma) > -1$, then $c(\Gamma) \geq 0$. Thus in this case there are no negative-cost cycles in A_f, and by Theorem 5.3 f is a minimum-cost circulation. □

Now the basic idea of the analysis is apparent. We start with an arbitrary circulation f which is C-optimal. If we assume that costs are integers, then by Lemma 5.17, when the circulation becomes ϵ-optimal, for $\epsilon < 1/n$, it will be a minimum-cost circulation. What we would now like to do is to show that the value of ϵ for which the current circulation f is ϵ-optimal is decreasing over the course of the algorithm. In order to discuss this, we would like to know the smallest value of ϵ such that f is ϵ-optimal, which gives rise to the following definition.

Definition 5.18: *For a given circulation f, let $\epsilon(f)$ denote the minimum value of ϵ for which f is ϵ-optimal.*

We will show that $\epsilon(f)$ is nonincreasing over the course of the algorithm, and that after some number of iterations it will have decreased by a certain factor. To prove that this decrease occurs, we need to show some relationship between $\epsilon(f)$ and the ratio $\mu(f)$ of a minimum-mean cycle. The following lemma shows that there is a very close relationship indeed between these two quantities.

Lemma 5.19: *If f is not a minimum-cost circulation, then $\epsilon(f) = -\mu(f)$.*

Proof First we show that $\mu(f) \geq -\epsilon(f)$. By the definition of $\epsilon(f)$, there exist potentials p such that $c_p(i, j) \geq -\epsilon(f)$ for all $(i, j) \in A_f$. Then for a minimum-mean cycle Γ in A_f,

$$\mu(f) = \frac{c(\Gamma)}{|\Gamma|} = \frac{c_p(\Gamma)}{|\Gamma|} \geq \frac{-\epsilon(f)|\Gamma|}{|\Gamma|} = -\epsilon(f),$$

as claimed, where the final inequality follows, since $c_p(i, j) \geq -\epsilon(f)$ for each $(i, j) \in \Gamma$.

Now we show that $-\epsilon(f) \geq \mu(f)$. Consider edge costs $\bar{c}(i, j) = c(i, j) - \mu(f)$ for all $(i, j) \in A$. Then for any cycle $\Gamma \subseteq A_f$, we must have that

$$\bar{c}(\Gamma) = c(\Gamma) - |\Gamma|\mu(f) \geq c(\Gamma) - |\Gamma|\frac{c(\Gamma)}{|\Gamma|} = 0,$$

since $\mu(f) \leq c(\Gamma)/|\Gamma|$ for all cycles Γ. Now we add a source node s to the residual graph G_f and arcs (s, j) of cost 0 and positive residual capacity for all $j \in V$ (as in Figure 5.2). Let $p(i)$ be the length of the shortest s-i path using arcs of positive residual capacity and using costs $\bar{c}(i, j)$ as the length of arc (i, j). We showed above that for the costs $\bar{c}$ there are no negative-cost cycles in G_f, and thus by Theorem 1.4, we can find the shortest s-i paths. Furthermore, it must be the case that $p(j) \leq p(i) + \bar{c}(i, j) = p(i) + c(i, j) - \mu(f)$. Thus we have potentials p such that $c(i, j) + p(i) - p(j) \geq \mu(f)$, and f is $-\mu(f)$-optimal. Hence $\epsilon(f) \leq -\mu(f)$, or $-\epsilon(f) \geq \mu(f)$.

Since it is also true that $\mu(f) \geq -\epsilon(f)$, then $\mu(f) = -\epsilon(f)$. □

The following corollary will be useful in a later section.

Corollary 5.20: *We can compute $\epsilon(f)$ and potentials p such that f is $\epsilon(f)$-optimal with respect to p in $O(mn)$ time.*

Proof The proof of the lemma shows how to compute the potentials using Theorem 1.4 and the value of $\mu(f)$; we can compute both in $O(mn)$ time. □

Suppose the algorithm has a circulation f at some iteration. We let $f^{(k)}$ be the resulting circulation after k iterations of the main loop. We will show that after m iterations, $\epsilon(f)$ has gone down by at least a factor of $1 - \frac{1}{n}$.

Lemma 5.21: $\epsilon(f^{(m)}) \leq \left(1 - \frac{1}{n}\right)\epsilon(f)$.

From this lemma we are able to deduce the following.

Theorem 5.22: *If costs c are integral, then the minimum-mean cycle canceling algorithm in Algorithm 5.4 takes $O(mn \ln(nC))$ iterations.*

Proof As we noted previously, any feasible circulation f is C-optimal, so that $\epsilon(f) \leq C$. After $k = mn \ln(nC)$ iterations, by Lemma 5.21, we have that

$$\epsilon(f^{(k)}) \leq \left(1 - \frac{1}{n}\right)^{n \ln(nC)} \epsilon(f) < e^{-\ln(nC)}\epsilon(f) \leq \frac{1}{nC} \cdot C = \frac{1}{n},$$

where we use $1 - x < e^{-x}$ for $x \neq 0$. Then by Lemma 5.17, the circulation $f^{(k)}$ must be optimal. □

We showed in Exercise 1.4 that we can find a minimum-mean cycle in $O(mn)$ time, so we have the following.

Theorem 5.23: *If costs c are integral, then the minimum-mean cycle canceling algorithm in Algorithm 5.4 takes $O(m^2 n^2 \ln(nC))$ time.*

Before we prove Lemma 5.21, we start by showing that $\epsilon(f)$ is nonincreasing.

Lemma 5.24: $\epsilon(f^{(1)}) \leq \epsilon(f)$.

Proof Let f be the circulation of the current iteration, Γ the minimum-mean cycle canceled in this iteration, and $f^{(1)}$ the resulting circulation. We know that there exist potentials p such that $c_p(i, j) \geq -\epsilon(f)$ for all arcs $(i, j) \in A_f$. Since Γ is the minimum-mean cycle of this iteration,

$$\mu(f) = \frac{c_p(\Gamma)}{|\Gamma|} \geq \frac{-\epsilon(f)|\Gamma|}{|\Gamma|} = -\epsilon(f).$$

However, by Lemma 5.19, $\mu(f) = -\epsilon(f)$, so it must be the case that $c_p(i, j) = -\epsilon(f)$ for all $(i, j) \in \Gamma$. We now claim that $c_p(i, j) \geq -\epsilon(f)$ for any arc (i, j) with $u_{f^{(1)}}(i, j) > 0$; that is, if (i, j) has positive residual capacity in the next iteration. The arc (i, j) has positive residual capacity in the next iteration if it has positive residual capacity in this iteration (that is, $u_f(i, j) > 0$) or if canceling Γ pushed flow on (j, i), so that $(j, i) \in \Gamma$. In the first case, we have $c_p(i, j) \geq -\epsilon(f)$, and in the second case, if $(j, i) \in \Gamma$, then $c_p(i, j) = -c_p(j, i) = \epsilon(f) \geq 0 \geq -\epsilon(f)$. Thus there exist potentials p such that $c_p(i, j) \geq -\epsilon(f)$ for any arc $(i, j) \in A_{f^{(1)}}$, which implies that $\epsilon(f^{(1)})$ cannot be larger than $\epsilon(f)$. $\qquad\square$

We can now prove Lemma 5.21.

Proof of Lemma 5.21 Let $\epsilon = \epsilon(f)$, and let p be the potentials p such that $c_p(i, j) \geq -\epsilon$ for all $(i, j) \in A_f$. We will consider a sequence of $k \leq m$ cycle cancellations. Let N_k denote the set of arcs that have positive residual capacity and negative reduced cost with respect to p after the kth cancellation.

We observe that in any iteration in which we cancel a cycle Γ such that all of its arcs are in N_k (that is, $\Gamma \subseteq N_k$), the size of N_k can only get smaller: if there is a new arc (i, j) in the residual graph after the kth cancellation because we pushed flow on (j, i) in canceling the kth cycle, it must have reduced cost $c_p(i, j) = -c_p(j, i) > 0$, since $(j, i) \in N_k$. Furthermore, because canceling Γ saturates some arc in Γ, it must be the case that $N_{k+1} \subset N_k$. Finally if each $(i, j) \in N_k$ has $c_p(i, j) \geq -\epsilon$, then since $N_{k+1} \subset N_k$, any $(i, j) \in N_{k+1}$ also has $c_p(i, j) \geq -\epsilon$.

We now consider two cases. First, suppose that each cycle Γ that we cancel has all negative reduced cost arcs with respect to the potentials p, so that $\Gamma \subset N_k$ for $0 \leq k \leq m$. Then by the argument above, $N_m \subset N_{m-1} \subset \cdots \subset N_0 \subseteq A$, so it must be the case that $N_m = \emptyset$. Hence if $f^{(m)}$ is the resulting circulation after the m cancellations, then for potentials p, we have that $c_p(i, j) \geq 0$ for all $(i, j) \in A_{f^{(m)}}$, and by Theorem 5.3, the circulation $f^{(m)}$ is optimal. In that case $\epsilon(f^{(m)}) = 0$, and the lemma follows.

Second, suppose that for $k - 1$ iterations each cycle Γ that we cancel has all negative reduced cost arcs with respect to the potentials p, but in the kth iteration, for $k < m$, it does not. Let Γ be the cycle canceled in the kth iteration. By the reasoning above, since initially for all $(i, j) \in N_0$, $c_p(i, j) \geq -\epsilon$, then for all $(i, j) \in N_k$, $c_p(i, j) \geq -\epsilon$. By hypothesis there exists some arc $(i, j) \in \Gamma$ such that $c_p(i, j) \geq 0$. Then

$$-\epsilon(f^{(m)}) \geq -\epsilon(f^{(k)}) = \mu(f^{(k)}) = \frac{c_p(\Gamma)}{|\Gamma|}$$
$$\geq \frac{|\Gamma| - 1}{|\Gamma|}(-\epsilon)$$
$$\geq \left(1 - \frac{1}{n}\right)(-\epsilon),$$

where the first inequality follows since $\epsilon(f^{(k)})$ is nonincreasing, the second inequality since at least one of the $|\Gamma|$ arcs has nonnegative reduced cost, and the remainder all have reduced cost at least $-\epsilon$, while the last inequality follows since $|\Gamma| \leq n$. Thus $\epsilon(f^{(m)}) \leq (1 - \frac{1}{n})\epsilon = (1 - \frac{1}{n})\epsilon(f)$. $\qquad\square$

To conclude this section, we present an alternate analysis of the minimum-mean cycle canceling algorithm, and show that the algorithm runs in strongly polynomial time. The basic idea of this analysis is to show that as we run the algorithm, the flow on certain arcs becomes *fixed*; that is, the amount of flow on the arc does not change in future iterations of the algorithm. In particular, we show that every $O(mn \ln n)$ iterations, a new arc becomes fixed. Since there are at most m arcs, this implies a running time of $O(m^2 n \ln n)$ iterations, or $O(m^3 n^2 \ln n)$ time overall. We now define what we mean by an arc becoming fixed.

Definition 5.25: *An arc $(i, j) \in A$ is ϵ-fixed if the flow $f(i, j)$ is the same for all ϵ-optimal circulations f.*

Before we show how we can determine when an arc is fixed, we will need the following lemma giving a basic property of circulations; namely that the flow out of any nontrivial cut must be 0 by skew symmetry and flow conservation.

Lemma 5.26: *Let f be any circulation. For any $S \subset V$, $S \neq \emptyset$,* $\sum_{(k,l) \in \delta^+(S)} f(k,l) = 0$.

Proof By flow conservation (5.4), we know for any $i \in V$ that $\sum_{k:(i,k) \in A} f(i,k) = 0$. Then

$$0 = \sum_{i \in S} \sum_{k:(i,k) \in A} f(i,k)$$

$$= \sum_{i \in S} \left(\sum_{k \notin S:(i,k) \in A} f(i,k) + \sum_{k \in S:(i,k) \in A} f(i,k) \right)$$

$$= 0 + \sum_{i \in S} \sum_{k \notin S:(i,k) \in A} f(i,k) = \sum_{(i,k) \in \delta^+(S)} f(i,k),$$

since by skew symmetry, the flow $f(i,k)$ on each arc (i,k) for $i,k \in S$ is canceled by the flow $f(k,i) = -f(i,k)$. $\qquad\qquad\qquad\qquad\qquad \square$

Now we can prove the main lemma showing that an arc must be ϵ-fixed if its reduced cost is very negative. We will show momentarily that such arcs must exist as the algorithm progresses. The main idea of the proof of the lemma is that if the reduced cost is very negative, then the arc must be saturated. If there is some other ϵ-optimal circulation f' using the arc such that it is not saturated, then there is a cycle in the residual graph of f' that includes the arc, and has a minimum-mean cost strictly less than $-\epsilon$. By Lemma 5.19, this contradicts the ϵ-optimality of f'.

Lemma 5.27: *Let $\epsilon > 0$, let f be a circulation, and let p be potentials such that f is ϵ-optimal with respect to the potentials p. If $c_p(i,j) \leq -2n\epsilon$, then (i,j) is ϵ-fixed.*

Proof We give a proof by contradiction. Suppose that arc (i,j) is not ϵ-fixed. Then there must exist another circulation f' that is ϵ-optimal such that $f'(i,j) \neq f(i,j)$. In fact, it must be the case that $f'(i,j) < f(i,j)$: Since f is ϵ-optimal with respect to p, it must be that $c_p(k,l) \geq -\epsilon$ for all $(k,l) \in A_f$. Thus since $c_p(i,j) < -2n\epsilon$, $(i,j) \notin A_f$, which implies that $u_f(i,j) = 0$ and $f(i,j) = u(i,j)$. Hence $f'(i,j) < f(i,j) = u(i,j)$.

Let $A_< = \{(k,l) \in A : f'(k,l) < f(k,l)\}$. Note that $(i,j) \in A_<$. We now wish to show that there is a cycle in $\Gamma \subseteq A_<$ such that $(i,j) \in \Gamma$. Let S be the set of all vertices reachable from j using arcs in $A_<$; we want to show that $i \in S$, since this together with $(i,j) \in A_<$ will imply the existence of a cycle $\Gamma \subseteq A_<$. Suppose not. Then by Lemma 5.26, we know that both $\sum_{(k,l) \in \delta^+(S)} f(k,l) = 0$ and $\sum_{(k,l) \in \delta^+(S)} f'(k,l) = 0$ so that

$\sum_{(k,l)\in\delta^+(S)}(f(k,l) - f'(k,l)) = 0$. Since we know that $f'(i,j) < f(i,j)$, then by skew symmetry $f'(j,i) > f(j,i)$, and since $(j,i) \in \delta^+(S)$, there must exist some arc $(k,l) \in \delta^+(S)$ such that $f'(k,l) < f(k,l)$ in order for the sum to be zero. But if $k \in S$ and $l \notin S$ and $f'(k,l) < f(k,l)$, then $(k,l) \in A_<$ and l should also be in S. Thus we have reached a contradiction, so $i \in S$, and the desired cycle Γ must exist.

Note that for any arc $(k,l) \in \Gamma$, $f'(k,l) < f(k,l) \leq u(k,l)$, so that $\Gamma \subseteq A_{f'}$. Also, for arc (l,k), $f(l,k) < f'(l,k) \leq u(l,k)$. Thus $(l,k) \in A_f$, and since f is ϵ-optimal, $c_p(l,k) \geq -\epsilon$, and thus $c_p(k,l) \leq \epsilon$. Now consider the cycle $\Gamma \subseteq A_{f'}$: we have that

$$
\begin{aligned}
\frac{c(\Gamma)}{|\Gamma|} = \frac{c_p(\Gamma)}{|\Gamma|} &= \frac{1}{|\Gamma|}\left(c_p(i,j) + \sum_{(k,l)\in\Gamma,\,(k,l)\neq(i,j)} c_p(k,l)\right) \\
&\leq \frac{1}{|\Gamma|}(-2n\epsilon + (|\Gamma| - 1)\epsilon) \\
&< \frac{1}{|\Gamma|}(-|\Gamma|\epsilon) \\
&= -\epsilon.
\end{aligned}
$$

Thus cycle Γ has mean cost less than $-\epsilon$, and $\mu(f') < -\epsilon$. But by Lemma 5.19, $\epsilon(f') = -\mu(f') > \epsilon$, and f' is not ϵ-optimal, which is a contradiction of our assumption that f' is an ϵ-optimal circulation. $\qquad\square$

Now we wish to show that once $\epsilon(f)$ has been reduced by a large enough factor, there must be some new arc with sufficiently negative reduced cost, so that it must be fixed.

Lemma 5.28: *Let f and f' be circulations such that $\epsilon(f') \leq \epsilon(f)/2n$, and such that f is not a minimum-cost circulation. Then there are strictly more $\epsilon(f')$-fixed arcs than $\epsilon(f)$-fixed arcs.*

Proof Since $\epsilon(f') < \epsilon(f)$, any $\epsilon(f)$-fixed arc is also $\epsilon(f')$-fixed. Thus we simply need to prove that there is some $\epsilon(f')$-fixed arc that is not $\epsilon(f)$-fixed. Let p be the potentials such that f is $\epsilon(f)$-optimal with respect to p. Since f is not a minimum-cost circulation, there is a negative-cost cycle in A_f; let Γ be the minimum-mean cycle in A_f. Then, as in the proof of Lemma 5.24, we have that

$$
-\epsilon(f) = \mu(f) = \frac{c_p(\Gamma)}{|\Gamma|} \geq \frac{-\epsilon(f)|\Gamma|}{|\Gamma|} = -\epsilon(f),
$$

so it must be the case that $c_p(i, j) = -\epsilon(f)$ for all $(i, j) \in \Gamma$. Note that none of the arcs in Γ are $\epsilon(f)$-fixed, since canceling Γ changes the flow on the arcs in f and the resulting flow is still $\epsilon(f)$-optimal by Lemma 5.24.

Now let f' be $\epsilon(f')$-optimal with respect to potentials p', and consider the same cycle Γ as above. Then

$$\frac{c_{p'}(\Gamma)}{|\Gamma|} = -\epsilon(f) \leq -2n\epsilon(f').$$

Since the average reduced cost of an arc is at most $-2n\epsilon(f')$, there must be some arc $(i, j) \in \Gamma$ such that $c_{p'}(i, j) \leq -2n\epsilon(f')$. Thus by Lemma 5.27, the arc (i, j) is $\epsilon(f')$-fixed, and we argued above that it was not $\epsilon(f)$-fixed. $\square$

Finally, we can prove what we claimed originally, and show that Algorithm 5.4 runs in strongly polynomial time.

Theorem 5.29: *Algorithm 5.4 takes $O(m^2 n \ln n)$ iterations and thus runs in $O(m^3 n^2 \ln n)$ time.*

Proof We claim a new arc is fixed after each additional $k = mn \ln(2n)$ iterations; this will give the claimed bound on the number of iterations. Pick an iteration, and let f be the current circulation. Then if $f^{(k)}$ is the circulation after k iterations, by Lemma 5.21,

$$\epsilon(f^{(k)}) \leq \left(1 - \frac{1}{n}\right)^{n \ln(2n)} \epsilon(f) < e^{-\ln(2n)} \epsilon(f) = \epsilon(f)/2n,$$

using $1 - x \leq e^{-x}$. By Lemma 5.28, an additional arc is fixed. Since there are m arcs altogether, after $O(m^2 n \ln n)$ iterations, all arcs are fixed, and we have found a minimum-cost circulation. $\square$

In Exercise 5.9, the reader will show that it is possible to derive a slightly faster implementation of minimum-mean cycle canceling.

5.4 A Capacity Scaling Algorithm

For our next algorithm for the minimum-cost circulation problem, we do not use a cycle-canceling algorithm as in Algorithm 5.1; we instead give an algorithm that uses an infeasible circulation called a *pseudoflow*. We again use the result from Theorem 5.3 that a circulation f is of minimum cost if and only if there are potentials p such that $c_p(i, j) \geq 0$ for all $(i, j) \in A_f$. The basic idea of the algorithm in this section is to maintain that $c_p(i, j) \geq 0$ for a subset of arcs A_f, and gradually convert the pseudoflow f to a circulation as we gradually expand the set of arcs to A_f. Once f is a circulation and $c_p(i,j) \geq 0$ for all arcs in A_f, we know that f is of minimum cost.

We begin with the definition of a pseudoflow. It is similar to a circulation, except that we do not impose the flow conservation constraints, and unlike the idea of a preflow used in the push-relabel algorithm of Section 2.8, we do not require that the net flow entering a node be nonnegative.

Definition 5.30: *A* pseudoflow $f : A \to \Re$ *is an assignment of reals to the arcs such that:*

- $f(i,j) \leq u(i,j)$ *for all* $(i,j) \in A$;
- $f(i,j) = -f(j,i)$ *for all* $(i,j) \in A$.

The excess *of a pseudoflow* f *at node* $i \in V$ *is the net flow entering* i, *or* $\sum_{k:(k,i)\in A} f(k,i)$, *and we denote it* $e_f(i)$.

Note that unlike the case of a preflow as used in Section 2.8, a pseudoflow can have nodes of positive excess and nodes of negative excess (sometimes called *deficits*). Also note that $\sum_{i\in V} e_f(i) = \sum_{i\in V} \sum_{k:(k,i)\in A} f(k,i) = \sum_{(i,j)\in A} f(i,j) = 0$ by skew symmetry, since the term $f(i,j)$ cancels the term $f(j,i)$.

In order for the algorithm to work, we need to make sure it is possible to push any amount of flow from any given node i to any other given node j. We modify the graph so that it is possible to do this but at infinite cost. We add two extra nodes x and y to the graph, and for each node $i \in V$, we add arcs (i,x) and (y,i) to the graph of cost $c(i,x) = c(y,i) = 0$ and capacity $u(i,x) = u(y,i) = \infty$ and $u(x,i) = u(i,y) = 0$. We also add an arc (x,y) of cost $c(x,y) = \infty$ and capacity $u(x,y) = \infty$, while $u(y,x) = 0$ so that $f(x,y) \geq 0$; see Figure 5.3. If capacities are integer, then by the Integrality Property (Property 5.5), there is a minimum-cost circulation f such that $f(x,y)$ is integer; clearly if $f(x,y) \geq 1$ then $c(f) = \infty$. So if there is any feasible circulation of non-infinite cost in the original graph G, then there is a minimum-cost circulation that does not use the arc (x,y) or any of the other newly introduced arcs.

We can now give the main idea of the algorithm. As discussed above, we maintain a pseudoflow f and potentials p. As in the capacity scaling algorithm in Section 2.6 for the maximum flow problem, we maintain a scaling parameter Δ, which is initially a power of two that is at least as large as the largest capacity U. We try to move flow in chunks of Δ units from any node that has excess at least Δ to nodes that have excess at most $-\Delta$ through arcs that have residual capacity at least Δ. To make this precise, we let $A_f(\Delta)$ be the arcs with residual capacity at least Δ; that is, $A_f(\Delta) = \{(i,j) \in A : u_f(i,j) \geq \Delta\}$.

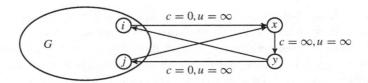

Figure 5.3 Modification of minimum-cost circulation instance for capacity scaling algorithm.

$f \leftarrow 0$

$p \leftarrow 0$

$\Delta \leftarrow 2^{\lceil \log_2 U \rceil}$

while $\Delta \geq 1$ **do**

    foreach $(i, j) \in A_f(\Delta)$ **do**

        if $c_p(i, j) < 0$ **then**

            $f(i, j) \leftarrow u(i, j)$

            $f(j, i) \leftarrow -u(i, j)$

    while $S_f(\Delta) \neq \emptyset$ and $T_f(\Delta) \neq \emptyset$ **do**

    Pick any $s \in S_f(\Delta), t \in S_f(\Delta)$

    Let P be the shortest s-t path using arcs in $A_f(\Delta)$ and costs

        $c_p(i, j)$

    Send Δ units of flow from s to t along P

    $\Delta \leftarrow \Delta / 2$

return f

Algorithm 5.5 A capacity-scaling algorithm for the minimum-cost circulation problem (first version).

We let $S_f(\Delta) = \{i \in V : e_f(i) \geq \Delta\}$ and $T_f(\Delta) = \{i \in V : e_f(i) \leq -\Delta\}$. We will maintain the property that $c_p(i, j) \geq 0$ for all $(i, j) \in A_f(\Delta)$. The algorithm repeatedly tries to move Δ units of flow from a node in $S_f(\Delta)$ to a node in $T_f(\Delta)$ using arcs in $A_f(\Delta)$. Once either $S_f(\Delta) = \emptyset$ or $T_f(\Delta) = \emptyset$, we will show that the total amount of excess in the network is small relative to Δ, and thus prove that the algorithm has made progress. We then divide Δ by two, and start again. In order to maintain the property that $c_p(i, j) \geq 0$ for all $(i, j) \in A_f(\Delta)$, once we divide Δ by two, we saturate all arcs (i, j) with $c_p(i, j) < 0$ that are now in $A_f(\Delta)$. We give a preliminary version of the algorithm in Algorithm 5.5; we will shortly give more details and modify the algorithm somewhat. Note that by our modification to the graph discussed previously, we can always find some path P of arcs in $A_f(\Delta)$ from any node s to any other node t.

While we need to provide some additional details about how we select the path P in each iteration, we can begin to reason about the algorithm as we have given it so far. In particular, we can prove that if we maintain the invariant that $c_p(i, j) \geq 0$ for all $(i, j) \in A_f(\Delta)$, then the pseudoflow f returned by the algorithm is a minimum-cost circulation.

Lemma 5.31: *Suppose that capacities u are integral, and that at the end of each iteration, before dividing Δ by two, $c_p(i, j) \geq 0$ for all $(i, j) \in A_f(\Delta)$. Then when the algorithm terminates, the pseudoflow f returned by the algorithm is a minimum-cost circulation.*

Proof First observe that Δ is initially a power of two, and so that in each iteration of the loop Δ is an integer. We modify the flow values by either saturating arcs, or by sending Δ units of flow along a path. Thus the flow values f are always integer, as are the residual capacities $u_f(i, j)$, since the capacities u are integral.

We now argue that f is a circulation. At the end of the iteration in which $\Delta = 1$, just before the algorithm divides Δ by two, we have that either $S_f(\Delta) = \emptyset$ or $T_f(\Delta) = \emptyset$. Suppose the former is true (the other case is similar). Then $\{i \in V : e_f(i) \geq 1\} = \emptyset$. Since the flow values are integer, it must be the case that for all $i \in V$, $e_f(i) \leq 0$. However, since the sum of the excesses is 0, it must be the case that for each $i \in V$, $e_f(i) = 0$, and thus flow conservation holds at each $i \in V$. Thus since f is a pseudoflow and obeys capacity constraints and skew symmetry, it must be a circulation.

Finally, we argue that f is a minimum-cost circulation. At the end of the iteration in which $\Delta = 1$, just before the algorithm divides Δ by two, we have $c_p(i, j) \geq 0$ for all $(i, j) \in A_f(\Delta)$. But since the residual capacities $u_f(i, j)$ are integer, if $c_p(i, j) \geq 0$ for all (i, j) such that $u_f(i, j) \geq 1$, then $c_p(i, j) \geq 0$ for all (i, j) such that $u_f(i, j) > 0$, or all $(i, j) \in A_f$. Thus by Theorem 5.3, f is a minimum-cost circulation. $\square$

We have so far been a little vague about how we maintain the invariant that $c_p(i, j) \geq 0$ for all $(i, j) \in A_f(\Delta)$ during the course of an iteration. Since at the beginning of an iteration we saturate all arcs $(i, j) \in A_f(\Delta)$ with $c_p(i, j) < 0$, clearly the invariant holds at the beginning of the iteration. In each iteration, we push Δ units of flow on a shortest s-t path P whose arcs are a subset of $A_f(\Delta)$; if the invariant holds, then all arcs in $A_f(\Delta)$ have nonnegative reduced costs and thus the shortest paths are well defined. Observe that if we push Δ units of flow on an arc $(i, j) \in A_f(\Delta)$ with $c_p(i, j) > 0$, then after pushing the flow, $u_f(j,i) \geq \Delta$ and thus $(j,i) \in A_f(\Delta)$ but then $c_p(j,i) < 0$. So ideally we would like to push flow on arcs (i,j) such that $c_p(i,j) = 0$, so that after the push, when (j,i) is added to $A_f(\Delta)$, we have $c_p(j,i) = 0$ and the invariant is maintained. We show below that by using the shortest s-t path P as indicated in the algorithm, we can adjust the potentials p so that $c_p(i,j) = 0$ for all $(i,j) \in P$, and thus maintain the invariant.

Lemma 5.32: *Let $s \in S_f(\Delta)$ be the vertex selected in an iteration of the algorithm, and let $\tilde{p}(i)$ be the cost of the shortest s-i path using arcs in $A_f(\Delta)$ and costs $c_p(i,j)$. Then if the algorithm updates the potentials $p(i)$ to be $p(i) + \tilde{p}(i)$ for all $i \in V$ in each iteration, then at the end of each iteration $c_p(i,j) \geq 0$ for all arcs $(i,j) \in A_f(\Delta)$.*

Proof We assume that initially $c_p(i,j) \geq 0$ for all arcs $(i,j) \in A_f(\Delta)$. Since $\tilde{p}(i)$ is the cost of the shortest s-i path using arcs in $A_f(\Delta)$ and costs $c_p(i,j)$, it follows that $\tilde{p}(j) \leq \tilde{p}(i) + c_p(i,j)$ for any $(i,j) \in A_f(\Delta)$. Furthermore, if P is a shortest s-t path, then for any arc $(i,j) \in P$, $\tilde{p}(j) = \tilde{p}(i) + c_p(i,j)$. Thus if we set $p'(i) = p(i) + \tilde{p}(i)$ for all $i \in V$, then for any arc $(i,j) \in A_f(\Delta)$,

$$c_p(i,j) + \tilde{p}(i) - \tilde{p}(j) \geq 0,$$

which implies that

$$c(i,j) + (p(i) + \tilde{p}(i)) - (p(j) + \tilde{p}(j)) \geq 0,$$

which implies that $c_{p'}(i,j) \geq 0$. Similarly, since for any arc $(i,j) \in P$, $c_p(i,j) + \tilde{p}(i) + \tilde{p}(j) = 0$, we derive that $c_{p'}(i,j) = 0$.

When we push Δ units of flow from s to t along the path P, for any arc $(i,j) \in P$, (j,i) will have residual capacity at least Δ after the push. But then $c_{p'}(j,i) = 0$. Thus after the push, for all arcs $(i,j) \in A_f(\Delta)$, it is the case that $c_{p'}(i,j) \geq 0$ and the invariant continues to hold.   □

We give the updated version of the algorithm in Algorithm 5.6.

We now show that we can bound the number of iterations taken by the algorithm. Since initially $\Delta \leq 2U$, and we divide Δ by two each time through the main while loop until $\Delta < 1$, there are at most $O(\log_2 U)$ iterations of the main while loop. We now need to bound the number of iterations of the inner while loop for each value of Δ. To do this, we bound the amount of excess present when we start executing the inner while loop. Let e_+ be the sum of the positive excesses, and e_- the absolute value of the sum of the negative excesses, so that $e_+ = \sum_{i \in V : e_f(i) > 0} e_f(i)$ and $e_- = -\sum_{i \in V : e_f(i) < 0} e_f(i)$. Since we know that $\sum_{i \in V} e_f(i) = 0$, it is the case that $e_+ = e_-$. We can now bound e_+ as follows.

$f \leftarrow 0$
$p \leftarrow 0$
$\Delta \leftarrow 2^{\lceil \log_2 U \rceil}$
while $\Delta \geq 1$ **do**
    foreach $(i, j) \in A_f(\Delta)$ **do**
        if $c_p(i, j) < 0$ **then**
            $f(i, j) \leftarrow u(i, j)$
            $f(j, i) \leftarrow -u(i, j)$
    while $S_f(\Delta) \neq \emptyset$ and $T_f(\Delta) \neq \emptyset$ **do**
        Pick any $s \in S_f(\Delta), t \in S_f(\Delta)$
        Let $\tilde{p}(i)$ be the length of the shortest s-i path using arcs in $A_f(\Delta)$
          and costs $c_p(i, j)$
        Let P be the shortest s-t path
        foreach $i \in V$ **do** $p(i) \leftarrow p(i) + \tilde{p}(i)$
        Send Δ units of flow from s to t along P
    $\Delta \leftarrow \Delta / 2$
return f

Algorithm 5.6 A capacity-scaling algorithm for the minimum-cost circulation problem (final version).

Lemma 5.33: *At the start of the inner while loop, $e_+ \leq 2\Delta(n + m)$.*

Proof At the start of the algorithm, $\Delta \geq U$. Prior to the start of the inner while loop, the algorithm saturates any arc (i, j) with $c_p(i, j) < 0$, which might create total positive excess of at most mU. Thus the first time the algorithm reaches the start of the inner while loop, $e_+ \leq mU \leq 2\Delta(n + m)$.

Now, at the completion of the inner while loop, prior to dividing Δ by two, $c_p(i, j) \geq 0$ for all $(i, j) \in A_f(\Delta)$ (by Lemma 5.32) and either $S_f(\Delta) = \emptyset$ or $T_f(\Delta) = \emptyset$. In the former case, $e_+ \leq n\Delta$ and in the latter case $e_- \leq n\Delta$. However, since $e_+ = e_-$, in either case $e_+ \leq n\Delta$. After dividing Δ by two, $e_+ \leq 2n\Delta$. Then prior to the next start of the inner while loop, we saturate all arcs $(i, j) \in A_f(\Delta)$ with $c_p(i, j) < 0$. Notice that we will only need to saturate an arc (i, j) if $\Delta \leq u_f(i, j) < 2\Delta$: At the completion of the inner while loop, prior to dividing Δ by two, we had that $c_p(i, j) \geq 0$ for all $(i, j) \in A_f(\Delta)$, so after dividing Δ by two, $c_p(i, j) \geq 0$ for all $(i, j) \in A_f(2\Delta)$. Since we only saturate arcs (i, j) with $u_f(i, j) < 2\Delta$, the total increase in positive excess due to saturating these arcs is at most $2m\Delta$. Hence at the start of the inner while loop, we have that $e_+ \leq 2\Delta(n + m)$. $\quad\square$

We can finally bound the overall running time of the algorithm. The running time is dominated by the shortest path computations in each iteration of the inner while loop. Since the costs on the arcs in each shortest path computation are nonnegative, we can use the $O(m + n \log n)$ time implementation of Dijkstra's algorithm mentioned at the end of Section 1.1.

Theorem 5.34: *The algorithm requires $O(m \log U)$ shortest path computations, and takes $O((m \log U)(m + n \log n))$ time.*

Proof We observed previously that there are $O(\log U)$ iterations of the main while loop. For each iteration of the main while loop, we can have at most $2(n + m)$ iterations of the inner while loop: at the start of the inner while loop, $e_+ \leq 2\Delta(n + m)$, and each iteration of the inner while loop reduces the amount of positive excess by Δ. Thus there are $O(m)$ iterations of the inner while loop per iteration of the main while loop, giving $O(m \log U)$ iterations overall. $\square$

In Exercise 5.8, we give another cycle-canceling algorithm that uses some of the capacity scaling ideas of the algorithm of this section.

5.5 Successive Approximation

In the algorithm in this section, we once again use the ideas of pseudoflows, as we did with the capacity scaling algorithm in Section 5.4. In that algorithm, we used pseudoflows to move flow excesses around in large chunks, which gradually became smaller over the course of the algorithm. Here we will reuse some of the analysis from the minimum-mean cycle canceling algorithm; we initially start with a C-optimal circulation, and we gradually transform it into an ϵ-optimal circulation for $\epsilon < 1/n$. Then if costs are integer, Lemma 5.17 tells us that the resulting circulation is of minimum cost. In fact, we explicitly make this idea the framework of the algorithm, and we will worry later about how to fill in the details. We start with any feasible circulation f, the potentials $p = 0$, and $\epsilon = C$, so that the circulation is ϵ-optimal with respect to the potentials p. In each iteration, we will divide ϵ by two, and find a new circulation f and potentials p such that f is ϵ-optimal. Once $\epsilon < 1/n$, we are done. We give this framework in Algorithm 5.7, and the theorem below follows immediately.

Theorem 5.35: *Algorithm 5.7 takes $O(\log(nC))$ iterations to compute a minimum-cost circulation.*

Let f be any feasible circulation
$p \leftarrow 0$
$\epsilon \leftarrow C$
while $\epsilon \geq 1/n$ **do**
$\quad \epsilon \leftarrow \epsilon/2$
$\quad f, p \leftarrow \text{Find}\epsilon\text{OptCirc}(f, \epsilon, p)$
return f

Algorithm 5.7 Polynomial-time successive approximation framework for minimum-cost circulation algorithm.

We invoke a subroutine FindϵOptCirc that will take as input a circulation f, potentials p, and an ϵ such that f is 2ϵ-optimal with respect to p, and return a new circulation f' and potentials p' such that f' is ϵ-optimal with respect to p'. In order to implement the subroutine FindϵOptCirc we will reuse many ideas from the push-relabel algorithm for the maximum flow problem that we studied in Section 2.8.

We can also use ideas of Section 5.3 to give a strongly polynomial-time variant of the algorithm, assuming that we have a strongly polynomial-time subroutine. We give the strongly polynomial-time variant in Algorithm 5.8. In this variant, we use Corollary 5.20 to compute the potentials p such that f is $\epsilon(f)$-optimal in each iteration; if $\epsilon(f) = 0$ (that is, if f is 0-optimal), then we know that f is a minimum-cost circulation and the algorithm terminates. Otherwise we set ϵ to $\epsilon(f)/2$, and invoke the subroutine to find a new circulation that is $\epsilon(f)/2$-optimal.

Lemma 5.36: *Algorithm 5.8 takes* $O(m \log n)$ *iterations to compute a minimum-cost circulation.*

Proof Pick a given iteration with circulation f. After $\log_2(2n)$ iterations, the algorithm will have computed a new circulation f' such that $\epsilon(f') \leq \epsilon(f)/2n$. Thus by Lemma 5.28, an additional arc is fixed. Thus after $m \log_2(2n)$ iterations, all arcs will be fixed, and the algorithm must terminate. $\square$

Corollary 5.37: *Algorithm 5.8 takes* $O(\min(\log(nC), m \log n))$ *iterations to compute a minimum-cost circulation.*

We now need to give the required subroutine that takes as input ϵ, a circulation f, and potentials p such that f is 2ϵ-optimal with respect to p, and gives as output a circulation f' and potentials p' such that f' is ϵ-optimal with respect to p'. To do this, we create from the 2ϵ-optimal circulation an

---

Let f be any feasible circulation
while $\epsilon > 0$ **do**
    Compute $\epsilon(f)$, potentials p such that f is $\epsilon(f)$-optimal
    if $\epsilon(f) > 0$ **then**
        $\epsilon \leftarrow \epsilon(f)/2$
        $f, p \leftarrow$ FindεOptCirc (f, ϵ, p)
    else
        return f
  return f

Algorithm 5.8 Strongly polynomial-time successive approximation framework for minimum-cost circulation algorithm.

ϵ-optimal pseudoflow: as stated in Section 5.4, a pseudoflow is a flow that obeys the capacity constraints and the skew symmetry constraints, but not the flow conservation constraints. We then convert the ϵ-optimal pseudoflow to an ϵ-optimal circulation by gradually enforcing the flow conservation constraints. We can do this conversion in many ways; here we show how to do it by a push-relabel style subroutine. Recall that the excess of a pseudoflow f at node $i \in V$ is the net flow entering i, or $\sum_{k:(k,i) \in A} f(k,i)$, and we denote it $e_f(i)$. Recall also that it is possible for i to have a deficit, corresponding to $e_f(i) < 0$.

We can easily convert the 2ϵ-optimal circulation f to an ϵ-optimal pseudoflow by saturating every arc $(i,j) \in A_f$ with $-2\epsilon \leq c_p(i,j) < -\epsilon$. Then we have a pseudoflow f, and $c_p(i,j) \geq -\epsilon$ for all $(i,j) \in A_f$. However, we will do something stronger by initially saturating every arc of negative reduced cost.

Now we would like to convert the ϵ-optimal pseudoflow to an ϵ-optimal circulation by moving the flow from nodes with excess to nodes with deficit in such a way that ϵ-optimality is maintained. As mentioned above, we will use ideas from the push-relabel algorithm to do this. In order to maintain the capacity constraints and ϵ-optimality, we will only push on arcs (i,j) with positive residual capacity ($u_f(i,j) > 0$) and negative reduced cost ($c_p(i,j) < 0$), so that if the push on (i,j) causes (j,i) to have positive residual capacity, then we know that the reduced cost of (j,i) is positive (since $c_p(j,i) = -c_p(i,j) > 0$). Any arc (i,j) with $u_f(i,j) > 0$ and $c_p(i,j) < 0$ we will call *admissible*. We say that node i is *active* if $e_f(i) > 0$. Thus if we have an active node i and there is an admissible arc (i,j), we can push $\delta = \min(e_f(i), u_f(i,j))$ units of flow from i to j. We need to relabel if we have a node i with $e_f(i) > 0$ and for all arcs (i,j) with positive residual capacity $u_f(i,j) > 0$ it is the case that $c_p(i,j) \geq 0$. In this case, we relabel by changing

$$\delta \leftarrow \min(e_f(i), u_f(i,j))$$
$$f(i,j) \leftarrow f(i,j) + \delta$$
$$f(j,i) \leftarrow f(j,i) - \delta$$

Procedure Push(i, j)

$$p(i) \leftarrow \max_{(i,j) \in A_f}(p(j) - c(i,j) - \epsilon)$$

Procedure Relabel(i)

for $(i,j) \in A_f$ such that $c_p(i,j) < 0$ **do**
    $f(i,j) \leftarrow u(i,j); f(j,i) \leftarrow -u(i,j)$
while there is an active i ($e_f(i) > 0$ for $i \in V$) **do**
    if there is j such that (i,j) is admissible ($u_f(i,j) > 0$ and
    $c_p(i,j) < 0$) **then**
        Push$((i,j))$
    else
        Relabel(i)
return f, p

Algorithm 5.9 An implementation of FindϵOptCirc(f, ϵ, p) via a push-relabel-style algorithm.

the potential $p(i)$. We want to relabel so that ϵ-optimality is maintained, and so that at least one arc (i,j) of positive residual capacity has negative reduced cost. To do this we set $p(i)$ to be the maximum of $p(j) - c(i,j) - \epsilon$ over all arcs $(i,j) \in A_f$. Then for any arc $(i,j) \in A_f, c_p(i,j) = c(i,j) + p(i) - p(j) \geq -\epsilon$ and for the arc (i,j) achieving the maximum, $c_p(i,j) = -\epsilon$. Since prior to the relabel all arcs $(i,j) \in A_f$ had $c_p(i,j) \geq 0$, we must have decreased $p(i)$ by at least ϵ. Also notice that since any arc $(k,i) \in A_f$ entering i had $c_p(k,i) \geq -\epsilon$, after we relabeling i, it must be that $c_p(k,i) \geq 0$; that is, there are no longer any admissible arcs entering i. We summarize the subroutine in Algorithm 5.9.

To begin our analysis of Algorithm 5.9, we show a lemma that is an analog of Lemma 2.40 for the push-relabel algorithm: there is a path from any node in the pseudoflow f that has excess to another that has deficit, and this path has particular properties that will let us later show that it is short with respect to the potentials. For our proofs, we will frequently be invoking the fact that the subroutine has at its start an initial 2ϵ-optimal circulation; we will call this circulation f'.

Lemma 5.38: *Let f be a pseudoflow, and let f' be a circulation. For any node i such that $e_f(i) > 0$, there exists a path $P \subseteq A_f$ to a node j such that $e_f(j) < 0$. Furthermore, for each arc $(k,l) \in P$, $(l,k) \in A_{f'}$.*

Proof We claim that we can find the desired path P in the set of arcs $A_< = \{(k,l) \in A : f(k,l) < f'(k,l)\}$; observe that for any arc $(k,l) \in A_<$, $f(k,l) < f'(k,l) \leq u(k,l)$ implies that $(k,l) \in A_f$. Thus if $P \subseteq A_<$, then $P \subseteq A_f$. Furthermore, if $(k,l) \in P$, then $f(k,l) < f'(k,l)$ implies that $f'(l,k) < f(l,k) \leq u(l,k)$ (by skew symmetry), and so $(l,k) \in A_{f'}$.

Pick a node i such that $e_f(i) > 0$, and let S be the set of all vertices reachable from i via arcs in $A_<$. Then

$$
-\sum_{k \in S} e_f(k) = -\sum_{k \in S} \sum_{l:(l,k) \in A} f(l,k) = \sum_{k \in S} \sum_{l:(k,l) \in A} f(k,l)
$$

$$
= \sum_{k \in S} \left(\sum_{l \in S:(k,l) \in A} f(k,l) + \sum_{l \notin S:(k,l) \in A} f(k,l) \right)
$$

$$
= 0 + \sum_{k \in S} \sum_{l \notin S:(k,l) \in A} f(k,l)
$$

$$
= \sum_{(k,l) \in \delta^+(S)} f(k,l),
$$

where the second-to-last equality follows by skew symmetry; for $k,l \in S$, $f(k,l)$ is canceled by $f(l,k)$. For any $(k,l) \in \delta^+(S)$ it must be the case that $f(k,l) \geq f'(k,l)$, since otherwise $(k,l) \in A_<$, l would be reachable from i via arcs in $A_<$, and then $l \in S$, a contradiction. Hence we have that

$$
-\sum_{k \in S} e_f(k) = \sum_{(k,l) \in \delta^+(S)} f(k,l) \geq \sum_{(k,l) \in \delta^+(S)} f'(k,l).
$$

Since f' is a circulation, we know by Lemma 5.26 that $\sum_{(k,l) \in \delta^+(S)} f'(k,l) = 0$, so we have that $-\sum_{k \in S} e_f(k) \geq 0$, or $\sum_{k \in S} e_f(k) \leq 0$. We know that $i \in S$, and $e_f(i) > 0$; hence it must be the case that there is some $j \in S$ such that $e_f(j) < 0$. Furthermore, j is reachable from i via arcs of $A_<$, so there is an i-j path P using arcs in $A_<$, and we are done. $\qquad \square$

The following lemma uses the previous one to help us bound the amount by which any potential can change during the course of the algorithm. This will bound the number of relabel operations performed by the algorithm, and, as we saw in the analysis of the push-relabel algorithm, once we have bounded the number of relabel operations, we can then bound the number of push operations.

Lemma 5.39: *For any* $i \in V$, $p(i)$ *decreases by at most* $3n\epsilon$ *during the execution of the subroutine in Algorithm 5.9.*

Proof Let f' and p' be the 2ϵ-optimal circulation and the potentials, respectively, that are the input to the subroutine, such that f' is 2ϵ-optimal with respect to p'. Let f and p be the pseudoflow and the potentials at some point during the execution of the algorithm; recall that we maintain that f is ϵ-optimal with respect to p. If $p(i)$ is relabeled, then i was active and $e_f(i) > 0$. By Lemma 5.38, there is some $j \in V$ such that $e_f(j) < 0$ and some i-j path P such that $P \subseteq A_f$. Let P' be the j-i path that is the reverse of P; by the lemma $P' \subseteq A_{f'}$. Since each arc $(k,l) \in P$ is in A_f, it has reduced cost at least $-\epsilon$ with respect to potentials p. Thus

$$-\epsilon|P| \leq \sum_{(k,l) \in P} c_p(k,l)$$

$$= \sum_{(k,l) \in P} (c(k,l) + p(k) - p(l)) = p(i) - p(j) + \sum_{(k,l) \in P} c(k,l).$$

Since each arc $(l,k) \in P'$ is in $A_{f'}$, it has reduced cost at least -2ϵ with respect to potentials p'. Thus

$$-2\epsilon|P| \leq \sum_{(l,k) \in P'} c_{p'}(l,k)$$

$$= \sum_{(l,k) \in P'} (c(l,k) + p'(l) - p'(k)) = p'(j) - p'(i) + \sum_{(l,k) \in P'} c(l,k).$$

Because P and P' are the reverse of each other and $c(k,l) = -c(l,k)$, then

$$\sum_{(k,l) \in P} c(k,l) + \sum_{(l,k) \in P'} c(l,k) = 0.$$

Thus if we add the two inequalities together, we obtain

$$-3\epsilon|P| \leq p(i) - p'(i) + p'(j) - p(j).$$

Note that during the course of the algorithm, we never create a new node with a deficit, so if $e_f(j) < 0$, then node j has always had a deficit, and thus has never been an active node. In particular, $p'(j) = p(j)$. Then we have that $p'(i) - p(i) \leq 3\epsilon|P| \leq 3n\epsilon$. Since this is true at any point in the execution of the algorithm for which i is an active node and can be relabeled, it is the case that $p(i)$ can decrease by at most $3n\epsilon$ from its initial value of $p'(i)$. $\square$

The following lemma is now an easy consequence of the previous one.

Lemma 5.40: *The number of relabel operations is* $O(n^2)$.

Proof In each relabel operation for $i \in V$, we decrease $p(i)$ by at least ϵ. Since we can decrease $p(i)$ by at most $3n\epsilon$ overall, we perform at most $3n$ relabel operations on i. Since there are n nodes in total, we perform at most $3n^2$ relabel operations.   □

As before, we distinguish between saturating pushes (which push $\delta = u_f(i, j)$ units of flow on (i, j)) and nonsaturating pushes (which push $\delta = e_f(i) < u_f(i, j)$ units of flow on (i, j)). We can bound the number of saturating and nonsaturating pushes in the algorithm with proofs similar to those for the push-relabel algorithm. First, we bound the number of saturating pushes.

Lemma 5.41: *The number of saturating push operations is $O(mn)$.*

Proof Pick any arc (i, j). Initially $c_p(i, j) \geq 0$, and so we need to relabel i before we can perform a saturating push on (i, j). Since $u_f(i, j) = 0$ after a saturating push, to be able to push flow on (i, j) again, we first need to push flow on (j, i), and in order for (j, i) to be admissible, it must be that $c_p(j, i) < 0$. Then $c_p(i, j) = -c_p(j, i) > 0$. Hence in order to push flow on (i, j) after flow is pushed on (j, i), we need to relabel i again. Hence we must relabel i before any saturating push on (i, j), which means we can perform at most $3n$ saturating pushes on (i, j). Thus there are at most $3mn$ saturating push operations.   □

Before we can bound the number of nonsaturating push operations, we need the following lemma.

Lemma 5.42: *The set of admissible arcs is acyclic.*

Proof Initially, there are no admissible arcs, since $c_p(i, j) \geq 0$ for all arcs (i, j). A push operation can remove an admissible arc (by saturating it), but cannot add any arcs to the set of admissible arcs: if we push flow on (i, j), we may make $u_f(j, i) > 0$, but since we only push flow on (i, j) if $c_p(i, j) < 0$, then $c_p(j, i) = -c_p(i, j) > 0$, and (j, i) is not admissible. A relabel operation on node $i \in V$ decreases $p(i)$ by at least ϵ, and causes at least one arc (i, j) to become admissible. Recall that we previously argued that after relabeling i, no arcs entering i are admissible; thus the set of admissible arcs continues to be acyclic.   □

Lemma 5.43: *The number of nonsaturating push operations is $O(mn^2)$.*

Proof We use a potential function argument. Let $\Phi(i)$ be the number of vertices reachable from i via admissible arcs; note that $\Phi(i) \geq 1$, since i can always reach itself. Let $\Phi = \sum_{i \text{ active}} \Phi(i)$. Initially $\Phi \leq n$, since there are no admissible arcs, and Φ is always nonnegative. At the end of the subroutine $\Phi = 0$, since there are no active nodes at termination. Now we consider what makes Φ increase and decrease over the execution of the subroutine. Each nonsaturating push decreases Φ, since a nonsaturating push takes a currently active node i and makes it inactive, thus removing i from the sum. Since a nonsaturating push on an arc (i, j) requires (i, j) to be admissible, note that $\Phi(i) > \Phi(j)$, because i can reach all nodes that j can reach via admissible arcs, but i can also reach itself and j cannot reach i, since by Lemma 5.42 the set of admissible arcs is acyclic. Thus even if the nonsaturating push on i makes j active, the change in Φ is $\Phi(j) - \Phi(i) \leq -1$. The increases in Φ are due to relabel operations and saturating pushes. A saturating push on (i, j) can increase Φ by making j active, and increases Φ by $\Phi(j) \leq n$. A relabel of i can make $\Phi(i)$ increase from 1 to at most n; however, it cannot increase $\Phi(j)$ for any $j \neq i$, since a relabel of i causes all arcs entering i to become inadmissible. Thus the total increase in Φ over the course of the subroutine is $O(n(n^2 + mn)) = O(mn^2)$. Thus the total number of nonsaturating pushes in $O(mn^2)$. $\square$

Putting everything together, we have the following.

Theorem 5.44: *The subroutine in Algorithm 5.9 can be implemented in $O(mn^2)$ time.*

Since the framework in Algorithm 5.7 takes $O(\min(\log(nC), m \log n))$ calls to the subroutine, we have the following theorem.

Theorem 5.45: *Algorithm 5.7 finds a minimum-cost circulation in $O(mn^2 \min (\log(nC), m \log n))$ time.*

As with the push-relabel algorithm for maximum flow, various heuristics can be introduced to help the algorithm run faster in practice. We give two (set relabeling and price refinement) in Exercises 5.10 and 5.11.

In Exercise 5.12, we show it is possible to implement the analogue of the FIFO push-relabel algorithm from Exercise 2.10 in order to implement the subroutine, and that it can be made to run in $O(n^3)$ time. In Exercise 5.13, we show that it is possible to implement the subroutine FindϵOptCirc via a blocking flow computation in $O(mn \log n)$ time. This implementation of the subroutine implies that we can find a circulation in $O(mn \log n \min(\log(nC), m \log n))$ time.

5.6 Network Simplex

In this section, we introduce one last algorithm for computing a minimum-cost circulation. This algorithm is a specialization of the simplex method for linear programming; the minimum-cost circulation problem can be expressed as a linear program. This specialization of the simplex method is usually called the network simplex algorithm. The simplex method has a particularly simple form in the case of the minimum-cost circulation problem, such that we do not need to give the more general algorithm. The network simplex algorithm has very good performance in practice; see the Chapter Notes for a discussion.

The network simplex algorithm maintains a feasible circulation f, an (undirected) spanning tree T, and potentials p such that the following invariants are maintained:

1. If both (i, j) and (j, i) have positive residual capacity, then the undirected edge $\{i, j\}$ is in the tree T.
2. For each tree edge $\{i, j\}$, the reduced costs of (i, j) and (j, i) are zero (that is, $c_p(i, j) = c_p(j, i) = 0$).

For Invariant 1, the converse need not be true; that is, if $\{i, j\}$ is in the tree, then it need not be the case that both (i, j) and (j, i) have positive residual capacity. We will say that an arc (i, j) is a *tree arc* if $\{i, j\}$ is an edge in the tree T. Otherwise (i, j) is a *nontree arc*.

We now show how to start with a feasible circulation f, and from f find a tree T, potentials p, and a corresponding circulation f' with $c(f') \leq c(f)$ such that the invariants are obeyed. We look at the undirected edges in $E = \{\{i, j\} : (i, j), (j, i) \in A_f\}$. If there is an undirected cycle $C \subseteq E$, then observe that we can push flow around either direction of the cycle C; call the two directed cycles Γ' and Γ''. Since for each arc $(i, j) \in \Gamma'$, $(j, i) \in \Gamma''$, and $c(i, j) = -c(j, i)$, it is the case that $c(\Gamma') = -c(\Gamma'')$. Thus one of the two cycles has nonpositive cost; suppose, without loss of generality, that $c(\Gamma') \leq 0$. Then we cancel Γ'; let f' be the resulting circulation. Notice that because an arc of Γ' was saturated, there is some $\{i, j\} \in C$ such that either $(i, j) \notin A_{f'}$ or $(j, i) \notin A_{f'}$. Thus we have at least one fewer edge in E. We continue until we have no cycles in E. If E does not contain a spanning tree, then we add any $\{i, j\}$ to E needed to get a spanning tree. Then we have a circulation f' such that $c(f') \leq c(f)$, and Invariant 1 is obeyed.

Given a tree T, it is particularly easy to compute potentials p such that Invariant 2 is obeyed. We root the tree at an arbitrary node r, and we set $p(r) = 0$. Then suppose that we have computed the potential $p(i)$ for a node i, and j is a child node of i. We set $p(j) = c(i, j) + p(i)$, since then $c_p(i, j) = c(i, j) + p(i) - p(j) = 0$; it follows that $c_p(j, i) = -c_p(i, j) = 0$. We can continue down the tree computing the potentials of the nodes; thus we can compute the potentials in $O(n)$ time.

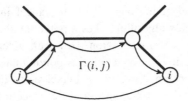

Figure 5.4 A basic cycle $\Gamma(i, j)$. The thick edges belong to the tree T.

Let f be any feasible circulation
Find f, T, p obeying Invariants 1 and 2
while there is a nontree arc $(i, j) \in A_f$ such that $c_p(i, j) < 0$ **do**
 Cancel $\Gamma(i, j)$
 Update f, T, p
return f

Algorithm 5.10 The network simplex algorithm.

The network simplex algorithm is also a negative-cost cycle canceling algorithm, as with Klein's algorithm in Algorithm 5.1. However, it considers a very limited set of cycles defined by the tree T. In particular, each nontree arc $(i, j) \in A_f$ defines a *basic cycle*, which we denote $\Gamma(i, j)$; the cycle consists of the arc (i, j) and the directed j-i path in T (see Figure 5.4). Because the reduced cost of all the arcs in the directed j-i path in T is zero, the cost of the cycle $\Gamma(i, j)$ is negative if and only if $c_p(i, j) < 0$, since $c(\Gamma(i, j)) = c_p(\Gamma(i, j)) = c_p(i, j)$. Now we need to consider what happens to the tree if we cancel a basic cycle $\Gamma(i, j)$. We know that some arc (k, ℓ) in the cycle is saturated (possibly (i, j) itself), and it may now be the case that both (i, j) and (j, i) have positive residual capacity. Thus to maintain Invariant 5.6, we add $\{i, j\}$ to the tree T, and remove $\{k, \ell\}$ so that T remains a tree (if $(k, \ell) = (i, j)$, we do not modify the tree T). We use language from the simplex method, and say that $\{i, j\}$ *enters* the tree T, $\{k, \ell\}$ *leaves* the tree T, and we *pivot on* the arc (i, j). We can now give an overview of the network simplex algorithm in Algorithm 5.10.

It is not hard to see the following.

Theorem 5.46: *At termination, f is a minimum-cost circulation.*

Proof At termination, all tree arcs (i, j) have $c_p(i, j) = 0$, and all nontree arcs $(i, j) \in A_f$ have $c_p(i, j) \geq 0$. Thus by Theorem 5.3, f must be a minimum-cost circulation. $\qquad \square$

It is possible to select the basic cycle to cancel in each iteration such that the network simplex algorithm takes a polynomial number of iterations; see the Chapter Notes for a discussion. However, given our previous cycle canceling algorithms, it is easy to give a polynomial-time version of the network simplex algorithm if we allow ourselves to pivot on nontree arcs (i, j) such that $c_p(i, j) \geq 0$. Suppose a cycle canceling algorithm (such as Wallacher's algorithm in Section 5.2 or the minimum-mean cycle canceling algorithm in Section 5.3) would next cancel cycle Γ. We show that with at most n pivots we can also cancel Γ. Pick some node k that is in Γ, and follow the arcs in the cycle until there is some arc $(i, j) \in \Gamma$ that is a nontree arc. We pivot on (i, j); if we saturate (i, j) or we saturate some tree arc in Γ, we have canceled Γ. Otherwise, we have saturated a tree arc $(k, \ell) \notin \Gamma$, and $\{k, \ell\}$ leaves the tree T and $\{i, j\}$ enters T. We then continue following arcs in Γ from node j until again we reach a nontree arc. Since each pivot either cancels Γ or adds some $\{i, j\}$ from Γ to the tree T, after at most $n - 1$ pivots, the tree T must contain edges corresponding only to arcs in Γ. Then the basic cycle canceled by the next pivot contains only arcs in Γ, and some arc of Γ must be saturated, canceling Γ.

Theorem 5.47: *For any negative-cost cycle canceling algorithm as in Algorithm 5.1 that takes $O(K)$ iterations to find a minimum-cost circulation, the network simplex algorithm takes $O(nK)$ pivots to find a minimum-cost circulation if it is allowed to pivot on nontree arcs (i, j) with $c_p(i, j) \geq 0$.*

5.7 Application: Maximum Flow Over Time

To conclude this chapter, we show how one can use the minimum-cost circulation to solve another flow problem, one that involves a dimension of time. There are many problems that have an extra dimension of time, but we will consider just the simplest one, the *maximum s-t flow problem over time*. We are given the same input as the maximum s-t flow problem, but in addition we are also given a nonnegative integer T, called the time bound, and for each arc we are given integer *transit times* $\tau(i, j) \geq 0$ for all $(i, j) \in A$. The idea is that $\tau(i, j)$ is the amount of time it takes for a unit of flow to traverse the arc (i, j); a unit of flow entering node i at time θ will arrive at j at time $\theta + \tau(i, j)$. The capacity $u(i, j)$ limits the rate of flow entering the arc (i, j); over a unit of time, at most $u(i, j)$ units of flow may enter arc (i, j). The goal of the problem is to find the maximum amount of flow that can be sent from s starting at time 0 to arrive at sink t by time T.

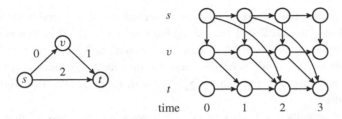

Figure 5.5 The graph on the right is the time-expanded network corresponding to the graph on the left for $T = 3$, where the labels of the arcs represent the transit times.

There is an easy approach to this problem, although it does not yield a polynomial-time algorithm: we create a new network called the *time-expanded network* in which there is a copy of each node for each time step θ. So, for example, for each node i we create $T + 1$ copies, $i(0), i(1), \ldots, i(T)$. Then for each arc (i, j) with transit time $\tau(i, j)$, we create $T + 1 - \tau(i, j)$ copies of the arc, one from $i(\theta)$ to $j(\theta + \tau(i, j))$ for $\theta = 0, \ldots, T - \tau(i, j)$. We also create arcs $i(\theta)$ to $i(\theta + 1)$ for each $\theta = 0, \ldots, T - 1$; these arcs are called *holdover arcs*, and represent the possibility that flow can stay at node i between time periods. We give a small example of a time-expanded network in Figure 5.5. Then we can compute the maximum s-t flow problem over time by computing a maximum $s(0)$-$t(T)$ flow problem in the time-expanded network. This algorithm is not a polynomial-time algorithm, since the size of the network is exponential in the size of the input number T when T is represented in binary.

There is, however, a polynomial-time algorithm for the problem that uses the solution to a minimum-cost circulation problem. We begin as follows. We define the transit time of a path P as $\tau(P) \equiv \sum_{(i,j) \in P} \tau(i, j)$. Suppose there is an s-t path P in the input graph with transit time at most T; that is, $\tau(P) \leq T$. If $\delta = \min_{(i,j) \in P} u(i, j)$, then we can send δ units of flow along path P at each time step θ for $\theta = 0, 1, \ldots, T - \tau(P)$. We call this repeated flow along path P a *temporally repeated flow*. We now give a connection between our usual notion of an s-t flow and the value of a flow over time that we can achieve via temporally repeated flows.

Lemma 5.48: *Given a standard s-t flow f and a decomposition of flow f into flows $f_1, \ldots, f_\ell$ on s-t paths $P_1, \ldots, P_\ell$ (as in Lemma 2.20) such that $\tau(P_k) \leq T$ for $k = 1, \ldots, \ell$, then the value of the flow created by temporally repeating flow along these paths is*

$$(T + 1)|f| - \sum_{(i,j) \in A} \tau(i, j) f(i, j).$$

Proof An intuitive view of the lemma statement is that we send the value $|f|$ of the flow f for all $T + 1$ time units, but subtract all the flow that is still in transit in the graph at time $T + 1$, which amounts to $\sum_{(i,j)\in A} \tau(i,j) f(i,j)$. Alternatively, we don't send flow that would remain in the graph at time $T + 1$, and this also amounts to $\sum_{(i,j)\in A} \tau(i,j) f(i,j)$. We now formalize this intuition.

More formally, for each $k = 1, \ldots, \ell$, we send $|f_k|$ units of flow along path P_k at each time step $t = 0, \ldots, T - \tau(P_k)$. We first should ask if this gives a valid flow over time; that is, is it the case that at any time t, the flow entering arc (i, j) is at most the capacity? We observe that at any time t, the total flow entering (i, j) is at most $\sum_{k:(i,j)\in P_k} f_k(i,j) = f(i,j) \leq u(i,j)$, where the equality holds because f_k is a flow decomposition of f, and the capacity constraint is obeyed because f is an s-t flow.

The total amount of flow sent by temporally repeating paths in this way is

$$\sum_{k=1}^{\ell} |f_k|((T+1) - \tau(P_k)) = \sum_{k=1}^{\ell} |f_k|(T+1) - \sum_{k=1}^{\ell} |f_k|\tau(P_k)$$

$$= |f|(T+1) - \sum_{k=1}^{\ell} |f_k| \sum_{(i,j)\in P_k} \tau(i,j)$$

$$= |f|(T+1) - \sum_{(i,j)\in A} \tau(i,j) \sum_{k:(i,j)\in P_k} f_k(i,j)$$

$$= |f|(T+1) - \sum_{(i,j)\in A} \tau(i,j) f(i,j).$$

$\square$

We would like now to compute an s-t flow with a decomposition as given in Lemma 5.48 that maximizes the total amount of flow $(T + 1)|f| - \sum_{(i,j)\in A} \tau(i,j) f(i,j)$. Notice that such a flow will give us the best possible temporally repeated flow, although it is not clear that such a flow gives the maximum s-t flow over time. To compute the temporally repeated flow that maximizes the total amount of flow, we compute a minimum-cost circulation in a new graph $G' = (V, A')$. Let $G = (V, A)$ be the input graph to the maximum s-t flow over time problem, with capacities $u(i, j) \geq 0$ and transit times $\tau(i, j) \geq 0$. For each arc $(i, j) \in A$ with transit time $\tau(i, j)$, we add arc (j, i) to A', and set $c(i, j) = \tau(i, j)$, $c(j, i) = -\tau(i, j)$, and $u(j, i) = 0$. We also add additional arcs (t, s) and (s, t) with $u(t, s) = \infty$, $u(s, t) = 0$, $c(t, s) = -(T + 1)$, and $c(s, t) = (T + 1)$; see Figure 5.6. We observe that any negative-cost cycle in this instance must use the arc (t, s), since all other arcs

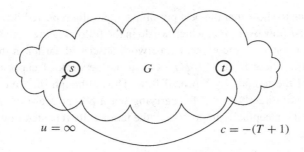

Figure 5.6 Minimum-cost circulation instance for computing maximum temporally repeated flow.

with positive capacity have nonnegative cost. Thus each such cycle consists of an s-t path P plus the arc (t,s). Because $c(t,s) = -(T+1)$, in order for the cycle to have negative cost, it must be that the cost of the path P is at most T, so that $\tau(P) \le T$. We also observe that the minimum-cost circulation f has cost

$$c(f) = \frac{1}{2} \sum_{(i,j)\in A'} c(i,j)f(i,j) = \sum_{(i,j)\in A} \tau(i,j)f(i,j) - (T+1)f(t,s),$$

where the factor of 1/2 is absorbed by skew-symmetry and the flow on reverse arcs that are in A' but not A.

Suppose we find a decomposition of the circulation f as in Lemma 5.7 into circulations $f_1, \ldots, f_\ell$ such that $f = \sum_{i=1}^{\ell} f_i$, $c(f) = \sum_{i=1}^{\ell} c(f_i)$, and for each i, the arcs of f_i with positive flow have positive capacity and form a simple cycle. We observe that each circulation f_k has negative cost, since otherwise $f - f_k$ would have cost $c(f - f_k) = c(f) - c(f_k) \le c(f)$, and is also a circulation: $f - f_k$ obeys flow conservation and skew symmetry, since both f and f_k do. For any arc (i,j) on which f_k has positive flow, $f(i,j) - f_k(i,j) \le u(i,j) - f_k(i,j) \le u(i,j)$, and on the reverse arc (j,i) it must be the case that $u(j,i) = 0$ and $f_h(j,i) \le 0$ for all $1 \le h \le \ell$, since each f_h has positive flow only on arcs of positive capacity. Thus $f(j,i) - f_k(j,i) = \sum_{h \ne k} f_h(j,i) \le 0 = u(j,i)$. Since each circulation f_k has negative cost and has positive flow on a simple cycle, it must be the case that it has positive flow on the arc (t,s) and an s-t path P_k such that $\tau(P_k) \le T$. Thus if we consider f just on the arcs in A (excluding the reverse arcs and (t,s) and (s,t)), we will have a flow f with the decomposition as required in Lemma 5.48 which maximizes $(T+1)|f| - \sum_{(i,j)\in A} \tau(i,j)f(i,j)$, since it minimizes $c(f) = \sum_{(i,j)\in A} \tau(i,j)f(i,j) - (T+1)f(t,s)$, and $f(t,s) = |f|$.

It remains to show that the best possible temporally repeated flow gives the maximum s-t flow over time, which we do in the following theorem. The proof strategy is to use the time-expanded network described earlier in the section, and show that there is an $s(0)$-$t(T)$ cut in the network of capacity at most the value of the temporally repeated flow. Thus although the time-expanded network is not directly useful for carrying out a polynomial-time algorithm, we can use it conceptually to prove that the temporally repeated flow is indeed maximum.

Theorem 5.49 (Ford and Fulkerson [66]): *The value of the maximum s-t flow over time equals the value of the maximum temporally repeated flow.*

Proof As suggested above, we will find an $s(0)$-$t(T)$ cut in the time-expanded network of capacity at most the value of the temporally repeated flow found by the minimum-cost circulation f as described above. We begin with some observations about the reduced cost of the circulation that we will need later on. Let p be the potentials as given in Theorem 5.3 such that for the circulation f, $c_p(i, j) \geq 0$ for all $(i, j) \in A'_f$. We observe that the inequality implies that if $c_p(i, j) < 0$, then $f(i, j) = u(i, j)$ for any arc $(i, j) \in A$ and $f(i, j) = 0$ if $(j, i) \in A$. Furthermore, we observe that as argued above, the cost of the circulation is $c(f) = \sum_{(i,j) \in A} \tau(i, j) f(i, j) - (T + 1) f(t, s)$. By Exercise 5.3, $c(f) = c_p(f)$. Then since

$$c(f) = c_p(f) = \frac{1}{2} \sum_{(i,j) \in A'} c_p(i, j) f(i, j) = \sum_{(i,j) \in A' : c_p(i,j) < 0} c_p(i, j) f(i, j),$$

we have that

$$\sum_{(i,j) \in A' : c_p(i,j) < 0} c_p(i, j) f(i, j) = \sum_{(i,j) \in A} \tau(i, j) f(i, j) - (T + 1) f(t, s).$$

$$(5.8)$$

We assume that $f(t, s) > 0$ so that the circulation does indeed have negative cost. We now define a cut S in the time-expanded network, where

$$S = \{i(\theta) : p(i) - p(s) \leq \theta\};$$

see Figure 5.7. Recall from Corollary 5.4 that since the transit times $\tau(i, j)$ are integer, and thus the costs $c(i, j)$ are integer, we can assume that the potentials p are integer. Thus if $\theta = p(i) - p(s)$, we get the nodes $i(\theta)$, $i(\theta + 1), \ldots, i(T) \in S$. We observe then that $s(0) \in S$, since $p(s) - p(s) = 0$, which implies that all copies of s are in S; that is, $s(0), \ldots, s(T) \in S$. Since $u_f(t, s) = u(t, s) - f(t, s) = \infty$, and $u_f(s, t) = u(s, t) - f(s, t) = 0 - f(s, t) = f(t, s) > 0$, both (s, t) and (t, s) are in A_f, so that by the choice

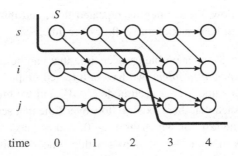

Figure 5.7 Example of cut S used in proof of Theorem 5.49.

of the potentials p, it must be the case that $c_p(t,s) \geq 0$ and that $c_p(s,t) \geq 0$. Since $c_p(s,t) = -c_p(t,s) \leq 0$, it must be the case that $c_p(t,s) = 0$. Thus $c(t,s)+p(t)-p(s) = 0$, or $-(T+1)+p(t)-p(s) = 0$, or $p(t)-p(s) = T+1$. Thus by the definition of S, $t(T) \notin S$. Therefore, S is an $s(0)$-$t(T)$ cut in the residual graph.

We would now like to determine the capacity of the cut S. We observe that the definition of S implies that there is no holdover arc $i(\theta)$-$i(\theta + 1)$ in $\delta^+(S)$. We get a copy of the arc (i,j) in the cut for each integer θ such that $p(i) - p(s) \leq \theta$ and $p(j) - p(s) > \theta + \tau(i,j)$, so that we get $\max(0, p(j) - p(s) - \tau(i,j) - (p(i) - p(s))) = \max(0, p(j) - p(i) - \tau(i,j))$ copies of arc (i,j) in the cut (again since we can assume that the potentials p are integer). Thus we have that

$$
\begin{aligned}
u(\delta^+(S)) &= \sum_{(i,j)\in A'} u(i,j) \cdot \max(0, p(j) - p(i) - \tau(i,j)) \\
&= \sum_{(i,j)\in A'} u(i,j) \cdot \max(0, -c_p(i,j)) \\
&= -\sum_{(i,j)\in A':c_p(i,j)<0} u(i,j)c_p(i,j) \\
&= -\sum_{(i,j)\in A':c_p(i,j)<0} c_p(i,j)f(i,j) \\
&= (T+1)f(t,s) - \sum_{(i,j)\in A} \tau(i,j)f(i,j),
\end{aligned}
$$

where the penultimate equality follows since we argued that $f(i,j) = u(i,j)$ for all $(i,j) \in A'$ with $c_p(i,j) < 0$, and the last equality follows from Equation (5.8). Thus we have an $s(0)$-$t(T)$ cut S whose capacity is equal to the value of an $s(0)$-$t(T)$ flow, the temporally repeated flow, and thus this temporally repeated flow must be a maximum s-t flow over time.   □

There are several other problems over time that can be considered. In the *quickest transshipment problem*, we have a directed graph with transit times on the arcs and a value $b(i)$ at each node $i \in V$, and we must determine the shortest time T such that there exists a flow over time that sends flow of value $b(i)$ from each node i for which $b(i) > 0$, and for each node i such that $b(i) < 0$, a flow of value $-b(i)$ arrives within time T. This problem can be solved in polynomial time, but the algorithm is complex; see the Chapter Notes for more discussion. The quickest minimum-cost flow problem is already an NP-hard problem.

Exercises

5.1   Prove Lemma 5.7.

5.2   Prove that given an instance of the minimum-cost circulation problem, we can transform it into an instance of the minimum-cost flow problem, such that from the optimal solution to the minimum-cost flow problem we can easily recover the optimal solution to the minimum-cost circulation problem.

5.3   Prove that for any circulation f and any potentials p, $c(f) = c_p(f)$.

5.4   Consider the instance of the minimum-cost circulation problem below, using the definition of a circulation from Definition 5.1, in which capacities u are given on the arcs, capacities $\ell = 0$ for all arcs, M is a large number, and all arcs have cost 0 except for the arc from t to s, which has cost -1. Show that an algorithm that chooses arbitrary negative-cost cycles from the residual graph to cancel does not run in polynomial time.

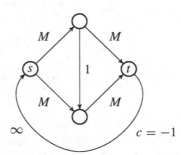

5.5   In this exercise, we consider the idea of trying to find a negative-cost
       cycle in the residual graph such that canceling this cycle gives the largest
       improvement in overall cost, as discussed at the end of Section 5.1.

       (a) Show that it is NP-hard to find such a cycle in general.
       (b) Show that if you can find and cancel such a cycle that Inequality
           (5.6) must hold.

5.6   In this problem, we consider the *minimum-cost perfect matching problem
       in bipartite graphs*. In this problem, we are given as input a bipartite
       graph $G = (X, Y, E)$ with $|X| = |Y|$, with costs $c(i, j)$ for each $(i, j) \in$
       E, where $i \in X$ and $j \in Y$. The goal is to find a minimum-cost subset of
       edges $F \subseteq E$ such that each node in X and each node in Y is adjacent to
       exactly one edge of F (a *perfect matching*). Of course, there may not be
       any $F \subseteq E$ that meets this condition, in which case the correct output is
       to say "no perfect matching".

       We can model this problem as a minimum-cost circulation problem
       as follows. Given the bipartite graph G, we add two nodes s and t, arcs
       (s, i) and (i, s) for each $i \in X$ of costs $c(s, i) = c(i, s) = 0$ and capacities
       $u(s, i) = 1$ and $u(i, s) = 0$, and arcs (j, t) and (t, j) for each $j \in Y$ of
       costs $c(j, t) = c(t, j) = 0$ and capacities $u(j, t) = 1$ and $u(t, j) = $
       0. We also add arcs (t, s) and (s, t) of costs $c(s, t) = c(t, s) = 0$ and
       capacities $u(t, s) = n$ and $u(s, t) = -n$. Finally, for each edge (i, j) in
       G with $i \in X$ and $j \in Y$ we add arcs (i, j) and (j, i) of costs $c(i, j)$
       (and $c(j, i) = -c(i, j)$) and capacities $u(i, j) = 1$ and $u(j, i) = 0$. See
       Figure 5.8.

       (a) Argue that there is a feasible solution to the minimum-cost circula-
           tion instance if and only if there is a perfect matching in the bipartite
           graph G, and that the minimum-cost circulation gives a minimum-
           cost perfect matching.
       (b) Argue that we can find a minimum-cost perfect matching in a
           bipartite graph in $O(mn^2)$ time.

       We now give an algorithm to find a minimum-cost perfect matching in a
       bipartite graph in $O(n(m + n \log n))$ time by solving the minimum-cost
       circulation problem by solving a sequence of n shortest path problems.
       We set the capacity of $u(t, s)$ and $u(s, t)$ to 0, and in each iteration
       of the algorithm, we increase $u(t, s)$ by one, decrease $u(s, t)$ by one,
       and augment the previous circulation to a new circulation by solving
       a shortest path problem. When $u(t, s) = u(s, t) = 0$, clearly $f = 0$ is
       a minimum-cost circulation. We claim that in each iteration by finding a

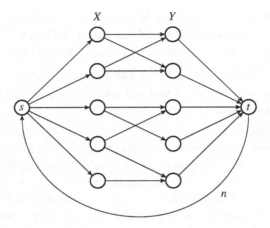

Figure 5.8 Reduction of minimum-cost perfect matching in bipartite graphs to the minimum-cost circulation problem.

$$
\begin{aligned}
&f \leftarrow 0 \\
&u(t,s) \leftarrow 0 \\
&u(s,t) \leftarrow 0 \\
&\textbf{for } k \leftarrow 1 \textbf{ to } n \textbf{ do} \\
&\quad \text{Find a shortest } s\text{-}t \text{ path } P \subseteq A_f \text{ using costs } c(i,j) \\
&\quad f'(i,j) \leftarrow \begin{cases} 1 & \text{if } (i,j) \in P \text{ or } (i,j) = (t,s) \\ -1 & \text{if } (j,i) \in P \text{ or } (i,j) = (s,t) \\ 0 & \text{otherwise} \end{cases} \\
&\quad u(t,s) \leftarrow k \\
&\quad u(s,t) \leftarrow -k \\
&\quad f \leftarrow f + f' \\
&\textbf{return } f
\end{aligned}
$$

Algorithm 5.11 An algorithm for finding a minimum-cost perfect matching in a bipartite graph.

shortest s-t path P in the set of edges A_f of positive residual capacity, and sending a unit of flow on P and the arc (t,s), we will have found a minimum-cost circulation for the problem in which $u(t,s)$ has been increased by one and $u(s,t)$ decreased by one. We summarize the algorithm in Algorithm 5.11.

(c) Argue inductively that when we compute the shortest s-t path in iteration k, there must be no negative-cost cycle in the arcs A_f, and

$f \leftarrow 0$

$u(t,s) \leftarrow 0$

$u(s,t) \leftarrow 0$

Let $p_0(i)$ be length of shortest s-i path in A_f using costs $c(i,j)$ for all $i \in V$

for $k \leftarrow 1$ **to** n **do**

   Let $c_k(i,j) = c(i,j) + p_{k-1}(i) - p_{k-1}(j)$

   Find a shortest s-t path $P \subseteq A_f$ using costs $c_k(i,j)$

   Let $p_k(i)$ be length of shortest s-i path in A_f using costs $c_k(i,j)$ for all $i \in V$

$$f'(i,j) \leftarrow \begin{cases} 1 & \text{if } (i,j) \in P \text{ or } (i,j) = (t,s) \\ -1 & \text{if } (j,i) \in P \text{ or } (i,j) = (s,t) \\ 0 & \text{otherwise} \end{cases}$$

   $u(t,s) \leftarrow k$

   $u(s,t) \leftarrow -k$

   $f \leftarrow f + f'$

return f

Algorithm 5.12 An algorithm for finding a minimum-cost perfect matching in a bipartite graph (take two).

that at the end of each iteration k, f is a minimum-cost circulation for the problem in which $u(t,s)$ is k.

(d) Because edge costs can be negative, in each iteration we must use the Bellman-Ford algorithm of Section 1.2. Conclude that the algorithm finds a minimum-cost circulation in the graph with $u(t,s) = n$ and $u(s,t) = -n$ in $O(mn^2)$ time.

We'd now like to replace the use of the Bellman-Ford algorithm by Dijkstra's algorithm. To that end, we compute potentials $p_k(u)$ in each iteration k as the shortest path from s to u using costs $c_k(i,j) \equiv c(i,j) + p_{k-1}(i) - p_{k-1}(j)$. We argue that $c_k(i,j) \geq 0$ in each iteration for all $(i,j) \in A_f$, so that we can use Dijkstra's algorithm to perform the shortest path calculations. We give the new algorithm in Algorithm 5.12.

(e) Argue that the new algorithm finds the same s-t path P as the previous algorithm in each iteration, and thus terminates with a minimum-cost circulation f for $u(t,s) = n$, $u(s,t) = -n$.

(f) Argue that $c_k(i,j) \geq 0$ for all $(i,j) \in A_f$ when we calculate shortest paths in iteration k.

(g) Argue that the algorithm runs in time $O(n(m + n \log n))$ time.

The minimum-cost perfect matching problem in bipartite graphs is also
sometimes called the *assignment problem*.

5.7   As shown in Exercise 5.5, finding a cycle to cancel that gives the most
improvement in the objective function is an NP-hard problem. However,
we can find in polynomial-time a collection C of node-disjoint cycles
such that canceling all cycles in C improves the objective function as
much as the most improving single cycle. In this problem, we will give
an algorithm that will find such a collection C.

To give such an algorithm, it may help to consider the minimum-cost
perfect matching problem in bipartite graphs defined in Exercise 5.6.

(a) Let f be any circulation, and let Γ be the cycle in G_f that results
in the greatest improvement in objective by canceling C; that is,
if circulation $\hat{f}$ is the circulation that results by canceling Γ,
then Γ is chosen to maximize $\delta = c(f) - c(\hat{f})$. Prove that in
$O(mn(m + n \log n))$ time we can find a collection C of node-disjoint
cycles such that if f' results from canceling all cycles in C, then
$c(f) - c(f') \geq \delta$.

(b) Conclude that we can obtain a $O(m^2 n(m + n \log n) \log(mUC))$ time
algorithm for the minimum-cost circulation problem.

5.8   In Wallacher's algorithm from Section 5.2, we cancel cycles that trade
off cost versus residual capacity. In this exercise, we consider another
way of doing this that uses some ideas from the capacity scaling
algorithm of Section 5.4. One way to improve the situation is to make
sure that every iteration of cycle canceling considers only arcs with
"large enough" residual capacity. Given a circulation f, potentials p
and a parameter Δ, let $A_f(\Delta) = \{(i,j) \in A_f : u_f(i,j) \geq \Delta\}$. Call
an arc $(i,j) \in A_f$ *admissible* if $c_p(i,j) < 0$ and Δ-*admissible* if (i,j)
is admissible and $(i,j) \in A_f(\Delta)$. Let's say that cycle Γ is a Δ-*cycle*
if $\Gamma \subseteq A_f(\Delta)$, $c_p(i,j) \leq 0$ for all $(i,j) \in \Gamma$, and $c_p(i,j) < 0$ for
some $(i,j) \in \Gamma$. Note that this implies $c_p(\Gamma) = c(\Gamma) < 0$. We give a
procedure $\mathrm{Find}\Delta\mathrm{Cycle}(p,i,j)$ that takes as input node potentials p
and some Δ-admissible arc (i,j), and uses them to find a Δ-cycle Γ.

We can then use this subroutine in Algorithm 5.13, $\mathrm{Cancel}\Delta\mathrm{Cycles}$.

(a) Prove that the subroutine $\mathrm{Find}\Delta\mathrm{Cycle}$ does not create any new
Δ-admissible arcs.

(b) Prove that if the subroutine $\mathrm{Find}\Delta\mathrm{Cycle}$ returns a cycle, it is a
Δ-cycle.

(c) Prove that either $\mathrm{Find}\Delta\mathrm{Cycle}$ returns a cycle containing (i,j) or
makes (i,j) inadmissible.

$\Gamma \leftarrow \emptyset$
Let S be the set of nodes reachable from j via arcs in $A_f(\Delta) - \{(j,i)\}$
if $i \notin S$ **then**
$$p(k) \leftarrow \begin{cases} p(k) + c_p(i,j) & \text{if } k \in S \\ p(k) & \text{otherwise} \end{cases}$$
else
    Compute shortest j-k path distance $\tilde{p}(k)$ for all $k \in S$ using arcs in
    $A_f(\Delta)$ and costs $\max(0, c_p(i,j))$
    $\tilde{p}_{max} = \max_{k \in S} \tilde{p}(k)$
$$p(k) \leftarrow \begin{cases} p(k) + \tilde{p}(k) - \tilde{p}_{max} & k \in S \\ p(k) & \text{otherwise} \end{cases}$$
    if $c_p(i,j) < 0$ **then**
        Let $\Gamma = \{(i,j)\}$ + shortest path from j to i
return Γ, p'

Procedure Find$\triangle$Cycle(p,i,j)

$f \leftarrow 0$
$p \leftarrow 0$
$\Delta \leftarrow 2^{\lceil \log U \rceil}$
while $\Delta \geq 1$ **do**
    while there is a Δ-admissible arc (i,j) **do**
        $(\Gamma, p) \leftarrow$ Find$\triangle$Cycle (p,i,j)
        if $\Gamma \neq \emptyset$ **then**
            Cancel Γ
            Update f
    $\Delta \leftarrow \Delta/2$
return f

Algorithm 5.13 Another cycle-canceling algorithm, Cancel$\triangle$Cycles.

(d) Prove that at the start of the inner while loop of Cancel$\triangle$Cycles, $u_f(i,j) < 2\Delta$ for each admissible arc (i,j), and that this remains true through the execution of the while loop.

(e) Prove that in each iteration of the inner while loop of Cancel$\triangle$ Cycles, the number of Δ-admissible arcs strictly decreases.

(f) Prove that if the algorithm terminates, it correctly returns a minimum-cost circulation.

Let f be any feasible circulation
Compute potentials p such that $c_p(i, j) \geq -\epsilon(f)$ for all $(i, j) \in A_f$
while f is not a minimum-cost circulation **do**
    while there exists an admissible cycle Γ **do**
        Cancel Γ
        Update f
        Update potentials p so that $c_p(i, j) \geq -\epsilon(f)$ for all $(i, j) \in A_f$
return f

Algorithm 5.14 The cancel-and-tighten algorithm for the minimum-cost circulation problem.

(g) Recall from the end of Section 1.1 that we can use Dijkstra's algorithm to computing shortest paths in graphs with nonnegative edge lengths in $O(m + n \log n)$ time. Prove that the algorithm runs in time $O((m \log U)(m + n \log n))$.

5.9   In this problem we consider another algorithm for the minimum-cost circulation problem, based on the minimum-mean cycle canceling algorithm given in Section 5.3. Call an arc (i, j) *admissible* with respect to potentials p if $c_p(i, j) < 0$ and $u_f(i, j) > 0$. A cycle is admissible if it consists entirely of admissible arcs. The algorithm will repeatedly cancel admissible cycles until no such cycles exist for the current potentials p. It can be shown that it takes $O(m)$ time plus $O(n)$ time per admissible cycle canceled to cancel all admissible cycles. We then update the potentials p so that $c_p(i, j) \geq -\epsilon(f)$ for all $(i, j) \in A_f$; we previously showed how to do this in Corollary 5.20. Now consider Algorithm 5.14; it is known as *cancel-and-tighten*.

In the analysis below, assume that the arc costs c are integral.

(a) Prove that when updating the potentials, $\epsilon(f)$ has decreased by a factor of $(1 - 1/n)$ since the last update.

(b) Prove that in each iteration of the main loop, at most m cycles are cancelled.

(c) Prove that at most $O(n \log(nC))$ iterations of the main loop are needed to obtain an optimal circulation f.

(d) Prove that the overall running time of the algorithm is $O(mn^2 \log(nC))$.

5.10 In Algorithm 5.9, it is sometimes possible to relabel many nodes at once. Let S be a set that contains at least one node with positive excess, and no nodes with negative excess. Suppose that there are no admissible arcs entering S; that is, for all $(i, j) \in \delta^-(S)$, either $(i, j) \notin A_f$ or $c_p(i, j) \geq 0$. Prove that we can decrease $p(i)$ for each $i \in S$ by ϵ such that f continues to be ϵ-optimal ($c_p(i, j) \geq -\epsilon$ for all $(i, j) \in A_f$) and the set of admissible arcs continues to be acyclic. This heuristic is called *set relabeling*.

5.11 In Algorithm 5.7, it is possible that after we have divided ϵ by two that there exist potentials p' such that the current circulation f is ϵ-optimal. In this case we do not need to call FindϵOptCirc. Give an $O(mn)$ time algorithm to find such potentials p' if they exist. If we call this algorithm each time we divide ϵ by two, does this change the overall running time of the algorithm? This heuristic is called *price refinement*.

5.12 Consider the successive approximation algorithm for the minimum-cost circulation problem given in Section 5.5. We used a push-relabel subroutine for converting a 2ϵ-optimal circulation to an ϵ-optimal circulation in FindϵOptCirc; this subroutine's running time was dominated by the $O(n^2 m)$ nonsaturating pushes taken by the algorithm.

Just as we improved the running time of push-relabel for the maximum flow problem from $O(n^2 m)$ to $O(n^3)$ in Exercise 2.10 by carefully ordering the push and relabel operations (resulting in FIFO push-relabel), we can do the same thing in this case.

(a) Show that in $O(m)$ time one can find an ordering of the nodes such that any push operation on an admissible arc will push from a node earlier in the ordering to one later in the ordering.

The algorithm will consider nodes in the order given by the ordering. When considering node i, we continue to push excess from node i until either there is no longer any excess at node i (after a nonsaturating push) or there are no admissible arcs out of node i.

(b) Prove that if we must relabel i, we can move i to be the first node in the ordering and have the resulting ordering satisfy the properties of the ordering in part (a).

After relabeling i, the algorithm moves i to the beginning of the ordering. It moves back to the beginning of the ordering (with node i) and considers nodes in the new order.

(c) Argue that if we reach the end of the ordering without a relabel operation, then we have a feasible circulation and the subroutine terminates.

---

for $(i, j) \in A$ **do**
   if $c_p(i, j) < 0$ **then**
      $f(i, j) \leftarrow u(i, j); f(j, i) \leftarrow -u(i, j)$
while f is not a circulation **do**
   $S \leftarrow \{i \in V : \exists j \in V$ such that $e_f(j) > 0, i$ reachable from j in $G_A\}$
   for $i \in S$ **do** $p(i) \leftarrow p(i) - \epsilon$
   Form network N from G_A by adding source s, sink t, arc (s, i) of
   capacity $e_f(i)$ for all $i \in V$ with $e_f(i) > 0$, arc (i, t) of capacity
   $e_f(i)$ for all $i \in V$ with $e_f(i) < 0$
   Find blocking flow b on N
   $f \leftarrow f + b$
return f, p

Algorithm 5.15 Algorithm for Exercise 5.13.

(d) Argue that the number of nonsaturating pushes is at most $O(n^3)$ and that the overall running time of the subroutine is now $O(n^3)$.

5.13 In Section 5.5, we gave a push-relabel based implementation of the subroutine `FindϵOptCirc` for converting a 2ϵ-optimal circulation to an ϵ-optimal circulation via a push-relabel algorithm, which resulted in an $O(n^2 m \min(\log(nC), m \log n))$ time algorithm for the minimum-cost circulation problem. In this problem, we will give a subroutine for the same problem based on blocking flows; consider the subroutine given in Algorithm 5.15, in which we let G_A be the graph of currently admissible arcs (that is, $c_p(i, j) < 0$ and $(i, j) \in A_f$). Given a blocking flow algorithm that runs in $O(m \log n)$ time when there are no cycles of positive residual capacity, prove that the subroutine is correct and runs in $O(mn \log n)$ time. This gives a $O(mn \log n \min(\log(nC), m \log n))$ time algorithm for the minimum-cost circulation problem.

Chapter Notes

The method does not seem to lend itself to machine calculation but may be efficient for hand computation on matrices of small order.

                  – Julia Robinson [174]

Schrijver ([176],[177, section 21.13e]) gives a historical overview of the transportation problem, an important special case of the minimum-cost flow problem in which the graph is bipartite and has no capacity constraints. As with the maximum flow problem, one of the first applications of the problem was to the railway networks of the former Soviet Union, although in this case Soviet researchers were attempting to minimize the cost of railway shipments of goods. Schrijver points out that an 1930 article of Tolstoi observes that the existence of a negative-cost cycle proves that the solution is not optimal.

Ahuja, Magnanti, and Orlin [3, 4] and Goldberg, Tardos, and Tarjan [91] provide surveys of the minimum-cost flow problem.

For the optimality conditions of Theorem 5.3, there were several precursors to the theorem showing that the circulation is optimal if and only if there are no negative-cost cycles in the residual graph; see Schrijver [176] for details. Robinson [174] states the condition for the transportation problem. Busacker and Saaty [30, theorem 7-8] provide an early statement of the theorem in the form we use it. The optimality of a circulation if and only if there are potentials p such that $c_p(i, j) \geq 0$ for all arcs (i, j) with positive residual capacity follows from linear programming duality, and appears in Fulkerson [74] and Ford and Fulkerson [66]. The negative-cost cycle canceling algorithm in Algorithm 5.1 is due to Klein [132].

Weintraub [205] shows the observation at the beginning of Section 5.2 that an algorithm finding the most improving cycle would converge quickly, and further argues that an algorithm finding a cycle, or a collection of cycles, making improvement of the same order as the most improving cycle would likewise converge quickly. The algorithm of Section 5.2 is from a technical report of Wallacher [201]. Although this algorithm was developed later chronologically than the other algorithms of the chapter, because its analysis duplicates that of a most improving cycle, we put it first in the chapter. Despite never appearing as a journal publication, the ideas from Wallacher's technical report have been influential. The minimum-mean cycle-canceling algorithm of Section 5.3 is due to Goldberg and Tarjan [93]. The first strongly-polynomial time algorithm for the minimum-cost circulation problem is due to Tardos [188]; her analysis was adapted to the minimum-mean cycle canceling algorithm by Goldberg and Tarjan [93, 94]. Tardos's algorithm was a major breakthrough. The capacity scaling algorithm of Section 5.4 is from Ahuja, Magnanti, and Orlin [4, section 10.2]; Ahuja, Magnanti, and Orlin cite the algorithm as a variant of an algorithm of Edmonds and Karp [57] developed by Orlin [157]. Other scaling techniques include scaling of costs; the idea of cost scaling for minimum-cost flow algorithms was developed independently by Röck [175] and by Bland and Jensen [25]. The algorithm using successive approximation that we give in Section 5.5 is due to Goldberg and Tarjan [94]. The network simplex algorithm of Section 5.6 was developed by Dantzig [47] for the transportation problem, and was generalized by him to the capacitated version of the problem [48, chapters 17-18]. Tarjan [193] and Goldfarb and Hao [97] independently made the observation of Theorem 5.47 that network simplex runs in polynomial-time if pivots are allowed that increase the cost. Orlin [158] gives a polynomial-time variant of network simplex in which such pivots are not allowed. The maximum flow over time problem and algorithm in Section 5.7 are due to Ford and Fulkerson [64] (see also [66, chapter III, section 9]). Problems involving flow over time were originally called dynamic flows. Skutella [181] gives a nice survey of problems and algorithms for flows over time. Hoppe and Tardos [111] give a polynomial-time algorithm for the quickest transshipment problem mentioned at the end of Section 5.7.

Orlin [157] gives the fastest known strongly polynomial-time algorithm for the minimum-cost flow problem; it runs in $O(m \log n(m + n \log n))$ time.

The Robinson quote above is from 1950 and concerns the negative-cost cycle canceling algorithm in the case of the transportation problem. Over the decades, many implementation studies of the algorithms of this chapter have been performed, and while negative-cost cycle canceling has indeed been implemented, it has been not been found to be competitive with other algorithms. Goldberg and Kharitonov [87], Goldberg [84], and Bünnagel, Korte, and Vygen [29] all study implementations of the Goldberg-Tarjan successive approximation algorithm of Section 5.5, and introduce various heuristics that help it to run faster in practice, including the set relabeling of Exercise 5.10 and the price refinement of Exercise 5.11; Goldberg [84] and Kovács [136] find that particular implementations of price refinement are helpful. Other helpful heuristics include *push lookahead*, to ensure that flow pushed from node i to node j will not simply be pushed back to i again. Goldberg [84] compares his code to the RELAX code of Bertsekas and Tseng [21] and some network simplex codes, and finds that it usually (but not always) outperforms these codes. Bünnagel et al. compare their code against a successive shortest path algorithm, and find that their code with heuristics added is substantially better. Löbel [145] compares a network simplex implementation of his own versus Goldberg's code, another network simplex code, and an updated version of RELAX [22] on instances drawn primarily from large vehicle scheduling problems, and finds his network simplex code outperforms the others.

Joshi, Goldstein, and Vaidya [118] and Resende and Veiga [172] compare LP-based interior-point algorithms for minimum-cost flow problems to a network simplex algorithm and the Bertsekas-Tseng RELAX algorithm, and find the interior-point algorithms better on sufficiently large problems. Portugal, Resende, Veiga, and Júdice [166] find an implementation of the Goldberg-Tarjan successive approximation algorithm is in general a better performer than an interior-point algorithm and a network simplex implementation on most instance classes.

Kovács [136] performs a recent and wide-ranging study of algorithms for the minimum-cost flow problem. He finds the minimum-mean cycle canceling algorithm of Section 5.3 (and its cancel-and-tighten variant in Exercise 5.9) and the capacity scaling algorithm of Section 5.4 to be uncompetitive. Other candidate algorithms he considers includes a number of different network simplex codes and the interior-point code of Portugal et al. Kovács finds that his own implementation of the network simplex algorithm outperforms the other algorithms in most instances, while an implementation of the Goldberg-Tarjan successive approximation algorithm outperforms other algorithms on large sparse instances.

More recent work on interior-point algorithms have yielded theoretically faster algorithms for the minimum-cost flow problem. Lee and Sidford [140] give an $\tilde{O}(m\sqrt{n}\log^{O(1)}(CU))$-time algorithm for finding a minimum-cost flow. Cohen, Mądry, Sankowski, and Vladu [43] have used electrical flows and ideas from interior-point algorithms to obtain an $\tilde{O}(m^{10/7}\log C)$-time algorithm for the minimum-cost flow problem in which $U = 1$. These algorithms use fast Laplacian solvers; some of this work will be discussed in Chapter 8 and its Chapter Notes.

The algorithm for minimum-cost perfect matching in bipartite graphs given in Exercise 5.6 uses an algorithm for the minimum-cost flow problem called *successive shortest paths*. Ahuja, Magnanti, and Orlin [3] attribute the application of successive shortest paths via Dijkstra's algorithm by using reduced costs in each iteration to observations by Edmonds and Karp [57] and Tomizawa [194]. Exercise 5.7 is due to Barahona and Tardos [15], following the observation of Weintraub mentioned earlier. Exercise 5.8 is due to Sokkalingam, Ahuja, and Orlin [183]. Exercise 5.9 is due to Goldberg and Tarjan [93]. Exercises 5.12 and 5.13 are due to Goldberg and Tarjan [94].

6

Generalized Flow Algorithms

...and this time it vanished quite slowly, beginning with the end of the tail,
and ending with the grin, which remained some time after the rest of it had
gone.

"Well! I've often seen a cat without a grin," thought Alice; "but a grin
without a cat! It's the most curious thing I ever saw in my life!"
                                                    – Lewis Carroll, *Alice in Wonderland*

God made the integers, all else is the work of man.
                                                    – Leopold Kronecker

In this chapter, we turn to *generalized flow problems*; in particular, we look
at the generalized maximum flow problem. In generalized flow problems, for
each arc (i, j) we additionally have a *gain* $\gamma(i, j) > 0$ that denotes a scaling
of the flow on (i, j), so that if $f(i, j)$ units of flow enters (i, j) from node i,
then $f(i, j)\gamma(i, j)$ units of flow leave (i, j) into node j. This gain factor can
be used to model losses on the arcs due to leakage, transaction costs, friction,
noise, taxes, and so on. We can also use the gains to model transformations of
the flow along the arcs. For instance, see Figure 6.1: each node represents a
currency, and the gain factor $\gamma(i, j)$ represents the exchange rate for changing
currency i into currency j. In generalized flow problems, we can then consider
problems of trying to maximize our holdings in a certain currency given all the
possible ways of exchanging currencies.

In the *generalized maximum flow problem*, we are given as input a directed
graph $G = (V, A)$ with capacities $u(i, j) \geq 0$ and gains $\gamma(i, j) > 0$ on all the
arcs $(i, j) \in A$. We assume that the capacities are integers and the gains are
expressed as the ratio of integers; let B be the largest integer used in expressing
both the capacities and the gains. We also have a sink vertex $t \in V$. Our goal
will be to maximize the net flow entering the sink t. It might seem curious to

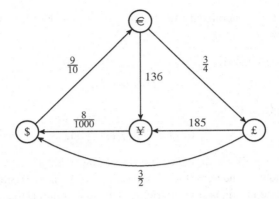

Figure 6.1 Example of generalized flow as modeling currency exchange. Arcs are labeling with their gain, and we assume for each arc (i, j) with gain $\gamma(i, j)$ there is an arc (j, i) with gain $1/\gamma(i, j)$.

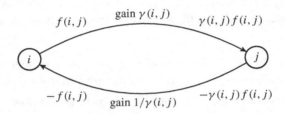

Figure 6.2 Example showing skew symmetry for generalized flow.

have a flow without a source, like having a grin without a cat. But we will see shortly that generalized flow problems upend some of the intuitions that we have accumulated about the nature of flow problems, and having a flow with no source is only one of the oddities we will encounter.

We will immediately give a formulation of the problem involving a skew symmetry condition. We assume that if there is an arc $(i, j) \in A$, there is also an arc $(j, i) \in A$, and that $\gamma(i, j) = 1/\gamma(j, i)$. Then pushing 1 unit of flow from i to j on (i, j) results in $\gamma(i, j)$ units at j, while pushing the $\gamma(i, j)$ units back on (j, i) results in the original single unit of flow. Our skew symmetry condition cannot simply be $f(i, j) = -f(j, i)$; we want it to be the case that the flow entering i from (j, i) is the negative of the flow leaving i on (i, j). Thus since $f(i, j)$ units leave i on (i, j) and $\gamma(j, i)f(j, i)$ enter i from (j, i), we want $f(i, j) = -\gamma(j, i)f(j, i)$. See Figure 6.2. We can now define the notion of a generalized pseudoflow, in which the flow obeys both capacity and skew symmetry constraints.

Definition 6.1: *A* generalized pseudoflow $f : A \rightarrow \Re$ *is an assignment of reals to arcs such that:*

- *for all arcs* $(i, j) \in A$,

$$f(i, j) \leq u(i, j); \tag{6.1}$$

- *for all arcs* $(i, j) \in A$,

$$f(i, j) = -\gamma(j, i)f(j, i). \tag{6.2}$$

We would now like to define the notion of an excess at a node, so that we can define a flow as one with flow conservation everywhere except at the sink. But again, the definition is slightly tricky. Our usual notion is that the excess is the net flow entering a node, which previously skew symmetry allowed us to express as the sum of the flows on the arcs entering the node. But here again, the flow entering a node i on arc (k, i) is not $f(k, i)$ but $\gamma(k, i)f(k, i)$. By the skew symmetry condition (6.2), this is equal to $-f(i, k)$. Thus we can write the net flow entering a node as the negative of the sum of flows on arcs leaving the node.

Definition 6.2: *The* excess *of a generalized pseudoflow f at node $i \in V$ is the net flow entering i, or* $- \sum_{k:(i,k)\in A} f(i, k)$*, and we denote it* $e_f(i)$.

We can now define what we mean by a flow and a proper flow.

Definition 6.3: *A* generalized flow *(or* flow*) f is a pseudoflow such that $e_f(i) \geq 0$ for all $i \in V$. A generalized* proper flow *(or* proper flow*) f is a flow such that $e_f(i) = 0$ for all $i \in V$, $i \neq t$.*

The goal of the generalized maximum flow problem is to find a (proper) flow that maximizes the excess at the sink. We call the excess at the sink the value of the flow.

Definition 6.4: *The* value *of a (proper) flow f is $e_f(t)$ and is denoted $|f|$.*

For the moment, we will concentrate on proper flows.

6.1 Optimality Conditions

We now begin a discussion of how we can tell whether a given proper flow f is maximum. As in previous chapters, the notion of a residual graph $G_f = (V, A)$ is useful. For a pseudoflow f, the residual capacity is $u_f(i, j) = u(i, j) - f(i, j)$ for all $(i, j) \in A$. We will also let A_f denote the arcs with positive residual capacity, so that $A_f = \{(i, j) \in A : u_f(i, j) > 0\}$.

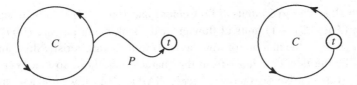

Figure 6.3 Two examples of generalized augmenting paths; the right example has an empty path from the cycle C to the sink t.

In order to discuss the analog of an augmenting path, we need to introduce the concept of the gain of a path and the gain of a cycle. The gain of a path P is simply the product of the gains of the arcs on the path, and we denote it $\gamma(P)$, so that $\gamma(P) = \prod_{(i,j) \in P} \gamma(i,j)$. Similarly, the gain of a cycle C is the product of the gains of the arcs on the cycle, and we denote it $\gamma(C)$, so that $\gamma(C) = \prod_{(i,j) \in C} \gamma(i,j)$. We distinguish various types of cycles depending on their gain.

Definition 6.5: *A cycle C is* flow-generating *if $\gamma(C) > 1$,* flow-absorbing *if $\gamma(C) < 1$, and* unit-gain *if $\gamma(C) = 1$.*

We note that if we push a unit of flow around a flow-generating cycle C starting at some $i \in C$, then the net flow entering i is positive: one unit leaves i and more than one unit enters i. Similarly, pushing a unit of flow around a flow-absorbing cycle C starting at some $i \in C$ yields less than a unit of flow entering i, and thus a negative net flow entering i.

We can now give the analog of an augmenting path for generalized flow, called a *generalized augmenting path*, or GAP for short. See Figure 6.3 for examples.

Definition 6.6: *A* generalized augmenting path *(GAP) is a flow-generating cycle C in A_f together with a path P in A_f (possibly empty) from some $i \in C$ to the sink t.*

The natural analog of the augmenting path algorithm for the maximum flow problem turns out to be true: a proper flow f is maximum if and only if there are no generalized augmenting paths in the arcs of positive residual capacity A_f.

We now show that sending flow along a GAP in A_f increases the value of the flow. To this end, we let $\chi(\Gamma)$ denote the *characteristic flow* on a GAP $\Gamma \subseteq A_f$: If the GAP has a path to t starting at node i on the cycle C, and arc (i,j) is the arc on C leaving i, the characteristic flow is what results from sending a unit of flow on the arc (i,j) of the GAP. Then $\gamma(C)$ units of flow enter i; to maintain flow conservation, we send $\gamma(C) - 1$ units of flow along the

i-t path P, so that $\gamma(C)$ units of flow enter i and $1 + (\gamma(C) - 1)$ units leave i. Then $\gamma(P)(\gamma(C) - 1)$ units of flow enter the sink t. For any arc $(i, j) \in \Gamma$, let $\chi(\Gamma, i, j)$ be the amount of flow on (i, j) in the characteristic flow, and let $|\chi(\Gamma)|$ be the flow entering t from the characteristic flow, so that $|\chi(\Gamma)| = \gamma(P)(\gamma(C) - 1)$. We say that we *cancel* a GAP $\Gamma \subseteq A_f$ if we find a scaling of the characteristic flow $\chi(\Gamma)$ such that the residual capacities are all respected and some arc (i, j) is saturated; that is, we find some $\delta > 0$ such that $0 \leq \delta \cdot \chi(\Gamma, i, j) \leq u_f(i, j)$ for all $(i, j) \in \Gamma$ and $\delta \cdot \chi(\Gamma, i, j) = u_f(i, j)$ for some $(i, j) \in \Gamma$. Thus $\delta = \min_{(i, j) \in \Gamma} u_f(i, j) / \chi(\Gamma, i, j)$. We then update f by setting

$$f'(i, j) = \begin{cases} f(i, j) + \delta \cdot \chi(\Gamma, i, j) & \forall (i, j) \in \Gamma \\ f(i, j) - \gamma(i, j) \cdot \delta \cdot \chi(\Gamma, j, i) & \forall (j, i) \in \Gamma \\ f(i, j) & \forall (i, j) : (i, j), (j, i) \notin \Gamma \end{cases}$$

(6.3)

We leave it as an exercise to the reader (Exercise 6.1) to prove that f' is a (proper) flow if f is a (proper) flow. We observe that canceling the GAP Γ increases the net flow into the sink by $\delta |\chi(\Gamma)|$, so that $|f'| = |f| + \delta |\chi(\Gamma)| = |f| + \delta(\gamma(C) - 1)\gamma(P) > |f|$.

Finally, to prove our optimality theorem it will be useful to introduce the concept of a *labeling* of the nodes of the graph. Node labels play a role very similar to node potentials for the minimum-cost circulation problem, and they are similarly useful in devising algorithms for the generalized maximum flow problem.

Definition 6.7: *A labeling* $\mu : V \to \Re^{\geq 0}$ *is an assignment of nonnegative reals to the nodes of the graph such that* $\mu(t) = 1$.

It is helpful to think of μ as a change in units of measurement at the nodes of the graph; as an example, consider again the currency conversion application shown in Figure 6.1. Rather than thinking about converting dollars to euros, we could think about converting cents to euros. We let $\mu(i)$ be the ratio of new units to old units; in the case of switching from dollars to cents, $\mu(i) = 100$. The change in units affects the capacities, gains (conversion rates), flows, and excesses: If before we could convert at most u dollars to euros at a rate of γ, now we can convert at most $100u$ cents to euros at at a rate of γ. Also, if the conversion rate was γ euros per dollar before, the rate becomes $\gamma/100$ euros per cent. A flow of f converting dollars to euros becomes a flow $100f$ converting cents to euros, and an excess of e dollars becomes an excess of $100e$ cents. Thus given a labeling μ, we have *relabeled* capacities, gains, flows, and excesses that we denote u^μ, γ^μ, f^μ, and e_f^μ respectively. These are related to the initial values via the labels as follows:

$$u^\mu(i,j) = u(i,j)\mu(i),$$

$$\gamma^\mu(i,j) = \gamma(i,j)\frac{\mu(j)}{\mu(i)},$$

$$f^\mu(i,j) = f(i,j)\mu(i),$$

$$e_f^\mu(i) = e_f(i)\mu(i).$$

Since capacities are also relabeled, the relabeled residual capacity is $u_f^\mu(i,j) = u^\mu(i,j) - f^\mu(i,j)$. Then we let A_f^μ be the arcs of positive residual capacity, so that $A_f^\mu = \{(i,j) \in A : u^\mu(i,j) - f^\mu(i,j) > 0\}$. Observe that $(i,j) \in A_f^\mu$ if and only if $(i,j) \in A_f$ and $\mu(i) > 0$. We further note that after relabeling, we still have that the relabeled gain $\gamma^\mu(i,j)$ is the reciprocal of the relabeled gain $\gamma^\mu(j,i)$ of the arc in the opposite direction, since

$$\gamma^\mu(i,j) = \gamma(i,j)\frac{\mu(j)}{\mu(i)} = \frac{1}{\gamma(j,i)}\frac{\mu(j)}{\mu(i)} = \frac{1}{\gamma^\mu(j,i)}.$$

Also, we note that since we require that $\mu(t) = 1$ for any labeling, the relabeled excess at the sink, $e_f^\mu(t)$, is the same as the original excess, $e_f(t)$. Thus relabeling does not change the value of the flow: $|f^\mu| = |f|$.

There is a particular labeling that is useful in some of the algorithms described in this chapter called the *canonical* labeling. In the canonical labeling, $\mu(i)$ is the gain of the highest gain path from i to the sink in the residual graph; that is,

$$\mu(i) = \max_{i\text{-}t \text{ paths } P \subseteq A_f} \gamma(P);$$

we assume $\mu(i) = 0$ if there is no path from i to t in A_f. Using $\mu(i)$ is potentially problematic for relabeling gains, since it is possible we might divide a number by 0. We will assume that $\gamma(i,j)\mu(j)/\mu(i) = \gamma(i,j)$ if both $\mu(i) = \mu(j) = 0$. Note that it cannot be the case that $\mu(i) = 0$ while $\mu(j) > 0$ for an arc $(i,j) \in A_f$, since if j can reach t in A_f and $(i,j) \in A_f$, then i can reach t in G_f as well.

We can find the canonical labeling by using shortest path computations in the following way: We set $c(i,j) = -\log\gamma(i,j)$. Then we observe that for any path P,

$$\sum_{(i,j)\in P} c(i,j) = -\sum_{(i,j)\in P}\log\gamma(i,j) = -\log\prod_{(i,j)\in P}\gamma(i,j) = -\log\gamma(P).$$

Thus finding an i-t path P of minimum cost gives the path of maximum gain. We know from Section 1.2 that in order for the shortest paths to the sink t to be well defined, there cannot be any negative-cost cycles that can reach t. A cycle C has negative cost if and only if

$$\sum_{(i,j)\in C} c(i,j) < 0,$$

which holds if and only if

$$\sum_{(i,j)\in C} \log \gamma(i,j) > 0,$$

which holds if and only if

$$\log \gamma(C) > 0,$$

which is true if and only if $\gamma(C) > 1$; that is, if and only if C is flow-generating. Thus we can compute canonical labels via a shortest-path computation when there are no flow-generating cycles that can reach the sink t in A_f; namely, we can compute canonical labels when there are no generalized augmenting paths in A_f.

Note that in the same sense that node potentials verify that there are no negative-cost cycles for the minimum-cost circulation problem, a canonical labeling verifies that there are no generalized augmenting paths: If a canonical labeling exists, then for any arc $(i,j) \in A_f$ such that j can reach the sink, it must be the case that $\mu(i) \geq \gamma(i,j)\mu(j)$, since the gain of the highest gain path from i to t in A_f is at least gain $\gamma(i,j)$ times the gain of the highest gain path from j to t in A_f. Thus $\gamma^\mu(i,j) = \gamma(i,j)\mu(j)/\mu(i) \leq 1$. If $\gamma^\mu(i,j) \leq 1$ for all arcs $(i,j) \in A_f$ such that j can reach the sink, then it is clear that there cannot be any flow-generating cycles with a vertex j that can reach t, since

$$\gamma(C) = \prod_{(i,j)\in C} \gamma(i,j)\frac{\mu(j)}{\mu(i)} = \gamma^\mu(C) \leq 1$$

for all $C \subseteq A_f$ where some vertex $j \in C$ can reach t; the first equality holds because all the labels $\mu(i)$ cancel going around cycle C. Thus there cannot be any generalized augmenting paths in A_f.

We can finally state and prove our optimality theorem.

Theorem 6.8: *The following three statements are equivalent for a proper flow f:*

1. *f is a maximum proper flow;*
2. *there is no generalized augmenting path in A_f;*
3. *there are labels μ such that $\gamma^\mu(i,j) \leq 1$ for all $(i,j) \in A_f^\mu$.*

Proof We have already shown that if there is a GAP Γ in A_f, then f is not a maximum proper flow. Thus we have shown that (1) implies (2).

To show that (2) implies (3), let $S \subseteq V$ be the nodes that can reach t via arcs in A_f. Then, since there are no GAPs in the residual graph, this implies that there are no negative-cost cycles in the nodes of S using the costs $c(i,j) = -\log \gamma(i,j)$. Thus we can compute a canonical labeling μ as described above. We observe that $\mu(i) > 0$ if $i \in S$, and $\mu(i) = 0$ if $i \notin S$, so that $(i,j) \in A_f^\mu$ if and only if $(i,j) \in A_f$ and $i \in S$. For any $(i,j) \in A_f^\mu$ with $i, j \in S$, we note that the properties of the canonical labeling imply that $\mu(i) \geq \gamma(i,j)\mu(j)$; if this is not the case, then there is a higher gain i-t path by using arc (i,j) together with the path of gain $\mu(j)$ from j to the sink. Therefore, for all $(i,j) \in A_f^\mu$ with $i, j \in S$,

$$\gamma^\mu(i,j) = \gamma(i,j)\frac{\mu(j)}{\mu(i)} \leq 1.$$

If $i \notin S$, then $(i,j) \notin A_f^\mu$. If $i \in S$, $j \notin S$, then $\gamma^\mu(i,j) = 0 \leq 1$, since $\mu(j) = 0$.

Finally, we show that (3) implies (1). Suppose we have a proper flow f and the given labeling μ. Consider any other proper flow $\tilde{f}$. Pick any arbitrary $(i,j) \in A$. If $f^\mu(i,j) < \tilde{f}^\mu(i,j) \leq u^\mu(i,j)$, then $f^\mu(i,j) < u^\mu(i,j)$ implies that $(i,j) \in A_f^\mu$ and $\gamma^\mu(i,j) \leq 1$. If $f^\mu(i,j) > \tilde{f}^\mu(i,j)$, then by skew symmetry $-\gamma(j,i)f^\mu(j,i) > -\gamma(j,i)\tilde{f}^\mu(j,i)$ or $f^\mu(j,i) < \tilde{f}^\mu(j,i)$. Following the same logic as previously, then $\gamma^\mu(j,i) \leq 1$, so that $\gamma^\mu(i,j) \geq 1$. Thus for any $(i,j) \in A$ we have that $(\gamma^\mu(i,j) - 1)(f^\mu(i,j) - \tilde{f}^\mu(i,j)) \geq 0$. Summing over all arcs, we get that

$$\sum_{(i,j)\in A} (\gamma^\mu(i,j) - 1)(f^\mu(i,j) - \tilde{f}^\mu(i,j)) \geq 0.$$

Rewriting, we have

$$\sum_{(i,j)\in A} \gamma^\mu(i,j)(f^\mu(i,j) - \tilde{f}^\mu(i,j)) - \sum_{(i,j)\in A} (f^\mu(i,j) - \tilde{f}^\mu(i,j)) \geq 0,$$

or, by skew symmetry,

$$\sum_{(j,i)\in A} (\tilde{f}^\mu(j,i) - f^\mu(j,i)) - \sum_{(i,j)\in A} (f^\mu(i,j) - \tilde{f}^\mu(i,j)) \geq 0. \qquad (6.4)$$

Recall that $e_f^\mu(i) = -\sum_{k:(i,k)\in A} f^\mu(i,k)$ and similarly for $\tilde{f}$. Since the inequality above sums over all arcs, it implies that

$$\sum_{i\in V} e_f^\mu(i) - \sum_{i\in V} e_{\tilde{f}}^\mu(i) \geq 0. \qquad (6.5)$$

Since both f and $\tilde{f}$ are proper flows, we have that $e_f^{\mu}(i) = e_{\tilde{f}}^{\mu}(i) = 0$ for all $i \neq t$. Thus

$$e_f^{\mu}(t) \geq e_{\tilde{f}}^{\mu}(t),$$

or, since $\mu(t) = 1$,

$$e_f(t) \geq e_{\tilde{f}}(t),$$

so that $|f| \geq |\tilde{f}|$. Thus f is a maximum proper flow, since $\tilde{f}$ was an arbitrary proper flow. □

As usual, our optimality theorem implies a natural algorithm in which we repeatedly find and cancel GAPs in the residual graph; we give the algorithm in Algorithm 6.1. However, unlike the maximum flow problem and the minimum-cost circulation problem, we cannot draw the usual conclusion of an integrality property or a pseudopolynomial-time algorithms. Because gains are not integer valued, it is not the case that flow values are integral, and residual capacities are therefore not integral even if capacities are integral. We used the integrality property for flows and circulations in many ways. One way in which we used the integrality property was in determining when we had a maximum flow (or a minimum-cost circulation): if the difference between the maximum flow value and our current flow value is less than one, then we must have a maximum flow. Similarly, if the difference in cost between the cost of our circulation and the minimum-cost circulation is less than one, then we must have a minimum-cost circulation. In the case of generalized flows, we do not have this convenience. One may or may not agree with the Kronecker quote at the beginning of the chapter, but the lack of the integrality property for generalized flows makes some issues considerably less than divine. Partially for this reason, we will often focus only on computing near-optimal solutions. We define a near-optimal solution as follows. Unfortunately, the name is similar to that used in a different way for ϵ-optimal circulations and pseudoflows in the previous

---

$f \leftarrow 0$
while there is a GAP Γ in A_f **do**
    Cancel Γ
    Update f
return f

Algorithm 6.1 GAP-canceling algorithm for the generalized maximum flow problem.

chapter; however, because it is standard in the literature, we will use the name despite the possibility for confusion.

Definition 6.9: *A proper flow f is an ϵ-optimal proper flow if $|f| \geq (1 - \epsilon)$ $|f^*|$, for f^* a maximum proper flow.*

We can indeed find a maximum proper flow when we have found an ϵ-optimal flow for ϵ sufficiently small; but ϵ must be quite small. We state the following theorem without proof. Recall that we assume that the capacities are integers and the gains are expressed as the ratio of integers, and we let B denote the largest integer used in expressing both the capacities and the gains.

Theorem 6.10: *If we find an ϵ-optimal proper flow with $\epsilon < 1/(m! \cdot B^{2m})$, then we can find a maximum proper flow in $O(m^2 n)$ time.*

Nevertheless, we are able to compute ϵ-optimal proper flows and maximum proper flows in polynomial time, as we will see in the next few sections.

We conclude this section by discussing a variant of the flow problem above. We have so far discussed computing proper flows and our optimality theorem is for proper flows, but it is sometimes useful to think about computing maximum generalized flows in which excesses can exist at nodes. Furthermore, it is also sometimes useful to consider the case in which there are supplies that are part of the input to the problem; we did not earlier discuss this possibility in order to focus on the issue of flow creation via flow-generating cycles and GAPs. Thus we have as an additional input a supply $b(i) \geq 0$ for all $i \in V$. Then the excess $e_f(i)$ of flow f at node i is

$$e_f(i) = b(i) - \sum_{k:(i,k)\in A} f(i,k).$$

If we introduce labels μ, then the relabeled supply $b^\mu(i) = b(i)\mu(i)$, so that again $e_f^\mu(i) = b^\mu(i) - \sum_{k:(i,k)\in A} f^\mu(i,k) = e_f(i)\mu(i)$. In this case, we may have *augmenting paths* that push flow from nodes with positive excess to the sink. Then our optimality theorem becomes the following.

Theorem 6.11: *The following three statements are equivalent for a generalized flow f:*

1. *f is a maximum flow;*
2. *there is no generalized augmenting path or augmenting path in A_f;*
3. *there are labels μ such that $\gamma^\mu(i, j) \leq 1$ for all $(i, j) \in A_f^\mu$ and $e_f^\mu(i) = 0$ for all $i \neq t$.*

Proof The proof is similar to the proof of Theorem 6.8. Clearly if there is a GAP or an augmenting path from a node with positive excess to the sink in the residual graph, the flow is not maximum, so we have that (1) implies (2).

The proof that (2) implies (3) is similar to the proof of the same implication for Theorem 6.8. The only remaining item to note is that (2) implies that the only nodes with positive excess $e_f(i) > 0$ are those that cannot reach the sink t via arcs in A_f. Thus in the canonical labeling, such nodes i receive a label $\mu(i) = 0$, so that $e_f^\mu(i) = 0$ for all $i \in V$.

Finally, to prove that (3) implies (1), we note that we did not use the fact that f or $\tilde{f}$ were proper flows to derive Inequality (6.4); it is sufficient that they are flows. By adding and subtracting $2\sum_{i \in V} b^\mu(i)$ to the left-hand side of Inequality (6.4), we obtain

$$2\sum_{i \in V} b^\mu(i) - 2\sum_{i \in V} b^\mu(i) + \sum_{(j,i) \in A} (\tilde{f}^\mu(j,i) - f^\mu(j,i))$$
$$- \sum_{(i,j) \in A} (f^\mu(i,j) - \tilde{f}^\mu(i,j)) \geq 0.$$

From this we can rederive Inequality (6.5) (recall that in this setting, $e_f^\mu(i) = b^\mu(i) - \sum_{k:(i,k) \in A} f^\mu(i,k)$), so that we have that

$$\sum_{i \in V} e_f^\mu(i) - \sum_{i \in V} e_{\tilde{f}}^\mu(i) \geq 0.$$

By hypothesis, $e_f^\mu(i) = 0$ for all $i \neq t$, so that Inequality (6.5) implies that

$$e_f^\mu(t) \geq \sum_{i \in V} e_{\tilde{f}}^\mu(i) \geq e_{\tilde{f}}^\mu(t),$$

since $\tilde{f}$ is a flow. Thus $e_f(t) \geq e_{\tilde{f}}(t)$, since $\mu(t) = 1$, and $|f| \geq |\tilde{f}|$. Since $\tilde{f}$ was an arbitrary flow, f must be maximum.   □

6.2 A Wallacher-Style GAP-Canceling Algorithm

For this section, we assume that we are trying to find a maximum generalized proper flow, so that $b(i) = 0$ for all $i \in V$. Our first polynomial-time algorithm for generalized flow is an adaptation of Wallacher's algorithm of Section 5.2 for the minimum-cost circulation problem.

In order to analyze Wallacher's algorithm, we needed a flow decomposition lemma for circulations, which the reader proved in Exercise 5.1. The analogous decomposition for generalized flows is somewhat more complicated.

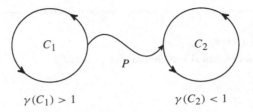

Figure 6.4 A bicycle consists of a flow-generating cycle C_1 connected to a flow-absorbing cycle C_2 by a path P.

It can be shown that a proper flow can be decomposed into generalized augmenting paths, unit-gain cycles, or a structure called a *bicycle*, which is a flow-generating cycle connected by a path to a flow-absorbing cycle; see Figure 6.4. We have the reader prove the following lemma in Exercise 6.2.

Lemma 6.12: *Any proper flow f can be decomposed into proper flows $f_1, f_2, \ldots, f_\ell, \ell \leq m$, such that $f = \sum_{i=1}^{\ell} f_i$, $|f| = \sum_{i=1}^{\ell} |f_i|$, and for each i, the arcs of f_i of positive flow are a generalized augmenting path, a unit-gain cycle, or a bicycle.*

Recall the characteristic flow $\chi(\Gamma)$ for a GAP Γ. Suppose we have a proper flow f. If we cancel a GAP Γ in A_f, then we increase the flow on arcs in Γ by $\delta \cdot \chi(\Gamma)$ where $\delta = \min_{(i,j) \in \Gamma} u_f(i,j)/\chi(\Gamma,i,j)$. The increase in flow value is $\delta|\chi(\Gamma)|$. Thus if we want to find the GAP that results in the greatest improvement in the value of the flow, we would find the GAP that maximizes

$$|\chi(\Gamma)| \cdot \min_{(i,j) \in \Gamma} \frac{u_f(i,j)}{\chi(\Gamma,i,j)} = \frac{|\chi(\Gamma)|}{\max_{(i,j) \in \Gamma} \frac{\chi(\Gamma,i,j)}{u_f(i,j)}}.$$

As we did in Wallacher's algorithm, we replace the max in the denominator with a sum, so that for a given Γ, we have the ratio

$$\beta(\Gamma) = \frac{|\chi(\Gamma)|}{\sum_{(i,j) \in \Gamma} \frac{\chi(\Gamma,i,j)}{u_f(i,j)}}.$$

For a given proper flow f, we search for the GAP Γ in A_f that maximizes the ratio; that is, we want the GAP that achieves

$$\beta(f) = \max_{\Gamma \subseteq A_f} \frac{|\chi(\Gamma)|}{\sum_{(i,j) \in \Gamma} \frac{\chi(\Gamma,i,j)}{u_f(i,j)}}.$$

We summarize the resulting algorithm in Algorithm 6.2.

As with Wallacher's algorithm for the minimum-cost circulation problem, we show that canceling the GAP Γ that achieves $\beta(f)$ increases the value of

$f \leftarrow 0$
repeat $m \ln \frac{1}{\epsilon}$ **times**
  Let Γ be a GAP in A_f such that $\beta(\Gamma) = \beta(f)$
  Cancel Γ
  Update f
return f

Algorithm 6.2 An ϵ-approximate Wallacher-style GAP-canceling algorithm for the generalized maximum flow problem.

proper flow f by at least a $1/m$ factor of the difference between the maximum flow value and the current flow value.

Lemma 6.13: *Let f be a proper flow and f^* a maximum proper flow. Then $\beta(f) \geq \frac{1}{m}(|f^*| - |f|)$.*

Proof By a standard argument (at this point), we can show that $f^* - f$ is a proper flow in G_f of value $|f^*| - |f|$. By using Lemma 6.12, we can decompose $f^* - f$ into $f_1, \ldots, f_h$ corresponding to at most m GAPs, bicycles, and unit-gain cycles. Let $\Gamma_1, \ldots, \Gamma_\ell$ be the GAPs, and let δ_k be such that $f_k = \delta_k \cdot \chi(\Gamma_k)$ for $k = 1, \ldots, \ell$. Then

$$|f^*| - |f| = \sum_{k=1}^{\ell} |f_k| = \sum_{k=1}^{\ell} \delta_k |\chi(\Gamma_k)|$$

$$= \sum_{k=1}^{\ell} \beta(\Gamma_k) \left(\sum_{(i,j) \in \Gamma_k} \frac{\delta_k \cdot \chi(\Gamma_k, i, j)}{u_f(i,j)} \right)$$

$$\leq \beta(f) \sum_{k=1}^{\ell} \left(\sum_{(i,j) \in \Gamma_k} \frac{\delta_k \cdot \chi(\Gamma_k, i, j)}{u_f(i,j)} \right)$$

$$= \beta(f) \sum_{(i,j) \in A_f} \frac{1}{u_f(i,j)} \sum_{k:(i,j) \in \Gamma_k} \delta_k \cdot \chi(\Gamma_k, i, j),$$

$$\leq \beta(f) \cdot m,$$

because for each arc $(i,j) \in A_f$, $\sum_{k:(i,j) \in \Gamma_k} \delta_k \cdot \chi(\Gamma_k, i, j) \leq u_f(i,j)$, as $\delta_k \cdot \chi(\Gamma_k)$ gives a decomposition of a flow in G_f. $\square$

Lemma 6.14: *Let f be a proper flow and let Γ be a GAP in A_f. Canceling Γ increases the value of the flow by at least $\beta(\Gamma)$. In particular, if $\beta(\Gamma) \geq \hat{\beta}$ for some $\hat{\beta}$, then the value of the flow is increased by at least $\hat{\beta}$.*

Proof Recall that we increase the flow f on the arcs of Γ by $\delta \cdot \chi(\Gamma)$, where $\delta = \min_{(i,j) \in \Gamma} u_f(i,j)/\chi(\Gamma,i,j)$. Thus the value of the flow increases by

$$\delta|\chi(\Gamma)| = \beta(\Gamma) \left(\sum_{(i,j)\in\Gamma} \delta \cdot \frac{\chi(\Gamma,i,j)}{u_f(i,j)} \right) \geq \beta(\Gamma) \geq \hat{\beta},$$

since $\delta = u_f(i,j)/\chi(\Gamma,i,j)$ for some arc $(i,j) \in \Gamma$. $\qquad\square$

We can now combine the previous two lemmas into a theorem with a proof very similar to that of Theorem 5.6 for the most improving algorithm for the minimum-cost circulation problem. The only significant difference is the termination condition.

Theorem 6.15: *Algorithm 6.2 terminates with an ϵ-optimal proper flow in $m \ln \frac{1}{\epsilon}$ iterations.*

Proof The iteration count is by construction of the algorithm. Let $f^{(k)}$ be the proper flow resulting from the algorithm after k iterations if we start with proper flow f. If in each iteration we cancel a GAP Γ such that $\beta(f) = \beta(\Gamma)$, we get from Lemmas 6.13 and 6.14 that the resulting proper flow $f^{(1)}$ has value at least

$$|f^{(1)}| \geq |f| + \beta(f) \geq |f| + \frac{1}{m}(|f^*| - |f|).$$

Thus

$$|f^*| - |f^{(1)}| \leq \left(1 - \frac{1}{m}\right)(|f^*| - |f|),$$

and after k iterations,

$$|f^*| - |f^{(k)}| \leq \left(1 - \frac{1}{m}\right)^k (|f^*| - |f|).$$

Thus if we set $k = m \ln \frac{1}{\epsilon}$ and use $1 - x < e^{-x}$ for $x \neq 0$, we have that

$$|f^*| - |f^{(k)}| < e^{-\ln(1/\epsilon)}|f^*| = \epsilon|f^*|,$$

so that $|f^{(k)}| > (1 - \epsilon)|f^*|$ and hence $f^{(k)}$ is an ϵ-optimal proper flow. $\qquad\square$

Rather than explain how to find the GAP Γ such that $\beta(f) = \beta(\Gamma)$, we turn instead to a scaling version of the algorithm, just as we had a scaling version of the most improving path algorithm for the maximum flow problem (in Section 2.5) and a scaling version of Wallacher's algorithm for the minimum-cost circulation problem (in Section 5.2). As before, we maintain a scaling parameter $\hat{\beta}$, and we find GAPs such that $\beta(\Gamma) \geq \hat{\beta}$. To do this, we introduce costs on the arcs: we let $c(i, j) = \hat{\beta}/u_f(i, j)$, and we introduce a new sink t', and a new arc (t, t') of cost $c(t, t') = -1$ and gain $\gamma(t, t') = 1$. Let G'_f denote this new residual graph with costs and the extra arc (t, t'). We consider the cost of a GAP $c(\Gamma)$, which we define to be $\sum_{(i,j)\in\Gamma} c(i, j)\chi(\Gamma, i, j)$; that is, the cost of each arc gets multiplied by the characteristic flow for the GAP on the arc. We say that Γ has negative-cost if and only if $c(\Gamma) < 0$. Then we have the following.

Lemma 6.16: *For a GAP Γ, $c(\Gamma) < 0$ in the new graph G'_f if and only if $\beta(\Gamma) > \hat{\beta}$ in the original residual graph G_f.*

Proof Clearly the cost is negative if and only if

$$c(\Gamma) = \hat{\beta} \sum_{(i,j)\in\Gamma:(i,j)\neq(t,t')} \frac{\chi(\Gamma, i, j)}{u_f(i, j)} - |\chi(\Gamma)| < 0,$$

which holds if and only if

$$\hat{\beta} < \frac{|\chi(\Gamma)|}{\sum_{(i,j)\in\Gamma:(i,j)\neq(t,t')} \frac{\chi(\Gamma, i, j)}{u_f(i, j)}} = \beta(\Gamma)$$

in the original residual graph G_f. □

Then the algorithmic idea is clear: we find negative-cost GAPs in G'_f (if they exist) and cancel them in G_f. If none exist, we divide $\hat{\beta}$ by 2, and repeat. To start with, we initialize $\hat{\beta}$ to B^2: Canceling any GAP can increase the value of flow by at most the maximum capacity of an arc times the maximum gain. We can upper bound both the arc capacity and the maximum gain by B, so that B^2 upper bounds the amount by which the value can increase by canceling any GAP. We summarize these ideas in Algorithm 6.3.

Of course, in order for this algorithm to work, we need to have a subroutine that will detect and return a negative-cost GAP if one exists. In Section 6.3, we will show the following theorem. The algorithm is very similar to the Bellman–Ford algorithm of Section 1.3 for detecting negative-cost cycles, although the analysis is somewhat more involved. For the algorithm to work, the graph must not have a negative-cost unit gain cycle or a negative-cost bicycle. In our algorithm, the only arc in G'_f with negative cost is the edge (t, t'), and there are no arcs out of t', so there cannot be any negative-cost unit gain cycles or bicycles in G'_f.

Theorem 6.17: *We can detect and return a negative-cost GAP in $O(mn)$ time if the graph has no negative-cost unit gain cycles and no negative-cost bicycles.*

$f \leftarrow 0$
$\hat{\beta} \leftarrow B^2$
while $\hat{\beta} > \frac{\epsilon}{2m}|f|$ **do**
    Create G'_f by adding t', (t,t') with $\gamma(t,t') = 1$ to G_f
    Set $c(t,t') = -1$, $c(i,j) = \hat{\beta}/u_f(i,j)$ in G'_f for all $(i,j) \in A_f$
    if there is GAP Γ in G'_f with $c(\Gamma) < 0$ **then**
        Cancel Γ
        Update f
    else
        $\hat{\beta} \leftarrow \hat{\beta}/2$
return f

Algorithm 6.3 A scaling version of the Wallacher-style GAP-canceling algorithm for the generalized maximum flow problem.

The analysis of Algorithm 6.3 is similar to that of the scaling algorithms mentioned previously. We define a $\hat{\beta}$-*scaling phase* to be the iterations of the algorithm for a fixed value of $\hat{\beta}$. We show that we cannot have too many iterations per $\hat{\beta}$-scaling phase.

Lemma 6.18: *There are at most $2m$ iterations per $\hat{\beta}$-scaling phase.*

Proof We argued previously that canceling any GAP can increase the value of the flow by at most B^2, and we know from Lemma 6.14 that canceling any GAP Γ increases the value of the flow by at least $\beta(\Gamma)$. Because we initialize $\hat{\beta}$ to B^2, we know that initially $\beta(\Gamma) \leq \hat{\beta}$ for any GAP $\Gamma \subseteq A_f$. Furthermore, by Lemma 6.16, when there are no more negative-cost GAPs in G'_f, ending the current $\hat{\beta}$-scaling phase, it is the case that $\beta(\Gamma) \leq \hat{\beta}$ for any GAP $\Gamma \subseteq A_f$; this is true also for the GAP $\Gamma \subseteq A_f$ such that $\beta(f) = \beta(\Gamma)$. Thus by Lemma 6.13, at the end of a $\hat{\beta}$-scaling phase, $\hat{\beta} \geq \beta(f) \geq \frac{1}{m}(|f^*| - |f|)$. At the end of the $\hat{\beta}$ scaling phase, we divide $\hat{\beta}$ by 2, so that at the start of the next $\hat{\beta}$-scaling phase, $\hat{\beta} \geq \frac{1}{2m}(|f^*| - |f|)$. If we start with flow f at the beginning of this $\hat{\beta}$-scaling phase, by Lemma 6.16 each GAP canceled increases the value of the flow by at least $\beta(\Gamma) > \hat{\beta} \geq \frac{1}{2m}(|f^*| - |f|)$. Thus after k cancelations, the value of the flow is at least $|f| + \frac{k}{2m}(|f^*| - |f|)$. So after $2m$ iterations, the value of the flow is at least $|f^*|$, so that there are no additional iterations possible in the $\hat{\beta}$-scaling phase. $\qquad \square$

We also need to argue that we have an ϵ-optimal proper flow when we terminate.

Lemma 6.19: *Algorithm 6.3 terminates with an ϵ-optimal proper flow.*

Proof As we argued in the proof of Lemma 6.18, at the start of a $\hat{\beta}$-scaling phase, $\hat{\beta} \geq \frac{1}{2m}(|f^*| - |f|)$. Thus if $\hat{\beta} \leq \frac{\epsilon}{2m}|f|$, we have that $|f^*| - |f| \leq \epsilon|f| \leq \epsilon|f^*|$, which implies that $|f| \geq (1 - \epsilon)|f^*|$.   □

We will show in Section 6.3 how we can find a negative-cost GAP in $O(mn)$ time, given that there are no negative-cost unit-gain cycles or bicycles in G'_f. Given this running time, we can bound the running time of Algorithm 6.3. We assume that $|f^*| > 0$. We can remove this assumption by using the negative-cost GAP algorithm to initially test whether there are any GAPs in the residual graph G_f for $f = 0$. If not, then $f = 0$ is optimal. Otherwise it must be the case that $|f^*| > 0$. We need this assumption in order to invoke the following lemma, whose proof we omit; see the Chapter Notes for a pointer to a proof.

Lemma 6.20: *If $|f^*| > 0$, then $|f^*| \geq 1/(m!\,B^{2m})$.*

We can now bound the number of iterations of the algorithm.

Theorem 6.21: *Assuming $|f^*| > 0$, Algorithm 6.3 computes an ϵ-optimal proper flow in $O(m^2 n \log \frac{mB}{\epsilon})$ time.*

Proof We split the $\hat{\beta}$-scaling phases into two types: those before the first GAP is canceled, and those afterwards. For those of the first type, we need only one negative-cost GAP detection per $\hat{\beta}$-scaling phase. From the proof of Lemma 6.18 and from Lemma 6.20, we know that at the start of each such $\hat{\beta}$-scaling phase, $\hat{\beta} \geq \frac{1}{2m}(|f^*| - |f|) = \frac{1}{2m}|f^*| \geq \frac{1}{2m \cdot m!\,B^{2m}}$, since $|f| = 0$ until the first GAP is canceled. Thus we can have at most $O(\log(2m \cdot m!\,B^{2m})) = O(m \log(mB))$ $\hat{\beta}$-scaling phases of the first type, and thus at most $O(m \log(mB))$ negative-cost GAP subroutine calls for scaling phases of the first type. Once the first GAP is canceled, we have by Lemma 6.14 that the value of the flow becomes $|f| \geq \hat{\beta}$. From this point on, $|f|$ only increases and $\hat{\beta}$ only decreases, so that it must take at most $O(\log \frac{2m}{\epsilon})$ $\hat{\beta}$-scaling phases of the second type before $\hat{\beta} \leq \frac{\epsilon}{2m}|f|$. We have at most $2m$ negative-cost GAP detections per $\hat{\beta}$-scaling phase of the second type, for $O(m \log \frac{2m}{\epsilon})$ negative-cost GAP subroutine calls for the $\hat{\beta}$-scaling phases of the second type. Thus we need $O(m \log(mB)) + O(m \log \frac{m}{\epsilon}) = O(m \log \frac{mB}{\epsilon})$ negative-cost GAP subroutine calls overall, for a total running time of $O(m^2 n \log \frac{mB}{\epsilon})$.   □

Corollary 6.22: *We can compute a maximum proper flow in $O(m^3 n \log(mB))$ time.*

Proof If we set $\epsilon < 1/m!\,B^{2m}$, then we can apply Theorem 6.10 and compute a maximum proper flow from an ϵ-optimal flow.   □

6.3 Negative-Cost GAP Detection

In this section, we give the subroutine used to find a negative-cost GAP in the algorithm of Section 6.2. We are given as input a graph $G = (V, A)$ with costs $c(i, j)$ for all $(i, j) \in A$. The subroutine will find a negative-cost GAP if one exists assuming the graph does not have any negative-cost unit-gain cycles or bicycles. We argued previously that Algorithm 6.3 calls this subroutine with graphs that do not have negative-cost unit-gain cycles or negative-cost bicycles.

As mentioned previously, the algorithm we give will be similar to the adaptation of the Bellman–Ford algorithm for finding negative-cost cycles given in Section 1.3. We will compute a value $d_k(i)$, which will be the minimum cost needed to send a single unit of flow starting at i and ending at t on a path (possibly non-simple) of exactly k arcs. Then inductively we have that

$$d_k(i) = \min_{(i, j) \in A} (c(i, j) + \gamma(i, j)d_{k-1}(j)),$$

since we incur a cost of $c(i, j)$ to send one unit of flow from i to j on arc (i, j); $\gamma(i, j)$ units of flow arrive at j, and it costs $\gamma(i, j)d_{k-1}(j)$ to send $\gamma(i, j)$ units of flow from j to t on a path of exactly $k - 1$ arcs. The details are given in Algorithm 6.4. Unlike the Bellman–Ford algorithm, we run the algorithm for $2n$ iterations. We let $d(i)$ be the minimum value of $d_k(i)$ over all of the values

---

$d_0(t) \leftarrow 0; d_0(i) \leftarrow \infty$ for all $i \neq t$
for $k \leftarrow 1$ to $2n$ **do**
    for $i \in V$ **do**
        $d_k(i) \leftarrow \min_{(i,j) \in A} (c(i, j) + \gamma(i, j)d_{k-1}(j))$
for $i \in V$ **do**
    $d(i) \leftarrow \min_{k=0,\dots,2n-1} d_k(i)$
if $d_{2n}(i) \geq d(i)$ for all $i \in V$ **then**
    return ("No negative-cost GAP")
for all $i \in V$ **do**
    Let k be the smallest value in $[0, \dots, 2n - 1]$ such that $d_k(i) = d(i)$
    Trace back k arc walk defining $d(i)$ to last repeated j before sink (if any). Let C be cycle, if it exists, P the j-t path.
    if C exists and $\gamma(C) > 1$ **then**
        Let GAP $\Gamma = C + P$
        return (Γ)
return ("No negative-cost GAP")

Algorithm 6.4 Algorithm for negative-cost GAP detection.

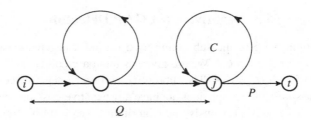

Figure 6.5 Example of non-simple path created from i to t by dynamic program of Algorithm 6.4.

of k from 0 to $2n - 1$. If for all $i \in V$, we have $d_{2n}(i) \geq d(i)$, then we can show that there is no negative-cost GAP; this is similar to the last iteration of the negative-cost cycle detection algorithm in Algorithm 1.6. Otherwise, for each $i \in V$, we look for the smallest value of k such that $d_k(i) = d(i)$ and trace the (possibly non-simple) path that defines $d_k(i)$ back to the sink t. If the path is non-simple, we look for the repeated vertex j that is closest to the sink, and use this to define a cycle C (that contains the repetition of the vertex j) and a simple path P from j to the sink t (see Figure 6.5). If the cycle C is such that $\gamma(C) > 1$, then we have found a GAP. We claim that the GAP must have negative cost, and we return it. If we do not find a GAP after checking each $i \in V$, then we claim that there is no negative-cost GAP. Below we prove our claims to establish the correctness of the algorithm.

In what follows, we let the characteristic flow of C starting at node j be denoted $\chi(C, j)$ and let it be the circulation that results on C that has a single unit of flow on the arc $(j, \ell) \in C$ directed out of j. Let $\chi(C, j, h, \ell)$ be this characteristic flow on the arc (h, ℓ). Then we denote the cost of C by $c(C, j) = \sum_{(h, \ell) \in C} c(h, \ell) \cdot \chi(C, j, h, \ell)$. Similarly, for sending a unit of flow on a path P starting at node j, let $\chi(P, j)$ be the characteristic flow on the path P, and denote the cost of the path P by $c(P, j) = \sum_{(h, \ell) \in P} c(h, \ell) \cdot \chi(P, j, h, \ell)$.

Lemma 6.23: *Let k be the smallest value in $0, 1, \ldots, 2n - 1$ such that $d_k(i) = d(i)$. Consider the length k path from i to t that defines $d_k(i)$, and suppose that the path is non-simple. Let j be the vertex that is closest to the sink that is repeated in the path, and C the cycle in the path from the second-to-last appearance of j to the last appearance of j, and P the path from the last appearance of j in the path to t, as in Figure 6.5. Then $d_{|P|+|C|}(j) < d_{|P|}(j)$.*

Proof Let Q be the (possibly non-simple) path from i to the second-to-last appearance of j in the path that defines $d_k(i)$. We have that $d(i) = d_k(i) = c(Q, i) + \gamma(Q) d_{|P|+|C|}(j)$. Also, since there is a path of $k - |C|$ arcs from

i to t, of the path Q followed by the path P, by the properties of the dynamic program, it must be the case that $d_{k-|C|}(i) \leq c(Q,i) + \gamma(Q)d_{|P|}(j)$. Then if $d_{|P|+|C|}(j) \geq d_{|P|}(j)$ it follows by combining the previous two inequalities that

$$d(i) = d_k(i)$$
$$= c(Q,i) + \gamma(Q)d_{|P|+|C|}(j) \geq c(Q,i) + \gamma(Q)d_{|P|}(j) \geq d_{k-|C|}(i),$$

which contradicts either our definition of $d(i)$ (if $d(i) > d_{k-|C|}(i)$) or our choice of k. $\qquad\square$

Lemma 6.24: *If the algorithm returns a GAP Γ, then $c(\Gamma) < 0$.*

Proof Suppose we are given path P and cycle C with node j as defined in the statement of the previous lemma; because the algorithm returns a GAP, we know that $\gamma(C) > 1$ and C is flow-generating, so that Γ is indeed a GAP. By Lemma 6.23, $d_{|P|+|C|}(j) < d_{|P|}(j)$. It is clear that

$$d_{|P|+|C|}(j) = c(C,j) + \gamma(C)d_{|P|}(j),$$

and $d_{|P|}(j) = c(P,j)$. Thus

$$0 > d_{|P|+|C|}(j) - d_{|P|}(j)$$
$$= c(C,j) + \gamma(C)c(P,j) - c(P,j)$$
$$= c(C,j) + (\gamma(C) - 1)c(P,j)$$
$$= c(\Gamma),$$

so that the lemma statement is proven. $\qquad\square$

Lemma 6.25: *If the algorithm does not return a negative-cost GAP, then there is no negative-cost GAP.*

Proof We prove the lemma by contradiction. Suppose there is a negative-cost GAP Γ consisting of a i-t path P (possibly empty) and a flow-generating cycle C containing i. Let k be the smallest value in $[0,1,\ldots,2n-1]$ such that $d(i) = d_k(i)$. Let Q be the (possibly non-simple) length k path from i to t such that $d_k(i) = c(Q,i)$.

We first claim that Q cannot be a simple i-t path. Suppose otherwise. Then

$$c(Q,i) = d_k(i) = d(i) \leq d_{|P|}(i) = c(P,i).$$

Then we claim that the GAP formed by the flow-generating cycle C and the i-t simple path Q is also a negative-cost GAP Γ'. To see this we note that

$$c(\Gamma') = c(C,i) + (\gamma(C) - 1)c(Q,i) \leq c(C,i) + (\gamma(C) - 1)c(P,i) = c(\Gamma) < 0.$$
$$\tag{6.6}$$

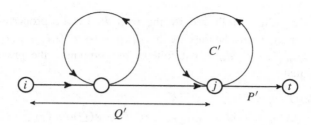

Figure 6.6 Example of non-simple path Q created from i to t by dynamic program in the proof of Lemma 6.25.

From this inequality, we conclude that

$$c(C,i) + \gamma(C)c(Q,i) < c(Q,i) = d(i).$$

But this implies that the walk that starts at i, follows C and then Q, is a i-t path of cost less than $d(i)$, so that $d_{|C|+|Q|}(i) < d(i)$. However, since $|C| + |Q| \leq 2n - 1$, this contradicts the choice of k that defined $d(i) = d_k(i)$.

Since Q is non-simple, we now partition Q into three parts. Let j be the last repeated vertex on the path Q from i to t, and let C' be the cycle defined by Q between the second-to-last appearance of j in Q and the last appearance of j. Let P' be the path on Q from the last appearance of j to t. Let Q' be the path from i to the second-to-last appearance of j in Q (See Figure 6.6). By Lemma 6.23, $d_{|C'|+|P'|}(j) < d_{|P'|}(j)$, so that it must be the case that $c(C',j) + \gamma(C')c(P',j) < c(P',j)$, or

$$c(C',j) + (\gamma(C') - 1)c(P',j) < 0. \tag{6.7}$$

We now argue that it cannot be the case that C' is flow-generating, unit-gain, or flow-absorbing, and thus the non-simple path Q cannot exist, completing the contradiction.

If C' is flow-generating, then the algorithm will return the GAP formed by C' and P', and by Inequality (6.7) it will be a negative-cost GAP.

If C' is unit-gain, then by Inequality (6.7) we have that $c(C',j) < 0$. Then C' is a negative-cost unit-gain cycle, and by hypothesis there are no such cycles.

If C' is flow-absorbing, then we will show that the walk formed by the flow-generating cycle C, the path Q', and the flow-absorbing cycle C' forms a negative-cost bicycle, and by hypothesis there are no negative-cost bicycles. We start by determining the cost of a flow on the bicycle starting with a unit flow from i on C. The cost $c(C,i)$ the cost of the flow on the cycle C, resulting in $\gamma(C) - 1$ units of flow to send along the path Q' at cost $(\gamma(C) - 1)c(Q',i)$, resulting in $(\gamma(C) - 1)\gamma(Q')$ units of flow that are absorbed in the flow-absorbing cycle C' at cost

$$(\gamma(C) - 1)\gamma(Q')c(C',j)\left[1 + \gamma(C') + \gamma(C')^2 + \gamma(C')^3 + \cdots\right]$$
$$= (\gamma(C) - 1)\gamma(Q')\left[c(C',j)/(1 - \gamma(C'))\right].$$

Thus the cost of the bicycle is

$$c(C,i) + (\gamma(C) - 1)c(Q',i) + (\gamma(C) - 1)\gamma(Q')c(C',j)/(1 - \gamma(C')). \quad (6.8)$$

We will now show that this cost is negative. We know by Inequality (6.7) that

$$c(C',j) + \gamma(C')c(P',j) < c(P',j),$$

so that

$$c(P',j) > c(C',j)/(1 - \gamma(C')).$$

From Inequality (6.6), we know that

$$c(C,i) + (\gamma(C) - 1)c(Q,i) < 0.$$

Then, after observing that

$$c(Q,i) = c(Q',i) + \gamma(Q')c(C',j) + \gamma(Q')\gamma(C')c(P',j),$$

we get that

$$0 > c(C,i) + (\gamma(C) - 1)[c(Q',i) + \gamma(Q')c(C',j) + \gamma(Q')\gamma(C')c(P',j)]$$
$$> c(C,i) + (\gamma(C) - 1)[c(Q',i) + \gamma(Q')c(C',j)$$
$$+ \gamma(Q')\gamma(C')c(C',j)/(1 - \gamma(C'))]$$
$$= c(C,i) + (\gamma(C) - 1)\left[c(Q',i) + \gamma(Q')c(C',j)\left(1 + \frac{\gamma(C')}{1 - \gamma(C')}\right)\right]$$
$$= c(C,i) + (\gamma(C) - 1)[c(Q',i) + \gamma(Q')c(C',j)/(1 - \gamma(C'))],$$

where the final expression is the cost of the bicycle from (6.8), showing that the cost of the bicycle is negative.

Thus we have reached a contradiction, and it must be the case that if no negative-cost GAP is returned, then none exists. □

6.4 Lossy Graphs, Truemper's Algorithm, and Gain Scaling

In this section, we turn to the case in which supplies $b(i)$ may be nonzero and we compute a maximum generalized flow, rather than a proper flow. In

Section 6.2, we gave an algorithm that used the part of the optimality theorem, Theorem 6.8, that says that a proper flow is maximum if and only if there are no GAPs. In this section, we use the other optimality theorem (Theorem 6.11) and give an algorithm that uses the other condition: namely, a proper flow is maximum if and only if there are labels μ such that $\gamma^\mu(i, j) \leq 1$ for all arcs $(i, j) \in A_f^\mu$ and $e_f^\mu(i) = 0$ for all $i \neq t$.

We first argue that in the case of finding a flow (instead of a proper flow), we can reduce to the case of a *lossy graph*: a lossy graph is one in which all arcs (i, j) of positive capacity have gain $\gamma(i, j) \leq 1$. To reduce to the case of a lossy graph, we cancel all flow-generating cycles, which allows us to compute labels such that the resulting relabeled residual graph is lossy. In Exercise 6.4, we have the reader show that we can use our previous negative-cost cycle-canceling algorithms to cancel all flow-generating cycles in $O(m^2 n^3 \log(nB))$ time. In particular, for a flow-generating cycle C, we pick some arc $(i, j) \in C$. If we push δ units of flow on (i, j) to cancel C, then an excess of $\delta(\gamma(C) - 1)$ units of flow results at node i, and we increase $b(i)$ by $\delta(\gamma(C) - 1)$. Recall from Section 6.1 that we can compute canonical labels by setting costs $c(i, j) = -\log \gamma(i, j)$ when there are no flow-generating cycles that can reach the sink, and the resulting labels μ are such that $\gamma^\mu(i, j) \leq 1$ for each arc (i, j) of positive residual capacity. Thus the relabeled residual graph is lossy, and has nonnegative supplies $b^\mu(i)$ for all nodes i. See Algorithm 6.5 for a summary.

We now show that if we can find a maximum flow in the lossy graph returned by Algorithm 6.5, then we can find a maximum flow in the original graph.

Lemma 6.26: *Let $\bar{f}$ be the flow computed by Algorithm 6.5, and $\bar{\mu}$ be the canonical labels. Then for a maximum flow f computed in the output lossy graph, the flow $f + \bar{f}^{\bar{\mu}}$ is maximum for the original input graph relabeled by $\bar{\mu}$.*

Algorithm: ReduceToLossy($\bar{G}, \bar{u}, \bar{\gamma}, \bar{b}$)

$\bar{f} \leftarrow 0$

while there is a flow-generating cycle C in $\bar{A}_{\bar{f}}$ **do**

    Pick $i \in C$, let δ be amount of flow needed to cancel C

    Cancel C and update $\bar{f}$

$\bar{b} \leftarrow e_{\bar{f}}$

Compute canonical labels $\bar{\mu}$ in $\bar{G}_{\bar{f}}$

return $(\bar{G}, \bar{u}_{\bar{f}}^{\bar{\mu}}, \bar{\gamma}^{\bar{\mu}}, \bar{b}^{\bar{\mu}}, \bar{f}^{\bar{\mu}})$

Algorithm 6.5 Algorithm to reduce to case of lossy graphs.

Proof Let $\bar{G}$ be the original input graph, with capacities $\bar{u}$, gains $\bar{\gamma}$, and supplies $\bar{b}$. The algorithm computes flow $\bar{f}$ and labels $\bar{\mu}$, and outputs graph $G = \bar{G}$ with capacities $u = \bar{u}_{\bar{f}}^{\bar{\mu}}$, gains $\gamma = \bar{\gamma}^{\bar{\mu}}$, and supplies $b = e_{\bar{f}}^{\bar{\mu}}$. If we compute a maximum flow f in the output graph, we have labels μ such that $\gamma^{\mu}(i, j) \leq 1$ for all arcs $(i, j) \in A_f$, and $e_f^{\mu}(i) = 0$ for all $i \neq t$. We now wish to argue that $g^{\bar{\mu}} = f + \bar{f}^{\bar{\mu}}$ is a maximum flow for the original input instance relabeled with $\bar{\mu}$.

The flow g obeys capacity constraints in the original (relabeled) instance, since for any $(i, j) \in A$,

$$f(i, j) \leq u(i, j) = \bar{u}_{\bar{f}}^{\bar{\mu}}(i, j) = \bar{u}^{\bar{\mu}}(i, j) - \bar{f}^{\bar{\mu}}(i, j) \qquad (6.9)$$

so that $f(i, j) + \bar{f}^{\bar{\mu}}(i, j) \leq \bar{u}^{\bar{\mu}}(i, j)$. Furthermore, g obeys skew-symmetry, since both f and $\bar{f}^{\bar{\mu}}$ obey skew-symmetry, so that

$$\begin{aligned} g^{\bar{\mu}}(i, j) = f(i, j) + \bar{f}^{\bar{\mu}}(i, j) &= -\gamma(j, i) f(j, i) - \bar{\gamma}^{\bar{\mu}}(j, i) \bar{f}^{\bar{\mu}}(j, i) \\ &= -\bar{\gamma}^{\bar{\mu}}(j, i) f(j, i) - \bar{\gamma}^{\bar{\mu}}(j, i) \bar{f}^{\bar{\mu}}(j, i) \\ &= -\bar{\gamma}^{\bar{\mu}}(j, i) g^{\bar{\mu}}(j, i). \end{aligned}$$

Given input supplies $\bar{b}$ for the original instance, we have that

$$\begin{aligned} e_g^{\bar{\mu}}(i) &= \bar{b}^{\bar{\mu}}(i) - \sum_{k:(i,k)\in A} g^{\bar{\mu}}(i, k) \\ &= \bar{b}^{\bar{\mu}}(i) - \sum_{k:(i,k)\in A} f(i, k) - \sum_{k:(i,k)\in A} \bar{f}^{\bar{\mu}}(i, k) \\ &= \bar{b}^{\bar{\mu}}(i) + (e_f(i) - b(i)) + (e_{\bar{f}}^{\bar{\mu}}(i) - \bar{b}^{\bar{\mu}}(i)) \\ &= e_f(i), \end{aligned}$$

using that $b(i) = e_{\bar{f}}^{\bar{\mu}}(i)$. Thus $e_g^{\bar{\mu}}(i) = e_f(i) \geq 0$ for all $i \neq t$, and we have shown that $g^{\bar{\mu}}$ is a feasible flow in the original input instance relabeled with $\bar{\mu}$.

We now want to show that the flow g is maximum. Since we know that f is a maximum flow in the instance output by the algorithm, we know there are labels μ such that $\gamma^{\mu}(i, j) \leq 1$ for all arcs $(i, j) \in A_f$, and $e_f^{\mu}(i) = 0$ for all $i \neq t$. So if there is positive residual capacity on the arc (i, j) for the flow $g^{\bar{\mu}}$, then by Inequality (6.9), $g^{\bar{\mu}}(i, j) < \bar{u}^{\bar{\mu}}(i, j)$ implies that $f(i, j) < \bar{u}_{\bar{f}}^{\bar{\mu}}(i, j)$ or $f(i, j) < u(i, j)$, so that $\gamma^{\mu}(i, j) \leq 1$ for this arc. Additionally, we know from above that $e_g^{\bar{\mu}}(i) = e_f(i)$ for all $i \neq t$, so that $e_g^{\bar{\mu}}(i)\mu(i) = e_f(i)\mu(i) = e_f^{\mu}(i) = 0$ for all $i \neq t$. Thus for the labels $\bar{\mu} \cdot \mu$, we have that in the original input instance $\bar{\gamma}^{\bar{\mu}\mu}(i, j) \leq 1$ for arcs (i, j) with positive residual capacity for flow g, and $e_g^{\bar{\mu}\mu}(i) = 0$ for all $i \neq t$, which proves that g is maximum for the original input instance.   □

Corollary 6.27: *Let $\bar{f}$ be the flow computed by Algorithm 6.5, and $\bar{\mu}$ be the canonical labels. Then if f is an ϵ-approximate flow computed in the output lossy graph, the flow $f + \bar{f}^{\bar{\mu}}$ is an ϵ-approximate flow for the original input graph relabeled by $\bar{\mu}$.*

Proof If f^* is the maximum flow in the output graph of Algorithm 6.5, we have that $|f| \geq (1 - \epsilon)|f^*|$, or that $e_f(t) \geq (1 - \epsilon)e_{f^*}(t)$. From the lemma, we know that $g = f^* + \bar{f}^{\bar{\mu}}$ is a maximum generalized flow for the original input graph, and from the proof we know that $e_g^{\bar{\mu}}(t) = e_{f^*}(t)$. Following the same logic, we have that flow $h = f + \bar{f}^{\bar{\mu}}$ is feasible, and $e_h^{\bar{\mu}}(t) = e_f(t)$, so that

$$e_h^{\bar{\mu}}(t) = e_f(t) \geq (1 - \epsilon)e_{f^*}(t) = (1 - \epsilon)e_g^{\bar{\mu}}(t),$$

and the corollary statement follows.   □

   Given a lossy graph, we will then push excesses from the supplies to the sink along augmenting paths P. Once there are no excesses at nodes that can reach the sink, the relabeled excesses are all 0, and by Theorem 6.11, the flow must be maximum.

   Our first algorithm for pushing excesses to the sink works as follows. Given the lossy graph, we know there cannot be any flow-generating cycles in the graph, so that we can compute canonical labels μ. We then push as much excess to the sink as possible along paths consisting of arcs whose relabeled gains $\gamma^\mu(i, j) = 1$; we do this by computing a maximum s-t flow (in the sense of Chapter 2) on these arcs with a new source vertex added. If a relabeled gain $\gamma^\mu(i, j) = 1$, then we have that $\mu(i) = \gamma(i, j)\mu(j)$. Since for a canonical labeling, $\mu(i)$ is the gain of the highest gain path from i to t, if $\mu(i) = \gamma(i, j)\mu(j)$, then the arc (i, j) must be on the highest gain path from i to t. After pushing excess to the sink on these arcs, we then recompute canonical labels, and continue until there are no more paths from nodes with positive excess to the sink. This algorithm is due to Truemper [198], and hence is known as Truemper's algorithm. We summarize Truemper's algorithm in Algorithm 6.6.

   We first show that the flow f remains feasible in each iteration.

Lemma 6.28: *The flow f remains feasible in the lossy graph throughout the algorithm.*

$(G, u, \gamma, b, \bar{f}) \leftarrow \texttt{ReduceToLossy}(\bar{G}, \bar{u}, \bar{\gamma}, \bar{b})$
$f \leftarrow 0$
while there is i with $e_f(i) > 0$ and i can reach t in G_f **do**
    Compute canonical labels μ
    $A' \leftarrow \{(i, j) \in A_f : \gamma^\mu(i, j) = 1\}$
    $u'(i, j) \leftarrow u_f^\mu(i, j)$
    Add vertex s'
    $A' \leftarrow A' \cup \{(s', i) : e_f^\mu(i) > 0, i \neq t\}, u'(s', i) = e_f^\mu(i), i \neq t$
    Compute s'-t max flow f' in $(V \cup \{s\}, A')$ with capacities u'
    $f^\mu \leftarrow f^\mu + f'$
return $f + \bar{f}$

Algorithm 6.6 Truemper's algorithm.

Proof Initially, for $f = 0$, we have $e_f(i) = b(i) \geq 0$ for all $i \in V$, and $f(i, j) \leq u(i, j)$ for all $(i, j) \in A$. In each iteration, we compute canonical labels μ and a flow f' such that $f'(i, j) \leq u_f^\mu(i, j)$ for all $(i, j) \in A$, and by the choice of the capacities $u'(s', i)$, we have that the net flow f' leaving i is at most $e_f^\mu(i)$ for each $i \neq t$; that is, $\sum_{k:(i,k)\in A} f'(i,k) \leq e_f^\mu(i)$. We set the new flow to be $f^\mu + f'$. Then the relabeled flow on arc (i, j) is at most $f^\mu(i, j) + u_f^\mu(i, j) = u^\mu(i, j)$. The relabeled excess at node $i \neq t$ is

$$b^\mu(i) - \sum_{k:(i,k)\in A} (f^\mu(i,k) + f'(i,k)) = e_f^\mu(i) - \sum_{k:(i,k)\in A} f'(i,k) \geq 0.$$

Thus the new flow is feasible. $\qquad\square$

In order to be able to compute canonical labels in each iteration, we need to ensure that the new flow f^μ created at the end of each iteration maintains the property that the residual graph is lossy.

Lemma 6.29: *At the start of each iteration of the main loop of Algorithm 6.6, the residual graph G_f is lossy.*

Proof We prove the statement by induction on the algorithm. This initial graph is lossy, so that at the beginning of the first iteration, after we compute canonical labels, we have that $\gamma^\mu(i, j) \leq 1$ for every $(i, j) \in A_f$. In each iteration, we only modify flow on arcs (i, j) such that $\gamma^\mu(i, j) = 1$. Thus we only introduce new residual arcs on arcs (j, i) such that $\gamma^\mu(j, i) = 1/\gamma^\mu(i, j) = 1$. Thus it continues to be the case at the end of the iteration that $\gamma^\mu(i, j) \leq 1$ for every $(i, j) \in A_f$. $\qquad\square$

We can bound the number of iterations of the main loop in terms of the number of different possible gains of paths. While this bound does not give a polynomial-time algorithm, it prepares us for a polynomial-time algorithm that we will present shortly.

Lemma 6.30: *The number of iterations of the main loop of Algorithm 6.6 is no more than the number of different possible gains of simple paths to the sink; that is, the number of iterations is at most* $|\{\gamma(P) : P \text{ an } i\text{-}t \text{ path for any } i\}|$.

Proof At the end of each iteration, there is no path P in A_f from a node with positive excess to the sink such that $\gamma^\mu(P) = 1$, since otherwise we would have pushed some of the excess to the sink along this path. Thus for any such path $P \subseteq A_f, \gamma^\mu(P) < 1$.

Now consider the canonical labels $\tilde{\mu}$ computed in the next iteration. For each $\ell \in V$, $\tilde{\mu}(\ell) = \gamma(P)$ for some simple ℓ-t path $P \subseteq A_f$. We now show that $\tilde{\mu}(\ell) < \mu(\ell)$. To see this, we consider $\tilde{\mu}(\ell)/\mu(\ell)$. Then

$$\frac{\tilde{\mu}(\ell)}{\mu(\ell)} = \frac{1}{\mu(\ell)}\gamma(P) = \frac{\mu(t)}{\mu(\ell)} \prod_{(i,j)\in P} \gamma(i,j)$$

$$= \prod_{(i,j)\in P} \gamma(i,j)\frac{\mu(j)}{\mu(i)}$$

$$= \gamma^\mu(P) < 1.$$

Thus $\tilde{\mu}(\ell) < \mu(\ell)$, and since $\tilde{\mu}(\ell) = \gamma(P)$ for some ℓ-t path P, the number of iterations cannot be more than the number of possible gains of the paths to t. □

Theorem 6.31: *Algorithm 6.6 computes a maximum generalized flow f.*

Proof To prove the statement we consider computing canonical labels μ at the termination of the algorithm; we can do so because by Lemma 6.29, the residual graph is lossy at the end of the algorithm and so there are no flow-generating cycles. Thus we know that $\gamma^\mu(i,j) \leq 1$ for all $(i,j) \in A_f$. Furthermore, when the algorithm terminates, there is no vertex i with positive excess such that i can reach t in G_f. Thus we know that any vertex i with $e_f(i) > 0$ is given a canonical label $\mu(i) = 0$, so that $e_f^\mu(i) = 0$. Then by Theorem 6.11, the flow f must be optimal for the lossy graph returned by the ReduceToLossy subroutine. By Lemma 6.26, the returned flow $f + \bar{f}$ is maximum for the original (relabeled) input instance. □

Lemma 6.30 then gives a natural idea for modifying Truemper's algorithm to run in polynomial time: we modify the gains so that there are only a polynomial number of different possible gains for simple paths. For a given $\epsilon > 0$, we set

$$d = (1 + \epsilon)^{1/n}.$$

Then for each arc (i, j) with gain $\gamma(i, j) \leq 1$, we round down $\gamma(i, j)$ to the nearest power of d, so that

$$\hat{\gamma}(i, j) = d^{\lfloor \log_d \gamma(i,j) \rfloor}$$

and

$$\hat{\gamma}(j, i) = 1/\hat{\gamma}(i, j).$$

Since the gain of any simple path is at most B^n and at least B^{-n}, the number of different gains for simple paths is at most

$$\log_d B^{2n} = \frac{2n \log B}{\log d} = \frac{2n^2 \log B}{\log(1 + \epsilon)},$$

and this number is polynomial in the input size for constant ϵ. Thus if we run Algorithm 6.6 with the gains $\hat{\gamma}$, the algorithm runs in time polynomial in the input size. The idea of modifying the gains by making them powers of d is called *gain scaling*.

However, gain scaling creates another issue in that we need to relate the flow in the network with the scaled gains to a flow in the lossy network with the gains as given by ReduceToLossy. Suppose we use Algorithm 6.6 to find a maximum flow h in the graph with the scaled gains $\hat{\gamma}$. We then *interpret* flow h as a flow f for the lossy network with gains γ by setting

$$f(i, j) = \begin{cases} h(i, j) & \text{if } h(i, j) \geq 0 \\ -\gamma(j, i)h(j, i) & \text{if } h(i, j) < 0 \end{cases},$$

so that the flow f meets the skew symmetry condition. We now summarize the modified algorithm in Algorithm 6.7.

We will show that Algorithm 6.7 finds a nearly optimal flow f for the lossy graph returned by ReduceToLossy; Corollary 6.27 implies that the algorithm returns a nearly optimal flow for the original input instance. We first need the modification of the decomposition lemma (Lemma 6.12) for the case that f is a flow (rather than a proper flow) and the graph is lossy. We leave its proof as another exercise (Exercise 6.3).

Lemma 6.32: *Any flow f in a lossy network can be decomposed into generalized pseudoflows $f_1, f_2, \ldots, f_\ell$, $\ell \leq m$, such that $f = \sum_{i=1}^{\ell} f_i$, $|f| = \sum_{i=1}^{\ell} |f_i|$, and for each i, the arcs of f_i of positive flow are a simple*

Algorithm: GainScalingTruemper$(\bar{G}, \bar{u}, \bar{\gamma}, \bar{b}, \epsilon)$

$(G, u, \gamma, b, \bar{f}) \leftarrow$ ReduceToLossy$(\bar{G}, \bar{u}, \bar{\gamma}, \bar{b})$

$h \leftarrow 0$

$d \leftarrow (1 + \epsilon)^{1/n}$

foreach $(i, j) \in A$ **do**

    if $\gamma(i, j) \leq 1$ **then**

        $\hat{\gamma}(i, j) \leftarrow d^{\lfloor \log_d \gamma(i,j) \rfloor}$

    else

        $\hat{\gamma}(i, j) \leftarrow d^{-\lfloor \log_d \gamma(j,i) \rfloor}$

while there is i with $e_h(i) > 0$ and i can reach t in G_h **do**

    Compute canonical labels μ for gains $\hat{\gamma}$

    Add vertex s'

    $A' \leftarrow \{(i, j) \in A_h : \hat{\gamma}^\mu(i, j) = 1\}$

    $u'(i, j) \leftarrow u_h^\mu(i, j)$

    $A' \leftarrow A' \cup \{(s', i) : e_h(i) > 0\}$

    Compute s'-t max flow h' in $(V \cup \{s'\}, A')$ with capacities u'

    $h^\mu \leftarrow h^\mu + h'$

foreach $(i, j) \in A$ **do**

    if $h(i, j) \geq 0$ **then**

        $f(i, j) \leftarrow h(i, j)$

    else

        $f(i, j) \leftarrow -\gamma(i, j)h(j, i)$

return $f + \bar{f}$

Algorithm 6.7 Truemper's algorithm with gain scaling.

path from some j to the sink t, a unit-gain cycle, or a path connected to a flow-absorbing cycle; only for the simple paths to t is $|f_i| > 0$.

Theorem 6.33: *Algorithm 6.7 finds an ϵ-optimal generalized flow in the original (relabeled) input graph in the time for $O(n^2 \log B / \log(1 + \epsilon))$ maximum s-t flow computations, plus time $O(m^2 n^3 \log(nB))$ for reducing to the lossy graph.*

Proof We initially reduce to a lossy graph. By construction of the gains γ, we have that gains $\hat{\gamma}(i, j) \leq \gamma(i, j) \leq 1$ for all arcs (i, j) with positive capacity in the lossy graph. Then the residual graph G_h must be lossy throughout the rest of the algorithm by Lemma 6.29.

First we argue that the interpretation f of h computed by the algorithm is a flow in the lossy graph: namely, that $e_f(i) \geq 0$ for all $i \in V$. In the lossy graph, all arcs with positive flow in h must be on arcs with gain $\gamma(i, j) \leq 1$, since only these arcs have positive capacity. Thus if $h(i, j) < 0$, then $h(j, i) > 0$ by skew-symmetry, so that $\hat{\gamma}(j, i) \leq \gamma(j, i) \leq 1$. Then

$$
\begin{aligned}
e_f(i) &= b(i) - \sum_{j:(i,j)\in A} f(i, j) \\
&= b(i) - \sum_{j:(i,j)\in A, h(i,j)>0} h(i, j) + \sum_{j:(i,j)\in A: h(i,j)<0} \gamma(j,i)h(j, i) \\
&\geq b(i) - \sum_{j:(i,j)\in A, h(i,j)>0} h(i, j) + \sum_{j:(i,j)\in A: h(i,j)<0} \hat{\gamma}(j,i)h(j, i) \\
&= b(i) - \sum_{j:(i,j)\in A} h(i, j) \\
&= e_h(i),
\end{aligned}
$$

so that $e_f(i) \geq 0$ for all $i \in V$, since $e_h(i) \geq 0$ for all $i \in V$. Note that this also implies that the value of the interpretation f in the lossy graph is at least the value of flow h, since $|f| = e_f(t) \geq e_h(t) = |h|$.

Next, we argue that f is an ϵ-optimal flow in the lossy graph given by ReduceToLossy. Let f^* be a maximum generalized flow in the lossy graph. We use f^* to argue that there exists a generalized flow in the graph of scaled gains of value at least $(1 - \epsilon)|f^*|$, so that maximum generalized flow value in the graph with scaled gains is at least this amount. By Lemma 6.32, we can decompose f^* into pseudoflows f_i^*. Since $|f_i^*| > 0$ only for simple paths to t, we do not consider the other pseudoflows into which f^* is decomposed. Let P_i be the path ending at t given by f_i^*, and let δ_i be the amount of flow initially pushed along path P_i by f_i^*, so that $|f^*| = \sum_i |f_i^*| = \sum_i \delta_i \gamma(P_i)$. Note that for paths P_i starting at j, the sum of the δ_i is at most the supply at j, $b(j)$. Since the graph is lossy, we have that $\hat{\gamma}(i, j) \leq \gamma(i, j) \leq 1$ for all arcs (i, j) in the lossy graph of positive capacity. Thus if we push the same amount of flow along the same paths with gains $\hat{\gamma}$ as in f^*, the resulting flow must obey the capacity constraints because the amount of flow that results on each arc with positive capacity can only be less. The excess at each node $j \neq t$ will be nonnegative, since the total flow on paths P_i starting at j is at most $b(j)$, and the flow on intermediate nodes on each path will be conserved. Furthermore, we have that the value of the flow is

$$
\begin{aligned}
\sum_i \delta_i \hat{\gamma}(P_i) &\geq \sum_i \delta_i \gamma(P_i)/d^{|P_i|} \\
&\geq \sum_i \delta_i \gamma(P_i)/(1 + \epsilon)
\end{aligned}
$$

$$\geq (1 - \epsilon) \sum_i \delta_i \gamma(P_i)$$

$$= (1 - \epsilon)|f^*|.$$

Since this generalized flow has value at least $(1 - \epsilon)|f^*|$, the maximum generalized flow in the graph with scaled gains must have value at least the same amount. Thus $e_f(t) \geq e_h(t) \geq (1 - \epsilon)|f^*|$, as desired. Finally, by Corollary 6.27, computing an ϵ-optimal flow f in the lossy graph implies that $f + \bar{f}$ is an ϵ-optimal flow in the original (relabeled) input graph.

For the running time of the algorithm, the reduction to a lossy graph takes $O(m^2 n^3 \log(nB))$ time to cancel all the flow-generating cycles, as shown in Exercise 6.4. As argued in Lemma 6.30, the number of maximum s-t flow computations is at most the number of different possible gains of simple paths, and we argued previously that there are at most $2n^2 \log B / \log(1 + \epsilon)$ different possible scaled gains $\hat{\gamma}$. This gives the running time claimed in the theorem statement.   □

In Exercise 6.5, we have the reader show that we can replace Truemper's algorithm in the gain-scaling Algorithm 6.7 with a push-relabel style algorithm, resulting in a faster overall running time.

6.5 Error Scaling

From Theorem 6.10 for Algorithm 6.7, we know that if we compute an ϵ-optimal flow for $\epsilon < 1/(m! \cdot B^{2m})$, then we can in $O(m^2 n)$ time compute a generalized maximum flow. Unfortunately, for this value of ϵ, the number of maximum flow computations of Algorithm 6.7 is $2n^2 \log B / \log(1 + \epsilon) = \Omega(1/\epsilon) = \Omega(m! \cdot B^{2m})$, so that the algorithm is not polynomial-time for ϵ in this range.

However, we can do the following, given any polynomial-time algorithm to compute an $\frac{1}{2}$-approximate generalized maximum flow, such as Algorithm 6.7. We set f to 0, then repeat the following $\log_2(1/\epsilon)$ times: we find a $\frac{1}{2}$-optimal generalized flow f' in G_f using the algorithm, and update f to be $f + f'$; each time we pass the current excess $e_f(i)$ as the supply $b(i)$ (observe that in the first iteration, when $f = 0$, $e_f(i) = b(i)$). We prove below that after i iterations the resulting flow is 2^{-i}-optimal, so that after $\lceil \log_2(1/\epsilon) \rceil$ iterations the flow is ϵ-optimal. By setting $\epsilon < 1/(m! \cdot B^{2m})$ we can get an ϵ-optimal flow in $O(\log(m! \cdot B^{2m})) = O(m \log(mB))$ calls to the algorithm and thus we can find a generalized maximum flow in polynomial time. We call this process

---

$f \leftarrow 0$
for $i \leftarrow 1$ to $\lceil \log_2(1/\epsilon) \rceil$ **do**
$\qquad f' \leftarrow$ ApproximateGeneralizedFlow(G_f, u_f, γ, e_f)
$\qquad f \leftarrow f' + f$
return f

Algorithm 6.8 Error scaling using a subroutine `ApproximateGeneralized`
`Flow`(G, u, γ, b) that returns a $\frac{1}{2}$-optimal flow on graph G with capacities u, gains γ, and supplies b.

error scaling: each iteration finds a flow of at least half the remaining value in the residual graph, so that the error converges quickly. We summarize the algorithm in Algorithm 6.8.

Lemma 6.34: *Let f^* be a maximum generalized flow for G with supplies b. Then for any flow f with supplies b, the flow $f^* - f$ is a maximum generalized flow in the residual graph G_f with capacities u_f and supplies e_f.*

Proof Let $g = f^* - f$. We observe that g obeys skew symmetry because both f^* and f do, and $g(i, j) = f^*(i, j) - f(i, j) \leq u(i, j) - f(i, j) = u_f(i, j)$, so capacity constraints are obeyed. Since the supply at i is $e_f(i)$, we have that

$$
\begin{aligned}
e_g(i) &= e_f(i) - \sum_{k:(i,k)\in A} g(i,k) \\
&= e_f(i) - \sum_{k:(i,k)\in A} (f^*(i,k) - f(i,k)) \\
&= e_f(i) + \left(b(i) - \sum_{k:(i,k)\in A} f^*(i,k) \right) - \left(b(i) - \sum_{k:(i,k)\in A} f(i,k) \right) \\
&= e_f(i) + e_{f^*}(i) - e_f(i) \\
&= e_{f^*}(i) \geq 0.
\end{aligned}
$$

Thus g is a feasible flow for residual graph G_f with capacities u_f and supplies e_f. To prove that it is maximum, let μ be the labels that prove that f^* is maximum in G via Theorem 6.11. By the optimality theorem, we know that $\gamma^\mu(i, j) \leq 1$ whenever $f^*(i, j) < u(i, j)$ and $\mu(i) = 0$ whenever $e_{f^*}(i) > 0$. Then $g(i, j) = f^*(i, j) - f(i, j) = u_f(i, j)$ if and only if $f^*(i, j) = u(i, j)$, so that when $g(i, j) < u_f(i, j)$, then $\gamma^\mu(i, j) \leq 1$. Similarly $e_g(i) > 0$ if and only if $e_{f^*}(i) > 0$ so that $e_g^\mu(i) = 0$ for all $i \neq t$. Thus by Theorem 6.11, $f^* - f$ is a maximum generalized flow in G_f. $\qquad \square$

Theorem 6.35: *Algorithm 6.8 returns an ϵ-optimal flow in the time for $O(\log \frac{1}{\epsilon})$ calls to an algorithm that produces a $\frac{1}{2}$-optimal generalized maximum flow.*

Proof We first argue that f is always a flow with supplies b. Clearly this is true for $f = 0$. Let f' be a flow in G_f with capacities u_f and supplies e_f, and $g = f + f'$. Clearly g obeys skew-symmetry, since f and f' do. Also, $f'(i, j) \leq u_f(i, j) = u(i, j) - f(i, j)$, so that $g(i, j) \leq u(i, j)$. Furthermore, for all $i \neq t$, $e_{f'}(i) \geq 0$, so that $e_f(i) - \sum_{k:(i,k)\in A_f} f'(i, k) \geq 0$, or

$$0 \leq b(i) - \sum_{k:(i,k)\in A} f(i, k) - \sum_{k:(i,k)\in A_f} f'(i, k)$$

$$= b(i) - \sum_{k:(i,k)\in A} (f(i, k) + f'(i, k))$$

$$= b(i) - \sum_{k:(i,k)\in A} g(i, k) = e_g(i),$$

so that $e_g(i) \geq 0$ for all $i \in V$ and the new flow g is a flow with supplies b.

We now argue by induction that at the end of i iterations, the algorithm returns a 2^{-i}-optimal flow. Let f^* be a maximum generalized flow. After the first iteration f is a $1/2$-optimal flow. Suppose that at the end of the $(i-1)$st iteration, f is a $2^{-(i-1)}$-optimal flow, so that $|f| \geq \left(1 - \frac{1}{2^{i-1}}\right)|f^*|$. Then in the next iteration, f' is a $1/2$-optimal flow in G_f, so that by Lemma 6.34, $|f'| \geq \frac{1}{2}(|f^*| - |f|)$. Then the new flow at the end of the iteration has value at least

$$|f| + \frac{1}{2}(|f^*| - |f|) = \frac{1}{2}\left(|f^*| + |f|\right)$$

$$\geq \frac{1}{2}|f^*| + \frac{1}{2}\left(1 - \frac{1}{2^{i-1}}\right)|f^*|$$

$$= |f^*| - \frac{1}{2^i}|f^*| = \left(1 - \frac{1}{2^i}\right)|f^*|.$$

We make $O(\log \frac{1}{\epsilon})$ calls to the algorithm `ApproximateGeneralized Flow`. □

Corollary 6.36: *Algorithm 6.8 finds an optimal generalized flow in $O(m^3 n^3 \log^2(mB))$ time plus the time for $O(mn^2 \log(mB) \log B)$ maximum flow computations.*

Proof As we argued previously, for $\epsilon < 1/(m! \cdot B^{2m})$ we can get an ϵ-optimal flow with $O(m \log(mB))$ calls to Algorithm 6.7, and then use $O(m^2 n)$ time to compute a generalized maximum flow via Theorem 6.10. □

Still faster algorithms are known for generalized maximum flow, as are strongly polynomial-time algorithms; see the Chapter Notes for more information.

Exercises

6.1   Prove that if f is a proper flow, and f' is the result of canceling a GAP as given in Equation (6.3), then f' is also a proper flow.

6.2   Prove Lemma 6.12.

6.3   Prove Lemma 6.32.

6.4   For the minimum-cost circulation problem we showed in Theorem 5.23 of Section 5.3 that we can cancel all negative-cost cycles in $O(m^2 n^2 \log(nC))$ time. When considering the generalized maximum flow problem, we can also cancel all flow generating cycles by using this algorithm. We do this by considering costs $c(i,j) = -\log \gamma(i,j)$ and canceling negative-cost cycles. However, the costs $c(i,j)$ are no longer integer, which was an assumption needed to prove the running time above. Assume that the gains $\gamma(i,j)$ are ratios of integers that are bounded in absolute value by B. Show that in this case, the running time of the cycle canceling algorithm is $O(m^2 n^3 \log(nB))$.

6.5   In this problem, we will consider a push/relabel style of algorithm for the generalized maximum flow problem. We say that an arc (i,j) is *admissible* if it has relabeled gain $\gamma^\mu(i,j) > 1$ and positive residual capacity. We say that a node i is *active* if it can reach the sink and it has positive excess (that is, $e_f^\mu(i) > 0$). Consider Algorithm 6.9.

(a) Prove that the algorithm maintains a flow h and labels μ such that $\hat\gamma^\mu(i,j) \le d^{1/n}$ for all residual arcs $(i,j) \in A_h$.

(b) Prove that during the course of the algorithm, the graph of admissible arcs is acyclic.

(c) Prove that during the course of the algorithm G_h has no flow-generating cycles.

(d) Prove that on termination the algorithm outputs an ϵ-optimal flow.

(e) Prove that there are at most $O(\frac{1}{\epsilon} n^3 \log B)$ relabels per node.

(f) Prove that there are at most $O(\frac{1}{\epsilon} mn^3 \log B)$ saturating pushes.

(g) Prove that there are at most $O(\frac{1}{\epsilon} mn^4 \log B)$ nonsaturating pushes.

Assuming that we can implement both the push and relabel operations in $O(\log n)$ time, we can thus find an ϵ-optimal flow in

---

Algorithm: GainScalingPushRelabel$(\bar{G}, \bar{u}, \bar{\gamma}, \bar{b}, \epsilon)$

$(G, u, \gamma, b, \bar{f}) \leftarrow$ ReduceToLossy$(\bar{G}, \bar{u}, \bar{\gamma}, \bar{b})$

$h \leftarrow 0$

$d \leftarrow (1 + \epsilon)^{1/n}$

foreach $(i, j) \in A$ **do**

    if $\gamma(i, j) \leq 1$ **then**

        $\hat{\gamma}(i, j) \leftarrow d^{\lfloor \log_d \gamma(i, j) \rfloor}$

    else

        $\hat{\gamma}(i, j) \leftarrow d^{-\lfloor \log_d \gamma(j, i) \rfloor}$

Compute canonical labels μ for gains $\hat{\gamma}$

while there is an active node i **do**

    if there is an admissible arc (i, j) **then**

        Push: Send $\min(e_h^\mu(i), u_h^\mu(i, j))$ units of flow on (i, j), update h^μ

    else

        Relabel: $\mu(i) \leftarrow \mu(i)/d^{1/n}$

foreach $(i, j) \in A$ **do**

    if $h(i, j) \geq 0$ **then**

        $f(i, j) \leftarrow h(i, j)$

    else

        $f(i, j) \leftarrow -\gamma(i, j)h(j, i)$

return $f + \bar{f}$

Algorithm 6.9 A push/relabel generalized maximum flow algorithm with gain scaling.

$O(\frac{1}{\epsilon} mn^4 \log B \log n)$ time plus the time for the ReduceToLossy subroutine.

(h) Using the above algorithm as a subroutine, and assuming that the reduction to a lossy graph takes $O(mn^3 \log(nB))$ time, obtain an $O(m^2 n^4 \log^2 B \log n)$ time algorithm for the maximum generalized flow problem.

6.6   In the generalized minimum-cost circulation problem, we are given costs $c(i, j)$ in addition to gains $\gamma(i, j)$ and capacities $u(i, j)$. The goal is to find a *generalized circulation* f that minimizes $\sum_{(i, j) \in A} c(i, j) f(i, j)$. A generalized circulation is a generalized pseudoflow that has $e_f(i) = 0$ for all $i \in V$.

    Prove that a minimum-cost generalized circulation f is optimal if and only if there are no negative-cost unit gain cycles and no negative-cost bicycles in the residual graph G_f.

Chapter Notes

Generalized flow problems were introduced by Jewell [116] (see also Dantzig [48, chapter 21]). Onaga [156] shows that a generalized flow is optimal if and only if its residual graph has no generalized augmenting paths. Goldberg, Plotkin, and Tardos state the optimal criterion in terms of rescaled gains (see [89, lemma 4.4]), though this also follows directly from linear programming duality. They attribute the idea of relabeling to Glover and Klingman [80]. Goldberg, Plotkin, and Tardos [89] give the first combinatorial polynomial-time algorithms for the problem. Many other such results were obtain subsequently; see, for example, Cohen and Megiddo [41], Radzik [169, 170], Goldfarb and Jin [98], Goldfarb, Jin, and Orlin [100], and Goldfarb, Jin, and Lin [99]. It was unknown until recently whether there were strongly polynomial-time algorithms for computing generalized flows; in 2016, Vegh [200] gave the first strongly polynomial-time algorithm. Olver and Vegh [155] give a simpler strongly polynomial-time algorithm running in $O((m + n \log n)mn \log(n^2/m))$ time. Radzik [170] gives the fastest combinatorial weakly polynomial-time algorithm, running in $O((m + n \log n)mn \log B)$ time. Daitch and Spielman [46] provide algorithms using electrical flows that compute near-optimal solutions for some generalized flow problems in lossy graphs.

The proofs of Theorem 6.10 and Lemma 6.20 can be found as the proofs of Lemma 3.9 and Lemma 3.6 respectively in Restrepo and Williamson [173].

The algorithm we give in Section 6.2 is due to Restrepo and Williamson [173]. The negative-cost GAP detection algorithm of Section 6.3 is an adaptation of an algorithm in the thesis of Aspvall [11]. It has the downside of needing $\Omega(n^2)$ space. Restrepo and Williamson [173] give a linear-space negative-cost GAP detection algorithm. Truemper's algorithm in Section 6.4 is due to Truemper [197]. The ideas of gain scaling and error scaling for generalized flow are due to Tardos and Wayne [190] (see also Wayne's thesis [202]).

We are only aware of two implementation studies of combinatorial algorithms for generalized flow, one by Radzik and Yang [171] and the other by Restrepo and Williamson [173]. Both studies report that network simplex algorithms for generalized flow outperform the other combinatorial algorithms tested. For a combinatorial description of a network simplex algorithm for generalized flow problems, see Ahuja, Magnanti, and Orlin [4, chapter 15]

Exercise 6.5 is due to Tardos and Wayne [190].

7

Multicommodity Flow Algorithms

A man said to the universe:
"Sir, I exist!"
"However," replied the universe,
"The fact has not created in me
A sense of obligation."
                                    – Stephen Crane

We turn to a final set of problems and algorithms that generalize the maximum flow problem, the *multicommodity* flow problem. In the maximum flow problem, we are trying to ship as much of a single good as possible from the source s to the sink t. In the multicommodity flow problem, we now have multiple goods (or multiple *commodities*) that need to be sent between distinct sources and sinks, one source and sink per commodity. The commodities are not interchangeable, so a commodity entering the system via the source for its commodity may not exit the system at a sink designated for another commodity. The problem captures sending multiple different types of goods through the same network with capacity constraints on the distribution of all goods or sending different information streams through the network with different messages being sent between the various source-sink pairs.

We formalize the problem as follows. We are given as input a directed graph $G = (V, A)$ with capacities $u(i, j) \geq 0$ for all arcs (i, j). Additionally, we are given K source-sink pairs of vertices, $s_1\text{-}t_1, s_2\text{-}t_2, \ldots, s_K\text{-}t_K$; these nodes need not be distinct, so that, for example, the source s_3 may be the same as the sink t_5. For some variants of the problem, we are also given demands d_k for each $k = 1, \ldots, K$. A feasible solution gives an $s_k\text{-}t_k$ flow f_k for each k (according to Definition 2.1, without skew symmetry), such that a joint capacity constraint is satisfied on each arc; that is, we want it to be the case that the total flow over all commodities is at most the capacity, or that $\sum_{k=1}^{K} f_k(i, j) \leq u(i, j)$ for all $(i, j) \in A$.

Let $|f_k|$ denote the value of the flow f_k. There are a number of different possible goals for the problem. In the *maximum multicommodity flow problem*, we want to maximize the total amount of flow sent between all the source-sink pairs; that is, we want to maximize $\sum_{k=1}^{K} |f_k|$. In such a problem, however, we might well send a lot of one type of commodity and very little of another. If we have the demands d_k as input, we might also consider trying to maximize the proportion of each demand sent. In the *maximum concurrent flow problem*, we maximize a parameter λ so that $|f_k| \geq \lambda d_k$; that is, for each commodity k, we send at least a λ fraction of the demand d_k that we wanted to send.

7.1 Optimality Conditions

For our previous network flow problems, we have been able to give nice, combinatorial statements about how to tell when the flow is optimal; these statements have motivated our algorithms. Unfortunately, there are not similar theorems here for the multicommodity flow problem. Except in some restricted cases, we also do not have an integrality property, or an analog of a maximum flow/minimum cut theorem. As in the Stephen Crane quote at the beginning of the chapter, the existence and usefulness of the multicommodity flow problem has not created in the universe an obligation to have an elegant theory along the same lines as the previous flow problems we have studied.

To explore this deficiency somewhat further, consider the case of the multicommodity flow problem in which we are given demands d_k for each s_k-t_k pair. We will say that a graph obeys the *cut condition* if for all $S \subseteq V$,

$$\sum_{k:s_k \in S, t_k \notin S} d_k \leq u(\delta^+(S)); \tag{7.1}$$

that is, there is sufficient capacity in each cut S to support a flow of at least the sum of the demands d_k such that S is an s_k-t_k cut. Clearly this is a necessary condition in order to be able to send d_k units of flow from s_k to t_k for each k. We know in the single commodity case ($K = 1$) by Theorem 2.7 that we can find a flow of value d_1 if and only if the cut condition holds. However, the cut condition is not a sufficient condition in general. Consider the example shown in Figure 7.1. It is easy to check that the cut condition holds for the two commodities with $d_1 = d_2 = 1$ and all three arcs with a single unit of capacity, but we cannot send both units of flow. To see this, notice that to send a unit of flow from s_1 to t_1, the unit must traverse two arcs, and the same is true for sending a unit of flow from from s_2 to t_2. Thus we need at least four units of

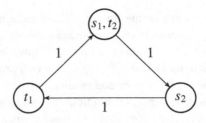

Figure 7.1 An example in which the cut condition does not hold. The demands are $d_1 = d_2 = 1$.

capacity to send both units of flow, but there are only three units of capacity in the network.

There are some limited cases in which the cut condition is sufficient; we consider one such case in the following section. In general, we can write multicommodity flow problems as linear programs, and we inherit some optimality conditions from the optimality conditions of linear programs. Consider, for example, the following linear program for the maximum multicommodity flow problem. We let the variable $f_k(i, j)$ indicate how much flow of commodity k is on the arc (i, j), and we can then write a linear program maximizing the total net flow out of each source subject to the conditions of a multicommodity flow, each of which can be written as a linear inequality in the $f_k(i, j)$ variables:

$$\text{Maximize} \sum_{k=1}^{K} \left(\sum_{j:(s_k, j) \in A} f_k(s_k, j) - \sum_{j:(j, s_k) \in A} f_k(j, s_k) \right)$$

subject to

$$\sum_{j:(j,i) \in A} f_k(j, i) - \sum_{j:(i, j) \in A} f_k(i, j) = 0, \qquad k = 1, \dots, K; i \neq s_k, t_k,$$

$$f_k(i, j) \geq 0, \qquad k = 1, \dots, K; (i, j) \in A,$$

$$\sum_{k=1}^{K} f_k(i, j) \leq u(i, j), \qquad (i, j) \in A.$$

It will be more useful to us, however, to write this linear program in a somewhat different form. Let $\mathcal{P}_k$ be the set of all s_k-t_k paths in the graph, and let $\mathcal{P} = \bigcup_k \mathcal{P}_k$ be the union of these sets over $k = 1, \dots, K$. By a simple generalization of the flow decomposition lemma (Lemma 2.20), we can decompose each of the flows f_k into flows along s_k-t_k paths. So we introduce a variable $x(P)$ to indicate how much flow is sent along the path P. Then we can express the maximum multicommodity flow problem as the following linear program:

$$\text{Maximize} \quad \sum_{P \in \mathcal{P}} x(P)$$

$$\text{subject to} \quad \sum_{P \in \mathcal{P}:(i,j) \in P} x(P) \le u(i,j), \quad (i,j) \in A, \qquad (7.2)$$

$$x(P) \ge 0, \qquad P \in \mathcal{P}.$$

It will be useful to consider the dual of this linear program, which is

$$\text{Minimize} \quad \sum_{(i,j) \in A} u(i,j)\ell(i,j)$$

$$\text{subject to} \quad \sum_{(i,j) \in P} \ell(i,j) \ge 1, \quad P \in \mathcal{P}, \qquad (7.3)$$

$$\ell(i,j) \ge 0, \qquad (i,j) \in A.$$

We can interpret the dual variable $\ell(i,j)$ as the length of the arc (i,j). Then the constraints of the dual say that the total length of each path $P \in \mathcal{P}$ should be at least one, or that for each k, then length of the shortest s_k-t_k path should be at least one.

7.2 The Two-Commodity Case

In this section, we give one case in which the cut condition is sufficient for $K = 2$ commodities. The example of the prior section shows that even in the case $K = 2$, the cut condition is not sufficient, so we must need some extra conditions for the cut condition to be sufficient. So far, we have been thinking of each commodity's flow f_k as a flow in the sense of Definition 2.1: the flow is nonnegative, but for this section it will be useful to think of each commodity's flow as a flow in the sense of Definition 2.3, so that we have skew-symmetry and $f_k(i,j) = -f_k(j,i)$. The additional condition we need is that $u(i,j) = u(j,i) > 0$ for all $(i,j) \in A$ (and recall in this case, we have $(j,i) \in A$ for each $(i,j) \in A$). With this particular definition of flows, we need to make sure that we don't allow one commodity's flow in the direction (i,j) cancel out the flow of another commodity in the direction (j,i), so the joint capacity constraint that we require is $\sum_{k=1}^{K} |f_k(i,j)| \le u(i,j)$; given skew-symmetry and $u(j,i) = u(i,j)$, this inequality poses the same requirement on both (i, j) and (j, i). Note that this different requirement on the flow capacity changes the cut condition, since the total capacity $u(\delta^+(S))$ limits flows both from $s_k \in S$ to $t_k \notin S$, and also those of a different commodity ℓ from $s_\ell \notin S$ to $t_\ell \in S$. Thus the cut condition in this case becomes

$$u(\delta^+(S)) \geq \sum_{k: |S \cap \{s_k, t_k\}| = 1} d_k. \tag{7.4}$$

Given this setting, we can prove the following theorem. We say that a flow f is *half-integral* if $2f$ is integral.

Theorem 7.1: *Suppose that $K = 2$ and $u(i, j) = u(j, i)$ for all $(i, j) \in A$. Then the cut condition (7.4) is sufficient to guarantee that multicommodity flow f_k exists satisying demands d_k. Furthermore, if the capacities $u(i, j)$ are integer and demands d_1 and d_2 are integer, then f_1 and f_2 are half-integral.*

Proof We first construct two different flows in $G = (V, A)$. For the first flow, consider an new graph G_1 in which we have added a source vertex s and a sink vertex t to G, and arcs (s, s_1) and (t_1, t) of capacity d_1, and arcs (s, s_2) and (t_2, t) of capacity d_2 (the capacity of the reverse arcs are all 0). For each $(i, j), (j, i) \in A$, we add (i, j) and (j, i) to G_1, both of capacity $u(i, j)$. See Figure 7.2 for an illustration of obtaining G_1 from G. We compute a maximum s-t flow g_1 in this graph G_1 (of the kind given in Definition 2.3). We observe that for any s-t cut S that contains s_1 but not s_2, $u(\delta^+(S)) \geq d_1 + d_2$ (because of the cut condition and the capacity of arc (s, s_2)), while if S contains s_2 but not s_1, $u(\delta^+(S)) \geq d_1 + d_2$ (because of the cut condition and the capacity of arc (s, s_1)), while if S contains both s_1 and s_2, then $u(\delta^+(S)) \geq d_1 + d_2$ (because of the cut condition and the capacity of the arcs to t). Thus the value of the s-t flow g_1 in graph G_1 will be $d_1 + d_2$ and the newly added arcs (s, s_1), (s, s_2), (t_1, t), and (t_2, t) will all be saturated. Furthermore we will have that for the original arcs A

$$\sum_{k: (i, k) \in A} g_1(i, k) = \begin{cases} 0 & i \neq s_1, t_1, s_2, t_2, \\ d_1 & i = s_1, \\ -d_1 & i = t_1, \\ d_2 & i = s_2, \\ -d_2 & i = t_2. \end{cases}$$

For the second flow, consider a new graph G_2 in which we have added a source vertex s and a sink vertex t to G, and arcs (s, s_1) and (t_1, t) of capacity d_1, and arcs (s, t_2) and (s_2, t) of capacity d_2 (the capacity of the reverse arcs are all 0). For each $(i, j) \in A$, we add (i, j) and (j, i) to G_2, both of capacity $u(i, j)$. See Figure 7.2 for an illustration of obtaining G_2 from G. We compute a maximum s-t flow g_2 in this graph G_2 (of the kind given in Definition 2.3).

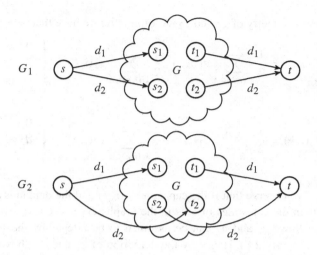

Figure 7.2 The graphs G_1 and G_2 used in Theorem 7.1.

We observe that for any s-t cut S that contains s_1 but not t_2, $u(\delta^+(S)) \geq d_1+d_2$ (because of the cut condition and the capacity of arc (s,t_2)), while if S contains t_2 but not s_1, $u(\delta^+(S)) \geq d_1+d_2$ (because of the cut condition and the capacity of arc (s,s_1)), while if S contains both s_1 and t_2, then $u(\delta^+(S)) \geq d_1 + d_2$ (because of the cut condition and the capacity of the arcs to t). Thus the value of the s-t flow g_2 in graph G_2 will be $d_1 + d_2$ and the newly added arcs (s,s_1), (s,t_2), (t_1,t), and (s_2,t) will all be saturated. Furthermore, we will have for the original arcs A

$$\sum_{k:(i,k)\in A} g_2(i,k) = \begin{cases} 0 & i \neq s_1, t_1, s_2, t_2, \\ d_1 & i = s_1, \\ -d_1 & i = t_1, \\ -d_2 & i = s_2, \\ d_2 & i = t_2. \end{cases}$$

From these two flows, g_1 and g_2, we now construct a multicommodity flow on the original graph G. We let $f_1(i,j) = \frac{1}{2}(g_1(i,j) + g_2(i,j))$ for all $(i,j) \in A$, and we let $f_2(i,j) = \frac{1}{2}(g_1(i,j) - g_2(i,j))$ for all $(i,j) \in A$. The capacity constraints are satisfied, since

$$\sum_{k=1}^{2} |f_k(i,j)| = \frac{1}{2}|g_1(i,j) + g_2(i,j)| + \frac{1}{2}|g_1(i,j) - g_2(i,j)|$$

$$= \max(|g_1(i,j)|, |g_2(i,j)|)$$

$$\leq \max(u(i,j), u(j,i)) = u(i,j),$$

by the skew-symmetry of g_1 and g_2. Additionally, we have that

$$\sum_{k:(i,k)\in A} f_1(i,k) = \frac{1}{2} \sum_{k:(i,k)\in A} g_1(i,k) + \frac{1}{2} \sum_{k:(i,k)\in A} g_2(i,k) = \begin{cases} 0 & i \neq s_1, t_1 \\ d_1 & i = s_1 \\ -d_1 & i = t_1, \end{cases}$$

and

$$\sum_{k:(i,k)\in A} f_2(i,k) = \frac{1}{2} \sum_{k:(i,k)\in A} g_1(i,k) - \frac{1}{2} \sum_{k:(i,k)\in A} g_2(i,k) = \begin{cases} 0 & i \neq s_2, t_2 \\ d_2 & i = s_2 \\ -d_2 & i = t_2, \end{cases}$$

as desired.

Finally, we observe that if the capacities $u(i,j)$ and the demands d_1, d_2 are integers, then the capacities of arcs in the graphs G_1 and G_2 will be integer, so that the flows g_1 and g_2 can be assumed to be integer by the Integrality Property (Property 2.8). Hence by the definition of f_1 and f_2 above, both f_1 and f_2 are half-integral.   □

There are other special cases in which the cut condition is sufficient for the existence of a multicommodity flow. We discuss some of these in the notes at the end of the chapter.

7.3 Intermezzo: The Multiplicative Weights Algorithm

At this point, we take what would appear to be a detour from our topic of multicommodity flows to discuss an algorithm that has had many applications in various fields: the multiplicative weights algorithm. In this section, we will discuss a particular form of it that will be of most use to us in our flow applications. The form is stated as that of making decisions over time so as to do almost as well as the best possible decision in hindsight. In particular, suppose that we must make a sequence of decisions over time. At each time step t, for $t = 1, \ldots, T$, we must choose one of N possible options. If we make decision i at time t, we get some unknown value $v_t(i) \in [0,1]$. We do not know the value of the $v_t(i)$ before we make the decision, but after we have selected decision i at time t, we learn all the values of the $v_t(j)$ for all $j = 1, \ldots, N$ before we must make the next decision at time $t+1$. We wish to maximize the total value resulting from the decisions that we have made. Quite surprisingly, we can give a very simple randomized algorithm that achieves, in expectation, a total value that is nearly as large as what could be obtained by choosing the best possible single decision j and making that decision over all time steps (which would result in total value $\max_j \sum_{t=1}^{T} v_t(j)$).

$w_1(i) \leftarrow 1$ for $i = 1, \ldots, N$

for $t \leftarrow 1$ to T **do**

    Make decision i with probability proportional to $w_t(i)$, get value $v_t(i)$

    $w_{t+1}(i) \leftarrow w_t(i)(1 + \epsilon v_t(i))$ for $i = 1, \ldots, N$

Algorithm 7.1 The multiplicative weights algorithm.

The central idea of the algorithm is that we will maintain a set of weights $w(i)$ for $i = 1, \ldots, N$, and we will make the decision i with probability proportional to weight $w(i)$. After each time step, we will update the weights to be proportionally larger for larger observed values $v_t(i)$. Thus decisions i that have had a prior history of having a good value $v_t(i)$ become more likely over time. Initially the weights $w(i)$ are 1 for all i, and after making each decision in time step t, we increase $w(i)$ by a multiplicative factor of $(1 + \epsilon v_t(i))$ for all i (for some fixed choice of $0 < \epsilon \leq 1/2$), hence the name of the algorithm. We will index the weights by t so that we can refer to the weight given to decision i at time t by $w_t(i)$. We make decisions over a time horizon $t = 1, \ldots, T$, although nothing in the algorithm uses any knowledge of T. We summarize the multiplicative weight algorithm in Algorithm 7.1.

Let $W_t = \sum_{i=1}^{N} w_t(i)$ be the total weight over all decisions at time step t, so that the probability we choose decision i at time t is $w_t(i)/W_t$; we denote this probability by $p_t(i)$. Thus the total expected value gained by the algorithm is $\sum_{t=1}^{T} \sum_{i=1}^{N} v_t(i) p_t(i)$. We now prove that the expected value gained by the algorithm is nearly as large as the maximum value given by any fixed decision j.

Theorem 7.2: *Assume $\epsilon \leq 1/2$. Then for any $j = 1, \ldots, N$,*

$$\sum_{t=1}^{T} \sum_{i=1}^{N} v_t(i) p_t(i) \geq (1 - \epsilon) \sum_{t=1}^{T} v_t(j) - \frac{1}{\epsilon} \ln N.$$

Proof The structure of the proof is quite simple. We derive both an upper bound and a lower bound on W_{T+1}, and then compare these two bounds in order to arrive at the desired result.

To obtain the upper bound, we observe that

$$W_{t+1} = \sum_{i=1}^{N} w_{t+1}(i) = \sum_{i=1}^{N} w_t(i)(1 + \epsilon v_t(i))$$

$$= W_t + \epsilon W_t \sum_{i=1}^{N} v_t(i) p_t(i)$$

$$= W_t \left(1 + \epsilon \sum_{i=1}^{N} v_t(i) p_t(i) \right)$$

$$\leq W_t \exp \left(\epsilon \sum_{i=1}^{N} v_t(i) p_t(i) \right),$$

where for the last inequality we use that $1 + x \leq e^x$. Thus we get that

$$W_{T+1} \leq W_T \exp \left(\epsilon \sum_{i=1}^{N} v_T(i) p_T(i) \right)$$

$$\leq W_{T-1} \exp \left(\epsilon \sum_{i=1}^{N} v_{T-1}(i) p_{T-1}(i) \right) \exp \left(\epsilon \sum_{i=1}^{N} v_T(i) p_T(i) \right)$$

$$\leq \cdots$$

$$\leq W_1 \prod_{t=1}^{T} \exp \left(\epsilon \sum_{i=1}^{N} v_t(i) p_t(i) \right)$$

$$= N \exp \left(\epsilon \sum_{t=1}^{T} \sum_{i=1}^{N} v_t(i) p_t(i) \right).$$

For the lower bound, we note that

$$W_{T+1} \geq w_{T+1}(j) = \prod_{t=1}^{T} (1 + \epsilon v_t(j))$$

$$\geq (1 + \epsilon)^{\sum_{t=1}^{T} v_t(j)},$$

using that $(1 + \epsilon x) \geq (1 + \epsilon)^x$ for $x \in [0, 1]$.

Now we can observe that the lower bound is no more than the upper bound, so that

$$(1 + \epsilon)^{\sum_{t=1}^{T} v_t(j)} \leq N \exp \left(\epsilon \sum_{t=1}^{T} \sum_{i=1}^{N} v_t(i) p_t(i) \right).$$

Taking the natural logarithm of both sides, we get that

$$\ln(1 + \epsilon) \sum_{t=1}^{T} v_t(j) \leq \ln N + \epsilon \sum_{t=1}^{T} \sum_{i=1}^{N} v_t(i) p_t(i).$$

Rearranging terms, we have

$$\sum_{t=1}^{T} \sum_{i=1}^{N} v_t(i) p_t(i) \geq \frac{1}{\epsilon} \ln(1 + \epsilon) \sum_{t=1}^{T} v_t(j) - \frac{1}{\epsilon} \ln N.$$

We can now use that $\ln(1 + \epsilon) \geq \epsilon - \epsilon^2$ for $\epsilon \in [0, 1/2]$ to obtain

$$\sum_{t=1}^{T} \sum_{i=1}^{N} v_t(i) p_t(i) \geq (1 - \epsilon) \sum_{t=1}^{T} v_t(j) - \frac{1}{\epsilon} \ln N.$$

$\square$

Observe that we are not using any assumptions about the values of the $v_t(j)$; we are not assuming that they are drawn from any probability distribution. Indeed, they could well be determined adversarially, and the bound still holds.

One of the great strengths of the algorithm is its flexibility; the basic algorithm and analysis can be adapted in many different ways. For example, suppose that instead of values $v_t(j) \in [0, 1]$ for decisions j we have costs $c_t(i) \in [-1, 1]$ and we wish to minimize the overall cost of our decisions. In Exercise 7.1, we ask the reader to show that a simple modification of the algorithm leads to a bound similar to that of Theorem 7.2.

As another example of the flexibility of the multiplicative weights algorithm, we show an example from optimization of finding a feasible solution to certain types of systems of inequalities. The most interesting case for our purposes is that of finding a near-feasible solution to a *packing problem*. We consider finding a feasible $x \in \Re^n$ such that

$$Mx \leq e \text{ and } x \in Q,$$

for Q a convex set, $M \in \Re^{m \times n}$, and e the vector of all 1s. We assume that $Mx \geq 0$ for all $x \in Q$. We could equally well have considered the inequalities $Mx \leq b$ instead of $Mx \leq e$, but we claim this is without loss of generality for $b > 0$, since we could easily divide the ith row of M by $b_i > 0$. The idea of this system is that Q represents constraints that are easy to optimize over, but the additional set of inequalities $Mx \leq e$ represents complicating side constraints.

In order for us to be able to apply the multiplicative weights algorithm to this problem, we assume that it is easy to optimize over Q in the sense that given a nonnegative vector $p \in \Re^m_{\geq 0}$, we have a subroutine that can find $x \in Q$ such that $p^T Mx \leq p^T e$ if such a vector x exists. We call the subroutine that either returns such an x or declares that there is no such x the *oracle* for Q. We observe that if there is no $x \in Q$ such that $p^T Mx \leq p^T e$ for $p \geq 0$, then the system $Mx \leq e$ and $x \in Q$ has no feasible solution. If we can optimize linear functions over Q, then it is easy to produce such an oracle, since $p^T Mx$ is a linear function in x, and all we need to do is minimize $p^T Mx$ over $x \in Q$; if a minimum $x \in Q$ has $p^T Mx \leq p^T e$, then we have found such an x, and otherwise the system is infeasible.

$w_1(i) \leftarrow 1$ for $i = 1, \ldots, m$
$T \leftarrow \frac{\rho}{\epsilon^2} \ln m$
for $t \leftarrow 1$ **to** T **do**
$\quad W_t \leftarrow \sum_{i=1}^m w_t(i)$, $p_t(i) \leftarrow w_t(i)/W_t$
$\quad$ Run oracle to find $x_t \in Q$ such that $p_t^T M x_t \leq p_t^T e$
$\quad v_t(i) \leftarrow \frac{1}{\rho} M_i x_t$ for $i = 1, \ldots, m$
$\quad w_{t+1}(i) \leftarrow w_t(i)(1 + \epsilon v_t(i))$ for $i = 1, \ldots, m$
return $\bar{x} \leftarrow \frac{1}{T} \sum_{t=1}^T x_t$

Algorithm 7.2 Multiplicative weights for packing problems.

To give our algorithm, we first need the concept of the *width* of the oracle for the system.

Definition 7.3: *Let M_i be the ith row of the matrix M. The* width ρ *of the oracle to be an upper bound on the maximum value of $M_i x$ over all rows i and all $x \in Q$ returned by the oracle; that is,*

$$\rho \geq \max_i \max_{\substack{x \in Q \\ \text{returned by oracle}}} M_i x. \tag{7.5}$$

Given that we want a solution x such that $M_i x \leq 1$, the width ρ is an upper bound on the multiplicative factor by which $M_i x$ can exceed its desired bound for any row i and any $x \in Q$ returned by the oracle.

In Algorithm 7.2, we give an algorithm that will find an $x \in Q$ that approximately satisfies the additional constraints; in particular, given $0 < \epsilon < 1/2$, it finds $x \in Q$ such that $Mx \leq (1+4\epsilon)e$. It is essentially the multiplicative weights algorithm given in Algorithm 7.1 in which each row of the matrix M corresponds to a decision. In each time step t, we run the oracle on the probability vector p_t to find $x_t \in Q$ such that $p_t^T M x_t \leq p_t^T e$. We then let the value $v_t(i)$ for the ith row be the quantity $\frac{1}{\rho} M_i x_t$. Note that since $Mx \geq 0$ for all $x \in Q$, by the definition of width given in (7.5), $v_t(i) \in [0, 1]$ for all $i = 1, \ldots, m$. Then for each row i, we increase its weight (and hence its probability) proportional to the value of $M_i x$, so that rows that exceed $M_i x \leq 1$ are given more weight and more probability mass, and hence future solutions x_t must be closer to satisfying these inequalities. We let the algorithm run for $T = \frac{\rho}{\epsilon^2} \ln m$ time steps, and at the end we return $\bar{x} = \frac{1}{T} \sum_{t=1}^T x_t$. We observe that because Q is convex and $x_t \in Q$ for each t, then $\bar{x} \in Q$.

Deriving the following theorem from Theorem 7.2 is now surprisingly simple.

Theorem 7.4: *If $\epsilon \leq 1/2$ and the oracle returns an x_t in each time step t, Algorithm 7.2 returns a solution $\bar{x} \in Q$ such that $M\bar{x} \leq (1 + 4\epsilon)e$ in $O(\frac{m\rho}{\epsilon^2} \ln m)$ time plus the time for $O(\frac{\rho}{\epsilon^2} \ln m)$ computations of the matrix-vector product Mx and for $O(\frac{\rho}{\epsilon^2} \ln m)$ oracle calls.*

Proof We run the main loop for $T = \frac{\rho}{\epsilon^2} \ln m$ iterations and make one oracle call and compute Mx_t once per iteration. We also spend $O(m)$ time per iteration updating v_t and w_{t+1}. Thus the running time bound is clear. We have also argued above that $\bar{x} \in Q$.

To show that $M\bar{x} \leq (1 + 4\epsilon)e$, we first observe that

$$\sum_{i=1}^{m} p_t(i)v_t(i) = \frac{1}{\rho}p_t^T Mx_t \leq \frac{1}{\rho}p_t^T e = \frac{1}{\rho},$$

since p_t is a probability distribution for any t and $\sum_{i=1}^{m} p_t(i) = 1$. Then we have that

$$\sum_{t=1}^{T}\sum_{i=1}^{m} p_t(i)v_t(i) \leq \frac{T}{\rho}.$$

Also, by applying Theorem 7.2, we have that for any $j \in \{1, \ldots, m\}$,

$$\sum_{t=1}^{T}\sum_{i=1}^{m} p_t(i)v_t(i) \geq (1 - \epsilon)\sum_{t=1}^{T} v_t(j) - \frac{1}{\epsilon}\ln m,$$

$$= (1 - \epsilon)\sum_{t=1}^{T} \frac{1}{\rho}M_j x_t - \frac{1}{\epsilon}\ln m,$$

$$= (1 - \epsilon)\frac{T}{\rho}M_j\bar{x} - \frac{1}{\epsilon}\ln m.$$

Then from the two inequalities we have that

$$(1 - \epsilon)\frac{T}{\rho}M_j\bar{x} - \frac{1}{\epsilon}\ln m \leq \frac{T}{\rho},$$

or, by rearranging terms, that

$$M_j\bar{x} \leq \frac{1}{1 - \epsilon}\left(1 + \frac{\rho \ln m}{\epsilon T}\right).$$

By the choice of $T = \frac{\rho}{\epsilon^2} \ln m$, we have that

$$M_j\bar{x} \leq \frac{1}{1 - \epsilon}(1 + \epsilon) \leq 1 + 4\epsilon,$$

where the last inequality holds for $\epsilon \leq 1/2$. Since the inequality holds for any $j \in \{1, \ldots, m\}$, then we have that

$$M\bar{x} \leq (1 + 4\epsilon)e,$$

as desired. $\square$

Once again, even this adaptation of the multiplicative weights algorithm is very flexible. Suppose, for instance, we wish to find an $x \in Q$, Q convex, such that $|Mx| \leq e$. Suppose that we have an oracle that for a vector $p \in \Re_{\geq 0}^m$ can find $x \in Q$ such that $\sum_{i=1}^m p(i)|M_i x| \leq p^T e$, or declare that no such x exists. Define the width ρ of the oracle to be an upper bound on the maximum of $|M_i x|$ over all rows i over all $x \in Q$ returned by the oracle. Then we ask the reader to show the following in Exercise 7.2.

Theorem 7.5: *If $\epsilon \leq 1/2$ and the oracle returns an x_t in each time step t, a modification of Algorithm 7.2 in which $v_t(i)$ is set to $\frac{1}{\rho}|M_i x_t|$ returns a solution $\bar{x} \in Q$ such that $|M\bar{x}| \leq (1 + 4\epsilon)e$ in $O(\frac{m\rho}{\epsilon^2} \ln m)$ time plus the time for $O(\frac{\rho}{\epsilon^2} \ln m)$ computations of the matrix-vector product Mx and for $O(\frac{\rho}{\epsilon^2} \ln m)$ oracle calls.*

We will see an application of this algorithm to the maximum flow problem in Section 8.2.

7.4 The Garg–Könemann Algorithm

In this section, we see how the multiplicative weights algorithm of the last section can be used to analyze an algorithm for the maximum multicommodity flow problem that we give here. We give the algorithm in Algorithm 7.3; it is due to Garg and Könemann [79], and thus is usually called the Garg–Könemann algorithm. The algorithm produces a nearly feasible, nearly optimal solution to the linear program (7.2) for the maximum multicommodity flow problem given in the initial section of the chapter.

The algorithm works as follows. Recall that $\mathcal{P}$ is the set of all s_k-t_k paths for all commodities k. The algorithm repeatedly finds the shortest path in $\mathcal{P}$ using lengths $\ell(i, j) = w(i, j)/u(i, j)$, where $w(i, j)$ is a weight for arc (i, j) maintained by the algorithm. Initially this weight is one; however, as we increase the flow on this arc, we increase the weight on the arc. This effectively increases the length of the arc and makes it less likely that the arc is part of a shortest path in future iterations. Each time we select path P, we let u be the capacity of the minimum capacity arc on path P (notice that this is the

$x(P) \leftarrow 0 \quad \forall P \in \mathcal{P}$
$f(i,j) \leftarrow 0, w(i,j) \leftarrow 1 \quad \forall (i,j) \in A$
while $f(i,j)/u(i,j) < (\ln m)/\epsilon^2 \ \forall (i,j) \in A$ **do**
   Let P be a shortest path in $\mathcal{P}$ using lengths $w(i,j)/u(i,j)$
   $u \leftarrow \min_{(i,j) \in P} u(i,j)$
   $x(P) \leftarrow x(P) + u$
   $f(i,j) \leftarrow f(i,j) + u \quad \forall (i,j) \in P$
   $w(i,j) \leftarrow (1 + \epsilon \frac{u}{u(i,j)}) w(i,j) \quad \forall (i,j) \in P$
$C \leftarrow \max_{(i,j) \in A} f(i,j)/u(i,j)$
return x/C;

Algorithm 7.3 The Garg–Könemann algorithm for the maximum multicommodity flow problem.

original capacity, not a residual capacity). We then increase the LP variable $x(P)$ by u. In order to keep track of the amount of flow on arc (i,j), we also increase a flow variable $f(i,j)$ for each arc $(i,j) \in P$ by u. We then perform an update to the weights of the arcs $(i,j) \in P$ inspired by the multiplicative weight algorithm, and increase the weight of each arc (i,j) in P by a factor of $(1 + \epsilon \frac{u}{u(i,j)})$; note that $0 \le u/u(i,j) \le 1$ by the choice of u. The algorithm continues until the flow $f(i,j)$ on some arc (i,j) is at least $(\ln m)/\epsilon^2$ times the arc's capacity $u(i,j)$. We then compute C, the maximum *congestion* of any arc, which is the ratio $f(i,j)/u(i,j)$ of the flow routed across the arc to the arc's capacity. By the termination condition of the algorithm, $C \ge (\ln m)/\epsilon^2$. We return $\hat{x} = x/C$; thus the flow across each arc in $\hat{x}$ is at most its capacity.

Notice that this algorithm is quite different from those we have previously seen for flow problems. There is no notion of a residual graph. The LP solution x constructed by the algorithm isn't even feasible; to produce a feasible solution, we scale x down by the maximum congestion so that the capacity constraints are obeyed.

To analyze the algorithm, let us first introduce some notation. Following our analysis of the multiplicative weights algorithm, let us index variables by t, denoting the value of the variable in the tth iteration of the algorithm. Thus in iteration t, $w_t(i,j)$ is the weight of arc (i,j), $f_t(i,j)$ is the flow across the arc (i,j), P_t is the path selected by the algorithm, and u_t is the amount of flow sent on path P_t. Let $W_t = \sum_{(i,j) \in A} w_t(i,j)$ be the total weight of all the arcs in A in iteration t. Let L_t be the length of the shortest path P_t found in iteration t, so that $L_t = \sum_{(i,j) \in P_t} \frac{w_t(i,j)}{u(i,j)}$. Let T be the number of iterations that the algorithm runs. Notice that the total value of the flow sent is $X \equiv \sum_{t=1}^{T} u_t = \sum_{P \in \mathcal{P}} x(P)$, though the value of the feasible flow $\hat{x}$ is the amount scaled down by C, or X/C. Let X^* be the value of a maximum multicommodity flow (that is, the value of an optimal solution to the LP (7.2)).

To analyze the performance of the algorithm, we will use feasible solutions to the dual linear program (7.3) to obtain a bound on X^*. In particular, if we scale down the lengths of the arcs by L_t, the length of the shortest path in the tth iteration, then we will have a feasible solution for the dual; that is, consider $\ell_t(i,j) = \frac{1}{L_t}(w_t(i,j)/u(i,j))$. Then for any path $P \in \mathcal{P}$, since L_t is the length of a shortest path in $\mathcal{P}$ in the tth iteration, $L_t \le \sum_{(i,j) \in P} \frac{w_t(i,j)}{u(i,j)}$, so that

$$\sum_{(i,j) \in P} \ell_t(i,j) = \frac{1}{L_t} \sum_{(i,j) \in P} \frac{w_t(i,j)}{u(i,j)} \ge 1,$$

showing that ℓ_t is a feasible solution for (7.3). By weak duality, the optimal multicommodity flow value X^* is at most the objective function value of the dual for any t, so that

$$X^* \le \sum_{(i,j) \in A} u(i,j)\ell_t(i,j) = \frac{1}{L_t} \sum_{(i,j) \in A} w_t(i,j) = \frac{W_t}{L_t}.$$

Given these preliminaries, we can now prove the following theorem.

Theorem 7.6: *The Garg–Könemann algorithm (Algorithm 7.3) computes a multicommodity flow of value at least $(1 - 2\epsilon)X^*$; that is, its value is within a factor of $(1 - 2\epsilon)$ of the value of a maximum multicommodity flow, when $0 < \epsilon \le 1/2$.*

Proof We begin by considering the ratio of X to X^*. Observe that

$$\frac{X}{X^*} = \frac{1}{X^*} \sum_{t=1}^{T} u_t \ge \sum_{t=1}^{T} \frac{u_t L_t}{W_t}$$

$$= \sum_{t=1}^{T} \frac{u_t}{W_t} \sum_{(i,j) \in P_t} \frac{w_t(i,j)}{u(i,j)}$$

$$= \sum_{t=1}^{T} \sum_{(i,j) \in P_t} \frac{u_t}{u(i,j)} \cdot \frac{w_t(i,j)}{W_t}. \tag{7.6}$$

We now take advantage of the similarity of our algorithm with the multiplicative weights algorithm. The weight update of the Garg–Könemann algorithm is exactly the same the weight update in Algorithm 7.1 with $v_t(i,j) = \frac{u_t}{u(i,j)} \in [0,1]$ for $(i,j) \in P_t$ (and $v_t(i,j) = 0$ for $(i,j) \notin P_t$)

and $p_t(i, j) = \frac{w_t(i,j)}{W_t}$, and in which each decision i from the multiplicative weights algorithm corresponds to an arc $(i, j) \in A$; thus the number of possible decisions is m. Theorem 7.2 tells us that for any decision $(h, k) \in A$,

$$\sum_{t=1}^{T} \sum_{(i,j)\in A} v_t(i, j) p_t(i, j) \geq (1 - \epsilon) \sum_{t=1}^{T} v_t(h, k) - \frac{1}{\epsilon} \ln m.$$

Plugging in the corresponding values for $v_t(i, j)$ and $p_t(i, j)$, the theorem implies that

$$\sum_{t=1}^{T} \sum_{(i,j)\in P_t} \frac{u_t}{u(i, j)} \cdot \frac{w_t(i, j)}{W_t} \geq (1 - \epsilon) \sum_{t=1}^{T} \frac{u_t}{u(h, k)} \cdot \mathbb{1}((h, k) \in P_t) - \frac{1}{\epsilon} \ln m,$$

where $\mathbb{1}((h, k) \in P_t)$ is 1 if $(h, k) \in P_t$ and 0 otherwise. Since $\sum_{t=1}^{T} u_t \cdot \mathbb{1}((h, k) \in P_t) = f(h, k)$, the inequality above is equivalent to

$$\sum_{t=1}^{T} \sum_{(i,j)\in P_t} \frac{u_t}{u(i, j)} \cdot \frac{w_t(i, j)}{W_t} \geq (1 - \epsilon) \frac{f(h, k)}{u(h, k)} - \frac{1}{\epsilon} \ln m.$$

Notice that from (7.6) the left-hand side is bounded above by X/X^*, so we have that

$$\frac{X}{X^*} \geq (1 - \epsilon) \frac{f(h, k)}{u(h, k)} - \frac{1}{\epsilon} \ln m.$$

Recall that we set $C = \max_{(i,j)\in A} f(i, j)/u(i, j)$, and that by the termination condition of the algorithm $C \geq (\ln m)/\epsilon^2$. Since the inequality above holds for any $(h, k) \in A$, it also holds for the arc achieving the maximum congestion C, so that

$$\frac{X}{X^*} \geq (1 - \epsilon)C - \frac{1}{\epsilon} \ln m \geq (1 - \epsilon)C - \epsilon C = (1 - 2\epsilon)C.$$

Since the value of the solution $\hat{x}$ returned by the algorithm is X/C, we then have that the value of the returned solution is

$$\frac{X}{C} \geq (1 - 2\epsilon)X^*,$$

proving the theorem. $\qquad\qquad\qquad\qquad\qquad\qquad\qquad\qquad\qquad\qquad\square$

We can bound the running time of the algorithm as follows.

Theorem 7.7: *The Garg–Könemann algorithm (Algorithm 7.3) takes $O((Km \ln m)/\epsilon^2)$ shortest path computations and thus takes $O\big(Km(m + n \log n)(\ln m)/\epsilon^2\big)$ time.*

Proof To prove the theorem, pick an arc (i, j). We note that a given arc (i, j) can be the minimum capacity arc on the selected shortest path at most $(\ln m)/\epsilon^2$ times before the algorithm terminates: Each time (i, j) is the minimum capacity arc and $u = u(i, j)$, the flow $f(i, j)$ increases by $u(i, j)$. Thus after $(\ln m)/\epsilon^2$ times in which (i, j) is the minimum capacity arc, $f(i, j)/u(i, j) \geq (\ln m)/\epsilon^2$, and the algorithm ends. Since there are m arcs altogether, and some arc must be the minimum capacity arc in each iteration, we can have at most $(m \ln m)/\epsilon^2$ iterations before the algorithm terminates. In each iteration, we must compute a shortest path for each of the K commodities to find the shortest overall path in $\mathcal{P}$, and so we must compute $(Km \ln m)/\epsilon^2$ shortest paths over the course of the algorithm. The running time of the algorithm follows, since we can compute a shortest path by using Dijkstra's algorithm in $O(m + n \log n)$ time. $\square$

In Exercise 7.3, we have the reader show that it is possible to reduce the running time to $O((m \ln m)/\epsilon^2)$ shortest path computations, which removes the dependence of the running time on the number of commodities K.

7.5 The Awerbuch–Leighton Algorithm

In this section, we look at another multicommodity flow algorithm for the maximum multicommodity flow problem, which is again quite different from the previous flow algorithms we have seen. This algorithm repeatedly iterates through all the edges and optimizes the amount of each commodity sent through each edge. If there exists a flow that sends d_k units of commodity k, then after a certain number of rounds, the algorithm can construct an overall multicommodity flow that sends at least $(1 - \epsilon)d_k$ of commodity k. The algorithm was given in the theoretical computer science literature by Awerbuch and Leighton [12], and hence we call it the Awerbuch–Leighton algorithm.

To simplify the presentation, we make a number of assumptions. We assume that $d_k = 1$ for commodities $k = 1, \ldots, K$. We assume that for each source s_k there is exactly one edge (s_k, j) leaving s_k; note that we can easily modify the graph to add such an edge if it does not exist. We assume there is a multicommodity flow f^* that sends 1 unit of commodity k between s_k and t_k for each commodity k; we let $f_k^*(i, j)$ be the flow of commodity k on arc (i, j). For the purposes of analysis we assume there exists a path decomposition of the flow f_k^*: we index the paths for each commodity k by r so that we have $x^*(P_{k,r}) \geq 0$ units of flow sent on path $P_{k,r}$, with $\sum_r x^*(P_{k,r}) = d_k = 1$ for all commodities k. Then $\sum_{r:(i, j) \in P_{k,r}} x^*(P_{k,r}) = f_k^*(i, j)$ for all commodities

k and arcs $(i, j) \in A$. We finally (and crucially) assume that there is a path from any node in the graph to any sink t_k such that every arc on the path has capacity at least 1. These assumptions can all be removed; see the Chapter Notes for further discussion.

In the algorithm, we treat the flow being sent as a fluid that can accumulate at nodes in the network. For each commodity k and each arc (i, j) such that $u(i, j) > 0$, we maintain two queues, one at i and one at j, which hold some amount of flow of commodity k. We let $q_k(i, (i, j))$ and $q_k(j, (i, j))$ denote the amount of flow being held in these two queues respectively. These amounts are always nonnegative. We will let q_k denote the amount of flow in the queue at the source s_k; recall that since there is a single edge leaving the source, this queue is well defined. The algorithm then repeatedly goes through the following four step process, which is also summarized in Algorithm 7.4:

1 (**Add Flow**) Add $1 - \epsilon$ units of flow to the queue q_k at s_k for each commodity k;

2 (**Push Flow**) For each arc $(i, j) \in A$, find $f_1(i, j), \ldots, f_K(i, j)$ that maximize the function

$$\sum_{k=1}^{K} f_k(i, j)[\Delta_k(i, j) - f_k(i, j)],$$

where $\Delta_k(i, j) = q_k(i, (i, j)) - q_k(j, (i, j))$ is the difference in the queue heights for commodity k at the tail and head of arc (i, j), subject to the constraints that $f_k(i, j) \geq 0$ and $\sum_{k=1}^{K} f_k(i, j) \leq u(i, j)$. Move $f_k(i, j)$ units of commodity k from $q_k(i, (i, j))$ to $q_k(j, (i, j))$.

3 (**Empty Flow**) Empty the commodity k queue at the sink t_k for all commodities k.

4 (**Balance Flow**) Balance the commodity k queues at each node $i \in V$ for all commodities k; that is, for each commodity k and each node i, sum the queues $q_k(i, (j, i))$ for arcs (j, i) entering i and $q_k(i, (i, h))$ for arcs (i, h) leaving i, then assign these queues the average taken over all of these arcs. The total amount of commodity k at node i in the queues will remain the same, and each queue $q_k(i, (j, i))$ and $q_k(i, (i, h))$ will have the same amount of commodity k.

The analysis of the algorithm uses a potential function to argue that there cannot be too much flow in the queues, which implies that over time the flow of commodity k entering the network at source s_k must leave the system at the sink t_k. We then run the algorithm for a certain number of iterations, and track the flow that both enters and leaves the graph. If the total amount of the

---

for $t \leftarrow 1$ to T **do**

    $q_k \leftarrow q_k + (1 - \epsilon)$ for all commodities k

    foreach $(i, j) \in A$ **do**

        $\Delta_k(i, j) \leftarrow q_k(i, (i, j)) - q_k(j, (i, j))$

        Compute $f_1(i, j), \ldots, f_K(i, j) \geq 0$ that maximize

        $\sum_{k=1}^{K} f_k(i, j)[\Delta_k(i, j) - f_k(i, j)]$ subject to

        $\sum_k f_k(i, j) \leq u(i, j)$

        $q_k(i, (i, j)) \leftarrow q_k(i, (i, j)) - f_k(i, j)$ for all k

        $q_k(j, (i, j)) \leftarrow q_k(j, (i, j)) + f_k(i, j)$ for all k

    $q_k(t_k, (j, t_k)) \leftarrow 0$ for all $(j, t_k) \in A$, for all commodities k

    foreach $i \in V$ **do**

        $n_i \leftarrow |\delta^+(i)| + |\delta^-(i)|$

        $a_k \leftarrow \frac{1}{n_i} \left(\sum_{(j,i) \in \delta^-(i)} q_k(i, (j, i)) + \sum_{(i,j) \in \delta^+(i)} q_k(i, (i, j)) \right)$ for

        all commodities k

        $q_k(i, (i, j)) \leftarrow a_k$ for all $(i, j) \in \delta^+(i)$ for all commodities k

        $q_k(i, (j, i)) \leftarrow a_k$ for all $(i, j) \in \delta^-(i)$ for all commodities k

---

Algorithm 7.4 The Awerbuch–Leighton algorithm.

flow in the queues is bounded, then after a certain number of iterations, the portion in the queues will be a small fraction of that which has been added to the source nodes, and so the remainder must have left at the sinks. We compute a multicommodity flow by averaging the flow that has left the graph. We give more details in the proof of our final theorem (Theorem 7.16).

Before we continue, we explain how we compute the flows in the Push Step of the algorithm. Recall that for each arc (i, j), we want to find find $f_1(i, j), \ldots, f_K(i, j) \geq 0$ that maximize the function

$$\sum_{k=1}^{K} f_k(i, j)[\Delta_k(i, j) - f_k(i, j)],$$

subject to $\sum_{k=1}^{K} f_k(i, j) \leq u(i, j)$. For a given arc (i, j) and $\lambda \geq 0$, we let

$$G(i, j) = \sum_{k=1}^{K} f_k(i, j)[\Delta_k(i, j) - f_k(i, j)] + \lambda \left(u(i, j) - \sum_{k=1}^{K} f_k(i, j) \right).$$

For the optimal flows $f_1(i, j), f_2(i, j), \ldots, f_K(i, j)$, we know that either $f_k(i, j) = 0$ or $\frac{\partial G}{\partial f_k} = 0$, where the latter implies that

$$\Delta_k(i, j) - 2f_k(i, j) - \lambda = 0.$$

Thus we have that

$$f_k(i, j) = \max\left(0, \frac{1}{2}(\Delta_k(i, j) - \lambda)\right),$$

and we want to choose λ so that

$$\sum_{k=1}^{K} \max\left(0, \frac{1}{2}(\Delta_k(i, j) - \lambda)\right) \leq u(i, j). \tag{7.7}$$

Notice that for all k with $\Delta_k(i, j) > \lambda$, $f_k(i, j) > 0$, so we can compute λ by sorting the $\Delta_k(i, j)$ in descending order, and performing bisection search on the prefixes of commodities in the sorted order. If S is the set of commodities in a given prefix, then we have that $\sum_{k \in S} f_k(i, j) = u(i, j)$ implies that

$$\frac{1}{2} \sum_{k \in S} (\Delta_k(i, j) - \lambda) = u(i, j).$$

Since $\lambda \geq 0$, we have then that

$$\lambda = \max\left(0, \frac{1}{|S|}\left(\sum_{k \in S} \Delta_k(i, j) - 2u(i, j)\right)\right).$$

Given this value of λ, we check if Inequality (7.7) holds. If it does, we can try a larger prefix S; if it doesn't, we try a smaller prefix S.

As we stated earlier, the analysis of the algorithm uses a potential function to argue that there can't be too much flow in the queues, which implies that over time the flow of commodity k entering the network at source s_k must leave the system at the sink t_k. To show that the total amount of flow in the queues must be bounded, we will use the potential function

$$\Phi = \sum_{(i, j) \in A} \sum_{k=1}^{K} \left(q_k(i, (i, j))^2 + q_k(j, (i, j))^2\right).$$

To analyze the algorithm, we analyze the change in this potential function for each of the four steps of the algorithm.

Lemma 7.8: *The Add Step of the algorithm increases the potential function Φ by*

$$2(1 - \epsilon) \sum_{k=1}^{K} q_k + (1 - \epsilon)^2 K.$$

Proof In the Add Step, the queues at the sources s_k each increase by $1 - \epsilon$, so that the increase in Φ due to the Add Step is

$$\sum_{k=1}^{K} \left([q_k + (1 - \epsilon)]^2 - q_k^2 \right) = \sum_{k=1}^{K} \left(2(1 - \epsilon)q_k + (1 - \epsilon)^2 \right)$$

$$= 2(1 - \epsilon) \sum_{k=1}^{K} q_k + (1 - \epsilon)^2 K.$$

$\square$

Observation 7.9: *The potential function Φ cannot increase during the Empty Step.*

For the Balance Step, we need the following well-known inequality.

Fact 7.10 (Cauchy–Schwarz Inequality): *For any two vectors of numbers $x = (x_1, \ldots, x_p)$ and $y = (y_1, \ldots, y_p)$, we have that*

$$\left(\sum_{i=1}^{p} x_i y_i \right)^2 \le \sum_{i=1}^{p} x_i^2 \sum_{i=1}^{p} y_i^2.$$

Lemma 7.11: *The potential function Φ cannot increase during the Balance Step.*

Proof If there are p arcs incident to node i, and z_j is the amount of flow in the queue for the jth arc incident to i for commodity k, and we set the queues to be $a_j = \frac{1}{p} \sum_{j=1}^{p} z_j$, then the change in the potential for commodity k across all arcs incident to i is

$$\sum_{j=1}^{p} \left(a_j^2 - z_j^2 \right) = p \left(\frac{1}{p} \sum_{j=1}^{p} z_j \right)^2 - \sum_{j=1}^{p} z_j^2 \le 0,$$

where the final inequality follows by applying the Cauchy–Schwarz Inequality in Fact 7.10 to the vectors $x = (z_1, \ldots, z_p)$ and $y = (\frac{1}{p}, \ldots, \frac{1}{p})$. $\square$

We now need to show that the decrease in the potential function from the Push Step can be used to balance out the increase from the Add Step.

Lemma 7.12: *The potential function Φ decreases during the Push Step by at least $2 \sum_{k=1}^{K} q_k + 2(1 - \epsilon)K - 2Km$, where q_k is the amount of commodity k in the queue at s_k at the start of the iteration.*

Proof We first show that the Push Step is designed to maximize the decrease in the potential function. Recall that we assume there is a multicommodity flow f^* that sends one unit of commodity k between s_k and t_k for each commodity k. We then use the existence of f^* to show that the potential function must decrease by at least the amount given in the statement of the lemma.

Suppose we move f units of flow from a queue of height x to a queue of height y, whose difference in height is $\Delta = x - y$. Then the total decrease in the potential function Φ due to this change is

$$
\begin{aligned}
x^2 + y^2 - (x - f)^2 - (y + f)^2 &= 2xf - 2yf - 2f^2 \\
&= 2f[(x - y) - f] \\
&= 2f[\Delta - f].
\end{aligned}
$$

Recall that for each edge (i, j) the Push Step maximizes $\sum_{k=1}^{K} f_k(i, j)$ $[\Delta_k(i, j) - f_k(i, j)]$ subject to $\sum_k f_k(i, j) \leq u(i, j)$. So the Push Step computes a flow on (i, j) that maximizes the potential decrease in Φ over all multicommodity flows. Thus the potential decrease realized by the flow f we compute must be at least the potential decrease of the multicommodity flow f^*. Hence we have that the drop in potential is

$$
2 \sum_{(i, j) \in A} \sum_{k=1}^{K} f_k(i, j)[\Delta_k(i, j) - f_k(i, j)]
$$

$$
\geq 2 \sum_{(i, j) \in A} \sum_{k=1}^{K} f_k^*(i, j)[\Delta_k(i, j) - f_k^*(i, j)]
$$

$$
= 2 \sum_{(i, j) \in A} \sum_{k=1}^{K} f_k^*(i, j)\Delta_k(i, j) - 2 \sum_{(i, j) \in A} \sum_{k=1}^{K} f_k^*(i, j)^2
$$

$$
\geq 2 \sum_{(i, j) \in A} \sum_{k=1}^{K} f_k^*(i, j)\Delta_k(i, j) - 2Km,
$$

where for the last step we use the fact that the demand $d_k = 1$ for each commodity k, so $f_k^*(i, j)^2 \leq 1$ for all $(i, j) \in A$. We now use the decomposition of the multicommodity flow f^* into paths; recall that $\sum_{r:(i, j) \in P_{k,r}} x^*(P_{k,r}) = f_k^*(i, j)$ for all commodities k and arcs $(i, j) \in A$, and $\sum_r x^*(P_{k,r}) = 1$. Thus

$$
\sum_{(i, j) \in A} \sum_{k=1}^{K} f_k^*(i, j)\Delta_k(i, j) = \sum_{k=1}^{K} \sum_r x^*(P_{k,r}) \sum_{(i, j) \in P_{k,r}} \Delta_k(i, j).
$$

We now observe that because of the Balance Step, for a given commodity k the queue heights of each node i for the edge coming into i and the edge leaving i must be the same during the Push Step: that is, for two consecutive edges in a path – say (i, j) and (j, ℓ) – we know that $q_k(j, (i, j)) = q_k(j, (j, \ell))$. Thus summing $\Delta_k(i, j)$ and $\Delta_k(j, \ell)$ gives the differences of the queues at i and ℓ:

$$\Delta_k(i, j) + \Delta_k(j, \ell) = [q_k(i, (i, j)) - q_k(j, (i, j))]$$
$$+ [q_k(j, (j, \ell)) - q_k(\ell, (j, \ell))]$$
$$= q_k(i, (i, j)) - q_k(\ell, (j, \ell)).$$

Extending the logic above, the sum of Δ_k along a path $P_{k,r}$, $\sum_{(i, j) \in P_{k,r}} \Delta_k(i, j)$, will leave only the queues at the start of the path (at s_k) and the end of the path (at t_k). At the start of the Push Step, we know that the queue for commodity k at s_k has $q_k + (1 - \epsilon)$ units of commodity k in it (where q_k is the content of the queue at s_k at the start of the iteration), and the queue for commodity k at t_k has 0 units in it. Recalling that $\sum_r x^*(P_{k,r}) = 1$, the decrease in the potential function Φ is at least

$$2\sum_{k=1}^{K} \sum_r x^*(P_{k,r}) \sum_{(i, j) \in P_{k,r}} \Delta_k(i, j) - 2Km \geq 2\sum_{k=1}^{K}(q_k + 1 - \epsilon) - 2Km$$

$$= 2\sum_{k=1}^{K} q_k + 2(1 - \epsilon)K - 2Km,$$

as desired. $\square$

The following observation is now easy to see from previous lemmas.

Lemma 7.13: *If at the start of an iteration, $\sum_{k=1}^{K} q_k \geq \frac{1}{\epsilon}Km$, then the potential function Φ will not increase during the iteration.*

Proof By Observation 7.9 and Lemma 7.11, the Empty and Balance Steps do not cause the potential function to increase. By Lemma 7.8, the Add Step causes the potential function Φ to increase by at most $2(1 - \epsilon) \sum_{k=1}^{K} q_k + (1 - \epsilon)^2 K$, while by Lemma 7.12, the Push Step causes the potential function Φ to decrease by at least $2 \sum_{k=1}^{K} q_k + 2(1 - \epsilon)K - 2Km$. The decrease is at least as much as the increase if

$$2\sum_{k=1}^{K} q_k + 2(1 - \epsilon)K - 2Km \geq 2(1 - \epsilon)\sum_{k=1}^{K} q_k + (1 - \epsilon)^2 K.$$

Rearranging, we get that the decrease is at least as much as the increase if

$$\sum_{k=1}^{K} q_k \geq \frac{1}{2\epsilon}[2Km + (1 - \epsilon)^2 K - 2(1 - \epsilon)K],$$

which is implied by $\sum_{k=1}^{K} q_k \geq \frac{1}{\epsilon}Km$, as desired. $\square$

Recall that our overall goal is to show that there cannot be too much flow in the network, so that most flow entering the network will eventually have to leave it. Our next lemma shows that if the condition of Lemma 7.13 is not met, and there is a large queue of flow somewhere in the network, the potential function will still decrease.

Lemma 7.14: *If at the start of an iteration, $\sum_{k=1}^{K} q_k < \frac{1}{\epsilon}Km$, but there exists a queue of height $q^* > \frac{1}{\epsilon}Km + n + \frac{1}{2}K$, then the potential function Φ will not increase during the iteration.*

Proof By Lemma 7.8 and the hypothesis of the lemma, we know that the Add Step increases the potential function by at most

$$2(1 - \epsilon)\sum_{k=1}^{K} q_k + (1 - \epsilon)^2 K < \frac{2}{\epsilon}Km + K.$$

We assumed that from any node in the graph, there is a path to any sink t_k for any k of arcs of capacity at least one. Suppose the queue of height q^* is at node i^* and is of commodity ℓ; let P be a path in the graph from i^* to t_ℓ. Consider a flow g_ℓ that sends one unit of flow from i^* to t_ℓ. By Lemma 7.12, we know that the potential function decreases by

$$2\sum_{(i,j)\in A}\sum_{k=1}^{K} f_k(i, j)[\Delta_k(i, j) - f_k(i, j)] \geq 2\sum_{(i,j)\in P} g_\ell(i, j)[\Delta_\ell(i, j) - g_\ell(i, j)]$$

$$= 2\sum_{(i,j)\in P}[\Delta_\ell(i, j) - 1]$$

$$\geq 2q^* - 2n,$$

using the reasoning as in the proof of Lemma 7.12 that the sum of the Δ_ℓ telescopes to the first queue in the path (at i^* of height q^*) and the last (at t_ℓ of height 0). So the potential function will decrease if

$$2q^* - 2n \geq \frac{2}{\epsilon}Km + K,$$

or

$$q^* \geq \frac{1}{\epsilon} K m + n + \frac{1}{2} K,$$

as desired.   □

From these results, we can give an upper bound on the potential Φ, and hence on the total amount of flow of any commodity k in the network.

Lemma 7.15: *For any commodity k, the total amount of flow of commodity k in the queues in the network is at most $\frac{9}{\epsilon} K^{3/2} m^2$.*

Proof Since there are $2mK$ queues in total, and by Lemma 7.14, each queue has height at most $\frac{1}{\epsilon} K m + n + \frac{1}{2} K \leq \frac{4}{\epsilon} K m$ before the potential function decreases (using $m \geq n$ and $\epsilon \leq 1$), and the queues at the sources have height at most $\frac{2}{\epsilon} K m$ before the potential function decreases, the potential function can never be larger than

$$2mK \left[\frac{4}{\epsilon} K m \right]^2 + \frac{2}{\epsilon} K m \leq \frac{34}{\epsilon^2} K^3 m^3.$$

Let M_k be the total amount of flow of commodity k in the queues of the network and assume that all flow in the queues is of commodity k. We get the worst-case upper bound on M_k by assuming that commodity k is the only contributor to the potential function, and that each queue has $M_k/2m$ units of commodity k. Then we have that

$$2m \left(\frac{M_k}{2m} \right)^2 \leq \frac{34}{\epsilon^2} K^3 m^3,$$

which implies

$$M_k \leq \frac{9}{\epsilon} K^{3/2} m^2.$$

                                                                               □

Now we can finally bound the number of iterations of the algorithm, as shown in the following theorem.

Theorem 7.16: *If we run Algorithm 7.4 for $\frac{9}{\epsilon^2} K^{3/2} m^2$ iterations, then we can compute a multicommodity flow that sends at least $1 - 2\epsilon$ units of flow of each commodity k.*

Proof Let $T = \frac{9}{\epsilon^2} K^{3/2} m^2$. As suggested earlier in this section, we let the algorithm run for T iterations and keep track of all the flow of each commodity that eventually exits the graph at its sink t_k. Let $F_k(i, j)$ be the amount of the commodity k that traverses edge (i, j) and is removed from the queue at t_k by the final iteration T. Let $g_k(i, j) = F_k(i, j)/T$. We claim that g_k is a multicommodity flow that sends at least $1 - 2\epsilon$ units of demand from s_k to t_k. For each commodity k, the Add Step of the algorithm adds $1 - \epsilon$ units of flow in each iteration of the algorithm, so $(1 - \epsilon)T$ units of commodity k get added over the T time steps. By Lemma 7.15, at most $\epsilon T = \frac{9}{\epsilon} K^{3/2} m^2$ units of commodity k can be in the queues of the graph at time T, so it must be the case that at least $(1 - \epsilon)T - \epsilon T$ units of commodity k have been removed from the sink t_k. Thus g_k sends at least $1 - 2\epsilon$ units of flow from s_k to t_k. Since in any iteration the total amount of flow sent over edge (i, j) is at most the capacity $u(i, j)$, it must be the case that $\sum_{k=1}^{K} g_k(i, j) \leq u(i, j)$. Finally, at any node $i \neq s_k, t_k$, the total flow that exits at the sink t_k entering i must be equal to the total flow exiting the sink leaving i, so flow conservation is maintained by g_k. $\qquad\square$

As with the push-relabel algorithm for the maximum flow problem, one strength of this algorithm is that all of its operations are very local. Rather than looking for augmenting paths in the graph and modifying flow along a path, we only modify flow on individual edges.

Exercises

7.1 Suppose $\epsilon \leq 1/2$, and $c_t(i) \in [-1, 1]$ for all t and i. Show that if we modify the multiplicative weight update step in Algorithm 7.1 to be $w_{t+1}(i) \leftarrow (1 - \epsilon c_t(i))w_t(i)$, then after T rounds, for any decision j, the expected cost of our solution is

$$\sum_{t=1}^{T}\sum_{i=1}^{N} c_t(i)p_t(i) \leq \sum_{t=1}^{T} c_t(j) + \epsilon \sum_{t=1}^{T} |c_t(j)| + \frac{1}{\epsilon} \ln N.$$

7.2 Prove Theorem 7.5.

7.3 Consider Algorithm 7.5, which is a modification of the Garg–Könemann algorithm given in Algorithm 7.3.

Algorithm 7.3 always computes the shortest path over all commodities, which requires K shortest path computations in each iteration of the main loop. We showed that the algorithm always terminates after augmenting flow on at most $\frac{m \ln m}{\epsilon^2}$ paths. Thus for Algorithm 7.3, we need $\frac{Km \ln m}{\epsilon^2}$ shortest path computations.

$x(P) \leftarrow 0 \quad \forall P \in \mathcal{P}$
$f(i, j) \leftarrow 0, w(i, j) \leftarrow 1 \quad \forall (i, j) \in A$
Let L be the length of the shortest path in $\mathcal{P}$ using lengths
$\quad \ell(i, j) = w(i, j)/u(i, j)$
while $f(i, j)/u(i, j) < (\ln m)/\epsilon^2 \, \forall (i, j) \in A$ **do**
$\quad L \leftarrow L(1 + \epsilon)$
$\quad$ **for** $k \leftarrow 1$ to K **do**
$\qquad$ **while** $\exists P \in \mathcal{P}_k$ with $\sum_{(i, j) \in P} \frac{w(i, j)}{u(i, j)} \le L$ and
$\qquad f(i, j)/u(i, j) < (\ln m)/\epsilon^2 \, \forall (i, j) \in A$ **do**
$\qquad\quad u \leftarrow \min_{(i, j) \in P} u(i, j)$
$\qquad\quad x(P) \leftarrow x(P) + u$
$\qquad\quad f(i, j) \leftarrow f(i, j) + u \quad \forall (i, j) \in P$
$\qquad\quad w(i, j) \leftarrow (1 + \epsilon \frac{u}{u(i, j)}) w(i, j) \quad \forall (i, j) \in P$
$C \leftarrow \max_{(i, j) \in A} f(i, j)/u(i, j)$
return x/C;

Algorithm 7.5 Modification of Algorithm 7.3.

(a) Prove that if in each iteration of Algorithm 7.3 we increase flow on a path whose length is at most $(1 + \epsilon)$ times the length of the shortest path in $\mathcal{P}$, the algorithm computes a multicommodity flow of value at least $(1 - 2\epsilon)/(1 + \epsilon)$ of the maximum multicommodity flow.

(b) Prove that in Algorithm 7.5, L is always at most $(1 + \epsilon)$ times the length of the shortest path in $\mathcal{P}$.

(c) Prove that in the course of Algorithm 7.5, the length of any edge can become at most $m^{2/\epsilon}$ times its original length.

(d) Prove that in Algorithm 7.5 there can be at most $O(\ln m/\epsilon^2)$ iterations of the outer while loop before the algorithm terminates.

(e) Prove that Algorithm 7.5 computes a multicommodity flow of value at least $(1 - 2\epsilon)/(1 + \epsilon)$ of the maximum multicommodity flow with $O((K + m)(\ln m)/\epsilon^2)$ shortest path computations.

(f) Recall that Dijkstra's algorithm for computing a shortest path computes the length of the shortest path from a given source node to all other nodes. Use this to prove that a simple modification of Algorithm 7.5 gives a multicommodity flow of value at least $(1 - 2\epsilon)/(1 + \epsilon)$ of the maximum multicommodity flow with $O((m \ln m)/\epsilon^2)$ shortest path computations.

Chapter Notes

Ford and Fulkerson [65] give an early reference for the maximum multicommodity flow problem. Early algorithms for the multicommodity flow problem focused on efficient implementations of the simplex method for solving the associated linear program; for instance, Ford and Fulkerson [65] give a column-generation-based version of the simplex method.

Theorem 7.1 on two-commodity flows in Section 7.2 is due to Hu [113]; the proof we give is due to Seymour [179]. Schrijver [177, section 70.11] surveys a number of cases in which the cut condition as given in Section 7.2 is sufficient for a multicommodity flow to exist; for example, a theorem of Okamura and Seymour [154] says that for planar graphs, if the graph can be drawn such that all s_k and t_k are on the exterior face, then the cut condition is sufficient.

Polynomial-time algorithms for multicommodity flow problems have so far been specializations of polynomial-time algorithms for linear programming. Vaidya [199] gives an $O(K^{2.5}n^2m^{1.5}\log(mDU))$ time algorithm, where $D = \max_k d_k$, by adapting an interior-point algorithm and using fast matrix multiplication. Kamath and Palmon [120] give several different algorithms based on interior-point methods. Tardos [189] gives a strongly polynomial-time algorithm for linear programs in which the coefficients of the constraints are bounded in the dimension of the problem; multicommodity flow problems have this structure, and consequently Tardos's algorithm gives a strongly polynomial-time algorithm for multicommodity flow.

Work on polynomial-time algorithms to find ϵ-optimal solutions to multicommodity flow problems began with a paper of Leighton, Makedon, Plotkin, Stein, Tardos, and Tragoudas [142]. Building on ideas of Shahrokhi and Matula [180] and Klein, Plotkin, Stein, and Tardos [133], they give a deterministic algorithm running in time $O(\frac{1}{\epsilon^2}K^2mn\log k\log^3 n)$ for the maximum concurrent flow problem; their algorithm repeatedly computes minimum-cost flows in which the cost of the edge is an exponential in its *congestion* (that is, the current ratio of the total amount of flow on the edge to its capacity). Radzik [168] shows how to improve the running time of this algorithm to $O(\frac{1}{\epsilon^2}Kmn\log k\log^3 n)$.

Subsequent generalizations of this exponential penalty method were made by Grigoriadis and Khachiyan [102] and Plotkin, Shmoys, and Tardos [164]. The multiplicative weights algorithm, introduced in Section 7.3, is from an excellent survey of Arora, Hazan, and Kale [10] on the multiplicative weights algorithm and its applications. The algorithm is introduced in the survey as an attempt to synthesize a number of different algorithms, including these algorithms using exponential penalties.

The Garg–Könemann algorithm of Section 7.4 is due to Garg and Könemann [79]. The perspective on the Garg–Könemann algorithm we give is from Arora, Hazan, and Kale [10].

The Awerbuch–Leighton algorithm is due to Awerbuch and Leighton [12]. Awerbuch and Leighton [13] also wrote a follow-up paper with better time bounds and a different potential function and balancing step than that given here; they achieve a running time of $O(\frac{1}{\epsilon^3}KL^2 m \ln^3(m/\epsilon))$, where L is the length of the longest simple path from a source to a sink in the graph (so that $L = O(n)$). Both papers handle arbitrary demands and capacities. The first paper has an extension to general directed graphs, and the second considers networks that change arbitrarily over time.

Some amount of experimental work with the exponential penalty algorithms of Leighton et al. [142] and Plotkin, Shmoys, and Tardos [164] has been performed. Leong, Shor, and Stein [143] find that the Leighton et al. algorithm for concurrent multicommodity flow outperforms a network simplex algorithm due to Kennington and an interior point algorithm due to Karmarkar and Ramakrishnan, though comparison tests were limited. Goldberg, Oldham, Plotkin, and Stein [88] performed computational testing for the minimum-cost multicommodity flow problem using an algorithm of Karger and Plotkin [121], as well as ideas drawn from Leighton et al. [142], Leong, Shor, and Stein [143], Plotkin, Shmoys, and Tardos [164], and Radzik [168]. They found their algorithm substantially outperformed simplex-based algorithms that solve the problem exactly, including the commercial code CPLEX [114]. They state that a modification of their algorithm is substantially faster than the implementation of Leong, Shor, and Stein for the concurrent flow problem. Bienstock [24] performs substantial experiments with algorithms based on the exponential penalty method; he applies his implementation to multicommodity flow problems as well as linear programs from network design problems. He found that his implementation substantially outperformed the CPLEX interior-point algorithm and dual simplex algorithm on concurrent flow problems, even when accounting for the moment when the algorithms had found an ϵ-optimal solution.

Exercise 7.3 is due to Fleischer [61].

8

Electrical Flow Algorithms

To carry the historical sketch another (and our last) step back in time might lead one to the Maxwell-Kirchoff theory of current distribution in an electrical network. Although this topic is closely related to the subject of the book, we have chosen not to include it. The reason for this is that we have limited the flow problems discussed to purely linear ones, and within this category, to those for which the assumption of integral data in the problem implies the existence of an integral solution. This sub-class of linear flow problems has, we feel, a simple elegance not shared by those outside the class. The first restriction, that of linearity, eliminates the Maxwell-Kirchoff electrical network problem, which, viewed as a programming problem, becomes one of minimizing a quadratic function subject to linear constraints. The second restriction eliminates, for example, linear problems that involve the simultaneous flow of several commodities, important as these may be in practical applications of linear programming.

> – L. R. Ford, Jr., and D. R. Fulkerson, *Flows in Networks*

One type of flow in a network that we have not yet considered is the well-studied topic of electrical flows in a network of resistors. Such flows are known to have many interesting connections to well-studied topics in graph theory. Recently they have been shown to have applications to the types of flows discussed in this book. In this chapter, we review concepts of electrical flows, and then show how they can be applied to computing maximum flows in undirected graphs (in Section 8.2) and to sparsifying graphs (in Section 8.3). We present an algorithm for computing such a flow in Section 8.4; the algorithm is surprisingly reminiscent of the network simplex algorithm given in Section 5.6.

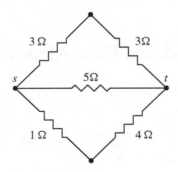

Figure 8.1 Example of an electrical network.

8.1 Optimality Conditions

Electrical Networks. We give an example of an electrical network in Figure 8.1. We can model it as an undirected graph $G = (V, E)$ in which each edge $(i, j) \in E$ has a *resistance* $r(i, j) > 0$. It will sometimes be useful to think of the inverse of the resistance, known as the *conductance* $c(i, j) = 1/r(i, j)$. We can determine a current flow f in the network via two physical laws. The first is one we know well, that of flow conservation, known in this context as *Kirchoff's Current Law*: at any node, the total current entering the node equals the total current leaving it. The second law, *Ohm's Law*, assumes that there is a potential $p(i)$ for each node i, and says that the flow across any edge is equal to the potential difference divided by the resistance of the edge (or multiplied by the conductance); thus

$$f(i, j) = \frac{p(i) - p(j)}{r(i, j)} = (p(i) - p(j))c(i, j).$$

Notice that we are treating $f(i, j)$ as the flow from i to j, and so we have a natural skew-symmetry property even though the graph is undirected: $f(j, i) = -f(i, j) = (p(j) - p(i))/r(i, j) = (p(j) - p(i))c(i, j)$. Because of the possibility for confusion in working with a flow that is directed in an undirected graph, where necessary we use the notation $\{i, j\} \in E$ for an undirected edge, so that there is no ordering on the elements of the edge. We also let $\vec{E}$ denote an arbitrary orientation of the edges of the undirected graph E, so that we have directed edges $(i, j) \in \vec{E}$.

For a given node i, we let $b(i)$ be the external current being supplied to node i, so that $b(i) > 0$ represents a supply of current to i, and $b(i) < 0$ represents a demand. Then by flow conservation we have that $b(i)$ must equal the net flow leaving i. Recalling that by skew-symmetry the net flow leaving i is $\sum_{j:\{i,j\}\in E} f(i,j)$, we have that

$$\sum_{j:\{i,j\}\in E} f(i,j) = b(i);$$

note that we are treating the sum over the undirected edges in E as a sum over unordered pairs $\{i,j\}$. Then

$$b(i) = \sum_{j:\{i,j\}\in E} f(i,j) = \sum_{j:\{i,j\}\in E} c(i,j)(p(i) - p(j))$$

$$= \sum_{j:\{i,j\}\in E} c(i,j)p(i) - \sum_{j:\{i,j\}\in E} c(i,j)p(j). \quad (8.1)$$

In our example network, suppose we put one unit of current in at node s and take a unit of current out at node t. Then we can calculate the flow $f(i,j)$ and potentials $p(i)$ for the arcs and nodes respectively. We show the result in Figure 8.2.

We will see later that a flow satisfying both the Kirchoff Current Law and Ohm's Law uniquely minimizes a certain function called the *energy* of the flow. For this reason, we will sometimes call such a flow an *optimal* electrical flow, and the associated potentials the *optimal* potentials.

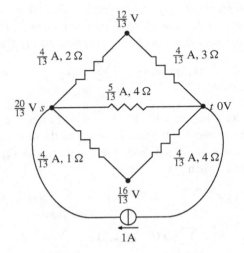

Figure 8.2 Example of a flow in an electrical network. We put in one unit of current (in amps) at s and remove one at t. The nodes show the potentials (in volts), and each edge has the current passing through it, followed by its resistance.

Another physical law, *Kirchoff's Potential Law*, is the equivalent of Ohm's Law. Kirchoff's Potential Law states that around any directed cycle C, it is the case that $\sum_{(i,j)\in C} r(i,j)f(i,j) = 0$. We prove the equivalence below.

Theorem 8.1: *Kirchoff's Potential Law is satisfied if and only if Ohm's Law is satisfied.*

Proof First we prove that if Ohm's Law holds, then Kirchoff's Potential Law holds. Assume that there exist potentials p such that $f(i,j) = (p(i) - p(j))/r(i,j)$ for any directed edge (i,j). Then we observe that for any directed cycle C of edges,

$$\sum_{(i,j)\in C} r(i,j)f(i,j) = \sum_{(i,j)\in C} (p(i) - p(j)) = 0.$$

Now suppose that Kirchoff's Potential Law holds for a flow f. We show that it is possible to define potentials p such that $f(i,j) = (p(i) - p(j))/r(i,j)$. To do this, pick an arbitrary spanning tree T of the undirected graph G, and pick an arbitrary root node r. Let P_i be the directed path in the tree T from $i \in V$ to r. Define $p(r) = 0$ and

$$p(i) = \sum_{(k,\ell)\in P_i} r(k,\ell)f(k,\ell).$$

We call such potentials *tree-defined potentials*, since they are defined with respect to the flows in the tree T. Now pick any edge $\{i,j\} \in T$; assume without loss of generality that j is closer to the root than i. Then

$$p(i) - p(j) = \sum_{(k,\ell)\in P_i} r(k,\ell)f(k,\ell) - \sum_{(k,\ell)\in P_j} r(k,\ell)f(k,\ell) = r(i,j)f(i,j),$$

(8.2)

as desired. Now consider any edge $\{i,j\} \in E - T$. Let $z \in V$ be the least common ancestor of i and j in the tree T, let P_{iz} be the directed path from i to z in T, let P_{jz} be the directed path from j to z in T, and let P_{zj} be the directed path from z to j in T. Then

$$
\begin{aligned}
p(i) - p(j) &= \sum_{(k,\ell)\in P_i} r(k,\ell)f(k,\ell) - \sum_{(k,\ell)\in P_j} r(k,\ell)f(k,\ell) \\
&= \sum_{(k,\ell)\in P_{iz}} r(k,\ell)f(k,\ell) - \sum_{(k,\ell)\in P_{jz}} r(k,\ell)f(k,\ell) \\
&= \sum_{(k,\ell)\in P_{iz}} r(k,\ell)f(k,\ell) + \sum_{(k,\ell)\in P_{zj}} r(k,\ell)f(k,\ell),
\end{aligned}
$$

where the second equality follows because the terms of the path from z to r cancel in both sums, and the last equation follows by skew symmetry. If we let C be the directed cycle that is the union of the directed path from i to z, the directed path from z to j, and the arc (j, i), then we have that

$$
\begin{aligned}
p(i) - p(j) &= \sum_{(k,\ell)\in P_{iz}} r(k,\ell)f(k,\ell) + \sum_{(k,\ell)\in P_{zj}} r(k,\ell)f(k,\ell) \\
&= \sum_{(k,\ell)\in C} r(k,\ell)f(k,\ell) - r(j,i)f(j,i) \qquad (8.3) \\
&= 0 + r(i,j)f(i,j),
\end{aligned}
$$

where we add and subtract $r(j,i)f(j,i)$ to obtain the second equality, and use Kirchoff's Potential Law and skew symmetry to obtain the last.   □

We will use the following corollary in Section 8.4.

Corollary 8.2: *Let p be tree-defined potentials for a tree T and a flow f, let the directed arc (i, j) be a non-tree edge, and let $\bar{C}$ be the directed cycle that consists of (i, j) plus the directed j-i path in T. Then*

$$
r(i,j)f(i,j) - (p(i) - p(j)) = \sum_{(k,\ell)\in\bar{C}} r(k,\ell)f(k,\ell).
$$

Proof Note that $\bar{C}$ is the reverse of the cycle C in the proof above. Applying skew symmetry, we have that $\sum_{(k,\ell)\in\bar{C}} r(k,\ell)f(k,\ell) = -\sum_{(k,\ell)\in C} r(k,\ell)f(k,\ell)$ and that $r(i,j)f(i,j) = -r(j,i)f(j,i)$. Substituting these terms into Equation (8.3) and rearranging gives the corollary.   □

Graph Laplacians. It will be useful for us to think of these equations in terms of matrix notation, and luckily there is a well-known concept at hand. Let e_i be the standard unit vector such that $e_i(j) = 1$ if $j = i$ and 0 if $j \neq i$. Then the *Laplacian* L_G of the undirected graph G is defined as

$$
L_G \equiv \sum_{\{i,j\}\in E} (e_i - e_j)(e_i - e_j)^T.
$$

Observe that each term $(e_i - e_j)(e_i - e_j)^T$ for $i \neq j$ is an $n \times n$ matrix that has -1 at the (i, j) and (j, i) entries, 1 at the diagonal entries for i and j, and zeroes everywhere else. Thus it is typical to observe that the Laplacian can also be expressed as the difference of two matrices, as follows. Let D be the diagonal matrix of node degrees of G, so that the ith entry on the diagonal is the degree of node i in G. Let $A = (a_{ij})$ be the *adjacency matrix* of the graph G, so that $a_{ij} = a_{ji} = 1$ if $\{i, j\} \in E$ and $a_{ij} = 0$ otherwise. Then it is easy to check that

$$L_G = D - A.$$

Given weights $w(i, j)$ on the edges, the *weighted Laplacian* L_G is defined as

$$L_G = \sum_{(i, j) \in E} w(i, j)(e_i - e_j)(e_i - e_j)^T.$$

As above, we can rewrite a weighted Laplacian as $L_G = D - W$, where D is the diagonal matrix whose ith diagonal entry is $\sum_{j:\{i, j\} \in E} w(i, j)$ and $W = (w_{ij})$ with $w_{ij} = w_{ji} = w(i, j)$ and $w_{ii} = 0$. Consider the weighted Laplacian L_G in which the weights are conductances from a network of resistors. Then we can write the expression of the vector of potentials in terms of the conductances in (8.1) in matrix notation as $L_G p = b$, since

$$L_G p = \sum_{\{i, j\} \in E} c(i, j)(e_i - e_j)(e_i - e_j)^T p = \sum_{\{i, j\} \in E} c(i, j)(e_i - e_j)(p(i) - p(j)).$$

Thus the ith coordinate of $L_G p$ is

$$\sum_{j:\{i, j\} \in E} c(i, j)(p(i) - p(j)) = b(i),$$

as given in (8.1).

We can also write the flow vector f in matrix notation as follows. If we let $C \in \Re^{m \times m}$ be a diagonal matrix of conductances, and $B \in \Re^{n \times m}$ be a matrix whose column corresponding to edge (i, j) is $(e_i - e_j)$, then by (8.1)

$$f = C B^T p$$

and the weighted Laplacian

$$L_G = \sum_{\{i, j\} \in E} c(i, j)(e_i - e_j)(e_i - e_j)^T = B C B^T.$$

Then

$$b = L_G p = B C B^T p = B f,$$

which expresses the flow conservation constraints for f.

Given the matrix notation, it becomes easy to make certain observations. For instance, suppose we have a supply vector b, potentials p, and a flow f such that $L_G p = b$, and $f = C B^T p$. Then if we have any scaling α of b, it follows that αp and αf are corresponding potentials and flow, since $L_G p = b$ implies $L_G(\alpha p) = \alpha b$, and $f = C B^T p$ implies $\alpha f = C B^T (\alpha p)$.

One of the reasons that interest in electrical flows has increased recently is that it has been shown that we can compute the potentials quickly, and these quick computations can be used to speed up certain applications. Recall that $\tilde{O}(f(n)) = O(f(n) \log^c n)$ for some constant c; that is, the $\tilde{O}$ notation hides polylogarithmic factors. Let e be the vector of all ones.

Theorem 8.3: *The solution p to $L_G p = b$ can be approximately computed in $\tilde{O}(m)$ time when G is connected and $b^T e = \sum_{i \in V} b(i) = 0$.*

Given the potentials p, we can compute the associated electrical flow f in $O(m)$ time, so that we get the following corollary.

Corollary 8.4: *The electrical flow f for a supply vector b can be approximately computed in $\tilde{O}(m)$ time when G is connected and $b^T e = 0$.*

We will give such an algorithm in Section 8.4. We will ignore the fact that the computation is only approximate in what follows. Note that the condition that $b^T e = 0$ makes sense as a physical condition on the system, since it enforces that the total of the current supplies/demands is zero. In this case, the total amount of current supplied to the network is equal to the total amount demanded, so that current is conserved in the supply vector b.

Effective Resistance. One extremely useful concept from electrical flows is that of the *effective resistance* between two nodes i and j. The effective resistance is the potential drop between i and j if we put one unit of current in at i and take one out at j. Another perspective is that the effective resistance reduces the behavior of the resistance of the network to a single number, as if there were just a single resistor between i and j. See Figure 8.3 for an example. We denote the effective resistance between i and j by $r_{\text{eff}}(i, j)$. Thus $r_{\text{eff}}(i, j) = p(i) - p(j)$ for the potentials p that are a solution to $L_G p = e_i - e_j$.

We will often be interested in the potentials p and flow f of an s-t *electrical flow*, which are the potentials p and flow f resulting from a unit of current put in at s and removed at t; the potentials are the solution to $L_G p = e_s - e_t$.

An incredibly useful alternate perspective on effective resistance relates electrical flows to spanning trees in the graph G. We assume G is connected. Let $\mathcal{T}$ be the set of all possible spanning trees of G. Let $r(T)$ be the product of all the resistances in a spanning tree T, so that $r(T) = \prod_{(i,j) \in T} r(i, j)$. Let $Z = \sum_{T \in \mathcal{T}} \frac{1}{r(T)}$; we will be using Z as a normalizing factor in what follows. For each tree $T \in \mathcal{T}$, let f_T be the result of sending one unit of current from s to t on the unique directed s-t path in T, so that $f_T(i, j) = 1$ if (i, j) is on the s-t path, $f_T(i, j) = -1$ if (j, i) is on the directed s-t path, and $f_T(i, j) = 0$ otherwise. Then the following theorem shows that we can define the s-t electrical flow as a weighted sum of these flows f_T.

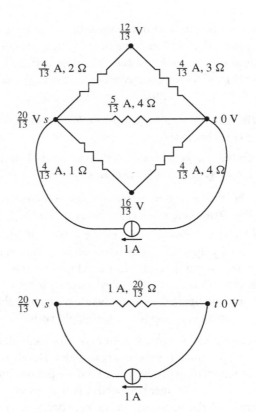

Figure 8.3 Example of effective resistance. We put in one unit of current (in amps) at s and remove one at t. The potential drop is $\frac{20}{13}$ volts from s to t, which is equivalent to having a single resistor between s and t of $\frac{20}{13}\Omega$.

Theorem 8.5: *Consider the flow*

$$f = \sum_{T \in \mathcal{T}} \frac{1}{Z \cdot r(T)} f_T.$$

Then f is an s-t electrical flow.

Proof Since each flow f_T sends a unit of current from s to t, and $\sum_{T \in \mathcal{T}} \frac{1}{Z \cdot r(T)} = 1$ by the definition of Z, f also sends a unit of flow from s to t. Since each flow f_T obeys flow conservation, the flow f will also obey flow conservation so that Kirchoff's Current Law is obeyed. We then only need to show that Kirchoff's Potential Law is obeyed. In particular, we wish to show that for any directed cycle C, $\sum_{(i,j) \in C} r(i,j) f(i,j) = 0$.

Let $\mathcal{S}$ be the set of all s-t cuts S such that the two graphs induced by S and $V - S$ are both connected. Let $\mathcal{T}[S]$ be the set of trees spanning S in the graph induced by S and similarly let $\mathcal{T}[V - S]$ be the set of trees spanning $V - S$ in the graph induced by $V - S$. Pick an arbitrary directed edge (i, j) and consider a tree T such that (i, j) is on the path directed from s to t. The removal of (i, j) from T partitions T into an s-t cut S and a set $V - S$, such that there is a tree $T_1 \in \mathcal{T}[S]$ and $T_2 \in \mathcal{T}[V - S]$ with $T = T_1 \cup T_2 \cup \{(i, j)\}$; if (j, i) is on the path directed from s to t, then removing (j, i) partitions T similarly. In the first case, $\delta^+(S) \cap T = \{(i, j)\}$, and in the second, $\delta^-(S) \cap T = \{(i, j)\}$. Hence we can write

$$f(i, j) = \sum_{T \in \mathcal{T}} \frac{1}{Z \cdot r(T)} f_T(i, j)$$

$$= \frac{1}{Z} \sum_{S \in \mathcal{S}} \left[\sum_{\substack{T = T_1 \cup T_2 \cup \{(i, j)\} \\ T_1 \in \mathcal{T}[S], T_2 \in \mathcal{T}[V-S], \\ i \in S, j \notin S}} \frac{1}{r(T)} - \sum_{\substack{T = T_1 \cup T_2 \cup \{(i, j)\} \\ T_1 \in \mathcal{T}[S], T_2 \in \mathcal{T}[V-S], \\ i \notin S, j \in S}} \frac{1}{r(T)} \right]$$

$$= \frac{1}{Z} \sum_{S \in \mathcal{S}} \left[\sum_{\substack{T_1 \in \mathcal{T}[S], \\ T_2 \in \mathcal{T}[V-S], \\ i \in S, j \notin S}} \frac{1}{r(T_1) r(T_2) r(i, j)} - \sum_{\substack{T_1 \in \mathcal{T}[S], \\ T_2 \in \mathcal{T}[V-S], \\ i \notin S, j \in S}} \frac{1}{r(T_1) r(T_2) r(i, j)} \right].$$

Pick any directed cycle C. We wish to show that $\sum_{(i, j) \in C} r(i, j) f(i, j) = 0$. Then $\sum_{(i, j) \in C} r(i, j) f(i, j)$ is equal to

$$\frac{1}{Z} \sum_{(i, j) \in C} r(i, j) \sum_{S \in \mathcal{S}} \left[\sum_{\substack{T_1 \in \mathcal{T}[S], \\ T_2 \in \mathcal{T}[V-S], \\ i \in S, j \notin S}} \frac{1}{r(T_1) r(T_2) r(i, j)} - \sum_{\substack{T_1 \in \mathcal{T}[S], \\ T_2 \in \mathcal{T}[V-S], \\ i \notin S, j \in S}} \frac{1}{r(T_1) r(T_2) r(i, j)} \right]$$

$$= \frac{1}{Z} \sum_{S \in \mathcal{S}} \sum_{(i, j) \in C} r(i, j) \left[\sum_{\substack{T_1 \in \mathcal{T}[S], \\ T_2 \in \mathcal{T}[V-S], \\ i \in S, j \notin S}} \frac{1}{r(T_1) r(T_2) r(i, j)} - \sum_{\substack{T_1 \in \mathcal{T}[S], \\ T_2 \in \mathcal{T}[V-S], \\ i \notin S, j \in S}} \frac{1}{r(T_1) r(T_2) r(i, j)} \right]$$

$$= \frac{1}{Z} \sum_{S \in \mathcal{S}} \sum_{\substack{T_1 \in \mathcal{T}[S], \\ T_2 \in \mathcal{T}[V-S]}} \frac{1}{r(T_1) r(T_2)} \left[|\delta^+(S) \cap C| - |\delta^-(S) \cap C| \right]$$

$$= 0,$$

since for any set $S \subset V$ and any directed cycle C, $|\delta^+(S) \cap C| = |\delta^-(S) \cap C|$; that is, the number of arcs on a cycle leaving any set S equals the number entering the set. $\square$

Another perspective on our definition of an s-t electrical flow above is that we sample tree $T \in \mathcal{T}$ with probability proportional to $1/r(T)$ (and equal to $1/(Z \cdot r(T))$), and the flow f is then the expected value of flow f_T sampled according to this distribution. Note that this probability distribution does not depend on the choice of s and t (although the flows f_T do depend on s and t). From this perspective, we get the following lemma relating effective resistance to the probability that a given edge is in the sampled tree.

Lemma 8.6: *For any edge $\{i, j\} \in E$, and $T \in \mathcal{T}$ sampled with probability* $1/(Z \cdot r(T))$,

$$\frac{r_{\text{eff}}(i, j)}{r(i, j)} = \Pr[\{i, j\} \in T].$$

Proof We let f be an i-j electrical flow, with associated potentials p. Then $r_{\text{eff}}(i, j) = p(i) - p(j)$. We note that for any tree $T \in \mathcal{T}$, if $\{i, j\} \in T$, then the edge (i, j) is the directed path from i to j in T, so that $f_T(i, j) = 1$, whereas if $\{i, j\} \notin T$, then $f_T(i, j) = 0$. Then

$$\begin{aligned}
\frac{r_{\text{eff}}(i, j)}{r(i, j)} &= \frac{p(i) - p(j)}{r(i, j)} \\
&= f(i, j) \\
&= \sum_{T \in \mathcal{T}} \frac{1}{Z \cdot r(T)} f_T(i, j) \\
&= \sum_{T \in \mathcal{T}: \{i, j\} \in T} \frac{1}{Z \cdot r(T)} \\
&= \Pr[\{i, j\} \in T]
\end{aligned}$$

by the definition of the probability distribution. $\square$

We can also now easily show the following result, which is sometimes known as Foster's Theorem.

Theorem 8.7 (Foster's Theorem [67]):

$$\sum_{\{i, j\} \in E} \frac{r_{\text{eff}}(i, j)}{r(i, j)} = n - 1.$$

Proof Using the definition of the probability distribution and Lemma 8.6, we have the following, where $\mathbb{1}[\{i, j\} \in T]$ is 1 if $\{i, j\} \in T$ and 0 otherwise:

$$
\begin{aligned}
\sum_{\{i,j\} \in E} \frac{r_{\text{eff}}(i, j)}{r(i, j)} &= \sum_{\{i,j\} \in E} \Pr[\{i, j\} \in T] \\
&= \sum_{\{i,j\} \in E} \sum_{T \in \mathcal{T}} \frac{1}{Z \cdot r(T)} \mathbb{1}[\{i, j\} \in T] \\
&= \sum_{T \in \mathcal{T}} \frac{1}{Z \cdot r(T)} \sum_{\{i,j\} \in E} \mathbb{1}[\{i, j\} \in T] \\
&= \sum_{T \in \mathcal{T}} \frac{1}{Z \cdot r(T)} (n - 1) = n - 1,
\end{aligned}
$$

using the fact that there are $n - 1$ edges in any spanning tree T. $\qquad\square$

Energy. One last concept we will need is that of the *energy* of the network for a particular current flow. For a single resistor of resistance r with current f flowing across it, the energy dissipated is $f^2 r$. The energy of the graph G with current flow $f(i, j)$ is the sum of the energy dissipated in the network, and is denoted $\mathcal{E}(f)$, so that

$$
\mathcal{E}(f) = \sum_{\{i,j\} \in E} f^2(i, j) r(i, j).
$$

If p are the potentials defining flow f, then

$$
\begin{aligned}
\mathcal{E}(f) &= \sum_{\{i,j\} \in E} f^2(i, j) r(i, j) \\
&= \sum_{\{i,j\} \in E} \frac{1}{r(i, j)} (p(i) - p(j))^2 \\
&= \sum_{\{i,j\} \in E} c(i, j) (p(i) - p(j))^2 \\
&= \sum_{\{i,j\} \in E} c(i, j) p^T (e_i - e_j)(e_i - e_j)^T p \\
&= p^T \left(\sum_{\{i,j\} \in E} c(i, j)(e_i - e_j)(e_i - e_j)^T \right) p \\
&= p^T L_G p.
\end{aligned}
$$

Then if the current flow f and potentials p are given by the s-t electrical flow, so that $L_G p = e_s - e_t$, we have that the energy is

$$\mathcal{E}(f) = p^T L_G p = p^T (e_s - e_t) = p(s) - p(t) = r_{\text{eff}}(s,t);$$

that is, the energy dissipated is the effective resistance between s and t. This is what we should expect, since the effective resistance treats the resistance of the entire network as a single number. Thus sending a single unit of current between s and t on a single resistor of resistance $r_{\text{eff}}(s,t)$ dissipates energy $r_{\text{eff}}(s,t)$.

It will be useful to show that the potentials p and current flows f minimize the overall energy in certain senses for the analysis of algorithms in subsequent sections. The first lemma states that an electrical flow f uniquely minimizes $\mathcal{E}(f)$ among all flows g such that $Bg = b$ (that is, all flows that obey flow conservation for a given supply vector b). The second lemma shows that the potentials p that define an electrical flow f for a supply vector b maximize the function $2b^T x - x^T L_G x$ among all vectors x. In these senses, both the electrical flow and the corresponding potentials are optimal flows/potentials for these particular objective functions.

Lemma 8.8: *Consider any b such that $b^T e = 0$. The electrical flow f minimizes $\mathcal{E}(f)$ among all flows g such that $Bg = b$.*

Proof Pick any flow g such that $Bg = b$, and let $h = g - f$. Then for any node $i \in V$, we have that

$$\sum_{j:\{i,j\}\in E} h(i,j) = \sum_{j:\{i,j\}\in E} g(i,j) - \sum_{j:\{i,j\}\in E} f(i,j) = b(i) - b(i) = 0,$$

$$(8.4)$$

where we sum over all edges incident on i in an undirected sense. Now consider the energy of g:

$$
\begin{aligned}
\mathcal{E}(g) &= \sum_{\{i,j\}\in E} g^2(i,j) r(i,j) \\
&= \sum_{\{i,j\}\in E} (f(i,j) + h(i,j))^2 r(i,j) \\
&= \sum_{\{i,j\}\in E} f^2(i,j) r(i,j) + 2 \sum_{\{i,j\}\in E} f(i,j) h(i,j) r(i,j) \\
&\quad + \sum_{\{i,j\}\in E} h^2(i,j) r(i,j)
\end{aligned}
$$

$$= \mathcal{E}(f) + 2 \sum_{\{i,j\} \in E} (p(i) - p(j))h(i,j) + \sum_{\{i,j\} \in E} h^2(i,j)r(i,j)$$

$$= \mathcal{E}(f) + 2 \sum_{i \in V} p(i) \sum_{j:\{i,j\} \in E} h(i,j) + \sum_{\{i,j\} \in E} h^2(i,j)r(i,j)$$

$$= \mathcal{E}(f) + \sum_{\{i,j\} \in E} h^2(i,j)r(i,j),$$

where the penultimate equality follows by the skew symmetry of h (since it is the difference of f and g, which both obey skew symmetry), and the final equality follows from (8.4). Finally, observe that unless $f = g$ (and $h = 0$), then the equations above show the $\mathcal{E}(g) > \mathcal{E}(f)$, as desired. $\qquad \square$

Lemma 8.9: *For a given supply vector b with $b^T e = 0$, the potentials p of the corresponding electrical flow f maximize $2b^T x - x^T L_G x$ over all vectors x.*

Proof Let $z(x) = 2b^T x - x^T L_G x$. Then at its maximum, we must have

$$\frac{\partial z}{\partial x(i)} = 0$$

for all i, which implies that

$$2b(i) - 2x(i) \sum_{j:\{i,j\} \in E} c(i,j) + 2 \sum_{j:\{i,j\} \in E} c(i,j)x(j) = 0,$$

which implies that

$$b(i) = \sum_{j:\{i,j\} \in E} c(i,j)(x(i) - x(j)),$$

which is exactly the equation (8.1) that defines the potentials p for the corresponding electrical flow. $\qquad \square$

Corollary 8.10: *For a given supply vector b with $b^T e = 0$, the maximum value of $2b^T x - x^T L_G x$ attained is $\mathcal{E}(f)$ for the corresponding electrical flow f.*

Proof Since the corresponding potentials p maximize the function and $L_G p = b$, we have that the maximum value of the function is

$$2b^T p - p^T L_G p = 2p^T L_G p - p^T L_G p = p^T L_G p = \mathcal{E}(f).$$

$\qquad \square$

8.2 Maximum Flow in Undirected Graphs

> Danny Ocean: Saul makes ten. Ten oughta do it, don't you think?
> Rusty Ryan: [*Silent, staring at TV, not looking at Danny*]
> Danny: You think we need one more?
> Rusty: [*Silent*]
> Danny: You think we need one more.
> Rusty: [*Silent*]
> Danny: All right, we'll get one more.
>
> – *Ocean's Eleven* (2001)

In this section, we give one more algorithm for computing a maximum flow. In particular, we show how computing an s-t electrical flow can be used in computing an approximate maximum s-t flow in an undirected graph. First, we must define what we mean by an s-t flow in an undirected graph $G = (V, E)$ with capacities $u(i, j) \geq 0$ for all $\{i, j\} \in E$. We choose an arbitrary orientation of the edges and denote the resulting set of directed edges by $\vec{E}$. Once again, we assume skew symmetry so that for any $(i, j) \in \vec{E}$, we have that $f(j, i) = -f(i, j)$. In order to satisfy the capacity constraints, we require that $-u(i, j) \leq f(i, j) \leq u(i, j)$ for all $(i, j) \in \vec{E}$; thus the positive flow can either be going from i to j or j to i, but in either case the amount of positive flow cannot exceed $u(i, j)$. Observe then that the flow conservation constraints are that

$$\sum_{j:(i,j)\in\vec{E}} f(i, j) - \sum_{j:(j,i)\in\vec{E}} f(j, i) = 0$$

for all $i \in V$, $i \neq s, t$.

To obtain our algorithm, we use the multiplicative weights algorithm for packing problems given in Section 7.3 and Algorithm 7.2, in particular Theorem 7.5. Recall that in the algorithm, we were able to provide an approximately feasible solution x to a system $|Mx| \leq e$, for e the all ones vector, and $x \in Q$ for Q a convex set. The algorithm assumes we have a subroutine, called an oracle. This oracle takes a nonnegative vector p and either finds an $x \in Q$ that satisfies the inequality $\sum_i p(i)|M_i x| \leq p^T e$, or correctly states that no such $x \in Q$ exists. The algorithm produces $\bar{x} \in Q$ such that $|M\bar{x}| \leq (1 + 4\epsilon)e$.

The central idea of this section is that we will use the computation of an s-t electrical flow as the oracle. Electrical flows obey flow conservation constraints but do not respect capacity constraints. Thus we will let the convex set Q

encode the flow conservation constraints, and let the matrix M encode the capacity constraints.

For the sake of simplicity, we will assume that the capacity $u(i, j) = 1$ for all arcs $(i, j) \in \vec{E}$. In what follows, we will give an algorithm that either computes a flow of value nearly k, assuming that a flow of value k exists, or correctly states that no flow of value k exists. Given such an algorithm, we can use bisection search to find a near maximum flow. Since the edge capacities are 1, we know that the value of the maximum flow is at least 0 and at most m, and since the capacities are integer, we know by the Integrality Property that the value of the maximum flow is also an integer. Hence with $O(\log m)$ calls to our algorithm, we will find a near-maximum flow.

We now give our algorithm in more detail. We put the capacity constraints into the matrix M, so that

$$-1 \le f(i, j) \le 1 \text{ for all } (i, j) \in \vec{E},$$

or

$$|f(i, j)| \le 1 \text{ for all } (i, j) \in \vec{E}.$$

We let Q encode the flow conservation constraints plus a constraint that the flow value is k, so that

$$Q = \left\{ f \in \Re^m : \sum_{j:(i, j) \in \vec{E}} f(i, j) - \sum_{j:(j,i) \in \vec{E}} f(j, i) = 0 \text{ for all } i \ne s, t \right.$$

$$\left. \text{and } \sum_{j:(s, j) \in \vec{E}} f(s, j) - \sum_{j:(j,s) \in \vec{E}} f(j, s) = k \right\}.$$

We give the algorithm in Algorithm 8.1; it is the algorithm for the packing problem (Algorithm 7.2) as given in Theorem 7.5 specialized to this particular case, with weights w_t, probabilities p_t, and values v_t for each edge $(i, j) \in \vec{E}$, since there is one constraint in the matrix M per edge (the capacity constraint). Recall from Definition 7.3 that ρ denotes the width of the oracle; in this context, the width is the relative amount by which the electrical flow can exceed the capacity constraint. We will show in Lemma 8.13 that for the s-t electrical flow oracle, $\rho \le \sqrt{2m/\epsilon}$; that is, an s-t electrical flow with the resistances r_t can send flow at most $\sqrt{2m/\epsilon}$ along each edge of unit capacity. Then for $T = \frac{1}{\epsilon^2} \rho \ln m$ iterations, we compute an s-t electrical flow f_t of value k using resistances $r_t(i, j)$ equal to the weight $w_t(i, j)$ for the edge plus $\frac{\epsilon}{m} W_t$. We update the values v_t and the weights w_t as given by Algorithm 7.2. Note that the weight of an edge increases the most for edges whose flow value is close to the width ρ, and consequently the resistance of an edge increases the

$w_1(i, j) \leftarrow 1$ for all $(i, j) \in \vec{E}$

$T \leftarrow \frac{1}{\epsilon^2} \rho \ln m$

for $t \leftarrow 1$ to T **do**

$\quad W_t \leftarrow \sum_{(i, j) \in \vec{E}} w_t(i, j)$

$\quad p_t(i, j) \leftarrow w_t(i, j) / W_t$ for all $(i, j) \in \vec{E}$

$\quad r_t(i, j) \leftarrow w_t(i, j) + \frac{\epsilon}{m} W_t$ for all $(i, j) \in \vec{E}$

$\quad$ Compute s-t electrical flow f_t of value k using resistances r_t

$\quad v_t(i, j) \leftarrow \frac{1}{\rho} |f_t(i, j)|$ for all $(i, j) \in \vec{E}$

$\quad w_{t+1}(i, j) \leftarrow w_t(i, j)(1 + \epsilon v_t(i, j))$ for all $(i, j) \in \vec{E}$

return $\bar{f} \leftarrow \frac{1}{T} \sum_{t=1}^{T} f_t$

Algorithm 8.1 Multiplicative weights algorithm for computing an approximate s-t flow via electrical s-t flows.

most for edges whose flow value is close to the width ρ. Since the resistance is higher, in future iterations, the flow value on this edge will be lower. At the end of the algorithm, we return a flow that is the average of the flows f_t over all T iterations.

We now argue that computing an s-t electrical flow can be used as an oracle in the multiplicative weights algorithm for packing problems. Recall that we need the oracle to find an $x \in Q$ such that $\sum_i p(i) |M_i x| \leq p^T e$ for probabilities p, or state that no such x exists; given that M captures the capacity constraints, we need that

$$\sum_{(i, j) \in \vec{E}} p_t(i, j) |f_t(i, j)| \leq \sum_{(i, j) \in \vec{E}} p_t(i, j) = 1.$$

Multiplying by W_t, we get that the oracle should find a flow $f_t \in Q$ such that

$$\sum_{(i, j) \in \vec{E}} w_t(i, j) |f_t(i, j)| \leq W_t. \tag{8.5}$$

Instead we prove a slightly weaker statement given in the statement of Lemma 8.12. We first recall the Cauchy–Schwartz Inequality from Fact 7.10, restated for vectors of edges.

Fact 8.11 (Cauchy–Schwarz Inequality): *For values* $a(k, \ell)$, $b(k, \ell)$ *on edges* $(k, \ell) \in \vec{E}$,

$$\left(\sum_{(k, \ell) \in \vec{E}} a(k, \ell) b(k, \ell) \right)^2 \leq \left(\sum_{(k, \ell) \in \vec{E}} a(k, \ell)^2 \right) \left(\sum_{(k, \ell) \in \vec{E}} b(k, \ell)^2 \right).$$

Lemma 8.12: *For the electrical flow f_t computed in iteration t of Algorithm 8.1,*

$$\sum_{(i,j)\in\vec{E}} w_t(i,j)|f_t(i,j)| \leq \sqrt{1+\epsilon} \cdot W_t.$$

Proof Let f^* be a maximum s-t flow. Recall from Lemma 8.8 that the electrical flow f_t minimizes the total energy among all flows obeying flow conservation, so that $\mathcal{E}(f_t) \leq \mathcal{E}(f^*)$. Thus

$$
\begin{aligned}
\mathcal{E}(f_t) = \sum_{(i,j)\in\vec{E}} f_t^2(i,j) r_t(i,j) &\leq \sum_{(i,j)\in\vec{E}} \left(f^*(i,j)\right)^2 r_t(i,j) \\
&\leq \sum_{(i,j)\in\vec{E}} r_t(i,j) \\
&= \sum_{(i,j)\in\vec{E}} \left(w_t(i,j) + \frac{\epsilon W_t}{m}\right) \\
&= (1+\epsilon)W_t, \qquad\qquad (8.6)
\end{aligned}
$$

where the second inequality follows, since $|f^*(i,j)| \leq 1$ because f^* obeys the capacity constraints.

Using the Cauchy–Schwarz inequality from Fact 8.11 with $a(k,\ell) = |f_t(k,\ell)|\sqrt{w_t(k,\ell)}$ and $b(k,\ell) = \sqrt{w_t(k,\ell)}$, we can show that

$$
\begin{aligned}
\left(\sum_{(i,j)\in\vec{E}} w_t(i,j)|f_t(i,j)|\right)^2 &\leq \left(\sum_{(i,j)\in\vec{E}} f_t^2(i,j)w_t(i,j)\right)\left(\sum_{(i,j)\in\vec{E}} w_t(i,j)\right) \\
&\leq \left(\sum_{(i,j)\in\vec{E}} f_t^2(i,j)r_t(i,j)\right) W_t \\
&\leq (1+\epsilon)W_t^2,
\end{aligned}
$$

where the final inequality follows from Inequality (8.6). Thus it follows that

$$\sum_{(i,j)\in\vec{E}} w_t(i,j)|f_t(i,j)| \leq \sqrt{1+\epsilon} \cdot W_t,$$

as desired.   □

Although the lemma above proves a weaker statement than what we need (as given in Inequality (8.5)), we can scale down the flow value by the factor of $\sqrt{1+\epsilon}$ to fix this problem, resulting in a loss of another small factor in the value of the final flow $\bar{f}$ that nearly satisfies the capacity constraints.

To finish the analysis of the algorithm, we need to determine the width of the oracle given by computing electrical flows.

Lemma 8.13: *The width ρ of the oracle computing electrical flows in Algorithm 8.1 is at most $\sqrt{2m/\epsilon}$ for $\epsilon \leq 1$.*

Proof By Definition 7.3, the width ρ is at upper bound the maximum value of $|f_t(i,j)|$ over all iterations t and all edges $(i,j) \in \vec{E}$ for the computed electrical flows f_t. To bound this quantity, we observe that the energy on a single edge (i,j) is at most the total energy, which is at most $(1+\epsilon)W_t$ from Inequality (8.6), so that

$$f_t^2(i,j)r_t(i,j) \leq (1+\epsilon)W_t.$$

Also, since we set the resistances $r_t = w_t(i,j) + \frac{\epsilon}{m}W_t$, it follows that

$$f_t^2(i,j)r_t(i,j) \geq f_t^2(i,j)\frac{\epsilon W_t}{m}.$$

Thus

$$f_t^2(i,j) \leq \frac{(1+\epsilon)m}{\epsilon},$$

which implies the statement of the lemma.   □

Then by plugging in Lemma 8.13 to Theorem 7.5, and using Corollary 8.4 (that states we can compute electrical flows in $\tilde{O}(m)$ time), we get the following theorem immediately.

Theorem 8.14: *Algorithm 8.1 computes an s-t flow $\bar{f}$ of value $k/\sqrt{1+\epsilon}$ (if a flow of value k exists) with $|\bar{f}(i,j)| \leq (1+4\epsilon)$ for all $(i,j) \in \vec{E}$ in $O((\sqrt{m}\ln m)/\epsilon^{2.5})$ electrical flow computations, or $\tilde{O}(m^{1.5}/\epsilon^{2.5})$ time.*

Using bisection search on the value of the flow as suggested at the start of this section yields that we can compute a flow $\bar{f}$ of value at least $|f^*|/\sqrt{1+\epsilon}$ that almost satisfies the capacity constraints in $\tilde{O}(m^{1.5}/\epsilon^{2.5})$ time.

We note that this algorithm is not an improvement over what we already know how to do for graphs with unit capacity: we showed in Section 4.2 that we could find the optimal flow in $O(m^{3/2})$ time. In Exercise 8.6 we show that it is possible to modify the algorithm to do better, and obtain an algorithm finding an approximately maximum flow in $\tilde{O}(m^{4/3}/\epsilon^3)$ time. Still faster algorithms for finding approximate maximum flows in undirected graphs have been devised; see the Chapter Notes for details.

8.3 Graph Sparsification

It is sometimes useful to get fast, nearly accurate solutions to network flow problems. One way we can do this is to work with sparse representations of the original input to the problem. In this section, we consider the case that we are interested in computing a cut in an undirected graph G (a minimum s-t cut, for example, or a global minimum cut). We will assume for simplicity that $u(i, j) = 1$ for all edges $(i, j) \in E$; while the results we present extend to general capacities, it will be easier for us to consider unit-capacity graphs. We will revert to our notation using (i, j) for an undirected edge, since we do not need to differentiate between edge directions in this section. Given an $\epsilon > 0$, we will say that an undirected graph $G' = (V, E')$ with capacities $u'(i, j)$ for all $(i, j) \in E'$ is a *cut sparsifier* of G if for all cuts S, the capacity of the cut S in G' is close to that of G: namely, we want that for all $S \subset V$, $S \neq \emptyset$,

$$|u'(\delta(S)) - u(\delta(S))| \leq \epsilon \cdot u(\delta(S)). \qquad (8.7)$$

Furthermore, we require that G' does not have many edges: in particular, we require that $|E'| = O((n \log n)/\epsilon^2)$. Given such a cut sparsifier G', we can run any algorithm for finding a cut on G' instead of G, and then the value of m in the running time in the algorithm becomes $O((n \log n)/\epsilon^2)$ instead. Furthermore, if we are finding a minimum cut of some sort, the cut we find in G' will have capacity within a factor of $1 + \epsilon$ of the minimum capacity cut in G.

The very high-level idea of creating a cut sparsifier is that we draw a random sample of the edges for our sparse representation G'. We then prove that the capacity of each cut in G' is close to its capacity in G. To do so, we use well-known results showing that values for certain types of random samples are close to their expected values with high probability. These types of results are known as *concentration of measure* results, and include (for example) the well-known Chernoff bounds; a full discussion of them is outside the scope of this book, but the Chapter Notes point to some resources on such results.

However, we need to be somewhat careful with this idea of drawing a random sample. Figure 8.4 shows that it is a bad idea to sample all edges uniformly with the same probability. If we do so, then we will get a good estimate of cuts that contain many edges but a bad estimate of the cut containing a single edge. So the successful modification of the random sampling idea is to sample an edge (i, j) with a probability proportional to $1/\lambda(i, j)$, where $\lambda(i, j)$ is a lower bound on the capacity of the minimum i-j cut in G. Of course, we also need to be able to compute the values of $\lambda(i, j)$ quickly relative to actually computing the capacity of a minimum i-j cut for

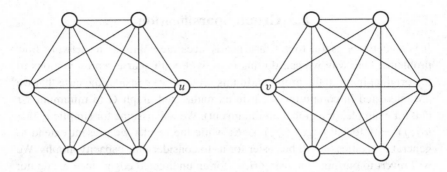

Figure 8.4 Example of a graph showing that uniform sampling of edges is unlikely to work well. Cuts containing many edges of the two cliques are likely to have an accurate estimate of the number of edges, but the cut containing just the edge (u, v) is unlikely to be accurate unless the sampling probability is close to 1.

all $(i, j) \in E$, since otherwise computing the sparse representation G' will be slower than solving the cut problem of interest in the original graph G.

There are many different values of $\lambda(i, j)$ that lead to good cut sparsifiers. In this section, we show that by setting the resistance of each edge to 1 and using the effective resistance (with $\lambda(i, j) = 1/r_{\text{eff}}(i, j)$) gives not only a good cut sparsifier but something even stronger, called a *spectral sparsifier*. We introduce the following notation. We say that for $n \times n$ symmetric square matrices A and B, $A \preceq B$ (or $B \succeq A$) if and only if $x^T A x \leq x^T B x$ for all $x \in \Re^n$. Thus for symmetric A, $A \succeq 0$ if and only if A is a positive semidefinite matrix. A spectral sparsifier G' of G is then one such that

$$(1 - \epsilon)L_G \preceq L_{G'} \preceq (1 + \epsilon)L_G, \tag{8.8}$$

where $L_{G'}$ is a weighted Laplacian with weights u' (recall that we are assuming the edges in G have unit capacity), and such that $|E'| = O((n \log n)/\epsilon^2)$.

We now show that any spectral sparsifier G' of a graph G is also a cut sparsifier of G. Recall that

$$L_G = \sum_{(i, j) \in E} (e_i - e_j)(e_i - e_j)^T,$$

so that

$$x^T L_G x = \sum_{(i, j) \in E} x^T (e_i - e_j)(e_i - e_j)^T x = \sum_{(i, j) \in E} (x(i) - x(j))^2.$$

Similarly, for a weighted Laplacian for G',

$$L_{G'} = \sum_{(i, j) \in E} u'(i, j)(e_i - e_j)(e_i - e_j)^T,$$

so that

$$x^T L_{G'} x = \sum_{(i,j) \in E} u'(i,j)(x(i) - x(j))^2.$$

Then for any $S \subseteq V$, let the vector $\chi_S \in \{0,1\}^n$ be such that $\chi_S(i) = 1$ if $i \in S$ and 0 otherwise. Then since $(\chi_S(i) - \chi_S(j))^2 = 1$ if and only if $(i,j) \in \delta(S)$,

$$\chi_S^T L_G \chi_S = \sum_{(i,j) \in E} (\chi_S(i) - \chi_S(j))^2 = u(\delta(S)),$$

and

$$\chi_S^T L_{G'} \chi_S = \sum_{(i,j) \in E} u'(i,j)(\chi_S(i) - \chi_S(j))^2 = u'(\delta(S)).$$

Then since we assumed G' is a spectral sparsifier, by Equation (8.8) and the definition of $\succeq$ we have that for any $S \subseteq V$,

$$(1 - \epsilon)u(\delta(S)) \leq u'(\delta(S)) \leq (1 + \epsilon)u(\delta(S)),$$

which implies that G' is a cut sparsifier by the definition in Equation (8.7).

We give our algorithm for computing a spectral sparsifier in Algorithm 8.2. The algorithm is quite simple: it computes the effective resistances of all edges in the graph, and then $K = (8n \ln n)/\epsilon^2 = O((n \ln n)/\epsilon^2)$ times it samples (with replacement) an edge $(i,j) \in E$ with probability $r_{\text{eff}}(i,j)/(n-1)$; we earlier proved Foster's Theorem (Theorem 8.7), which shows that $\sum_{(i,j) \in E} r_{\text{eff}}(i,j) = n-1$, so that $r_{\text{eff}}(i,j)/(n-1)$ is a probability distribution over edges in the graph. We update the capacity $u'(i,j)$ of the selected edge (i,j) by adding $(n-1)/K \cdot r_{\text{eff}}(i,j)$ (that is, by adding the reciprocal of K times the probability of sampling (i,j)). Since we sample an edge $(i,j) \in E$ a total of $O((n \log n)/\epsilon^2)$ times, it is clear that $|E'| = O((n \log n)/\epsilon^2)$.

$E' \leftarrow \emptyset$
$u'(i,j) \leftarrow 0$ for all $(i,j) \in E$
$K \leftarrow (8n \ln n)/\epsilon^2$
Compute $r_{\text{eff}}(i,j)$ for all $(i,j) \in E$
for $k \leftarrow 1$ to K **do**
    Sample one edge $(i,j) \in E$ with probability $r_{\text{eff}}(i,j)/(n-1)$
    $u'(i,j) \leftarrow u'(i,j) + (n-1)/(K \cdot r_{\text{eff}}(i,j))$
    $E' \leftarrow E' \cup \{(i,j)\}$
return $G' = (V, E')$ with capacities u'

Algorithm 8.2 Sampling algorithm for computing a spectral sparsifier.

We now prove that Equation (8.8) holds for the resulting G'; following the proof, we discuss the running time of the algorithm. Let Z_k be a random matrix giving an additive update of the weights of u' in the kth iteration of the algorithm, so that for the selected edge (i, j),

$$Z_k = \frac{n-1}{K \cdot r_{\text{eff}}(i, j)} (e_i - e_j)(e_i - e_j)^T.$$

Thus since we select (i, j) with probability $r_{\text{eff}}(i, j)/(n - 1)$,

$$E[Z_k] = \sum_{(i,j) \in E} \frac{r_{\text{eff}}(i, j)}{n-1} \cdot \frac{n-1}{K \cdot r_{\text{eff}}(i, j)} (e_i - e_j)(e_i - e_j)^T$$

$$= \frac{1}{K} \sum_{(i,j) \in E} (e_i - e_j)(e_i - e_j)^T = \frac{1}{K} L_G.$$

Then since $L_{G'} = \sum_{k=1}^{K} Z_k$, it follows that

$$E[L_{G'}] = E\left[\sum_{k=1}^{K} Z_k \right] = L_G,$$

so that in expectation, the resulting graph G' has a Laplacian exactly the same as G. To prove that G' is a spectral sparsifier, then, we need to invoke a result that states that with high probability, the resulting Laplacian $L_{G'}$ will be close to its expectation. To do this, we use the following concentration of measure result.

Theorem 8.15: *Let Z be a random $n \times n$ matrix that is symmetric and positive semidefinite ($Z \succeq 0$). Let $X = E[Z]$. Suppose that there is a scalar α such that for any realization of Z, $\alpha X - Z \succeq 0$. Let $Z_1, \ldots, Z_K$ be drawn independently from the distribution of Z. Then for any $\epsilon \in (0, 1)$,*

$$\Pr\left[(1 - \epsilon)X \preceq \frac{1}{K} \sum_{k=1}^{K} Z_k \preceq (1 + \epsilon)X \right] \geq 1 - 2n \exp(-\epsilon^2 K/4\alpha).$$

In order to apply the theorem, we will need to prove the following lemma.

Lemma 8.16:

$$\frac{n-1}{K} L_G - Z \succeq 0$$

for any matrix $Z = \frac{n-1}{K \cdot r_{\text{eff}}(i, j)} (e_i - e_j)(e_i - e_j)^T$ for edge $(i, j) \in E$.

We defer the proof of this lemma for a minute, and show that we can now derive the following.

Theorem 8.17: *The graph G' computed by Algorithm 8.2 is a spectral sparsifier with probability at least $1 - 2/n$.*

Proof We apply Theorem 8.15 with $K = (8n \ln n)/\epsilon^2$ and $\alpha = n - 1$; we use for Z in the theorem $Z = \frac{n-1}{K \cdot r_{\mathrm{eff}}(i,j)}(e_i - e_j)(e_i - e_j)^T$, for some edge $(i, j) \in E$ selected with probability $r_{\mathrm{eff}}(i, j)/(n - 1)$. Then we have already shown that $X = E[Z] = L_G/K$ and for the K independent draws $Z_1, \ldots, Z_K$ from the distribution of Z, we have that $\frac{1}{K}\sum_{k=1}^K Z_k = L_{G'}/K$. Lemma 8.16 shows that $\alpha X - Z = \frac{n-1}{K}L_G - Z \succeq 0$ for any realization of Z. Thus we have that

$$(1 - \epsilon)L_G/K \preceq L_{G'}/K \preceq (1 + \epsilon)L_G/K \tag{8.9}$$

holds with probability at least

$$1 - 2n \exp(-\epsilon^2 \cdot 8n \ln n/(4(n - 1)\epsilon^2)) \geq 1 - \frac{2n}{n^2} = 1 - 2/n.$$

Multiplying Inequality (8.9) through by K gives the desired Equation (8.8). $\square$

We now turn to the proof of Lemma 8.16.

Proof of Lemma 8.16 We want to show that

$$\frac{n-1}{K}L_G - Z \succeq 0.$$

We know that for some edge $(i, j) \in E$, $Z = \frac{n-1}{K \cdot r_{\mathrm{eff}}(i,j)}(e_i - e_j)(e_i - e_j)^T$, so that we want to show that

$$\frac{n-1}{K}L_G - \frac{n-1}{K \cdot r_{\mathrm{eff}}(i,j)}(e_i - e_j)(e_i - e_j)^T \succeq 0,$$

which is true if and only if

$$L_G - \frac{1}{r_{\mathrm{eff}}(i,j)}(e_i - e_j)(e_i - e_j)^T \succeq 0.$$

By the definition of positive semidefinite matrices, this holds if and only if for all $x \in \Re^n$,

$$x^T L_G x - x^T \left[\frac{1}{r_{\mathrm{eff}}(i,j)}(e_i - e_j)(e_i - e_j)^T\right] x \geq 0,$$

which is true if and only if

$$(x(i) - x(j))^2 \leq r_{\mathrm{eff}}(i, j) \cdot x^T L_G x.$$

If $x(i) = x(j)$, then the inequality holds trivially, since $r_{\mathrm{eff}}(i, j)$ and $x^T L_G x = \sum_{\{i,j\}\in E}(x(i) - x(j))^2$ are nonnegative. Otherwise, since this inequality holds under any scaling of x, it is true if we restrict ourselves to $x \in \Re^n$ such that

$x(i) - x(j) = r_{\text{eff}}(i, j)$, and thus the lemma is true if and only if for all such vectors x,

$$(r_{\text{eff}}(i, j))^2 \leq r_{\text{eff}}(i, j) \cdot x^T L_G x,$$

which holds if and only if

$$r_{\text{eff}}(i, j) \leq x^T L_G x.$$

We recall that $r_{\text{eff}}(i, j) = \mathcal{E}(f) = p^T L_G p$ for potentials p and i-j electrical flow f with $p(i) - p(j) = r_{\text{eff}}(i, j)$. By Lemma 8.9 and Corollary 8.10 we know that for $b = e_i - e_j$,

$$2b^T x - x^T L_G x \leq p^T L_G p = r_{\text{eff}}(i, j).$$

Since $b^T x = (x(i) - x(j)) = r_{\text{eff}}(i, j)$, we get

$$2r_{\text{eff}}(i, j) - x^T L_G x \leq r_{\text{eff}}(i, j),$$

or

$$r_{\text{eff}}(i, j) \leq x^T L_G x,$$

as desired. □

We now discuss the running time of Algorithm 8.2. We can sample an edge in each iteration as follows. Because $\sum_{(i,j) \in E} r_{\text{eff}}(i, j)/(n - 1) = 1$, we can partition the interval $[0, 1]$ into intervals, one per edge in E. Each time we wish to sample an edge, we draw a number uniformly at random from the interval $[0, 1]$ and choose the edge corresponding to the interval in which the number falls. Using bisection search, we can find the appropriate interval in $O(\log m)$ time. We assume such a random number can be drawn in unit time, so that the main loop of the algorithm can be executed in $O((n \log^2 n)/\epsilon^2)$ time. We can compute all effective resistances by computing an i-j electrical flow for each edge $(i, j) \in E$ in $\tilde{O}(m)$ time by Corollary 8.4, for a total of $\tilde{O}(m^2)$ time. By being a bit more clever, we can compute all effective resistances by computing an i-j electrical flow for each edge (i, j) in a spanning tree T of G, and using these flows to infer the effective resistances of all the non-tree edges; we give this as an exercise in Exercise 8.5. In this case, the total time is $\tilde{O}(mn)$. It is also possible to compute values for the effective resistances within a factor of $(1 + \epsilon)$ of the actual effective resistance for all edges in $O((m \log n)/\epsilon^2)$ time; see the Chapter Notes for a discussion. Having approximate values of the effective resistances is sufficient for the purposes of the algorithm. This leads to the following theorem.

Theorem 8.18: *Algorithm 8.2 can be implemented in $\tilde{O}(m/\epsilon^2)$ time.*

8.4 A Simple Laplacian Solver

In this section, we describe a simple randomized algorithm that runs in $\tilde{O}(m)$ time and finds a vector p that approximately satisfies the linear system $L_G p = b$ for an undirected graph G with resistances $r(i, j)$ for all $\{i, j\} \in E$; since directions are important in this section, we revert to our notation from previous sections in which $\vec{E}$ denotes an arbitrary orientation of the undirected edges of E. The algorithm has some similarity to the network simplex algorithm for the minimum-cost flow problem introduced in Section 5.6, although there are significant differences as well.

As with the network simplex algorithm, the algorithm starts with a spanning tree T of G. The tree is chosen to approximately minimize a parameter τ that we will discuss in a moment. We start with a flow $f^{(0)}$ that satisfies the demand vector b using only the edges in the tree T; to do this, for tree edge (i, j), let S be the cut induced by removing (i, j) from the tree, such that $i \in S$. Then $f^{(0)}(i, j) = \sum_{k \in S} b(k)$. In Exercise 8.4, we ask the reader to prove that $f^{(0)}$ is the unique flow satisfying the demand vector b using only the edges in T. We let $p^{(0)}$ be corresponding tree-defined potentials for $f^{(0)}$ and tree T as defined in the proof of Lemma 8.1. Since the flow satisfies flow conservation, we need only have it satisfy Kirchoff's Potential Law in order to find the potentials p that define the electrical flow, so that $L_G p = b$. To do this we repeatedly choose a non-tree edge $(h, \ell) \in \vec{E} - T$, and consider the directed basic cycle $\Gamma(h, \ell)$ created by adding (h, ℓ) to T; this is the cycle formed by (h, ℓ) plus the directed ℓ-h path in T (see Figure 8.5). We then modify the flow $f^{(k)}$ on the cycle $\Gamma(h, \ell)$ so that the Kirchoff potential law is satisfied on this cycle; that is, so that for resulting flow $f^{(k+1)}$, $\sum_{(i, j) \in \Gamma(h, \ell)} r(i, j) f^{(k+1)}(i, j) = 0$. By analogy with cycle-canceling for the minimum-cost circulation problem, we will say that we have *corrected* the cycle $\Gamma(h, \ell)$. After a certain number of iterations, we can show that the resulting flow must be close to the optimal electrical flow, and thus the resulting tree-defined potentials are also close to

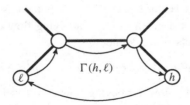

Figure 8.5 A basic cycle $\Gamma(h, \ell)$. The thick edges belong to the tree T.

Find tree T with low value of parameter τ
Find flow $f^{(0)}$ in T satisfying supplies b
Let $p^{(0)}$ be tree-defined potentials for $f^{(0)}$ with respect to tree T
$K \leftarrow \tau \ln((\tau + 2n)/\epsilon)$
for $k \leftarrow 1$ to K **do**
    Pick an $(h, \ell) \in \vec{E} - T$ with probability proportional to
    $R(\Gamma(h, \ell))/r(h, \ell)$
    Update $f^{(k-1)}$ to correct basic cycle $\Gamma(h, \ell)$
    Let $f^{(k)}$ be resulting flow
    Let $p^{(k)}$ be tree-defined potentials for $f^{(k)}$
return $f^{(K)}, p^{(K)}$

Algorithm 8.3 Simple combinatorial algorithm for approximately solving the linear system $L_G p = b$.

potentials p satisfying $L_G p = b$, and the algorithm terminates. We summarize the algorithm in Algorithm 8.3.

We now define a parameter τ, which is used in Algorithm 8.3 to define K, the number of iterations of the main loop. Let

$$R(\Gamma) = \sum_{\{i, j\} \in \Gamma} r(i, j)$$

denote the total resistance of the edges in cycle Γ.

Definition 8.19: *The* tree condition number τ *of tree T with resistances r is defined to be the sum over all non-tree arcs (i, j) of the ratio of the resistance of the cycle $\Gamma(i, j)$ to the resistance of the edge $r(i, j)$. Thus*

$$\tau \equiv \sum_{(i, j) \in \vec{E} - T} \frac{R(\Gamma(i, j))}{r(i, j)}.$$

To measure the progress of the algorithm, we will show that the energy of the flow $f^{(k)}$, $\mathcal{E}(f^{(k)})$, is converging to the energy of the optimal electrical flow f^* for the supply vector b. Let p^* be the potentials corresponding to the electrical flow f^*. For a given flow f satisfying flow conservation (so that $Bf = b$), and potentials p, we define

$$\text{gap}(f, p) \equiv \mathcal{E}(f) - [2b^T p - p^T L_G p].$$

By Lemma 8.8, for any flow f obeying flow conservation, $\mathcal{E}(f)$ is an upper bound on $\mathcal{E}(f^*)$, while by Corollary 8.10, for any potentials p, $2b^T p - p^T L_G p$ is a lower bound on $\mathcal{E}(f^*)$, so that $\text{gap}(f, p)$ is always nonnegative. It also follows that the difference between the energy of f and that of f^* is at most $\text{gap}(f, p)$, or

$$\mathcal{E}(f) - \mathcal{E}(f^*) \leq \text{gap}(f, p),$$

and we will use this inequality to measure how close the current flow f is to the electrical flow f^*. For our parameter τ, we will show that $\mathcal{E}(f^{(0)}) \leq (\tau + 2n)\mathcal{E}(f^*)$, and that each iteration of the algorithm reduces $\text{gap}(f, p)$ by a factor of $1 - \frac{1}{\tau}$. Thus after $\tau \ln((\tau + 2n)/\epsilon)$ iterations for some given $\epsilon > 0$, we will have that

$$\begin{aligned}
\mathcal{E}(f) - \mathcal{E}(f^*) &\leq \left(1 - \frac{1}{\tau}\right)^{\tau \ln((\tau+2n)/\epsilon)} (\tau + 2n)\mathcal{E}(f^*) \\
&\leq e^{-\ln((\tau+2n/\epsilon)} (\tau + 2n)\mathcal{E}(f^*) \\
&= \epsilon\mathcal{E}(f^*),
\end{aligned}$$

using $1 - x \leq e^{-x}$; the inequality implies that $\mathcal{E}(f) \leq (1 + \epsilon)\mathcal{E}(f^*)$. We will later show that this bound is good enough to prove that the resulting potentials are close to the potentials p^*.

We now show why correcting a cycle is useful: it reduces the energy of the flow. To see this, pick any directed cycle Γ in the graph. For a given flow f, we let

$$\Delta(\Gamma, f) \equiv \sum_{(i,j)\in\Gamma} f(i, j)r(i, j)$$

denote its distance from satisfying the Kirchoff Potential Law. If the cycle does not already satisfy the Kirchoff Potential Law, and $\Delta(\Gamma, f) \neq 0$, then we let f' be a flow in which we decrease the flow by some amount δ (possibly negative) on the arcs around Γ, so that

$$f'(i, j) = \begin{cases} f(i, j) - \delta & \forall (i, j) \in \Gamma, \\ f(i, j) + \delta & \forall (j, i) \in \Gamma, \\ f(i, j) & \forall (i, j) : (i, j), (j, i) \notin \Gamma. \end{cases}$$

Observe that if f obeys flow conservation, then so does f (as we argued for circulations in Section 5.1). Since we want $\Delta(\Gamma, f') = 0$, or $\sum_{(i,j)\in\Gamma} r(i, j)(f(i, j) - \delta) = 0$, solving for δ we get

$$\delta = \Delta(\Gamma, f)/R(\Gamma).$$

We can now show that if the cycle Γ does not obey the Kirchoff Potential Law, then the energy of f' is lower than that of f, so that correcting cycle Γ reduces the energy of the flow.

Lemma 8.20:

$$\mathcal{E}(f') - \mathcal{E}(f) = -\Delta(\Gamma, f)^2 / R(\Gamma).$$

Proof We see that

$$\mathcal{E}(f') - \mathcal{E}(f) = \sum_{(i,j)\in\Gamma} \left[r(i,j)(f(i,j) - \delta)^2 - r(i,j)f(i,j)^2 \right]$$

$$= \sum_{(i,j)\in\Gamma} r(i,j)[-2\delta f(i,j) + \delta^2]$$

$$= -2\delta\Delta(\Gamma, f) + \delta^2 R(\Gamma).$$

Then by our choice of $\delta = \Delta(\Gamma, f)/R(\Gamma)$, we have that

$$\mathcal{E}(f') - \mathcal{E}(f) = -2\frac{\Delta(\Gamma, f)^2}{R(\Gamma)} + \frac{\Delta(\Gamma, f)^2}{R(\Gamma)} = -\frac{\Delta(\Gamma, f)^2}{R(\Gamma)}.$$

$\square$

It is now possible to relate the amount by which the energy is reduced by correcting cycles Γ to the value of gap(f, p).

Lemma 8.21: *For a given flow f and the corresponding tree-defined potentials p in tree T,*

$$\mathrm{gap}(f, p) = \sum_{(i,j)\in\vec{E}-T} \frac{\Delta(\Gamma(i,j), f)^2}{r(i,j)}.$$

Proof By definition, we know that

$$\mathrm{gap}(f, p) = \mathcal{E}(f) - (2b^T p - p^T L_G p)$$

$$= \sum_{(i,j)\in\vec{E}} f(i,j)^2 r(i,j) - 2\sum_{i\in V} b(i)p(i) + \sum_{(i,j)\in\vec{E}} \frac{(p(i) - p(j))^2}{r(i,j)}.$$

Now by flow conservation, we know that $b(i) = \sum_{j:\{i,j\}\in E} f(i,j)$, so that by skew symmetry,

$$\sum_{i\in V} b(i)p(i) = \sum_{i\in V} p(i) \sum_{j:\{i,j\}\in E} f(i,j) = \sum_{(i,j)\in\vec{E}} f(i,j)(p(i) - p(j)).$$

Thus

$$
\begin{aligned}
\text{gap}(f, p) &= \sum_{(i,j)\in \vec{E}} f(i,j)^2 r(i,j) - 2 \sum_{(i,j)\in \vec{E}} f(i,j)(p(i) - p(j)) \\
&\quad + \sum_{(i,j)\in \vec{E}} \frac{(p(i) - p(j))^2}{r(i,j)} \\
&= \sum_{(i,j)\in \vec{E}} (r(i,j)f(i,j) - (p(i) - p(j)))^2 / r(i,j).
\end{aligned}
$$

As we showed in Equation (8.2) in the proof of Theorem 8.1, for any $(i,j) \in T$, since $p(i)$ and $p(j)$ are tree-defined potentials, $p(i) - p(j) = r(i,j)f(i,j)$, and the contribution of this edge to the sum is zero. As shown in Corollary 8.2, for any $(i,j) \in \vec{E} - T$,

$$
r(i,j)f(i,j) - (p(i) - p(j)) = \sum_{(k,\ell)\in \Gamma(i,j)} r(k,\ell)f(k,\ell) = \Delta(\Gamma(i,j), f).
$$

Thus we have that

$$
\text{gap}(f, p) = \sum_{(i,j)\in \vec{E}-T} \frac{\Delta(\Gamma(i,j), f)^2}{r(i,j)}.
$$

$\square$

We can now state the main idea of the algorithm. In each iteration of the algorithm, we will pick an edge $(i,j) \in \vec{E} - T$ with probability

$$
p(i,j) = \frac{1}{\tau} \frac{R(\Gamma(i,j))}{r(i,j)}.
$$

Note that

$$
\sum_{(i,j)\in \vec{E}-T} p(i,j) = \frac{1}{\tau} \sum_{(i,j)\in \vec{E}-T} \frac{R(\Gamma(i,j))}{r(i,j)} = 1,
$$

by the definition of τ, so that the $p(i,j)$ give a probability distribution. By Lemma 8.20, we know that if we pick (i,j), then the decrease in energy is $\Delta(\Gamma(i,j), f)^2 / R(\Gamma(i,j))$. Thus the overall expected decrease in energy in an iteration if we pick edges according to the given probability distribution is

$$
\sum_{(i,j)\in \vec{E}-T} p(i,j) \cdot \frac{\Delta(\Gamma(i,j), f)^2}{R(\Gamma(i,j))} = \frac{1}{\tau} \sum_{(i,j)\in \vec{E}-T} \frac{R(\Gamma(i,j))}{r(i,j)} \cdot \frac{\Delta(\Gamma(i,j), f)^2}{R(\Gamma(i,j))}
$$

$$= \frac{1}{\tau} \sum_{(i,j)\in\vec{E}-T} \frac{\Delta(\Gamma(i,j),f)^2}{r(i,j)}$$

$$= \frac{1}{\tau} \operatorname{gap}(f,p), \tag{8.10}$$

by Lemma 8.21.

Thus if f' is the flow resulting from a single iteration of the algorithm starting with flow f,

$$\mathcal{E}(f) - E[\mathcal{E}(f')] = \frac{1}{\tau} \operatorname{gap}(f,p) \geq \frac{1}{\tau} \left[\mathcal{E}(f) - \mathcal{E}(f^*) \right]. \tag{8.11}$$

Adding the energy of the electrical flow f^* to both sides, and rearranging, we obtain that

$$E[\mathcal{E}(f')] - \mathcal{E}(f^*) \leq \left(1 - \frac{1}{\tau} \right) \left[\mathcal{E}(f) - \mathcal{E}(f^*) \right].$$

If $f^{(k)}$ is the flow resulting from k iterations of the algorithm, then it is possible to prove that

$$E[\mathcal{E}(f^{(k)})] - \mathcal{E}(f^*) \leq \left(1 - \frac{1}{\tau} \right)^k \left[\mathcal{E}(f) - \mathcal{E}(f^*) \right];$$

we omit the details of the proof. Thus after sufficiently many iterations, the energy of $f^{(k)}$ is (in expectation) close to the energy of the optimal flow f^* if the initial flow f has energy that is not too large.

We now need to show that the energy of the initial flow $f^{(0)}$ is not too far away from the energy of the electrical flow f^*.

Lemma 8.22:

$$\mathcal{E}(f^{(0)}) - \mathcal{E}(f^*) \leq (\tau + 2n)\mathcal{E}(f^*).$$

Proof Let $P(k,\ell)$ be the directed path from k to ℓ in the tree T. Then consider the flow that results by sending $f^*(k,\ell)$ units of flow on $P(k,\ell)$ for each $(k,\ell) \in \vec{E}$. Then the total flow on an edge $(i,j) \in T$ is

$$\sum_{(k,\ell)\in\vec{E}:(i,j)\in P(k,\ell)} f^*(k,\ell).$$

We recall (from Exericse 8.4) that the flow satisfying the demands b using only the edges in T must be unique, so the flow given above must be the same as the flow $f^{(0)}$. Thus we have that

$$\mathcal{E}(f^{(0)}) = \sum_{(i,j)\in T} r(i,j) \left(\sum_{(k,\ell)\in\vec{E}:(i,j)\in P(k,\ell)} f^*(k,\ell) \right)^2.$$

For each edge $(i, j) \in T$, we use the Cauchy–Schwarz Inequality (8.11) with $a(k, \ell) = \sqrt{r(i, j)/r(k, \ell)}$ and $b(k, \ell) = \sqrt{r(k, \ell)} f^*(k, \ell)$ and derive

$$
r(i, j) \left(\sum_{(k,\ell)\in\vec{E}:(i,j)\in P(k,\ell)} f^*(k, \ell) \right)^2
$$

$$
\leq \left(\sum_{(k,\ell)\in\vec{E}:(i,j)\in P(k,\ell)} \frac{r(i, j)}{r(k, \ell)} \right) \left(\sum_{(k,\ell)\in\vec{E}:(i,j)\in P(k,\ell)} r(k, \ell) f^*(k, \ell)^2 \right)
$$

$$
\leq \left(\sum_{(k,\ell)\in\vec{E}:(i,j)\in P(k,\ell)} \frac{r(i, j)}{r(k, \ell)} \right) \mathcal{E}(f^*).
$$

Thus we have that

$$
\mathcal{E}(f^{(0)}) \leq \sum_{(k,\ell)\in\vec{E}} \sum_{(i,j)\in P(k,\ell)} \frac{r(i, j)}{r(k, \ell)} \mathcal{E}(f^*)
$$

$$
= \mathcal{E}(f^*) \left(\sum_{(k,\ell)\in T} \frac{r(k, \ell)}{r(k, \ell)} + \sum_{(k,\ell)\in\vec{E}-T} \frac{R(\Gamma(k, \ell)) - r(k, \ell)}{r(k, \ell)} \right)
$$

$$
= \mathcal{E}(f^*) \left(|T| + \tau - |\vec{E} - T| \right)
$$

$$
\leq \mathcal{E}(f^*)(\tau + 2|T|) \leq \mathcal{E}(f^*)(\tau + 2n).
$$

$\square$

Thus, as we have argued earlier, after $k = \tau \ln(\tau(\tau + 2n)/\epsilon)$ iterations,

$$
E[\mathcal{E}(f^{(k)})] - \mathcal{E}(f^*) \leq \left(1 - \frac{1}{\tau} \right)^k \mathcal{E}(f^{(0)})
$$

$$
\leq e^{-\ln(\tau(\tau+2n)/\epsilon)}(\tau + 2n)\mathcal{E}(f^*)
$$

$$
\leq \frac{\epsilon}{\tau} \mathcal{E}(f^*), \tag{8.12}
$$

using $1 - x \leq e^{-x}$.

While this proves that the expected energy of the resulting flow is close to the optimal energy, what we would like to show is that the resulting tree-defined potentials are in some sense close to the optimal potentials. We measure closeness with respect to a particular distance measure. Let $\|x\|_L = \sqrt{x^T L_G x}$ be the matrix norm with respect to the Laplacian L_G. Then we will prove the following lemma.

Lemma 8.23: *Let p^* be the potentials for the electrical flow f^*, and let $\hat{p}$ be the tree-defined potentials for a flow $\hat{f}$ such that*

$$\mathcal{E}(\hat{f}) - \mathcal{E}(f^*) \leq \frac{\epsilon}{\tau}\mathcal{E}(f^*).$$

Then

$$\|\hat{p} - p^*\|_L^2 \leq \epsilon\|p^*\|_L^2.$$

Proof Using that $(p^*)^T L_G p^* = \mathcal{E}(f^*)$, $b = L_G p^*$, and $b^T = (p^*)^T L_G$, we see that

$$
\begin{aligned}
\|\hat{p} - p^*\|_L^2 &= (\hat{p} - p^*)^T L_G(\hat{p} - p^*) \\
&= \hat{p}^T L_G \hat{p} - (p^*)^T L_G \hat{p} - \hat{p}^T L_G p^* + (p^*)^T L_G p^* \\
&= \hat{p}^T L_G \hat{p} - 2b^T \hat{p} + \mathcal{E}(f^*) \\
&= \mathrm{gap}(f^*, \hat{p}).
\end{aligned}
$$

By Equation (8.11), we know that if $\hat{f}'$ is the result of one more iteration of the algorithm starting with flow $\hat{f}$, then

$$\mathcal{E}(\hat{f}) - E[\mathcal{E}(\hat{f}')] = \frac{1}{\tau}\mathrm{gap}(\hat{f}, \hat{p}).$$

Thus it follows that

$$\mathcal{E}(\hat{f}) - \mathcal{E}(f^*) \geq \frac{1}{\tau}\mathrm{gap}(\hat{f}, \hat{p}),$$

so that

$$\mathrm{gap}(\hat{f}, \hat{p}) \leq \tau\left(\mathcal{E}(\hat{f}) - \mathcal{E}(f^*)\right).$$

Then

$$
\begin{aligned}
\|\hat{p} - p^*\|_L^2 &= \mathrm{gap}(f^*, \hat{p}) \\
&= \mathrm{gap}(\hat{f}, \hat{p}) - \left(\mathcal{E}(\hat{f}) - \mathcal{E}(f^*)\right) \\
&\leq (\tau - 1)\left(\mathcal{E}(\hat{f}) - \mathcal{E}(f^*)\right) \qquad\qquad (8.13) \\
&\leq \epsilon\mathcal{E}(f^*) \\
&= \epsilon(p^*)^T L_G p^* \\
&= \epsilon\|p^*\|_L^2,
\end{aligned}
$$

where we use the hypothesis of the theorem in the final inequality.   □

Corollary 8.24: *At the termination of Algorithm 8.3,*

$$E\left[\|\hat{p} - p^*\|_L^2\right] \leq \epsilon\|p^*\|_L^2.$$

Proof Taking expectations of both sides of Inequality (8.13) and plugging in Inequality (8.12), we get the Corollary.   □

Putting everything together, we get the following theorem.

Theorem 8.25: *Algorithm 8.3 finds a vector $\hat{p}$ of potentials such that $E\left[\|\hat{p} - p^*\|_L^2\right] \leq \epsilon \|p^*\|_L^2$ in $\tilde{O}(m \ln(m/\epsilon)))$ time.*

Proof There is an $\tilde{O}(m)$ algorithm to find a tree T with $\tau = \tilde{O}(m)$, and an $O(m)$ time algorithm to compute the probabilities $r(i,j)/R(\Gamma(i,j))$ for each edge; we give further details in the notes at the end of the chapter. As in Algorithm 8.2, we can sample an edge with probability $p(i,j)$ in $O(\log m)$ time. There are $k = \tau \ln(\tau(\tau + 2n)/\epsilon) = \tilde{O}(m \ln(m/\epsilon))$ total iterations until the difference of the expected energy of flow $f^{(k)}$ and the energy of the optimal flow f^* is at most $\frac{\epsilon}{\tau}\mathcal{E}(f^*)$. By Corollary 8.24, in expectation the potentials $p^{(k)}$ are then close to optimal potentials p^* as required by the theorem. We claim without proof that it takes $O(\log n)$ time to update the flow and potentials in each iteration; updating the flow in $O(\log n)$ time can be done via the dynamic tree data structure described in Exercise 4.3. Thus the overall time taken is $\tilde{O}(m \ln(m/\epsilon))$.   □

Exercises

8.1 Prove Rayleigh's Monotonicity Principle: Given a graph G, let $\mathcal{E}(f,r)$ be the energy of a flow f for supply vector b under resistances $r(i,j)$ for all $(i,j) \in \vec{E}$. Let f be the electrical flow for supply vector b under resistances $r(i,j)$, and let f' be the electrical flow for the same supply vector b under resistances $r'(i,j)$, where $r'(i,j) \geq r(i,j)$ for all $(i,j) \in \vec{E}$. Then Rayleigh's Monotonicity Principle states that

$$\mathcal{E}(f',r') \geq \mathcal{E}(f,r).$$

8.2 Let G be an electrical network with resistances r. Prove that effective resistances obey the triangle inequality; that is, for any i, j, k,

$$r_{\text{eff}}(i,k) \leq r_{\text{eff}}(i,j) + r_{\text{eff}}(j,k).$$

8.3 Let $e = (i,j)$ and $L_e = (e_i - e_j)(e_i - e_j)^T$. Assume that G is an unweighted graph. Prove that

$$L_e \preceq r_{\text{eff}}(i,j)L_G.$$

8.4 Prove that given a spanning tree T and demand vector b, the flow $f^{(0)}$ defined at the beginning of Section 8.4 is unique among all flows obeying flow conservation that have nonzero flow only on the edges of T.

8.5 Let T be a spanning tree of an undirected graph G. Suppose we compute the potentials p for an i-j flow for each edge $(i, j) \in T$; call the associated vector $p(i, j)$. Prove that the $p(i, j)$ for $(i, j) \in T$ can be used to find the effective resistance $r_{\text{eff}}(k, \ell)$ for any edge $(k, \ell) \in E$.

8.6 In this exercise, we show how it is possible to improve on the approximate maximum flow algorithm of Section 8.2, Algorithm 8.1. There is an immediate obstacle to improvement: it is possible to have a flow in a unit capacity graph in an iteration t such that $f_t(i, j) = \Theta(\sqrt{m})$. This implies that the algorithm will require at least $\Omega(\sqrt{m})$ oracle calls: we'll need $\Omega(\sqrt{m})$ iterations in which the flow on the edge (i, j) is small so that its average over the total number iterations is at most $1 + 4\epsilon$.

To improve the algorithm, we use the following idea. Whenever the oracle finds an edge with electrical flow strictly greater than $\hat{\rho}$, for some parameter $\hat{\rho}$, we will delete the edge and recompute the electrical flow, until the flow on each edge is at most $\hat{\rho}$. If this is the case, then the width of the oracle will be $\hat{\rho}$. If we do not delete too many edges, then the capacity of the minimum s-t cut will not be reduced too much and we will not have called the subroutine to compute the electrical flow too many times.

To make this intuition more precise, we let H be the set of deleted edges. We will use $\hat{\rho} = \frac{4}{\epsilon}(m \ln m)^{1/3}$, and show that for k the current value of the flow, and for $\epsilon \leq 1/3$, $|H| \leq \min[(m \ln m)^{1/3}, \frac{1}{8}\epsilon k]$. Thus we ensure that by removing at most $|H|$ edges, the value of the flow can decrease by a factor of at most $(1 - \frac{1}{8}\epsilon)$. Furthermore, since we recompute the electrical flow each time we remove an edge, there are at most $|H|$ additional electrical flow computations. We now restate the algorithm in Algorithm 8.4. Rather than deleting an edge if its electrical flow is too large, we set its resistance to infinity, which ensures that the electrical flow on it is zero in future iterations.

To prove the bound on the number of edges, we need to show that the energy of the electrical flow never decreases, and, for each edge removed, goes up by a certain factor. We also need to give a lower bound on the initial energy, and an upper bound on the final energy. A combination of all of these statements allows us to prove a bound on $|H|$.

(a) Show that the energy $\mathcal{E}(f_t)$ does not decrease throughout the execution of Algorithm 8.4 (Hint: use Exercise 8.1).

$w_1(i, j) \leftarrow 1$ for all $(i, j) \in \vec{E}$

$\hat{\rho} \leftarrow \frac{4}{\epsilon}(m \ln m)^{1/3}$

$H \leftarrow \emptyset$

$T \leftarrow \frac{1}{\epsilon^2} \hat{\rho} \ln m$

$t \leftarrow 1$

while $t \leq T$ **do**

$\quad W_t \leftarrow \sum_{(i,j) \in \vec{E}-H} w_t(i, j)$

$\quad p_t(i, j) \leftarrow w_t(i, j)/W_t$ for all $(i, j) \in \vec{E}$

$\quad r_t(i, j) \leftarrow \begin{cases} w_t(i, j) + \frac{\epsilon}{m} W_t & \text{if } (i, j) \notin H \\ \infty & \text{if } (i, j) \in H \end{cases}$

$\quad$ Compute s-t electrical flow f_t of value k using resistances r_t

$\quad$ **if** $f_t(i, j) > \hat{\rho}$ for some $(i, j) \notin H$ **then**

$\quad\quad H \leftarrow H \cup \{(i, j)\}$

$\quad$ **else**

$\quad\quad v_t(i, j) \leftarrow \frac{1}{\hat{\rho}}|f_t(i, j)|$ for all $(i, j) \in \vec{E} - H$

$\quad\quad w_{t+1}(i, j) \leftarrow w_t(i, j)(1 + \epsilon v_t(i, j))$ for all $(i, j) \in \vec{E} - H$

$\quad\quad t \leftarrow t + 1$

return $\bar{f} \leftarrow \frac{1}{T} \sum_{t=1}^{T} f_t$

Algorithm 8.4 Multiplicative weights algorithm for computing an approximate s-t flow via electrical s-t flows.

(b) Show that the initial energy $\mathcal{E}(f_1)$ is at least $1/m^2$.

(c) Show that the final energy $\mathcal{E}(f_{T+1})$ is at most $(1+\epsilon)m \exp\left(\frac{1}{\epsilon} \ln m\right)$.

(d) Show that the energy increases by at least a factor of $1 + \frac{\epsilon \hat{\rho}^2}{2m}$ for each edge removed from the graph (Hint: consider the potentials p for the flow f before removing the edge, and use the lower bound from Lemma 8.9 to bound the energy of the graph with the edge removed).

(e) Show that for $\hat{\rho} = \frac{4}{\epsilon}(m \ln m)^{1/3}$ and $\epsilon \leq 1/3$, it must be that $|H| \leq \frac{6}{16}(m \ln m)^{1/3}$. You may wish to use that $\ln(1 + x) \geq x/(1 + x)$.

(f) Argue that if the total flow value $k \leq \hat{\rho}$, then we will never remove any edges and $H = \emptyset$. Then assume that $k > \hat{\rho}$, and use this to infer that $|H| \leq \frac{1}{8}\epsilon k$.

(g) Prove that Algorithm 8.4 computes an s-t flow $\bar{f}$ of value at least $(1 - \frac{\epsilon}{8})k/\sqrt{1+\epsilon}$ (if a flow of value k exists) with $|\bar{f}(i, j)| \leq (1 + 4\epsilon)$ for all $(i, j) \in E$ in $O((m^{1/3} \ln^{4/3} m)/\epsilon^3)$ electrical flow computations, or $\tilde{O}(m^{4/3}/\epsilon^3)$ time.

Chapter Notes

Connections of electrical flow to topics in graph theory have been known for some time; for example, the classic textbook of Doyle and Snell [55] shows the connection of electrical flow to random walks (the Rayleigh Monotonicity Principle of Exercise 8.1 is described there). Other connections to topics in combinatorics and graph theory appear in Bollobás [26, chapter II]; the connection between electrical flow and randomly sampled spanning trees given in Section 8.1 is derived from the presentation of Bollobás.

However, the connections between electrical flow and the types of network flow in this book began with the $\tilde{O}(m)$ algorithm of Spielman and Teng [186] for finding an approximate solution p to $L_G p = b$ described in Theorem 8.3. This paper set off a flurry of work, both in improving the algorithm to solve $L_G p = b$ and using the algorithm as a subroutine for various other kinds of algorithms, as in Sections 8.2 and 8.3. The theoretically fastest algorithm known for the approximate solution of $L_G p = b$ as of this writing is due to Cohen, Kyng, Miller, Pachocki, Peng, Rao, and Xu [42] and runs in time $O(m \log^{1/2} n (\log \log n)^{3+\delta} \log \frac{1}{\epsilon})$ for any constant $\delta > 0$.

The maximum flow algorithm of Section 8.2, which uses electrical flows as the oracle within the multiplicative update algorithm, is due to Christiano, Kelner, Mądry, Spielman, and Teng [40], as is the improved algorithm of Exercise 8.6. The fastest known algorithm for finding a flow of value of at least $(1 - \epsilon)$ times the maximum is due to Peng [162], who gives an algorithm running in $O(m \log^{32} n (\log \log n)^2 \max(\log^9 n, 1/\epsilon^3))$ time. Lee and Sidford [140] use interior-point methods to give an $\tilde{O}(m \sqrt{n} \log^{O(1)} U)$ time algorithm for the maximum flow problem, while Mądry [146] gives a maximum flow algorithm running in $\tilde{O}(m^{10/7} U^{1/7})$ time using electrical flow computation as a black box; this running time is polynomial for interesting special cases (such as $U = 1$). Some of these ideas have been applied to minimum-cost flow problems as well. As mentioned in the notes for the minimum-cost circulation chapter, Cohen, Mądry, Sankowski, and Vladu [43] have used electrical flows to obtain an $\tilde{O}(m^{10/7} \log C)$-time algorithm for the minimum-cost flow problem in which $U = 1$. It does not seem like these algorithms are currently contenders for practical algorithms, but they may contain the ideas for such algorithms.

The idea of graph sparsification was introduced by Karger [122] for unweighted undirected graphs. Benczúr and Karger [20] extended these ideas to weighted graphs to obtain cut sparsifiers with $O((n \log n)/\epsilon^2)$ edges. Spielman and Teng [185] extended the idea of a cut sparsifier to a spectral sparsifier. Spielman and Srivastava [184] introduce the idea of sampling by effective resistances that we give in Section 8.3 to produce a spectral sparsifier with $O((n \log n)/\epsilon^2)$ edges. Spielman and Srivastava also explain how to approximate the effective resistances of all the edges of the graph in $O((m \log n)/\epsilon^2)$ time. The presentation we give is due to Harvey [105], including his version of Theorem 8.15, which was originally shown by Ahlswede and Winter [2]. Batson, Spielman, and Srivastava [16, 17] show how to deterministically obtain a spectral sparsifier with $O(n/\epsilon^2)$ edges; all previous algorithms involved random sampling. However, their algorithm needs time $O(n^3 m/\epsilon^2)$, which makes it slower than many algorithms running on the original non-sparsified graph. Lee and Sun [141] have shown how to find a sparsifier with $O(n/\epsilon^2)$ edges in $\tilde{O}(m/\epsilon^2)$ time.

Section 8.3 mentions concentration of measure results and uses the Ahlswede-Winter inequality of Theorem 8.15 as an example. Chernoff bounds are a typical case of concentration of measure inequalities used in computer science, and discussions of these bounds can be found in the text of Dubhashi and Panconesi [56] and books on uses of probability in computing, such as Mitzenmacher and Upfal [148] and Motwani and Raghavan [150]. The Ahlswede–Winter inequality is an example of the extension of Chernoff bounds for scalar random variables to matrix random variables. Many well-known results for scalar variables are extended to matrix variables in a paper of Tropp [195], and a book of Tropp [196] surveys these results.

The simple Laplacian solver of Section 8.4 is due to Kelner, Orecchia, Sidford, and Zhu [131]. There are some pieces of the result we did not show. In particular, we did not show how to find a tree with tree condition number $\tau = \tilde{O}(m)$. The tree condition number is an additive factor of $m - (n-1)$ away from the *stretch* of a spanning tree; the concept of the stretch of a spanning tree was introduced by Alon, Karp, Peleg, and West [8]. As of this writing, a spanning tree of stretch $\tilde{O}(m)$ can be found in $\tilde{O}(m)$ time due to a result of Abraham and Neiman [1]. Papp [161] provides a survey of algorithms to find low-stretch trees and includes some experimental work. Additionally, in order for the Laplacian solver to run in $\tilde{O}(m)$ time, we need to be able to update the flow on the tree T and the potentials in $O(\log n)$ time per iteration. As we mentioned in the proof of Theorem 8.25, we can update the flow using the dynamic tree data structure of Exercise 4.3, and a modification of that data structure allows us to update potentials as well. Kelner et al. also provide their own data structure for updating the flow and potentials in $O(\log n)$ time per iteration. Preliminary experimental work with the Kelner et al. solver by Boman, Deweese, and Gilbert [27] and Hoske, Lukarski, Meyerhenke, and Wegner [112] indicate that the solver is not competitive with traditional methods of solving linear systems, at least not without some additional algorithmic ideas.

Permissions

9

Open Questions

"Have you guessed the riddle yet?" the Hatter said, turning to Alice again.
"No, I give it up," Alice replied. "What's the answer?"
"I haven't the slightest idea," said the Hatter.
"Nor I," said the March Hare.

– Lewis Carroll, Alice in Wonderland

The area of network flows brings together several elements that are not always found simultaneously in the study of algorithms. First, it has a mathematically elegant theory, starting with Ford and Fulkerson's maximum flow-minimum cut theorem (Theorem 2.6). Second, it has beautiful algorithms with simple analyses, such as the push/relabel algorithm of Section 2.8 and the random contraction algorithm of Section 3.3. Third, these algorithms are often very efficient in practice, as we have tried to describe in the Chapter Notes throughout the book. Fourth, network flow problems are enormously useful in modeling a large variety of problems. The area is intellectually rich, aesthetically satisfying, and genuinely practical.

But there is still more work to be done! To conclude the book, we list a few significant open problems.

Problem 1: A simple $O(mn)$ time maximum flow algorithm. As mentioned in the notes at the end of Chapter 2, Orlin [159] gives an $O(mn)$ time algorithm for the maximum flow problem, which is currently the fastest strongly polynomial-time algorithm for the problem. In doing so, he answered a long-standing question in network flow theory about whether such an algorithm is possible. The algorithm is somewhat complex. Is it possible to achieve the same running time with a simpler algorithm, and without complex data structures? For instance, for the push-relabel algorithm of Section 2.8, the running time of the algorithm without accounting for nonsaturating pushes is

$O(mn)$; if a simple rule could be devised that allowed for nonsaturating pushes to run in $O(mn)$ time overall, then push-relabel would be $O(mn)$ time.

Problem 2: A Gomory-Hu tree without $n - 1$ flow computations. As we explained in Chapter 3, initially the only known way to find a global minimum cut in an undirected graph was to run $n - 1$ maximum flow computations, but then other, non-flow-based methods were devised, such as the MA ordering algorithm of Section 3.2 and the random contraction algorithm of Section 3.3. Is it possible to find a Gomory–Hu tree without using $n - 1$ maximum flow computations? Bhalgat, Hariharan, Kavitha, and Panigrahi [23] have made some progress on the problem in the case of unit capacity graphs.

Problem 3: A strongly polynomial-time algorithm for the generalized minimum-cost circulation problem. In Exercise 6.6, we defined the generalized minimum-cost circulation problem, which is similar to the minimum-cost circulation problem of Chapter 5: in addition to costs $c(i, j)$ and capacities $u(i, j)$, there are gains $\gamma(i, j) > 0$ for each arc in the graph, and if $f(i, j)$ units of flow enter arc (i, j) at node i, then $\gamma(i, j)f(i, j)$ units of flow leave arc (i, j) and enter node j. The goal of the problem is to find a minimum-cost circulation, so that capacity constraints are obeyed and flow conservation is maintained at all nodes. Wayne [204] has given a combinatorial polynomial-time algorithm, based on Wallacher's algorithm for minimum-cost circulations (Section 5.2). It was a major breakthrough in the mid-1980s when Tardos [188] gave the first strongly polynomial-time algorithm for the minimum-cost flow problem, and also recently when Vegh [200] gave a strongly polynomial-time algorithm for the generalized maximum flow problem. Is it possible to obtain a strongly polynomial-time algorithm for generalized minimum-cost circulation problem? Since network flow problems can be expressed as linear programs, obtaining such an algorithm would be the next step toward a strongly polynomial-time algorithm for linear programming.

Problem 4: A combinatorial, polynomial-time, exact algorithm for multicommodity flow. The known exact polynomial-time algorithms for the multicommodity flow problem are all based on polynomial-time linear programming algorithms, as with the interior-point algorithm of Vaidya [199], for example. The combinatorial algorithms, as with the Garg–Könemann algorithm (Section 7.4) and the Awerbuch–Leighton algorithm (Section 7.5) give approximate solutions. Is it possible to devise a combinatorial, polynomial-time algorithm for the problem that finds an optimal solution?

Problem 5: Combinatorial minimum-cost circulation algorithms as fast as interior-point algorithms. As mentioned in the notes for Chapter 5, Lee and Sidford [140] give an $\tilde{O}(m\sqrt{n}\log^{O(1)}(CU))$-time algorithm for finding a minimum-cost flow; this result is a specialization of an interior-point algorithm for linear programming. The minimum-cost flow algorithm uses the fast Laplacian solvers of the sort described in Section 8.4. Is it possible to find an $\tilde{O}(m\sqrt{n}\log(CU))$ algorithm for the minimum-cost circulation problem that is combinatorial in nature?

References

[1] I. Abraham and O. Neiman. Using petal-decompositions to build a low stretch spanning tree. In *Proceedings of the 44th Annual ACM Symposium on the Theory of Computing*, pages 395–406, 2012. Full version available at https://www.cs.bgu.ac.il/~neimano/spanning-full1.pdf. Accessed May 14, 2018.

[2] R. Ahlswede and A. Winter. Strong converse for identification via quantum channels. *IEEE Transactions on Information Theory*, 48:569–579, 2002.

[3] R. K. Ahuja, T. L. Magnanti, and J. B. Orlin. Network flows. In G. L. Nemhauser, A. H. G. Rinnooy Kan, and M. J. Todd, editors, *Optimization*, volume 1 of Handbooks in Operations Research and Management Science, pages 211–369. North-Holland, Amsterdam, The Netherlands, 1989.

[4] R. K. Ahuja, T. L. Magnanti, and J. B. Orlin. *Network Flows: Theory, Algorithms, and Applications*. Prentice Hall, Englewood Cliffs, NJ, USA, 1993.

[5] R. K. Ahuja and J. B. Orlin. A fast and simple algorithm for the maximum flow problem. *Operations Research*, 37:748–759, 1989.

[6] R. K. Ahuja and J. B. Orlin. Distance-directed augmenting path algorithms for maximum flow and parametric maximum flow problems. *Naval Research Logistics*, 38:413–430, 1991.

[7] R. K. Ahuja, J. B. Orlin, and R. E. Tarjan. Improved time bounds for the maximum flow problem. *SIAM Journal on Computing*, 18:939–954, 1989.

[8] N. Alon, R. M. Karp, D. Peleg, and D. West. A graph-theoretical game and its application to the k-server problem. *SIAM Journal on Computing*, 24:78–100, 1995.

[9] R. J. Anderson and J. Setubal. Goldberg's algorithm for maximum flow in perspective: A computational study. In D. S. Johnson and C. C. McGeoch, editors, *Network Flows and Matching, First DIMACS Implementation Challenge*, number 12 in DIMACS Series in Discrete Mathematics and Theoretical Computer Science, pages 1–18. American Mathematical Society, Providence, RI, USA, 1993.

[10] S. Arora, E. Hazan, and S. Kale. The multiplicative weights update method: A meta-algorithm and applications. *Theory of Computing*, 8:121–164, 2012.

[11] B. I. Aspvall. *Efficient Algorithms for Certain Satisfiability and Linear Programming Problems*. PhD thesis, Department of Computer Science, Stanford University, August 1980. Also appears as Technical Report STAN-CS-80-822.

[12] B. Awerbuch and T. Leighton. A simple local-control approximation algorithm for multicommodity flow. In *Proceedings of the 34th Annual IEEE Symposium on Foundations of Computer Science*, pages 459–468, 1993.

[13] B. Awerbuch and T. Leighton. Improved approximation algorithms for the multicommodity flow problem and local competitive routing in dynamic networks. In *Proceedings of the 26th Annual ACM Symposium on the Theory of Computing*, pages 487–496, 1994.

[14] G. Baier, E. Köhler, and M. Skutella. The k-splittable flow problem. *Algorithmica*, 42:231–248, 2005.

[15] F. Barahona and É. Tardos. Note on Weintraub's minimum-cost circulation algorithm. *SIAM Journal on Computing*, 18:579–583, 1989.

[16] J. Batson, D. A. Spielman, and N. Srivastava. Twice-Ramanujan sparsifiers. *SIAM Journal on Computing*, 41:1704–1721, 2012.

[17] J. Batson, D. A. Spielman, and N. Srivastava. Twice-Ramanujan sparsifiers. *SIAM Review*, 56:315–334, 2014.

[18] R. Bellman. On a routing problem. *Quarterly of Applied Mathematics*, 16:87–90, 1958.

[19] A. A. Benczúr and M. X. Goemans. Deformable polygon representation and near-mincuts. In M. Grötschel and G. O. H. Katona, editors, *Building Bridges*, number 19 in Boylai Society Mathematical Studies, pages 103–135. Springer, Berlin, Germany, 2008.

[20] A. A. Benczúr and D. R. Karger. Randomized approximation schemes for cuts and flows in capacitated graphs. *SIAM Journal on Computing*, 44:290–319, 2015.

[21] D. P. Bertsekas and P. Tseng. Relaxation methods for minimum cost ordinary and generalized network flow problems. *Operations Research*, 36:93–114, 1988.

[22] D. P. Bertsekas and P. Tseng. RELAX-IV: A faster version of the RELAX code for solving minimum flow problems. Technical Report LIDS-P-2276, Laboratory for Information and Decision Systems, Massachusetts Institute of Technology, November 1994.

[23] A. Bhalgat, R. Hariharan, T. Kavitha, and D. Panigrahi. An $\tilde{O}(mn)$ Gomory-Hu tree construction algorithm for unweighted graphs. In *Proceedings of the 39th Annual ACM Symposium on the Theory of Computing*, pages 605–614, 2007.

[24] D. Bienstock. *Potential Function Methods for Approximately Solving Linear Programming Problems: Theory and Practice*. Kluwer Academic Publishers, New York, NY, USA, 2002.

[25] R. G. Bland and D. L. Jensen. On the computational behavior of a polynomial-time network flow algorithm. *Mathematical Programming*, 54:1–39, 1992.

[26] B. Bollobás. *Modern Graph Theory*. Springer, New York, NY, USA, 1998.

[27] E. G. Boman, K. Deweese, and J. R. Gilbert. Evaluating the potential of a dual randomized Kaczmarz Laplacian linear solver. *Informatica*, 40:95–107, 2016.

[28] Y. Boykov and V. Kolmogorov. An experimental comparison of min-cut/max-flow algorithms for energy minimization in vision. *IEEE Transactions on Pattern Analysis and Machine Intelligence*, 26:1124–1137, 2004.

[29] U. Bünnagel, B. Korte, and J. Vygen. Efficient implementation of the Goldberg-Tarjan minimum-cost flow algorithm. *Optimization Methods and Software*, 10:157–174, 1998.

[30] R. G. Busacker and T. L. Saaty. *Finite Graphs and Networks: An Introduction with Applications*. McGraw-Hill Book Company, New York, NY, USA, 1965.

[31] B. G. Chandran and D. S. Hochbaum. A computational study of the pseudo-flow and push-relabel algorithms for the maximum flow problem. *Operations Research*, 57:358–376, 2009.

[32] C. S. Chekuri, A. V. Goldberg, D. R. Karger, M. S. Levine, and C. Stein. Experimental study of minimum cut algorithms. In *Proceedings of the 8th Annual ACM-SIAM Symposium on Discrete Algorithms*, pages 324–333, 1997.

[33] C. K. Cheng and T. C. Hu. Ancestor tree for arbitrary multi-terminal cut functions. *Annals of Operations Research*, 33:199–213, 1991.

[34] J. Cheriyan and S. N. Maheshwari. Analysis of preflow push algorithms for maximum network flow. *SIAM Journal on Computing*, 18:1057–1086, 1989.

[35] J. Cheriyan and K. Mehlhorn. An analysis of the highest-level selection rule in the preflow-push max-flow algorithm. *Information Processing Letters*, 69:239–242, 1999.

[36] B. V. Cherkasskii. A fast algorithm for constructing a maximum flow through a network. *American Mathematical Society Translations*, 158:23–30, 1994.

[37] B. V. Cherkassky and A. V. Goldberg. On implementing the push-relabel method for the maximum flow problem. *Algorithmica*, 19:390–410, 1997.

[38] B. V. Cherkassky and A. V. Goldberg. Negative-cycle detection algorithms. *Mathematical Programming*, 85:277–311, 1999.

[39] T.-Y. Cheung. Computational comparison of eight methods for the maximum flow problem. *ACM Transactions on Mathematical Software*, 6:1–16, 1980.

[40] P. Christiano, J. A. Kelner, A. Mądry, D. Spielman, and S.-H. Teng. Electrical flows, Laplacian systems, and faster approximation of maximum flow in undirected graphs. In *Proceedings of the 43rd Annual ACM Symposium on the Theory of Computing*, pages 273–282, 2011. Full version available at https://people.csail .mit.edu/madry/docs/maxflow.pdf. Accessed May 15, 2018.

[41] E. Cohen and N. Megiddo. New algorithms for generalized network flows. *Mathematical Programming*, 64:325–336, 1994.

[42] M. B. Cohen, R. Kyng, G. L. Miller, J. W. Pachocki, R. Peng, A. B. Rao, and S. C. Xu. Solving SDD linear systems in nearly $m \log^{1/2} n$ time. In *Proceedings of the 46th Annual ACM Symposium on the Theory of Computing*, pages 343–352, 2014.

[43] M. B. Cohen, A. Mądry, P. Sankowski, and A. Vladu. Negative-weight shortest paths and unit capacity minimum cost flow in $\tilde{O}(m^{10/7} \log W)$ time. In *Proceedings of the 28th Annual ACM-SIAM Symposium on Discrete Algorithms*, pages 752–771, 2017. Full version available at https://arxiv.org/pdf/1605.01717.pdf. Accessed June 8, 2018.

[44] W. J. Cook, W. H. Cunningham, W. R. Pulleyblank, and A. Schrijver. *Combinatorial Optimization*. John Wiley & Sons, New York, NY, USA, 1998.

[45] T. H. Cormen, C. E. Leiserson, R. L. Rivest, and C. Stein. *Introduction to Algorithms*. MIT Press, Cambridge, MA, USA, third edition, 2009.

[46] S. I. Daitch and D. A. Spielman. Faster approximate lossy generalized flow via interior-point algorithms. In *Proceedings of the 40th Annual ACM Symposium on the Theory of Computing*, pages 451–460, 2008. Full version available at https://arxiv.org/pdf/0803.0988.pdf. Accessed February 3, 2019.

[47] G. B. Dantzig. Application of the simplex method to a transportation problem. In T. C. Koopmans, editor, *Activity Analysis of Production and Allocation*, number 13 in Cowles Commission for Research in Economics, pages 359–373. John Wiley & Sons, New York, NY, USA, 1951.

[48] G. B. Dantzig. *Linear Programming and Extensions*. Princeton University Press, Princeton, NJ, USA, 1963.

[49] G. B. Dantzig and D. R. Fulkerson. On the max-flow min-cut theorem of networks. In H. W. Kuhn and A. W. Tucker, editors, *Linear Inequalities and Related Systems*, number 38 in Annals of Mathematics Studies, pages 215–222. Princeton University Press, Princeton, NJ, USA, 1956.

[50] U. Derigs and W. Meier. Implementing Goldberg's max-flow-algorithm – A computational investigation. *ZOR – Methods and Models of Operations Research*, 33:383–403, 1989.

[51] E. W. Dijkstra. A note on two problems in connexion with graphs. *Numerische Mathematik*, 1:269–271, 1959.

[52] E. A. Dinic. An algorithm for the solution of the max-flow problem with power estimation. *Doklady Akademii Nauk SSSR*, 194:754–757, 1970. In Russian. English version in *Soviet Mathematics Doklady* 11:1277–1280, 1970.

[53] E. A. Dinitz, A. V. Karzanov, and M. V. Lomonosov. O strukture sistemy minimal'nykh rebernykh razrezov grafa. In A. A. Fridman, editor, *Issledovaniya po Diskretnoĭ Optimizatsii*, pages 290–306. Nauka, Moscow, 1976. In Russian. English translation available at http://alexander-karzanov.net/ScannedOld/76_cactus_transl.pdf. Accessed February 14, 2018.

[54] Y. Dinitz. Dinitz' algorithm: The original version and Even's version. In O. Goldreich, A. L. Rosenberg, and A. L. Selman, editors, *Theoretical Computer Science: Essays in Memory of Shimon Even*, number 3895 in Lecture Notes in Computer Science, pages 218–240. Springer, Berlin, Germany, 2006.

[55] P. G. Doyle and J. L. Snell. *Random Walks and Electric Networks*. The Mathematical Association of America, Washington DC, USA, 1984. Online version available at https://arxiv.org/pdf/math/0001057.pdf. Accessed January 24, 2019.

[56] D. P. Dubhashi and A. Panconesi. *Concentration of Measure for the Analysis of Randomized Algorithms*. Cambridge University Press, New York, NY, USA, 2009.

[57] J. Edmonds and R. M. Karp. Theoretical improvements in algorithmic efficiency for network flow problems. *Journal of the ACM*, 19:248–264, 1972.

[58] P. Elias, A. Feinstein, and C. E. Shannon. A note on the maximum flow through a network. *IRE Transactions on Information Theory*, 2:117–119, 1956.

[59] S. Even and R. E. Tarjan. Network flow and testing graph connectivity. *SIAM Journal on Computing*, 4:507–518, 1975.

[60] L. Fleischer. Building chain and cactus representations of all minimum cuts from Hao-Orlin in the same asymptotic run time. *Journal of Algorithms*, 33:51–72, 1999.

[61] L. K. Fleischer. Approximating fractional multicommodity flow independent of the number of commodities. *SIAM Journal on Discrete Mathematics*, 13:505–520, 2000.

[62] L. R. Ford Jr. Network flow theory. Paper P-923, The RAND Corporation, Santa Monica, CA, USA, 1956.

[63] L. R. Ford Jr. and D. R. Fulkerson. Maximal flow through a network. *Canadian Journal of Mathematics*, 8:399–404, 1956.

[64] L. R. Ford Jr. and D. R. Fulkerson. Constructing maximal dynamic flows from static flows. *Operations Research*, 6:419–433, 1958.

[65] L. R. Ford Jr. and D. R. Fulkerson. A suggested computation for maximal multi-commodity network flows. *Management Science*, 5:97–101, 1958.

[66] L. R. Ford Jr. and D. R. Fulkerson. *Flows in Networks*. Princeton University Press, Princeton, NJ, USA, 1962.

[67] R. M. Foster. The average impedance of an electrical network. In *Reissner Anniversary Volume: Contributions to Applied Mechanics*, pages 333–340. J. W. Edwards, Ann Arbor, MI, USA, 1949.

[68] A. Frank. Connectivity and network flows. In R. L. Graham, M. Grötschel, and L. Lovász, editors, *Handbook of Combinatorics*, volume I, pages 111–178. Elsevier B.V., Amsterdam, The Netherlands, 1995.

[69] A. Frank. On the edge-connectivity algorithm of Nagamochi and Ibaraki. EGRES Quick Proof 2009-01, Department of Operations Research, Eötvös University, Budapest, Hungary, 2009. Available at http://www.cs.elte.hu/egres/qp/egresqp-09-01.pdf. Accessed September 11, 2012.

[70] M. L. Fredman, R. Sedgewick, D. D. Sleator, and R. E. Tarjan. The pairing heap: A new form of self-adjusting heap. *Algorithmica*, 1:111–129, 1986.

[71] M. L. Fredman and R. E. Tarjan. Fibonacci heaps and their uses in improved network optimization algorithms. *Journal of the ACM*, 34:596–615, 1987.

[72] S. Fujishige. Another simple proof of the validity of Nagamochi and Ibaraki's min-cut algorithm and Queyranne's extension to symmetric submodular function minimization. *Journal of the Operations Research Society of Japan*, 41:626–628, 1998.

[73] S. Fujishige. A maximum flow algorithm using MA ordering. *Operations Research Letters*, 31:176–178, 2003.

[74] D. R. Fulkerson. An out-of-kilter method for minimal-cost flow problems. *SIAM Journal on Applied Mathematics*, 9:18–27, 1961.

[75] D. R. Fulkerson and G. B. Dantzig. Computation of maximal flows in networks. *Naval Research Logistics Quarterly*, 2:277–283, 1955.

[76] H. N. Gabow. A matroid approach to finding edge connectivity and packing arborescences. *Journal of Computer and System Sciences*, 50:259–273, 1995.

[77] H. N. Gabow. The minset-poset approach to representations of graph connectivity. *ACM Transactions on Algorithms*, 12, 2016. Article 24.

[78] G. Gallo, M. D. Grigoriadis, and R. E. Tarjan. A fast parametric maximum flow algorithm and applications. *SIAM Journal on Computing*, 18:30–55, 1989.

[79] N. Garg and J. Könemann. Faster and simpler algorithms for multicommodity flow and other fractional packing problems. *SIAM Journal on Computing*, 37:630–652, 2007.

[80] F. Glover and D. Klingman. On the equivalence of some generalized network problems to pure network problems. *Mathematical Programming*, 4:269–278, 1973.

[81] F. Glover, D. Klingman, J. Mote, and D. Whitman. Comprehensive computer evaluation and enhancement of maximum flow algorithms. Research Report 356, Center for Cybernetic Studies, University of Texas, Austin, October 1979. Available at http://www.dtic.mil/dtic/tr/fulltext/u2/a081941.pdf. Accessed May 29, 2018.

[82] F. Glover, D. Klingman, J. Mote, and D. Whitman. An extended abstract of an indepth algorithmic and computational study for maximum flow problems. *Discrete Applied Mathematics*, 2:251–254, 1980.

[83] A. V. Goldberg. Finding a maximum density subgraph. Technical Report UCB/CSD-84-171, EECS Department, University of California, Berkeley, 1984. Available at http://www2.eecs.berkeley.edu/Pubs/TechRpts/1984/CSD-84-171.pdf. Accessed May 29, 2018.

[84] A. V. Goldberg. An efficient implementation of a scaling minimum-cost flow algorithm. *Journal of Algorithms*, 22:1–29, 1997.

[85] A. V. Goldberg. Two-level push-relabel algorithm for the maximum flow problem. In A. V. Goldberg and Y. Zhou, editors, *Algorithmic Aspects in Information and Management*, number 5564 in Lecture Notes in Computer Science, pages 212–225. Springer, Berlin, Germany, 2009.

[86] A. V. Goldberg, S. Hed, H. Kaplan, R. Kohli, R. E. Tarjan, and R. F. Werneck. Faster and more dynamic maximum flow by incremental breadth-first search. In N. Bansal and I. Finocchi, editors, *Algorithms – ESA 2015*, number 9294 in Lecture Notes in Computer Science, pages 619–630. Springer, Berlin, Germany, 2015.

[87] A. V. Goldberg and M. Kharitonov. On implementing scaling push-relabel algorithms for the minimum-cost flow problem. In D. S. Johnson and C. C. McGeoch, editors, *Network Flows and Matching, First DIMACS Implementation Challenge*, number 12 in DIMACS Series in Discrete Mathematics and Theoretical Computer Science, pages 1–18. American Mathematical Society, Providence, RI, USA, 1993.

[88] A. V. Goldberg, J. D. Oldham, S. Plotkin, and C. Stein. An implementation of a combinatorial approximation algorithm for minimum-cost multicommodity flow. In R. E. Bixby, E. A. Boyd, and R. Z. Ríos-Mercado, editors, *Integer Programming and Combinatorial Optimization, 6th International IPCO Conference*, volume 1412 of *Lecture Notes in Computer Science*, pages 338–352. Springer, Berlin, Germany, 1998.

[89] A. V. Goldberg, S. A. Plotkin, and É. Tardos. Combinatorial algorithms for the generalized circulation problem. *Mathematics of Operations Research*, 16:351–381, 1991.

[90] A. V. Goldberg and S. Rao. Beyond the flow decomposition barrier. *Journal of the ACM*, 45:783–797, 1998.

[91] A. V. Goldberg, É. Tardos, and R. E. Tarjan. Network flow algorithms. In B. Korte, L. Lovász, H. J. Prömel, and A. Schrijver, editors, *Paths, Flows, and VLSI-Layout*, pages 101–164. Springer, Berlin, Germany, 1990.

[92] A. V. Goldberg and R. E. Tarjan. A new approach to the maximum-flow problem. *Journal of the ACM*, 35:921–940, 1988.

[93] A. V. Goldberg and R. E. Tarjan. Finding minimum-cost circulations by canceling negative cycles. *Journal of the ACM*, 36:873–886, 1989.

[94] A. V. Goldberg and R. E. Tarjan. Finding minimum-cost circulations by successive approximation. *Mathematics of Operations Research*, 15:430–466, 1990.

[95] A. V. Goldberg and R. E. Tarjan. Efficient maximum flow algorithms. *Communications of the ACM*, 57:82–89, 2014.

[96] A. V. Goldberg and K. Tsioutsiouliklis. Cut tree algorithms: An experimental study. *Journal of Algorithms*, 83:51–83, 2001.

[97] D. Goldfarb and J. Hao. Polynomial-time primal simplex algorithms for the minimum cost network flow problem. *Algorithmica*, 8:145–160, 1992.

[98] D. Goldfarb and Z. Jin. A faster combinatorial algorithm for the generalized circulation problem. *Mathematics of Operations Research*, 21:529–539, 1996.

[99] D. Goldfarb, Z. Jin, and Y. Lin. A polynomial dual simplex algorithm for the generalized circulation problem. *Mathematical Programming*, 91:271–288, 2002.

[100] D. Goldfarb, Z. Jin, and J. B. Orlin. Polynomial-time highest-gain augmenting path algorithms for the generalized circulation problem. *Mathematics of Operations Research*, 22:793–802, 1997.

[101] R. E. Gomory and T. C. Hu. Multi-terminal network flows. *SIAM Journal on Applied Mathematics*, 9:551–570, 1961.

[102] M. D. Grigoriadis and L. G. Khachiyan. Fast approximation schemes for convex programs with many blocks and coupling constraints. *SIAM Journal on Optimization*, 4:86–107, 1994.

[103] D. Gusfield. Very simple methods for all pairs network flow analysis. *SIAM Journal on Computing*, 19:143–155, 1990.

[104] J. Hao and J. B. Orlin. A faster algorithm for finding a minimum cut in a directed graph. *Journal of Algorithms*, 17:424–446, 1994.

[105] N. Harvey. Lecture Notes from CPSC 536N: Randomized Algorithms, Winter 2012, Lectures 13 and 14. Available at http://www.cs.ubc.ca/~nickhar/W12/. Accessed May 14, 2018.

[106] M. Henzinger, S. Rao, and D. Wang. Local flow partitioning for faster edge connectivity. In *Proceedings of the 28th Annual ACM-SIAM Symposium on Discrete Algorithms*, pages 1919–1938, 2017.

[107] D. S. Hochbaum. The pseudoflow algorithm: A new algorithm for the maximum flow problem. *Operations Research*, 56:992–1009, 2008.

[108] A. J. Hoffman. Some recent applications of the theory of linear inequalities to extremal combinatorial analysis. In R. Bellman and M. Hall, Jr., editors, *Combinatorial Analysis*, volume X of *Proceedings of Symposia in Applied Mathematics*, pages 113–127, American Mathematical Society, Providence, RI, USA, 1960.

[109] A. J. Hoffman. On greedy algorithms that succeed. In I. Anderson, editor, *Surveys in combinatorics 1985: Invited papers for the Tenth British Combinatorial Conference*, number 103 in London Mathematical Society Lecture Note Series, pages 97–112. Cambridge University Press, Cambridge, UK, 1985.

[110] A. J. Hoffman. On simple combinatorial optimization problems. *Discrete Mathematics*, 106/107:285–289, 1992.

[111] B. Hoppe and É. Tardos. The quickest transshipment problem. *Mathematics of Operations Research*, 25:36–62, 2000.

[112] D. Hoske, D. Lukarski, H. Meyerhenke, and M. Wegner. Engineering a combinatorial Laplacian solver: Lessons learned. *Algorithms*, 9, 2016. Article 72.

[113] T. C. Hu. Multi-commodity network flows. *Operations Research*, 11:344–360, 1963.

[114] IBM ILOG. CPLEX. https://www.ibm.com/analytics/cplex-optimizer.

[115] H. Imai. On the practical efficiency of various maximum flow algorithms. *Journal of the Operations Research Society of Japan*, 26:61–82, 1983.

[116] W. S. Jewell. Optimal flow through networks with gains. *Operations Research*, 10:476–499, 1962.

[117] D. B. Johnson. Efficient algorithms for shortest paths in sparse networks. *Journal of the ACM*, 24:1–13, 1977.

[118] A. Joshi, A. S. Goldstein, and P. M. Vaidya. A fast implementation of a path-following algorithm for maximizing a linear function over a network polytope. In D. S. Johnson and C. C. McGeoch, editors, *Network Flows and Matching, First DIMACS Implementation Challenge*, number 12 in DIMACS Series in Discrete Mathematics and Theoretical Computer Science, pages 267–298. American Mathematical Society, Providence, RI, USA, 1993.

[119] M. Jünger, G. Rinaldi, and S. Thienel. Practical performance of efficient minimum cut algorithms. *Algorithmica*, 26:172–195, 2000.

[120] A. Kamath and O. Palmon. Improved interior point algorithms for exact and approximation solution of multicommodity flow problems. In *Proceedings of the 6th Annual ACM-SIAM Symposium on Discrete Algorithms*, pages 502–511, 1995.

[121] D. Karger and S. Plotkin. Adding multiple cost constraints to combinatorial optimization problems, with applications to multicommodity flows. In *Proceedings of the 27th Annual ACM Symposium on the Theory of Computing*, pages 18–25, 1995.

[122] D. R. Karger. Random sampling in cut, flow, and network design problems. *Mathematics of Operations Research*, 24:383–413, 1999.

[123] D. R. Karger. Minimum cuts in near-linear time. *Journal of the ACM*, 47:46–76, 2000.

[124] D. R. Karger and D. Panigrahi. A near-linear time algorithm for constructing a cactus representation of minimum cuts. In *Proceedings of the 20th Annual ACM-SIAM Symposium on Discrete Algorithms*, pages 246–255, 2009.

[125] D. R. Karger and C. Stein. A new approach to the minimum cut problem. *Journal of the ACM*, 43:601–640, 1996.

[126] R. M. Karp. A characterization of the minimum cycle mean in a digraph. *Discrete Mathematics*, 23:309–311, 1978.

[127] A. V. Karzanov. O nakhozhdenii maksimal'nogo potoka v setyakh spetsial'nogo vida i nekotorykh prilozheniyakh. In L. A. Lyusternik, editor, *Matematicheskie Voprosy Upravleniya Proizvodstvom*, volume 5, pages 81–94. Moscow State

University Press, Moscow, Russia, 1973. In Russian. English translation available at http://alexander-karzanov.net/ScannedOld/73_spec-net-flow_transl.pdf. Accessed February 3, 2019.

[128] A. V. Karzanov. Determining the maximal flow in a network by the method of preflows. *Soviet Mathematical Dokladi*, 15:434–437, 1974.

[129] A. V. Karzanov and E. A. Timofeev. Efficient algorithm for finding all minimal edge cuts of a nonoriented graph. *Cybernetics*, 22:156–162, 1986.

[130] K. Kawarabayashi and M. Thorup. Deterministic global minimum cut of a simple graph in near-linear time. In *Proceedings of the 47th Annual ACM Symposium on the Theory of Computing*, pages 665–674, 2015.

[131] J. A. Kelner, L. Orecchia, A. Sidford, and Z. A. Zhu. A simple combinatorial algorithm for solving SDD systems in nearly-linear time. In *Proceedings of the 45th Annual ACM Symposium on the Theory of Computing*, pages 911–920, 2013. Full version available at https://arxiv.org/pdf/1301.6628.pdf. Accessed May 14, 2018.

[132] M. Klein. A primal method for minimal cost flows with applications to the assignment and transportation problems. *Management Science*, 14:205–220, 1967.

[133] P. Klein, S. Plotkin, C. Stein, and É. Tardos. Faster approximation algorithms for the unit capacity concurrent flow problems with applications to routing and finding sparse cuts. *SIAM Journal on Computing*, 23:466–487, 1994.

[134] J. Kleinberg and É. Tardos. *Algorithm Design*. Addison Wesley, Boston, MA, USA, 2006.

[135] B. Korte and J. Vygen. *Combinatorial Optimization: Theory and Algorithms*. Springer, Berlin, Germany, Fifth edition, 2012.

[136] P. Kovács. Minimum-cost flow algorithms: an experimental evaluation. *Optimization Methods and Software*, 30:94–127, 2015.

[137] M. A. Langston. Fixed-parameter tractability, a prehistory. In H. L. Bodlaender, R. Downey, F. V. Formin, and D. Marx, editors, *The Multivariate Algorithmic Revolution and Beyond – Essays Dedicated to Michael R. Fellows on the Occasion of His 60th Birthday*, number 7370 in Lecture Notes in Computer Science, pages 3–16. Springer, Berlin, Germany, 2012.

[138] D. H. Larkin, S. Sen, and R. E. Tarjan. A back-to-basics empirical study of priority queues. In *Proceedings of the 16th Workshop on Algorithm Engineering and Experiments (ALENEX)*, pages 61–72, 2014.

[139] E. L. Lawler. Optimal cycles in doubly weighted directed linear graphs. In P. Rosenstiehl, editor, *Theory of Graphs, International Symposium*, pages 209–213. Gordon and Breach, New York, NY, USA, 1967.

[140] Y. T. Lee and A. Sidford. Path-finding methods for linear programming: Solving linear programs in $\tilde{O}(\sqrt{rank})$ iterations and faster algorithms for maximum flow. In *Proceedings of the 55th Annual IEEE Symposium on Foundations of Computer Science*, pages 424–433, 2014. Full versions available at https://arxiv.org/pdf/1312.6677.pdf and https://arxiv.org/pdf/1312.6713.pdf. Accessed June 8, 2018.

[141] Y. T. Lee and H. Sun. An SDP-based algorithm for linear-sized spectral sparsification. In *Proceedings of the 49th Annual ACM Symposium on the Theory*

of Computing, pages 678–687, 2017. Full version available at https://arxiv.org/pdf/1702.08415.pdf. Accessed May 14, 2018.

[142] T. Leighton, F. Makedon, S. Plotkin, C. Stein, É. Tardos, and S. Tragoudas. Fast approximation algorithms for multicommodity flow problems. *Journal of Computer and System Sciences*, 50:228–243, 1995.

[143] T. Leong, P. Shor, and C. Stein. Implementation of a combinatorial multicommodity flow algorithm. In D. S. Johnson and C. C. McGeoch, editors, *Network Flows and Matching, First DIMACS Implementation Challenge*, number 12 in DIMACS Series in Discrete Mathematics and Theoretical Computer Science, pages 387–405. American Mathematical Society, Providence, RI, USA, 1993.

[144] M. S. Levine. Experimental study of minimum cut algorithms. Master's thesis, Massachusetts Institute of Technology, May 1997. Available as MIT LCS Technical Report TR-719, from http://publications.csail.mit.edu/lcs/pubs/pdf/MIT-LCS-TR-719.pdf. Accessed February 12, 2018.

[145] A. Löbel. Solving large-scale real-world minimum-cost flow problems by a network simplex method. Technical Report SC 96-7, ZIB, 1996. Available at https://opus4.kobv.de/opus4-zib/frontdoor/index/index/docId/218. Accessed June 5, 2018.

[146] A. Mądry. Computing maximum flow with augmenting electrical flows. In *Proceedings of the 57th Annual IEEE Symposium on Foundations of Computer Science*, pages 593–602, 2016. Full version available at https://people.csail.mit.edu/madry/docs/aug_flow.pdf. Accessed June 8, 2018.

[147] K. Mehlhorn. Blocking flow algorithms for maximum network flow, Course notes, Summer 1999. Available at www.mpi-inf.mpg.de/~mehlhorn/ftp/Goldberg-Rao.ps. Accessed September 27, 2012.

[148] M. Mitzenmacher and E. Upfal. *Probability and Computing*. Cambridge University Press, Cambridge, UK, second edition, 2017.

[149] E. F. Moore. The shortest path through a maze. In *Proceedings of the International Symposium on the Theory of Switching*, pages 285–292, Harvard University Press, Cambridge, MA, USA, 1959.

[150] R. Motwani and P. Raghavan. *Randomized Algorithms*. Cambridge University Press, New York, NY, USA, 1995.

[151] H. Nagamochi and T. Ibaraki. Computing edge-connectivity in multigraphs and capacitated graphs. *SIAM Journal on Discrete Mathematics*, 5:54–66, 1992.

[152] H. Nagamochi, T. Ono, and T. Ibaraki. Implementing an efficient minimum capacity cut algorithm. *Mathematical Programming*, 67:325–341, 1994.

[153] Q. C. Nguyen and V. Venkateswaran. Implementations of the Goldberg-Tarjan maximum flow algorithm. In D. S. Johnson and C. C. McGeoch, editors, *Network Flows and Matching, First DIMACS Implementation Challenge*, number 12 in DIMACS Series in Discrete Mathematics and Theoretical Computer Science, pages 1–18. American Mathematical Society, Providence, RI, USA, 1993.

[154] H. Okamura and P. D. Seymour. Multicommodity flows in planar graphs. *Journal of Combinatorial Theory B*, 31:75–81, 1981.

[155] N. Olver and L. A. Végh. A simpler and faster strongly polynomial algorithm for generalized flow maximization. In *Proceedings of the 49th Annual ACM*

Symposium on the Theory of Computing, pages 100–111, 2017. Full version available at https://arxiv.org/pdf/1611.01778.pdf. Accessed July 30, 2018.

[156] K. Onaga. Optimum flows in general communications networks. *Journal of the Franklin Institute*, 283:308–327, 1967.

[157] J. B. Orlin. A faster strongly polynomial minimum cost flow algorithm. *Operations Research*, 41:338–350, 1993.

[158] J. B. Orlin. A polynomial time primal network simplex algorithm for minimum cost flows. *Mathematical Programming*, 78:109–129, 1997.

[159] J. B. Orlin. Max flows in $O(mn)$ time, or better. In *Proceedings of the 45th Annual ACM Symposium on the Theory of Computing*, pages 765–774, 2013. Full version available at https://dspace.mit.edu/openaccess-disseminate/1721.1/88020. Accessed May 25, 2018.

[160] M. Padberg and G. Rinaldi. An efficient algorithm for the minimum cut problem. *Mathematical Programming*, 47:19–36, 1990.

[161] P. A. Papp. Low-stretch spanning trees. BSc thesis, Eötvös Lorand University, May 2014. Available at http://web.cs.elte.hu/blobs/diplomamunkak/bsc_alkmat/2014/papp_pal_andras.pdf. Accessed May 14, 2018.

[162] R. Peng. Approximate undirected maximum flows in $O(m\text{polylog}(n))$ time. In *Proceedings of the 27th Annual ACM-SIAM Symposium on Discrete Algorithms*, pages 1862–1867, 2016. Full version available at https://arxiv.org/pdf/1411.7631.pdf. Accessed May 15, 2018.

[163] J.-C. Picard and M. Queyranne. On the structure of all minimum cuts in a network and applications. *Mathematical Programming Study*, 13:8–16, 1980.

[164] S. A. Plotkin, D. B. Shmoys, and É. Tardos. Fast approximation algorithms for fractional packing and covering problems. *Mathematics of Operations Research*, 20:257–301, 1995.

[165] B. D. Podderyugin. Algorithm for determining the edge connectivity of a graph. In *Voprosy Kibernetiki – Trudy Seminara po Kombinatornoĭ Matematike*, pages 136–141. Akademiya Nauk SSSR Nauchnyĭ Sovet po Kompleksnoĭ Probleme "Kibernetika", Moscow, USSR, 1973. In Russian.

[166] L. F. Portugal, M. G. C. Resende, G. Veiga, and J. J. Júdice. A truncated primal-infeasible dual-feasible network interior point method. *Networks*, 35:91–108, 2000.

[167] M. Queyranne. Minimizing symmetric submodular functions. *Mathematical Programming*, 82:3–12, 1998.

[168] T. Radzik. Fast deterministic approximation for the multicommodity flow problem. *Mathematical Programming*, 78:43–58, 1997.

[169] T. Radzik. Faster algorithms for the generalized network flow problem. *Mathematics of Operations Research*, 23:69–100, 1998.

[170] T. Radzik. Improving time bounds on maximum generalised flow computations by contracting the network. *Theoretical Computer Science*, 312:75–97, 2004.

[171] T. Radzik and S. Yang. Experimental evaluation of algorithmic solutions for the maximum generalised flow problem. Technical Report TR-01-09, Department of Computer Science, King's College London, 2001.

[172] M. G. Resende and G. Veiga. An efficient implementation of a network interior point method. In D. S. Johnson and C. C. McGeoch, editors, *Network Flows and*

Matching, First DIMACS Implementation Challenge, number 12 in DIMACS Series in Discrete Mathematics and Theoretical Computer Science, pages 299–348. American Mathematical Society, Providence, RI, USA, 1993.

[173] M. Restrepo and D. P. Williamson. A simple GAP-canceling algorithm for the generalized maximum flow problem. *Mathematical Programming, Series A*, 118:47–74, 2009.

[174] J. Robinson. A note on the Hitchcock-Koopmans problem. Research Memorandum RM-407, RAND Corporation, June 1950.

[175] H. Röck. Scaling techniques for minimal cost network flows. In U. Pape, editor, *Discrete Structures and Algorithms, Proceedings of the Workshop WG 79*, pages 181–192. Carl Hanser Verlag, München, Germany, 1980.

[176] A. Schrijver. On the history of the transportation and maximum flow problems. *Mathematical Programming, Series B*, 91:437–445, 2002.

[177] A. Schrijver. *Combinatorial Optimization: Polyhedra and Efficiency*. Springer, Berlin, Germany, 2003.

[178] B. L. Schwartz. Possible winners in partially completed tournaments. *SIAM Review*, 8:302–308, 1966.

[179] P. D. Seymour. A short proof of the two-commodity flow theorem. *Journal of Combinatorial Theory B*, 26:370–371, 1979.

[180] F. Shahrokhi and D. W. Matula. The maximum concurrent flow problem. *Journal of the ACM*, 37:318–334, 1990.

[181] M. Skutella. An introduction to network flows over time. In W. J. Cook, L. Lovász, and J. Vygen, editors, *Research Trends in Combinatorial Optimization*. Springer, Berlin, Germany, 2009.

[182] D. D. Sleator and R. E. Tarjan. A data structure for dynamic trees. *Journal of Computer and System Sciences*, 26:362–391, 1983.

[183] P. T. Sokkalingam, R. K. Ahuja, and J. B. Orlin. New polynomial-time cycle-canceling algorithms for minimum-cost flows. *Networks*, 36:53–63, 2000.

[184] D. A. Spielman and N. Srivastava. Graph sparsification by effective resistances. *SIAM Journal on Computing*, 40:1913–1926, 2011.

[185] D. A. Spielman and S.-H. Teng. Spectral sparsification of graphs. *SIAM Journal on Computing*, 40:981–1025, 2011.

[186] D. A. Spielman and S.-H. Teng. Nearly linear time algorithms for preconditioning and solving symmetric, diagonally dominant linear systems. *SIAM Journal on Matrix Analysis and Applications*, 35:835–885, 2014.

[187] M. Stoer and F. Wagner. A simple min-cut algorithm. *Journal of the ACM*, 44:585–591, 1997.

[188] É. Tardos. A strongly polynomial minimum cost circulation algorithm. *Combinatorica*, 5:247–255, 1985.

[189] É. Tardos. A strongly polynomial algorithm to solve combinatorial linear programs. *Operations Research*, 34:250–256, 1986.

[190] É. Tardos and K. D. Wayne. Simple generalized maximum flow algorithms. In R. E. Bixby, E. A. Boyd, and R. Z. Ríos-Mercado, editors, *Integer Programming and Combinatorial Optimization*, number 1412 in Lecture Notes in Computer Science, pages 310–324, Springer, Berlin, Germany, 1998.

[191] R. E. Tarjan. Shortest paths. Technical report, AT&T Bell Laboratories, Murray Hill, NJ, USA, 1981.

[192] R. E. Tarjan. *Data Structures and Network Algorithms*. Society for Industrial and Applied Mathematics, Philadelphia, PA, USA, 1983.

[193] R. E. Tarjan. Efficiency of the primal network simplex algorithm for the minimum-cost circulation problem. *Mathematics of Operations Research*, 14:272–291, 1991.

[194] N. Tomizawa. On some techniques useful for solution of transportation network problems. *Networks*, 1:173–194, 1971.

[195] J. A. Tropp. User-friendly tail bounds for sums of random matrics. *Foundations of Computational Mathematics*, 12:389–434, 2012.

[196] J. A. Tropp. An introduction to matrix concentration inequalities. *Foundations and Trends in Machine Learning*, 8(1–2):1–230, 2015. Also available at https://arxiv.org/pdf/1501.01571.pdf. Accessed May 15, 2018.

[197] K. Truemper. An efficient scaling procedure for gain networks. *Networks*, 6:151–159, 1976.

[198] K. Truemper. On max flows with gains and pure min-cost flows. *SIAM Journal on Applied Mathematics*, 32:450–456, 1977.

[199] P. M. Vaidya. Speeding-up linear programming using fast matrix multiplication. In *Proceedings of the 30th Annual IEEE Symposium on Foundations of Computer Science*, pages 332–337, 1989.

[200] L. A. Végh. A strongly polynomial algorithm for generalized flow maximization. *Mathematics of Operations Research*, 42:117–211, 2017.

[201] C. Wallacher. A generalization of the minimum-mean cycle selection rule in cycle canceling algorithms. Technical report, Abteilung für Optimierung, Institut für Angewandte Mathematik, Technische Universität Carolo-Wilhelmina, Braunschweig, Germany, 1991.

[202] K. D. Wayne. *Generalized Maximum Flow Algorithms*. PhD thesis, Cornell University, January 1999.

[203] K. D. Wayne. A new property and a faster algorithm for baseball elimination. *SIAM Journal on Discrete Mathematics*, 14:223–229, 2001.

[204] K. D. Wayne. A polynomial combinatorial algorithm for generalized minimum cost flow. *Mathematics of Operations Research*, 27:445–459, 2002.

[205] A. Weintraub. A primal algorithm to solve network flow problems with convex costs. *Management Science*, 21:87–97, 1974.

[206] D. P. Williamson and D. B. Shmoys. *The Design of Approximation Algorithms*. Cambridge University Press, New York, NY, USA, 2011.

Author Index

Of making many books there is no end, and much study wearies the body. Now all has been heard; here is the conclusion of the matter: Fear God and keep his commandments, for this is the duty of all mankind.

– Ecclesiastes 12:12b-13

Abraham, I. 289
Ahlswede, R. 289
Ahuja, R. K. ix, xii, 77–79, 185, 187, 223
Alon, N. 289
Anderson, R. J. 78
Arora, S. 251, 252
Aspvall, B. I. 223
Awerbuch, B. 240, 252

Baier, G. 79
Barahona, F. 187
Batson, J. 289
Bellman, R. 7, 21, 22
Benczúr, A. A. 115, 288
Berra, Y. 21
Bertsekas, D. P. 186
Bhalgat, A. 114, 292
Bienstock, D. 252
Bland, R. G. 185
Bollobás, B. 288
Boman, E. G. 289
Boykov, Y. 78
Bünnagel, U. 186
Busacker, R. G. 185

Carroll, L. 1, 188, 291
Chandran, B. G. 78
Chekuri, C. S. 114
Cheng, C. K. 115

Cheriyan, J. 77
Cherkassky, B. V. 22, 78
Cheung, T.-Y. 78
Christiano, P. 288
Cohen, E. 223
Cohen, M. B. 187, 288
Cook, W. J. xii
Cormen, T. H. xii, 21, 22
Crane, S. 224
Cunningham, W. H. xii

Daitch, S. I. 223
Dantzig, G. B. 77, 185, 186, 223
Derigs, U. 78
Deweese, K. 289
Dijkstra, E. W. 2, 21
Dinitz, Y. 77, 115, 130
Doyle, P. G. 288
Dubhashi, D. P. 289

Edmonds, J. 53, 77, 130, 185, 187
Elias, P. 77
Even, S. 130

Feinstein, A. 77
Fleischer, L. K. 115, 252
Ford Jr., L. R. xii, 7, 21, 22, 23, 29, 77, 100, 132, 174, 185, 186, 251, 253
Foster, R. M. 262
Frank, A. 78, 113

Fredman, M. L. 21
Fujishige, S. 113, 115
Fulkerson, D. R. xii, 23, 29, 77, 100, 132, 174, 185, 186, 251, 253

Gabow, H. N. 113, 115
Gail, A. B. 307
Gallo, G. 79
Garg, N. 236, 252
Gershwin, I. 116
Gilbert, J. R. 289
Glover, F. 78, 223
Goemans, M. X. 115
Goldberg, A. V. x, 22, 67, 77–79, 114–116, 130, 185–187, 223, 252
Goldfarb, D. 186, 223
Goldstein, A. S. 186
Gomory, R. E. 100, 114
Grigoriadis, M. D. 79, 251
Gusfield, D. 100, 114, 115

Hao, J. 82, 85, 114, 186
Hariharan, R. 114, 292
Harvey, N. 289
Hazan, E. 251, 252
Hed, S. 78
Henzinger, M. 114
Hochbaum, D. S. 78
Hoffman, A. J. 79, 130
Hoppe, B. 186
Hoske, D. 289
Hu, T. C. 100, 114, 115, 251

Ibaraki, T. 113, 114
Imai, H. 78

Jensen, D. L. 185
Jewell, W. S. 223
Jin, Z. 223
Johnson, D. B. 21
Joshi, A. 186
Júdice, J. J. 186
Jünger, M. 114

Kale, S. 251, 252
Kamath, A. 251
Kaplan, H. 78
Karger, D. R. 114, 115, 252, 288
Karp, R. M. 22, 53, 77, 130, 185, 187, 289
Karzanov, A. V. 77, 113, 115, 130
Kavitha, T. 114, 292
Kawarabayashi, K. 114
Kelner, J. A. 288, 289
Khachiyan, L. G. 251

Kharitonov, M. 186
Klein, M. 139, 185
Klein, P. 251
Kleinberg, J. xii, 21, 22
Klingman, D. 78, 223
Köhler, E. 79
Kohli, P. 78
Kolmogorov, V. 78
Könemann, J. 236, 252
Korte, B. xii, 186
Kovács, P. 186, 187
Kronecker, L. 188
Kyng, R. 288

Langston, M. A. 21
Larkin, D. H. 21
Lawler, E. L. 22
Lee, Y. T. 187, 288, 289, 293
Leighton, T. 240, 251, 252
Leiserson, C. E. xii, 21, 22
Leong, T. 252
Levine, M. S. 114
Lin, Y. 223
Löbel, A. 186
Lomonosov, M. V. 115
Lukarski, D. 289

Mądry, A. 187, 288
Magnanti, T. L. ix, xii, 78, 185, 187, 223
Maheshwari, S. N. 77
Makedon, F. 251, 252
Matula, D. W. 251
Megiddo, N. 223
Mehlhorn, K. 77, 130
Meier, W. 78
Meyerhenke, H. 289
Miller, G. L. 288
Mitzenmacher, M. 289
Montaigne ix
Moore, E. F. 21, 22
Mote, J. 78
Motwani, R. 289

Nagamochi, H. 113, 114
Neiman, O. 289
Nguyen, Q. C. 78
Niel, D. A. 307

Okamura, H. 251
Oldham, J. D. 252
Olver, N. 223
Onaga, K. 223
Ono, T. 114

Orecchia, L. 289
Orlin, J. B. ix, xii, 77–79, 82, 85, 114, 185–187, 223, 291

Pachocki, J. W. 288
Padberg, M. 114
Palmon, O. 251
Panconesi, A. 289
Panigrahi, D. 114, 115, 292
Papp, P. A. 289
Peleg, D. 289
Peng, R. 288
Picard, J.-C. 115
Plotkin, S. A. 223, 251, 252
Podderyugin, B. D. 113
Portugal, L. F. 186
Pulleyblank, W. R. xii

Qoholeth 307
Queyranne, M. 115

Radzik, T. 223, 251, 252
Raghavan, P. 289
Rao, A. B. 288
Rao, S. x, 78, 114, 116, 130
Resende, M. G. C. 186
Restrepo, M. x, 223
Rinaldi, G. 114
Rivest, R. L. xii, 21, 22
Robinson, J. 184, 185
Röck, H. 185

Saaty, T. L. 185
Sankowski, P. 187, 288
Schrijver, A. xii, 21, 22, 76, 184, 185, 251
Schwartz, B. L. 79
Sedgewick, R. 21
Sen, S. 21
Setubal, J. 78
Seymour, P. D. 251
Shahrokhi, F. 251
Shakespeare, W. xi
Shannon, C. E. 77
Shmoys, D. B. ix, 251, 252
Shor, P. 252
Sidford, A. 187, 288, 289, 293
Skutella, M. 79, 186
Sleator, D. D. 21, 130
Snell, J. L. 288

Sokkalingam, P. T. 187
Sondheim, S. 116
Spielman, D. A. 223, 288, 289
Srivastava, N. 288, 289
Stein, C. xii, 21, 22, 114, 115, 251, 252
Stoer, M. 113
Sun, H. 289

Tardos, É. xii, 21, 22, 78, 185–187, 223, 251, 252, 292
Tarjan, R. E. xii, 21, 22, 67, 77–79, 130, 185–187
Teng, S.-H. 288
Thienel, S. 114
Thorup, M. 114
Timofeev, E. A. 113
Tomizawa, N. 187
Tragoudas, S. 251, 252
Tropp, J. A. 289
Truemper, K. 212, 223
Tseng, P. 186
Tsioutsiouliklis, K. 115
Twain, M. 20

Upfal, E. 289
Uth, R. 307

Vaidya, P. M. 186, 251, 292
Végh, L. A. 223, 292
Veiga, G. 186
Venkateswaran, V. 78
Vladu, A. 187, 288
Vygen, J. xii, 186

Wagner, F. 113
Wallacher, C. x, 141, 185
Wang, D. 114
Wayne, K. D. 79, 223, 292
Wegner, M. 289
Weintraub, A. 185
Werneck, R. F. 78
West, D. 289
Whitman, D. 78
Williamson, D. P. ix, x, 223
Winter, A. 289

Xu, S. C. 288

Yang, S. 223

Zhu, Z. A. 289

Index

Λ, 120
ϵ-fixed arc, 151
ϵ-optimal, 147, 197

active node, 59, 67, 162
admissible arc, 58, 162, 182, 221
Ahlswede-Winter theorem, 274
amortized running time, 21
ancestor tree, 115
arc
  ϵ-fixed, 151
  admissible, 58, 162, 182, 221
  fixed, 151
  holdover, 171
  nontree, 168
  saturated, 29
  special, 123
  tree, 168
assignment problem, 180
augmenting path, 30, 197
  generalized, 191
  most improving, 50, 71
augmenting path algorithm, 32
  most improving, 47–50
  shortest, 53–55
Awerbuch-Leighton algorithm, 240–249

B (matrix), 258
B (scalar), 188
baseball elimination problem, 36–41,
  67, 70
basic cycle, 169
Bellman-Ford algorithm, 6–10, 205
bicycle, 199
binary search, 45
bisection search, 45

blocking flow, 116–117
  algorithm, 119–120, 128–130
  and dynamic trees, 128–130
  definition, 116–117
  in series-parallel graphs, 128
  in unit capacity graph, 128
bucket data structure, 64

C (matrix), 258
C (scalar), 139
cactus tree, 115
cancel-and-tighten, 182
canceling
  cycle, 135–136, 221
  GAP, 191–192
canonical labeling, 193–194
capacity constraint, 24, 133, 190
capacity scaling algorithm
  for maximum flow problem, 51–53
  for minimum-cost circulation problem,
    154–160
Cauchy-Schwarz inequality, 244, 268
characteristic flow, 191
Chernoff bounds, 289
circulation, 134–135
  definition, 132–133
concentration of measure, 271, 289
concurrent flow problem, see maximum
    concurrent flow problem
condition number
  tree, 278
conductance, 254
congestion, 237, 251
contraction, 90–91
cost scaling, 185

310

cut
  global minimum, 80
  s-t, capacity, 26
  s-t, definition, 26–27
  sparsifier, 271–273
  X-t, 82
cut condition, 225–226
  two commodities, 227–230
cut level, 84
cut-equivalent tree, 100
cycle, 1
  basic, 169
  canceling, 135–136, 221
  correction, 277
  flow-absorbing, 191
  flow-generating, 191
  minimum-mean, 146
  negative-cost, 6, 135
  simple, 1
  unit-gain, 191

DAG, 19
data structure
  bucket, 64
  dynamic trees, 67, 128–130, 285
  Fibonacci heap, 5, 21
  heap, 4–6
  pairing heap, 21
  queue, 9
deficit, 155
demand, 133, 254
density of a graph, 42
Dijkstra's algorithm, 2–6, 160
Dilworth's theorem, 77
Dinitz's algorithm, 116–120
directed acyclic graph, 19
discharge, 64
distance labels, 2, 53
  X-valid, 83
  valid, 57
distance level, 84, 120
  empty, 84
dynamic trees, 67, 128–130, 285

effective resistance, 259–263
electrical flow
  definition, 254–255
  energy, 255
  optimality conditions, 254–255
electrical network, 254–257
energy, 255, 263–265

error scaling, 218–219
excess, 57, 155, 190
excess scaling push-relabel algorithm, 72–73

Fibonacci heap, 5, 21, 90, 110
FIFO push-relabel algorithm, 72
fixed arc, 151
Fleischer's algorithm, 249–250
flow
  characteristic, 191
  generalized, 190
  interpretation, 215
  over time, 170
  proper, 190
  s-t, definition, 23–25
  temporally repeated, 171
  value, 24, 190
flow conservation constraint, 24, 133, 190
flow decomposition, 47, 142, 199
flow-absorbing cycle, 191
flow-equivalent tree, 101, 112
  algorithm, 112–113
flow-generating cycle, 191
Foster's theorem, 262
Fujishige's algorithm, 110

gain, 188
gain scaling, 214–215
GAP, see generalized augmenting path
GAP canceling, 191–192
gap relabeling, 68–69, 76
Garg-Könemann algorithm, 236–240,
      249–250
generalized
  circulation, 222, 292
  flow, 190
  proper flow, 190
  pseudoflow, 189
generalized augmenting path, 191
generalized maximum flow problem
  definition, 188–190
  GAP canceling algorithm, 196–197
  optimality condition, 190–198
generalized minimum-cost circulation
      problem, 222, 292
global minimum cut, 80
  α-approximate, 112
  in directed graphs, 80
  in undirected graphs, 80
  number, 112
global relabeling, 69

Goldberg-Rao algorithm, 122–128
Golden Snitch, 70
Gomory-Hu tree, 292
  algorithm, 104–108
  definition, 100–101
  for symmetric submodular functions,
    108–110
Gusfield's algorithm, 107

Hall's theorem, 77
Hao-Orlin algorithm, 82–89
heap, 4–6
  Fibonacci, 5, 21
  pairing, 21
highest label push-relabel algorithm, 65
Hoffman circulation theorem, 71, 133, 139
holdover arc, 171

image segmentation problem, 70
integrality property
  maximum flow problem, 32
  minimum-cost circulation problem, 139
interpreting flow, 215

König-Egerváry theorem, 77
Kirchoff Current Law, 254
Kirchoff Potential Law, 255

labeling, 192–193
  canonical, 193–194
Laplacian, 257–259
  solver, 277–285
lossy graph, 210
low-stretch spanning tree, 289

m, 2
MA ordering, 89–90, 110
  for global minimum cut, 90–93
  for maximum flow problem, 110
  for symmetric submodular functions,
    111–112
maximum adjacency ordering, *see* MA
  ordering
maximum concurrent flow problem, 224–225
maximum density subgraph problem, 41–46
  weighted, 71
maximum flow problem
  augmenting path algorithm, 32
  definition, 23–24
  integrality property, 32
  optimality conditions, 31

over time, 170–176
  parametric, 76
maximum flow-minimum cut theorem, 29
maximum multicommodity flow problem,
  224–225
minimum s-t cut problem, 29
minimum s-cut problem, 80–81
minimum X-t cut problem, 82
minimum cost-to-time ratio cycle problem, 20
minimum-cost circulation problem, 292–293
  cycle canceling algorithm, 139
  definition, 132–133
  generalized, 222, 292
  integrality property, 139
  optimality conditions, 137
minimum-cost flow problem, 133–134, 176
  quickest, 176
minimum-cost perfect matching problem,
  177–180
minimum-mean cycle, 146
  algorithm, 20
minimum-mean cycle canceling algorithm,
  146–154
most improving
  augmenting path, 47, 50, 71
  negative-cost cycle, 140, 176
multicommodity flow problem, 292
  cut condition, 225–226
  definition, 224–225
  optimality condition, 226–227
  two commodities, 227–230
multiplicative weights algorithm, 230–236
  for maximum flow, 266–270
  for multicommodity flow, 236–240
  for packing problems, 233–236
  with costs, 249

n, 2
negative-cost cycle, 6, 135
  detection, 11–19
  most improving, 176
negative-cost GAP, 202
  detection, 205–209
network reliability problem, 81–82
network simplex algorithm, 167–170
node
  active, 59, 67, 162
  contraction, 90–91
  demand, 133
  labeling, 192–193
  potential, 136, 254

price, 136
relabeling, 192–193
sink, 23, 188
source, 23
supply, 133
nonsaturating push, 166
nontree arc, 168

$\bar{O}$, 113, 259
Ocean's Eleven, 266
Ohm's Law, 254
oracle for convex set, 233
width, 233

packing problem, 233
pairing heap, 21
parallel composition, 128
parametric maximum flow, 76
parent
graph, 11
pointer, 3
path, 1
augmenting, 30
simple, 1
perfect matching, 177
polynomial time, 32
pseudo-, 32
strongly, 33
potential, 136, 254
tree-defined, 256, 277
potential function, 62–63
preflow, 56–57
X-preflow, 83
convert to flow, 67, 76
price, 136
price refinement, 183
proper flow, 190
pseudoflow, 78, 154
definition, 155
generalized, 189
pseudopolynomial time, 32
push, 58
nonsaturating, 62, 166
saturating, 62, 166
stack, 73
push-relabel algorithm, 56–69, 291
excess scaling, 72–73
FIFO, 72
highest label, 65
wave scaling, 73–76

queue, 9
quickest minimum-cost flow problem, 176
quickest transshipment problem, 176
quidditch elimination problem, 70

random contraction algorithm, 93–99
Rayleigh monotonicity principle, 285
recursive random contraction algorithm, 97–99
reduced cost, 136
relabel, 58
set, 182
relabeling, 192–193
RELAX, 186
residual graph, 29–30, 135, 190
resistance, 254
effective, 259–263

s-t cut
capacity, 26
definition, 26–27
s-t flow
definition, 23–25
saturated arc, 29
saturating push, 166
scaling
capacity, 51–53, 154–160
cost, 185
error, 218–219
gain, 214–215
scaling parameter, 51
scan, 8–9
series composition, 128
series-parallel graphs, 128
set relabeling, 182
shortest augmenting path algorithm, 53–55
simple
cycle, 1
path, 1
sink, 23, 188
skew symmetry, 24, 134, 189
source, 1, 23
sparsifier
cut, 271–273
spectral, 272–276
special arc, 123
spectral sparsifier, 272–276
stack push, 73
strongly polynomial time, 33, 292
submodular function, 102, 110–112
symmetric, 102, 110–111
Gomory-Hu tree, 108–110
minimization algorithm, 111–112

successive approximation, 160–167
supply, 133, 254
symmetric submodular function, *see*
        submodular function, symmetric

temporally repeated flow, 171
time-expanded network, 170
transit time, 170
transportation problem, 184
tree
    ancestor, 115
    arc, 168
    cactus, 115
    condition number, 278
    cut-equivalent, 100

flow-equivalent, 101, 112
    low-stretch, 289
tree-defined potential, 256, 277
Truemper's algorithm, 209–214

U (scalar), 32, 49, 139
unit capacity graph, 113, 120
    blocking flow, 128
unit-gain cycle, 191

value, 24, 190

Wallacher's algorithm, 140–146
wave scaling push-relabel algorithm, 73–76
width, 233

Printed in the United States
By Bookmasters